TRULY, MADLY

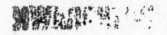

Also by Stephen Galloway

*Leading Lady: Sherry Lansing and the Making of a
Hollywood Groundbreaker*

TRULY, MADLY

VIVIEN LEIGH, LAURENCE OLIVIER AND THE ROMANCE OF THE CENTURY

STEPHEN GALLOWAY

GRAND CENTRAL
PUBLISHING

NEW YORK   BOSTON

Grand Central Publishing
Hachette Book Group
1290 Avenue of the Americas, New York, NY 10104
grandcentralpublishing.com
twitter.com/grandcentralpub

First edition: March 2022

Grand Central Publishing is a division of Hachette Book Group, Inc. The Grand Central Publishing name and logo is a trademark of Hachette Book Group, Inc.

The publisher is not responsible for websites (or their content) that are not owned by the publisher.

The Hachette Speakers Bureau provides a wide range of authors for speaking events. To find out more, go to www.hachettespeakersbureau.com or call (866) 376-6591.

Library of Congress Cataloging-in-Publication Data

Names: Galloway, Stephen (Journalist) author.
Title: Truly, madly : Vivien Leigh, Laurence Olivier, and the romance of the century / Stephen Galloway.
Description: New York : Grand Central Publishing, 2022.
Identifiers: LCCN 2021046444 | ISBN 9781538731970 (hardcover) | ISBN 9781538731963 (ebook)
Subjects: LCSH: Olivier, Laurence, 1907–1989. | Actors—Great Britain—Biography. | Olivier, Laurence, 1907–1989—Marriage. | Leigh, Vivien, 1913–1967. | Motion picture actors and actresses—Great Britain—Biography. | Leigh, Vivien, 1913–1967—Marriage.
Classification: LCC PN2598.O55 G35 2022 | DDC 792.02/80922 [B]—dc23
LC record available at https://lccn.loc.gov/2021046444

ISBNs: 9781538731970 (hardcover); 9781538731963 (ebook)

Printed in Canada

MRQ-T

10 9 8 7 6 5 4 3 2 1

For
June Wyndham-Davies and Norma West
and, in memoriam,
Pieter Rogers

PROLOGUE

―――・◦◦・―――

Around midnight on June 16, 1937, an anxious young man, dark-eyed and good-looking, slipped out of his London home, stole away from his wife and child, and set out to meet the woman he loved.

Two years after Laurence Olivier had first glimpsed Vivien Leigh, a woman of such transcendent beauty and intoxicating allure that she had left him drunk with desire, he was under her spell. Day in and day out, they would sneak off the set of their new movie or sit lost amid a swirl of dreams, real-life versions of the lovers they would later play, Romeo and Juliet, whose lesson they would have done well to learn, "violent delights have violent ends / And in their triumph die." "Whether they thought they were fooling anybody, I don't know," said a crew member. "But we all knew that here were two people hopelessly in love."

What drew them to each other with such fierce power, blinding them to all sense of duty and danger, even to right and wrong, and pushing them to the point where, this very night, they were about to run away? Was it simply lust, the devouring sexual greed that nobody who knew them could ignore? Or was it something else, an affinity of the heart, mind and soul? Long after their passion had faded, when their ecstasy had turned to agony and their turbulent romance had left them battered and scarred, Olivier searched for an explanation. It was a virus, he said, a disease, a compulsion as mighty as any in legend or myth. "It sometimes felt almost like an illness," he wrote, "but the remedy was unthinkable. Only an early Christian martyr could have faced it. Virtue seemed to work upside down: love was like an angel, guilt was a dark fiend. At its every surge *Macbeth* would haunt me: 'Then comes my fit again.'"

For cynics, this was self-aggrandizement; for others, mere indulgence. Only Larry's wife, Jill Esmond, collateral damage left in the wake of her husband's affair, understood what it was, even when it had turned into a fireball that incinerated her marriage. "Real passion—I've only seen it that once," she told their son. "If you are ever hit by it, God help you. There's nothing you can do."

And yet there was something Olivier could have done. Three weeks before he and Vivien fled, they had traveled to Denmark, planning to stage *Hamlet* in the place where it was set, with the thirty-year-old Larry as the prince and the twenty-three-year-old Vivien as Ophelia. Equipment, costumes and props had been loaded onto trucks; the trucks hauled across the North Sea; the cast and crew flown to the coastal town of Helsingor, where the actors were scheduled to perform for a week on the ramparts of Kronborg Castle. And then, hours before they were due to go on, all hell broke loose. A thunderstorm cracked open the sky; water flooded the battlements, along with thousands of makeshift seats; and any hope of salvaging the production as it had been conceived was doused by the storm. Moving indoors to a hotel ballroom, the troupe scrambled to reconfigure their work as theater in the round, with barely enough time to arrange their entrances and exits before an audience of royals and dignitaries began to filter in. The play seemed doomed. And yet somehow, despite the chaos, this *Hamlet* was a sensation, sealing Olivier's reputation as one of the most dazzling actors alive.

The next day, he was in the midst of rehearsals when an incident took place that shook him to the core. What happened is unclear, but after an explosive confrontation with Vivien, he reappeared before his colleagues, ashen, and said "something about Viv having gone bonkers, having attacked him, having had a fit of some kind," according to an early report. When Vivien emerged, she was unrecognizable from her usual vivacious self and spoke "not a word to anyone, just staring blankly into space."

This was more than a moment of pique, more than a terrified ingenue's temper tantrum; it was as if a flare had been sent up from the recesses of her psyche, warning Olivier of trouble ahead. Why she had erupted, he did not know; whether she would do so again, he could not predict. And yet it was obvious this exquisite diamond was flawed. Once, outsiders might have said she was possessed; now, two hundred and fifty years after the last witch had been burned at the stake, and decades into the age of Freud and Jung, people still knew so little about mental health that nobody understood she was seriously ill.

Larry could have walked away, could have ended his affair then and there and returned to Jill (who had accompanied him on this voyage, only to be shunted off on sightseeing tours with the young Alec Guinness). But he didn't. Rather than extricate himself, he plunged deeper; rather than step back, he surged forward. Once home, he and Vivien vowed, they would leave their spouses for good. Reason was powerless to stop them. Passion conquered all.

This book is a study of passion—not the soft, sentimental kind of Hollywood movies and Victorian romance but the sort that engulfs, overwhelms and sometimes destroys: the sort for which the Oliviers became famous.

Half a century since Vivien's death and more than three

decades since Larry's, they continue to haunt us. There are books and blogs about them, conferences and symposia; there are documentaries and exhibitions and even a collection of scholarly essays published by Manchester University Press. And yet they remain veiled, their story wrapped in half-truths, conundrums and lies, proof positive of Gabriel García Márquez's adage that all human beings have three lives: the public, the private and the secret.

They were emblems of a class and culture that's sunk as deep beneath the waves as the ocean liners that ferried them across the seas, but they didn't belong to that class and culture at all. They were lovers as famous as Burton and Taylor or Bogie and Bacall, but their kind of love often seemed closer to hate. And they were the first married couple since the advent of sound to become global celebrities, but they despised celebrity and even the medium that led to their fame.

They appeared to have it all; and yet in their own minds they were blighted, doomed by a mental illness neither understood that transformed their relationship from the stuff of dreams into a living nightmare.

CHAPTER 1

———◆———

Laurence Kerr Olivier was born on May 22, 1907, the son of an impoverished curate who had fallen far short of his goals. Living in a cramped two-up-two-down, built for the working classes in the country town of Dorking, the Oliviers could hardly feign gentility: their neighbor was a chimney sweep, the very archetype of what it meant to be poor.

"My father used to describe how he was frying sausages for Dr. Rawlings and himself when the doctor appeared in the kitchen doorway bearing a tiny but healthy-looking infant in his arms, as yet unwashed and smeared with blood," wrote Olivier in his 1982 memoir, *Confessions of an Actor.* "My father's telling of this always indicated a sense of slight disgust as Dr. Rawlings placed me in his arms."

Gerard Olivier, known to his son as "Fahv," was a mercurial man, a failed teacher who had only recently joined the church and lived in the shadow of his older brother, Sydney, soon to become secretary of state for India and later the first Baron Olivier. Father and son never bonded; instead, overwhelmed by three young children—Larry followed Sybille (born in 1901) and Dickie (born in 1904)—Gerard came to resent the infant and blamed him for siphoning off his wife's attention. While he meted out affection in tranches, just like the Sunday roast he would cut into wafer-thin slices (their very meagerness a source of pride), Agnes Olivier made up for her domestic disappointments by lavishing love on her youngest child. With so many mouths to feed and so little money to do so, the Oliviers' marriage grew strained, their arguments heated. On occasion, Gerard would explode in "a storming, raging tornado which he'd turn on Larry in a way he never did on my brother Dick and me," recalled Sybille. But Olivier had only the faintest memory of this, because in 1910 Gerard gave up his life as a country priest to minister in the London slums.

London was a sprawling, chaotic mess whose population had doubled in less than forty years. Its tenements were fetid, its drains foul, just a decade after a groundbreaking study had found twenty-eight percent of the slum population virtually swimming in their own excrement. "I see little glory," said Winston Churchill, then a young member of Parliament, "in an Empire which can rule the waves and is unable to flush its sewers."

It was in this empire that Gerard began to work, based in Notting Dale, the most "hopelessly degraded" part of London, according to a contemporary report, where he served in an area nicknamed "the potteries and the piggeries" for the brick kilns that lined its streets and the pigs that wallowed in its mud. A clay pit known as "the ocean" slopped with slime, while the homes were "mere hovels in a ruinous condition, filthy in the extreme, and containing vast accumulations of garbage and offal." Things were beginning to improve, but this was still "hell on earth to more than 4,000 people," writes one historian. "Its houses were densely overcrowded, many occupied by 20 people and more, [who] were largely made up of loafers, cab-runners, beggars, tramps, thieves, and prostitutes."

To these thieves and prostitutes, Gerard brought his ministry, operating out of a shack with the grandiose name of St. Gabriel's while his family lived a mile away in Elgin Crescent, a few doors down (if many layers socially) from the future residence of British prime minister Boris Johnson. As Agnes and her children settled in, Gerard devoted himself to his flock, urging them to keep up with the Bible when they could barely keep up with the rent. He was not so much a fish out of water as a whale, an intense and self-lacerating figure who did everything to stand out, draping himself in a black cassock and pointed hat (the garb of a Catholic priest, not a Protestant), and delivering fire-and-brimstone sermons when all his parishioners really wanted was his support.

Larry never questioned this. "Many sons react against their father's being in religion," he said later. "I didn't. I accepted everything." Rebellion was left to Sybille, who rebelled so much she made it a way of life. She left home to become an actress in her teens; lived "in sin" with another actor long before it was acceptable; and was possibly bisexual—she once told Larry she would have had "a thundering love affair" with his first wife if he hadn't gone and married her. She was a free spirit when women had no right to freedom or spiritedness.

A year after moving to London, Gerard was fired, precipitating the family's gravest crisis. His stubbornness, zealotry and extreme "High Church" brand of Christianity proved too much even for a local parish that desperately needed him, and so in the summer of 1911, homeless and penniless, he and his family began a meandering trek across the country, traipsing "from one seaside town to another," remembered Sybille, while Gerard searched for part-time clerical work. For weeks the family shuttled among the run-down resorts of the southern coast, the working-class havens that one of Olivier's most celebrated characters, Archie Rice, would call his own, while the temperature rose to a broiling ninety-nine degrees. The *Times* published lists of "deaths by heat" as water pumps burst and trees withered, asphalt melted on the roads, workingmen's button-on collars stuck to their skin, adults and children fainted and died.

Squeezed into sad, soggy rooms in cheap boardinghouses, Agnes was forced to cope alone while Gerard went wherever his services were required. By the time he had found a permanent post in London, he had lost his taste for domesticity and "never took kindly to family life again."

Rejected by his father, Larry turned to his mother. She was "the most enchanting person," wrote Sybille. "Hair so long she could sit on it. She absolutely made our childhood, and she adored Larry." "Mrs. Olivier was a darling," confirmed the actress Sybil Thorndike, a family friend, "and Larry was exactly like her. She was sturdy, with a face just like Larry's, rather gipsy-looking, rather larky. I'm sure he got all his humour from his mother."

Agnes believed in her son, lent ballast to his hopes and dreams. He was his mother's "baby" and her "darling old Kim" (an abbreviation of the nickname Larrykin that also called to mind Kipling's vagabond boy), whom she encouraged to aim high. Maybe he could go to India and work on a plantation, as his brother would do when Larry was fifteen. Maybe he could even buy his own plantation or do better still and become a politician, like Uncle Sydney, who had placed first in the nation's Civil Service exams, was a friend of Bernard Shaw and destined for high office. These were the hopes Agnes implanted in her favorite child, these the ideals that enflamed his imagination. And then, when Larry was twelve, a guillotine dropped down, severing his world in two.

His mother had begun to change. Soon she became weak and lost full control of her limbs. "Her disease was at first wrongly diagnosed as disseminated sclerosis [a form of multiple sclerosis]," wrote Sybille, "and she spent months in Addenbrooke's Hospital, Cambridge, where her sister Constance was at that time Matron, having electric treatment which unfortunately did no good at all. Her left side became partially paralysed, her left hand useless, and the left side of her mouth appeared pulled down so that her face was distorted into that of a much older woman."

Too late, the family learned she was suffering from a cerebral tumor, most likely glioblastoma, a pernicious cancer of the brain that would later kill US senators Edward M. Kennedy and John McCain. Its progress was swift and unstoppable, first causing headaches and nausea, then moodiness, vomiting and agonizing pain. Agnes probably never knew she was terminally ill: her doctors would not have told her, as was their practice, because cancer was taboo, an "abomination of the body," in the words of sociologist Erving Goffman. It was bad enough that Agnes was dying; it would have been shameful for her to know the cause.

One Saturday in March 1920, the Reverend Olivier brought his son home from boarding school and led him into the family's new residence in Letchworth, just north of London, where he was serving as vicar. "Larry came to the old Rectory to see his mother," wrote Sybille. "There he stood, Agnes' most precious child, at the open door with his cap in his hand, his dark hair rather rough and badly cut as usual, and his tweed overcoat shabby, smiling at his mother in the way she loved him best. There was no agony of parting for those two, just a laughing 'Goodbye Mummy,' as she lay there looking at him." Sybille played one of her mother's favorite hymns on the piano while they spoke: "Praise Him! Praise Him! Jesus, our blessed Redeemer! / Sing, ye saints! His wonderful love proclaim!"

On March 27, Agnes died; she was forty-eight years old.

The anguish of that experience haunts Olivier's memoirs, written sixty years after her death. "My heaven, my hope, my entire world, my own worshiped Mummy died when I was twelve," he wrote. The older he got, the more tenderly he spoke of her and the more he was unable to recall her without being overcome. "There was undoubtedly a paradise in my childhood, and it lasted until my mother died," he told the *Los Angeles Times*.

"I've been looking for her ever since, [for a] vanished Garden of Eden, paradise lost, [with] all the world's nostalgia for what has gone and cannot be recovered."

Olivier cherished his few mementos of Agnes, and her warm notes to him can be found in his archive at London's British Library, written on onionskin sheets and preserved in their tiny original envelopes, the word "Precious" scrawled on one in Larry's adult handwriting. "How she loved you," Sybille reminded him when they were old. "And how eternally grateful I am to have had her as long as I did."

After his wife's funeral, Gerard didn't utter her name for years—not at home, nor to his family, nor to the outside world. Losing her must have been devastating, no matter how great the tension between them. She had remained loyal throughout, even when he broke the one vow she had insisted he take as a precondition for their marriage: that he never join the church. He was alone now, and not just alone but destined to remain so, he thought, if he wished to remain true to his ideals: that a High Churchman should never remarry but should commit himself to God. As he turned deeper into himself, he turned further from his children, leaving them to struggle alone—especially his younger and so-vulnerable son. From then on, noted the critic Kenneth Tynan, Larry retained a "pipeline to childhood pain."

"There was this little gap inside [him], a little vortex after that," says the actress Sarah Miles. "He could play all of the archetypes. But in the center, something was missing."

Five thousand miles away, at the very time Agnes lay dying, a six-year-old child and her parents left their estate in Calcutta, India, and set out for the nearby port.

The humidity was oppressive on this March 2, 1920, and along with the humidity came stinkbugs and mosquitoes and disease: malaria, chikungunya and yellow fever, plagues that had left too many British invaders dead and the rest with a permanent itch called prickly heat. Once, these colonials had believed they could conquer India; now they knew India had conquered them.

Still, this was a small price to pay for success and at age thirty-eight Ernest Hartley had succeeded beyond his wildest dreams. Fifteen years since leaving his job as a low-level bank clerk in England, his gamble had paid off: he had risen to senior partner with the stockbrokers Pigott, Chapman & Co., his ascent only briefly interrupted by his obligatory military service in World War I. He was a horseman, a gambler, a ladies' man and an amateur actor—a fellow who loved the theater and all things theatrical, qualities his daughter would inherit. Now he was about to take her to the land of his birth.

If Gertrude Yackjee, thirty-one, lacked her husband's effervescence, she made up for it in beauty. She may have come from the lower rungs of Anglo society in India (where she was born, unlike him), but she was clever enough to use her looks well in a place where looks were the key to marriage and marriage was the key to everything else. With her cobalt-blue eyes and peachy skin, she floated above the boatloads of Englishwomen who washed up on Indian shores—the "Fishing Fleet," as they were collectively known: single women arriving each winter season in search of husbands. She had captured Ernest's heart from the start, despite the tut-tuts of his colleagues, horrified he might marry a woman country-born, whose grandmother had grown up in an orphanage and may even have been a "half-caste" at that.

None of this meant anything to the couple's restive daughter. Vital and charismatic, the young Vivian Hartley* was the most memorable of the three. Photos from the time show a

---

* Vivien changed the spelling of her name when she became an actress. The original spelling is only used here when referring to her as a child.

raven-haired girl with brilliant eyes, but fail to capture the energy others noted, the eagerness and excitement that could sometimes carry her away, which it did when she played a lion in one of her father's theatricals and bit her mother in the leg.

As the Hartleys crossed the narrow girder bridge that forded Tully's Creek and headed for the mighty port, their car crawling past hordes of migrants who were transforming this storied "city of palaces" into a synonym for urban squalor, did Vivian realize she was leaving her country for good? As they reached the docks and began boarding the seven-thousand-ton *City of Baroda*, with its hundred crewmen and two hundred passengers, all strictly segregated by race and class, did she understand she was bidding farewell to everything she had grown up with? And as the *Baroda* slipped from its berth, easing into the swirling Hooghly River—past jetties laden with bales of cotton and tea, past every vestige of the landscape she knew and loved—did she know she would never come home again?

Spring came late to England, where the ship docked in April, and with the dull, damp weather came the fog and the rain and the cold. Historians look back on the 1920s as the time of the Bright Young Things, the British version of America's flappers; but traces of the Great War, which had only just ended after four years of hell and the loss of twenty million lives, were all around. The euphoria of victory was long gone, and three million demobilized soldiers faced chronic unemployment, many left to wander the streets like ghosts, some mutilated, others carrying the shards of psychic wounds as sharp as shrapnel.

This was the London Vivian discovered. And yet, even as empty shells of human beings scrambled to survive, the city teemed with life. Bright lights sparkled outside the theaters, dozens in the capital alone. Here was *Pretty Peggy*, the story of a poor newsboy who switches identities with a millionaire; there was *The Shop Girl*, starring twenty-year-old Evelyn Laye and a real-life marching band; and a little farther off was *The Beggar's Opera*, which ran for a staggering 1,463 performances, the kind of hit that would have turned the older Larry green with envy. Vivian was in a frenzy of excitement as her parents took her out each day—to tea, to the theater, to the incense-filled Roman Catholic churches that Gertrude adored. London was heaven until it turned to hell.

Six months after arriving, Vivian and her mother drove out of the city, across the river Thames, over the lush fields that had not yet been plowed under for housing as the sprawling city gobbled up everything in its path to make way for new residents, all the way to the village of Roehampton, seven miles to the southwest, where they stopped outside a large Tudor estate hidden behind forbidding walls. This was the Convent of the Sacred Heart, a boarding school where Gertrude handed Vivian over to the reverend mother general before returning to the city alone.

The girl was distraught. What could she possibly have done wrong? How had she so alienated her parents that they would abandon her to a prison like this? In truth, they had little choice. For the affluent Anglos in India, this was the way of the world, the only solution to their terrible predicament: how to be both part of India and fully British. Gertrude would later regret her decision, but for a woman of her age and class, bringing up her own daughter was out of the question: the child would have been marginalized at best or would have learned to speak English with the "chichi" accent the upper classes abhorred, a revelation that she wasn't quite "pukka."

Gertrude was faced with "an agonising dilemma that few [Anglo mothers] could solve," writes the historian Anne de Courcy, "whether to abandon the husband who needed them, to live in England, probably on very little money, so that they could be with the children in the school holidays, or to stay with the husband they loved and leave their children with others." She left her child with others, with sisters who knew little of nature and less of nurture. After visiting her a few times, taking her to lunch or dinner or the zoo and then returning her to the convent amid a storm of tears, she and Ernest set sail for Calcutta.

Vivian was in torment. Woken each day at 6:30 a.m., with only a kitten to give her love (the nuns' one concession to her loneliness), she began her morning with the sound of a clanging bell and a voice chanting "Precious blood of our Lord Jesus Christ," to which she and the other girls would reply: "Wash away our sins." Mass followed, with the Angelus recited three times a day and the constant refrain: "Hail Mary, full of grace, / The Lord is with Thee."

An only child, used to a retinue of servants who functioned like serfs, she now shared her quarters with the other girls, scattered among twenty unheated dormitories, their beds ranked in serried rows with only the flimsiest of curtains to keep them apart. After having her own governess and amah (or nanny), she was forced to scrub and clean and adhere to a code of conduct so severe she couldn't even bathe without wearing a shift; nudity itself was an offense before God. Breakfast was bread and butter and a cup of coffee; too much fraternization among the children was discouraged; letters home were scrutinized and strictly censored. For punishment, a safety pin would be jabbed into Vivian's ear. "There was rigid discipline," writes one of her biographers, Hugo Vickers. "Good Catholics were urged to dwell 'constantly in the spiritual presence of death' and St. Teresa was quoted as having exclaimed at each striking of the hour: 'An hour nearer to death. An hour nearer to heaven or hell.'"

Was it surprising, in the midst of this, that the girl dreamed of escape, both literal and metaphorical? "If Vivian, in her misery and her loneliness, concocted a grander existence for herself, there was nothing to contradict the fantasy," says the actress

Victoria Tennant, daughter of the Oliviers' longtime manager, Cecil Tennant. "It's the stuff of movies and books: Orphans make up stories about being princesses as a compensation for the barrenness of their own reality. Maybe she just had to make up who she was."

When Ernest, back in India, took pity on his child and sent her an expensive doll, it arrived with its head shattered, a heartbreaking emblem of Vivian herself. Sixteen months passed before she saw her father again, sixteen long months before he and her mother returned, almost strangers, to visit the child they had left behind.

Over the years, Vivian adjusted—more than that, she came to embrace her new home and grew popular with the other girls. Years later, indeed, her convent friend Maureen O'Sullivan expressed surprise at the warmth with which Vivian spoke of her past, in contrast to herself. Still, the damage was done: the rift ran deep, the crack was permanent. Vivian would remain at Sacred Heart for eight years before leaving for good, hungry for the kind of love no nun could ever give her.

This was the young woman Larry would see for the first time when she was twenty-one, the adult version of the child who had gone through almost as much heartache as himself. By then she had a new life, a new career and a new name: Vivien Leigh.

CHAPTER 2

❧

I first set eyes upon the possessor of this wondrous, unimagined beauty on the stage of the Ambassadors Theatre," recalled Olivier. "Apart from her looks, which were magical, she possessed beautiful poise; her neck looked almost too fragile to support her head and bore it with a sense of surprise, and something of the pride of the master juggler who can make a brilliant maneuver appear almost accidental. She also had something else: an attraction of the most perturbing nature I had ever encountered."

Larry was twenty-eight and feeling jaded. More than a decade since leaving home—initially to become a student at the Central School of Speech Training and Dramatic Art, then as a member of the shambolic Lena Ashwell Players (the "Lavatory Players," he called them)—and five years after landing his big break opposite Noël Coward in the 1930 sensation *Private Lives*, he looked at his life and found it wanting. True, he had remade himself, filling the gap in his teeth, working out almost compulsively and transforming the shuffling, shaggy-haired adolescent into a young Adonis, an unparalleled act of self-reinvention, the sort that would mark his entire career. And true, he was a rising star, at least in the theater, where he was back on terra firma after a disastrous, two-year detour to Hollywood. But his personal life was a mess.

Seven years since he had appeared opposite Jill Esmond in a West End comedy, *Bird in Hand*, he was married and had begun to stray. Affairs, minor and major, complicated his domestic malaise, among them liaisons with the actresses Greer Garson and Ann Todd, along with an old friend from acting school, Peggy Ashcroft (who remained in love with him until Jill came hammering at her door, when she wisely chose to withdraw). But his marriage was on the rocks, and if Jill didn't know it, Larry most certainly did.

They had first met when Larry was only twenty-one. Unformed and inexperienced, he was still under the sway of his father, still in thrall to his belief that the spirit was willing but the flesh was weak. Intensely romantic, he was profoundly ignorant of sex; he was oblivious to the roiling Shakespearean emotions— green-eyed envy and thundering rage, devouring ambition and the thirst for power—let alone the one Shakespeare knew best: lust in action, "the expense of spirit in a waste of shame." He claimed he had been "alarmingly loose," but "loose" didn't mean what it does today: it meant flirtatious and spirited, not oversexed. Larry wasn't sexed at all. "There were no romantic adventures," he admitted later, "oh no, most certainly not—without marriage that would have been a mortal sin and I was well and truly steeped in religious thinking." A fellow this callow could easily confuse liking with love, as he may have done with Jill. Later, when he had forgotten everything he admired about her, when he had persuaded himself that she was bad in order to convince himself he was good, he would advise his son, Tarquin, to avoid "the cretinous romanticism of the Oliviers."

A year younger than Larry, Jill was pretty without being beautiful, handsome but not breathtaking. She wasn't "dazzling," as he put it, nor was she especially romantic. "There was nothing of the passionate personality about her," said a friend. Still, she had an impeccable pedigree, and for this upwardly mobile parson's

son, that may have mattered more. She came from theatrical royalty: her late father, Henry Esmond, had been a leading actor-
manager and her mother, Eva Moore, was a well-known actress.
They represented everything Olivier did not: success, sophistication, social standing. Love? That was almost beside the point.

So what if there were ominous signs, like the nickname Larry's friends bestowed on Jill, "the Colonel"? She was intelligent
and even intellectual, refined and—most important—able to
refine him. And so, within weeks of their meeting in 1927, Larry
proposed, only for Jill to turn him down. She wasn't ready, she
said, and neither was he. From that point on, the couple lurched
back and forth almost comically, one zigging while the other
zagged. Larry followed Jill to New York, where she went with a
play—only to be forced back to England when his own production flopped. At each step, something seemed to go wrong, not
least the couple's halfhearted stabs at making love. "[His] modesty was unnatural," writes Tarquin. "Any forward move from
Jill led to his prayers for forgiveness, on his knees."

"I suppose our happiest moment has just the faintest shadow
lurking somewhere near it," Larry wrote Jill from the ship bringing him home, "some doubt, or fear—fear perhaps of hurting
something, some ideal, God, perhaps or the moment itself."
What was it, Jill wondered? Was it their "imp"? Or the "dancing
teacher"? Or their "bigger devil," whatever that meant—surely
not Larry's premature ejaculation (which he would oddly reveal
in Confessions), because they hadn't had sex. Perhaps ambivalence on Jill's part as well as his? In the future, her liaisons would
be mainly with women, while Larry would become sexually rapacious, juggling affairs, whether he was married or not. But that
was later. For now, a priest said there was no cause for alarm and
that all would be fine if they only had faith in the Lord. Larry
proposed again. "All this gadding about is silly," he said. "We've
got to be married." "That's a noble idea," replied Jill. "When?"

On July 25, 1930, they tied the knot and, on the morning of their wedding at All Saints Church, London, Larry received a tender note from another woman: his stepmother, Isobel Buchanan (known as Ibo), whom Gerard had unexpectedly married in defiance of his own beliefs, four years after Agnes's death. "Kim Darling," she wrote kindly, "just a little word on your wedding morning. I wish I could come and wake you up and sit on your bed and have a little talk. But that can't be so I must send it on paper. It is such a big day for you and Jillie, there will be other big days in your lives, but nothing can be quite like this one. You said the other day, that you were both darling such strangers to one another—and that's just how it is—you are strangers—until that wonderful service—and afterwards you are just a complete 'one'!" She continued, blithely unaware of her double entendres: "Larry darling, it's just beautiful and every day you will, please God, find that oneness becoming bigger and bigger. Be very gentle with her, Darling, but be the leader."

Few men were less equipped to lead, and the day after his nuptials, still recovering from the shock of sex, Larry accidentally shaved off half his mustache, an act that would have made Freud proud.

Private pain was counterbalanced by professional pleasure. It was through Jill that Larry met Noël Coward; through Coward that he landed *Private Lives*; and through *Private Lives* that he got invited to Hollywood, where he had his initial and desultory experience with the movie business. Now, after five back-to-back motion picture flops, he had returned to London and triumph in the West End.

Trying to perk things up at home, he bought Jill a pet lemur named Tony, as if all she needed was another bushy-tailed male. "Olivier during the unhappy period of his first marriage, to Jill Esmond, made a desperate attempt to cheer his dreary home life by the purchase...from Harrods of a LEMUR," confided his close friend, actor-producer Anthony Bushell, in a letter to a young acquaintance. "This detestable beast terrorized his household....His favourite, + least attractive, trick, was to cling to the top of a curtain—hide in the [velvet] + stay there for hours until an incautious visitor would be rash enough to look out of the window. He would then drop on their back + gibber insanely into their faces."

When a maid accidentally let the lemur loose, he "bounded to the window, up to the roof, and swung from the eaves into the neighbour's bedroom where there was an enormously fat woman getting dressed," writes Tarquin. "He terrorised her, and was found by Jill prancing up and down, keeping the poor woman cornered in her underwear. As soon as Jill came to the rescue he clasped his hands to his face to show how sorry he was." Jill treasured him nonetheless. "In the garden he used to sit and spread his hands out to the sun, gurgling with contentment. He clung to Jill or Larry when frightened by a strange dog or a banging door. Perhaps he awakened Jill's maternal instinct, suppressed by her ambition as an actress. She used to wonder whether, if she had a child, she would love it as much."

She found out in late 1935, when she became pregnant and the lemur went berserk. Larry was in the midst of caressing him when Jill entered their room. "As soon as he saw her he knew: she was pregnant, and he flung himself at her in a screaming jealous rage," notes Tarquin. "He bit her hand and clenched his teeth. She had betrayed him. Larry managed to prize open his jaws, wrench him away, struggling, and put him back into his cage where he sat, glowering, shaking."

The couple decided he had to go. Taking him to the London Zoo, they left him with a female lemur who bullied him mercilessly. "Jill visited him, so did Larry," writes Tarquin, "but his delight at their arrival and his increasingly agonised screams at each departure only added to his torture."

*   *   *

Vivian's own torture had come to an end. At fourteen, she had left Sacred Heart and gone into the world, touring the finishing schools of Europe (schools where girls would be taught the social graces of upper-class life) while proving as irresistible to men as they were to her. She was liberal with her affections—libertine even, in her strict mother's eyes. It was all well and good for Ernest to have his mistresses: boys would be boys, and Gertrude had long tolerated his affairs enough to poke fun at him, once even inviting his lovers to dinner, along with their husbands. But girls were different, especially good Catholics. When Gertrude spotted Vivian kissing a local waiter, she slapped her face and plucked her out of school, only to plop her down in another, where the cycle resumed. By the time Vivian was eighteen, she was ready for more, which she found in the form of Leigh Holman.

Herbert Leigh Holman, thirty-one, could not have been more different from her. He was a staid and stolid fellow, a graduate of Harrow and Cambridge, and a lawyer like his father. Olivier would later declare him a spectacular bore, "a dull man, dry, cerebral, without sparkle," before changing his mind. But he was an island of stability in the eyes of a teenager who had next to none, especially following the crash of 1929, which cost her family almost everything it possessed. Hopping from one friend's home to another's, Vivian was living like a nomad, while her parents relocated to England and temporarily separated as they tried to reconstruct their lives. She had just enrolled at the Royal Academy of Dramatic Art (RADA), when she noticed Holman riding his horse in late December 1931. The next week, she recorded their first meeting in her diary: "Drove round and saw Holman estate met Leigh."

A few days later, they ran into each other again at a local ball and waltzed into the night. Another ball followed, and then they spent a day at the Henley Regatta. Soon Holman was smitten and doing everything he could to conquer his prize: he even invited Gertrude to chaperone them to a Jerome Kern musical, *The Cat and the Fiddle.* "Dinner + show with Leigh—7 o'clock," Vivian gushed. "*The* most marvellous night."

On December 20, 1932, the two were married at St. James's Roman Catholic Church in Marylebone, London. They made the sort of couple Dickens would have adored: one a picture of innocence, the other of experience—or such were the roles they chose to play. As the bride promised to love, cherish and obey her husband till death did them part, even dropping out of RADA to do so, she seemed as chaste as any of the nuns. "All I remember was how thin and shy she looked," said a guest. "Yes, a shy little bride in white satin. The bridesmaids wore peach satin with puff sleeves and carried chrysanthemums. But it is her demureness that remains in my memory."

Vivian was ecstatic: "I got married," she scribbled in her diary. "*Wonderful* day." Gertrude, however, was distraught and called the event "terribly sad." Perhaps her enthusiasm was tempered by her own marital woes (she had had enough of Ernest's womanizing and was openly in love with his best friend, Tommy Thomson, in a strange relationship that appears to have remained platonic). As soon as the wedding was over, she fled to the comfort food of a wafer-thin musical, *Tell Her the Truth,* while the newly named Mr. and Mrs. Leigh Holman set off on a European honeymoon.

Ten months after their return, in October 1933, Vivian gave birth to a baby girl, Suzanne. Ten months after that, she saw Olivier for the first time in the comedy *Theatre Royal.* Forgetting her wedding vows, she turned to a companion and whispered: "That's the man I'm going to marry."

Struggling to master his recalcitrant wife, Holman asked a friend for advice when she wished to return to RADA. "You can't stop her," said the friend, publisher Hamish Hamilton. "But it will be the end of your marriage." He was right. Soon, Vivian was out and about at all times, preferring the company of her new actor friends to that of her safe but stodgy husband—perhaps sexually, too. And then she abandoned all pretense at domesticity, striking out as an actress with new goals, new dreams and a new identity, merging her own name with Holman's to become Vivien Leigh.

Like Larry, she was reinventing herself, shedding one lifestyle and adopting another. Professional opportunities arose quickly— first a film, *Things Are Looking Up*, in which she had all of one line; and then two others, *The Village Squire* and *Gentleman's Agreement*, neither memorable. Along with these minor movie roles, Vivien made a small but undistinguished appearance in a short-lived play, *The Green Sash*, in February 1935. But she was a starlet, not a star, a pretender to the throne, not royalty itself, until she won the lead in *The Mask of Virtue*, a stage adaptation of Diderot's eighteenth-century novel *Jacques le fataliste et son maître*.

Sydney Carroll, its producer, had tried for months to find a woman who could play the prostitute who ensnares an aristocrat in an elaborate game of love and lust. He'd gone after such eminent actresses as Ashcroft and Anna Neagle, only to be spurned, and was on the point of losing hope when he laid eyes on this newcomer as she was having dinner with her agent, John Gliddon. Carroll was captivated, not just by her looks but by something in which he had more faith: the lines of her hand. "I was influenced solely by my own judgement plus a knowledge of palmistry," he bragged. "Vivien allowed me to read her hands and her remarkable line of success or destiny struck me as being unique."

Brought in to read for the role, she "literally shook from head to foot with fright," as she later remembered. But actress Lilian Braithwaite "gave me a smile of friendly encouragement, and somehow I managed to find my voice. After I stopped reading there was a moment's silence. Then [Braithwaite] said briskly: 'I think we have got the right girl, don't you, Sydney?'" Technically unsure and thin of voice, unaware of her own laugh lines and incapable of crying convincingly onstage, Vivien nevertheless possessed a rare charm that captivated audiences and critics alike when the play opened on May 15, 1935.

"The miracle had happened," she sighed. "I had arrived."

Days after the miracle, Larry saw her onstage. Then the two met in person at the Savoy Grill, where Vivien was dining with actor John Buckmaster. "[He] pointed across to Larry," she recalled, "and he said to me, 'Doesn't he look funny without his moustache?' and I was very indignant and I said rather pompously that he didn't look funny at all."

Soon, she accepted Olivier's invitation to a garden party he and Jill were hosting, where, she would recall, "we went and we played football, and I remember Larry roaring around one minute and then unaccountably falling fast asleep under the piano the next."

On January 27, 1936, they had lunch for the first time alone. They were not yet on intimate terms, as Larry's diary makes clear: he refers to his lunch date as "Vivien Leigh," using her full name. But "Vivien Leigh" soon gives way to "Vivien," and "Vivien" to "Viv," until finally she becomes "Vivling," not just a pet name but the very one Holman used. Olivier wasn't just stealing the man's wife; he was stealing his language.

When Larry joined John Gielgud in a celebrated production of *Romeo and Juliet*, where the two alternated the roles of Romeo and Mercutio, Vivien came to see him over and over again. Disappointing as Romeo, Larry was kinetic as the hotheaded Mercutio, projecting the kind of swashbuckling energy that would lead any young woman to fall head over heels. And Vivien did just that. Visiting him backstage, she made a move.

"I was making up for a matinée of *Romeo* when she popped into my dressing-room at the New Theatre," wrote Olivier. "It was ostensibly to invite us to something or other; she only stayed a couple of minutes, and then she gave me a soft little kiss on the shoulder and was gone."

So, alas, was Vivien's luck. After the sensation of *Mask*, she suddenly found herself out of a job. The play had ended quicker than expected, less of a box office draw than everyone had anticipated. If Vivien had been less distinctive, she might have gone straight from that to a host of other parts; but the very qualities that made her stand out—her breathtaking beauty, her unusual elegance—also made her hard to cast.

For a while, she clung to the hope of starring opposite Charles Laughton in a film version of Edmond Rostand's *Cyrano de Bergerac*, only for it to fritter away amid bickering between Laughton and his producer. Having turned down a new stage production of *Hamlet* (starring Leslie Howard) because of the film, she hurriedly tried to salvage Howard's offer to play Ophelia, only to find he had cast someone else. Instead, she took small roles in two back-to-back productions, neither of any significance: a short-lived Oxford run of *Richard II*, which Gielgud directed; and a brief revival of Max Beerbohm's *The Happy Hypocrite*. When she reunited with her *Mask* producer, Carroll, for an outdoor production of *Henry VIII*, she was walloped by the critics, who complained that her voice was too weak to be heard above the pigeons and the traffic.

Months after taking London by storm, she was floundering. Unsure how to revive her career and increasingly claustrophobic in her domestic environment, she was fast realizing that marriage was just another role in an interminable play, motherhood a repeat performance without the benefit of good writing. She had nothing to challenge her, nothing to keep her fertile mind busy except reading (which she did voluminously) and making the rounds of her many friends, while her husband tried to entertain her with the minutiae of his tedious work. She was ripe for change and even riper for an affair when the producer Alexander Korda approached her about a new film.

Korda was the kind of mogul London had never known, a larger-than-life, globe-trotting, heavily accented Hungarian émigré who had fled his authoritarian country in 1919 and arrived in England after stretches in Europe and America, during which he had lavished his talents on such pictures as the 1931 French classic *Marius* and the 1933 British drama *The Private Life of Henry VIII*. He had snapped Vivien up with a long-term contract the moment he saw her in *Mask*, strategically (if falsely) spreading the word that this was the most lucrative deal any newcomer had ever signed, as the British press trumpeted the putative £50,000 pact. Now, after several abortive attempts to relaunch his protégée's career, he cast her as Cynthia, a fictionalized lady-in-waiting to Elizabeth I, with Flora Robson as the Virgin Queen, in a swashbuckler about a dashing aristocrat, Michael Ingolby, who assumes the guise of a Spanish spy to infiltrate the court of King Philip II of Spain.

Fire Over England was one of Britain's first propaganda pieces since the Nazis had seized power, a summons to patriotism and self-sacrifice shot three years before England went to war. Korda was acutely aware of the danger Hitler posed; he had fled one dictatorship and was loath to flee another, though he remained largely ignored at a time when the British public was deeply divided. Such admired figures as King Edward VIII were sympathetic to the Nazis (after his abdication, the monarch would visit Hitler at his rural retreat) and several of the country's press barons strongly favored appeasement; indeed, the *Times* had refused to publish warnings by its Berlin correspondent of the threat the Nazis posed. But the apolitical Vivien wanted the part for another reason: Olivier was set to star.

On July 15, 1936, the two passed each other in a hallway at Denham Studios on their first day of work. "You know," Larry teased her, "before the picture's over we're going to be fighting. People who play together in pictures always get very sick of each other."

They didn't. Instead, Larry reserved his fighting for the camera as he battled the Spaniards, hurtling across a ship's deck and jumping into a fake ocean with such abandon that his director, William K. Howard, a veteran from the silent era, was afraid he'd broken his neck. Larry could have asked for a stuntman, but he was young and impetuous, too convinced that acting needed every ounce of authenticity ever to let another man take his place, and too keen to show off his manliness to Vivien.

Watching him today in the black-and-white film, exquisitely lit by one of the masters of the craft, cinematographer James Wong Howe, his beauty dazzles more than his performance. Slender and well-toned, elegant and athletic (helped by a little padding), he radiates virility, but only in rare moments does he allow his natural sly humor to slip in, adding an unexpected layer that Vivien's more one-dimensional performance lacks. As for her, never was she this beautiful, never so gorgeously shot, even if the camera failed to register the full force of her personality, which would emerge, startling and unheralded, only in *Gone with the Wind*.

Vivien and Larry could not keep apart. Together for protracted periods when others weren't around, they crossed the line from attraction to action, from admiration to an affair. Each moment they weren't working—and sometimes when they were—they would sneak off, find a private space where they could talk, laugh and touch. Hands, lips, limbs reached for each other with an urgency neither could control. When Larry asked the avuncular Korda if he could use his house for meetings with an unnamed woman, Korda sent a spy to find out who it was, as if he hadn't guessed. Melting in the August heat, and drowning in her heavy costumes, Vivien would tear them off as soon as she and Larry were alone. They were making love all the time— "every day, two, three times," Larry confided to a friend.

"I don't think I have ever lived quite as intensely ever since," Vivien said later. "I don't remember sleeping, ever; only every precious moment that we spent together."

When she developed a cough, Larry visited her at home, where he sat in her bedroom, dousing her with rum while Holman— away on one of his many boating trips—remained impervious to the truth. He "didn't pay it any attention," recalled his close friend, Oswald Frewen. "He assumed it was just another of those theatrical relationships."

Larry and Vivien thought they could keep things under wraps; but they were wrong, as they discovered when they confided in Korda. "We're in love and we're going to get married," exclaimed Vivien, assuming he would be surprised. "Don't be silly," said Korda. "I've known it for weeks and weeks."

Left alone in her little house in Chelsea, Jill could not have been blind to all this, though Frewen believed she never "had the whisper of an idea that Larry had more on his mind than helping out a young actress friend of both of them." She was "defenceless and looking her worst," observed Tarquin. She had smelled Vivien's perfume on her husband and yet discounted it or assumed the affair would blow over, as it had with Ashcroft. She was on her own, isolated for long stretches as she entered the final weeks of a tortured pregnancy, forced to remain still on doctor's orders out of fear she would lose her baby, and lacking even her beloved lemur, Tony, for company. Much as Larry's rapscallion friends may have disliked her, she was a supportive and devoted spouse, admired by many (not least Coward) for her talent and her belief in her husband. She'd brought Larry into her family fold, allowed their mantle of distinction to fall on him when he was an upstart, a mere parvenu, then followed him to Hollywood, only to leave at his insistence when he felt threatened by her success. Now, housebound, she clung to her husband even as he clung to Vivien.

On August 21, 1936, following an excruciating, fourteen-hour labor that ended with a C-section, weeks into *Fire*'s three-month shoot, she gave birth to her first and only child, Simon Tarquin. It was an agonizing experience, but at least Larry was with her the entire night, holding her hand as she held his, gripping it so hard that the skin was scratched raw. The baby almost died; it had "punctured the membrane and swallowed fluid," writes Tarquin, speaking of himself. "The doctor put it in cold water, then hot water, then cold again and just managed to bring it to life."

Larry was delighted and began reciting Shakespeare to him in his crib. But nothing could break his bond with Vivien and, with a deceitfulness that galled him, he brought her to see his newborn son. Then Jill made a tactical error: instead of drawing a red line between Vivien and herself, she pulled her rival closer, as if holding her tight could keep danger at bay. It was the beginning of a strange friendship in which the disparate couples—Vivien and Holman, Larry and Jill—spent more and more time together, even as two of the four were conducting a covert affair.

That culminated in October 1936, when Vivien left London for Italy, taking her first vacation without her husband or child, accompanied by Frewen, who had become her friend as well as Holman's, an older man willing to tag along. As for Holman, he was unable to join them, though he might have found a way had he known his wife's plans.

Setting out for Rome, they traveled by train to the far south, sleeping in adjacent compartments, their privacy maintained by a connecting door that was mostly left open. Vivien was "so natural," wrote Frewen, "that sex didn't obtrude," perhaps the only time in her adult life that it didn't. He was ignorant of her true goal: to meet the Oliviers, who were vacationing in Capri. And so he listened happily as she prattled on about life and art, about Holman and herself, as unaware of the subterfuge as her husband.

"I am restless to have you back, Vivling," wrote Holman, "but don't grudge you a moment of the sun. Perhaps the Mediterranean sun will make you brown, but brown or natural-tinted you will give me a happiness which has been suppressed for 10 days."

Black, rather than brown, was the color of the day and omnipresent on the Fascist uniforms, fourteen years after Mussolini had come to power; but Vivien paid them no heed. The regime had yet to introduce its most extreme racial policies; still, it was impossible to mistake the authoritarianism that had engulfed the nation and would soon overwhelm Europe. All this passed Vivien by as she crossed the country and arrived at Taormina's Domenico Hotel, overlooking Mount Etna. Here she revealed her true motive in a letter back home, couched in such casual language that only a polygraph could have detected it. She was thinking of heading to Capri, she mentioned to Holman, because "it would be fun to see Jill & Larry if they're still there."

While Etna smoked, ominous signs abounded. When Vivien's seaplane took off, bound for the small island nine miles off the coast, it struggled to rise, thudding like a skimmed stone over the waves. Terrified, Vivien muttered the name Thérèse over and over, perhaps not the wisest choice given that St. Thérèse of Lisieux had died at twenty-four.

Arriving safely in Capri, she found the Oliviers at the Hotel Quisisana, bored to tears. "Larry, the other side of the hall, cried in a loud voice 'Vivien!' and Viv, my side of the hall, cried loudly 'Darling!'" noted Frewen, "and Jill uttered further love-cries as all three met in the middle of what I could only describe as a joint passionate embrace, while I smiled agedly and with benignity!"

Not even age and benignity could hide the obvious: Larry and Vivien were in love. One of Frewen's photographs captures their predicament as Larry stands on the rocks with one arm snaking around Vivien, the other around Jill, staring at her warily. If Frewen still had doubts, they disappeared days later, when Larry and Vivien bade a tearful goodbye at the Naples train station while soldiers manned the doors. Hours later, Vivien suffered a "crise de nerfs," as Frewen put it, while he begged her to do nothing impetuous. She was sobbing, calling for Larry and no longer attempting to hide the truth.

Back in England, she started work on a new film, *Dark Journey*, appropriately about a double agent (who falls in love with a German spy), which kept her not only away from her husband but also at the same studio where Olivier was wrapping *Fire Over England*.

"I was so depressed Friday—last night—my darling," she wrote Holman, off on another trip. "It was very dismal without you." She missed him desperately, she insisted, and yet was terrified he'd come home. "I am so unhappy when you are in London, when you could be in the country or sailing which is so good for you. I think I'd almost rather you stayed on sailing my love. That isn't because I am not longing to see you & be with you but I feel so mean when you're waiting for me all that time, especially in this wonderful weather."

On December 7, 1936, Larry took Vivien to a reception following Tarquin's christening. He "had been away filming," recalled one guest, "but suddenly he appeared and he had this girl in slacks and a red jumper with him. It was Vivien. They didn't quite come in, but stood near the door and everyone was soon saying to themselves, Hello.... Oh that's it, is it? They were together—one couldn't mistake it. After a few minutes, they vanished. Vivien didn't come back, but Larry did—with what looked like lipstick on his cheek. I suppose it would have been considered scandalous in any ordinary group. But we were all theatricals—it was just something that happened."

Perhaps this explains why Jill never gave Larry an ultimatum, never tried to repel Vivien's siege, and indeed did just the opposite: she allowed the Holmans to sleep over and let Larry spend the night with them, though they lived only two miles apart. "Despite herself," writes Tarquin, "she could not help liking Vivien." And so she made Vivien her pupil, tried to shape her as she had previously shaped Larry. "She was astonished to find herself passing on all she could to Vivien, as though they were the closest of friends. Next time they met Vivien would have read what Jill had suggested and be keen to discuss it. She learnt fast."

Such proximity must have been agonizing for Jill, as it would have been for Holman if he'd had a clue what was going on. But unlike Esmond, he gave no sign of awareness and, with an almost reckless abandon, time and again he absented himself at the moments of gravest danger. His letters home come across as a heartbreaking counterpoint to his wife's betrayal. "I am loveless because you have it all, Viv," he wrote, unaware that his "Viv" was in love with another man. Doubt never crossed his mind, not even when Vivien began to adopt some of Larry's most distinctive traits: she grew enamored of Shakespeare, scoffed at the films (which she'd previously relished) and aped the expletives that peppered his every phrase. "Olivier," noted the actor Anthony Quayle, "was the very first person I ever heard use the word 'fucking' as a sort of free-and-easy embellishment in everyday speech. . . . Vivien caught this trick off him, I believe." Her language, he said, "would have caused the hair to curl on a rocking horse."

This was the beginning of a long period that later made Olivier shudder and that he regarded with a cocktail of horror and shame. It was "two years of furtive life, lying life. Sneaky," he wrote. He felt like "a really wormlike adulterer, slipping in between another man's sheets." But he was sick with desperation and desire, and so was Vivien. "All [Vivien] wanted to do was to talk about Larry," recalled Rex Harrison, who costarred with her in a new feature comedy, *Storm in a Teacup*.

Throughout, as Vivien segued to the films *A Yank at Oxford* and *St. Martin's Lane*, and Larry undertook his boldest stage work to date, turning his back on commercial ventures to join the Old Vic repertory company in a series of Shakespeares that would make his name, the lovers maintained their status quo. They were living in limbo, wrenched one way by their galvanic feelings and another by their guilt. Only when they appeared together onstage did their affair gain critical mass.

Hamlet was Olivier's bid to seize Gielgud's mantle, a tossing of the gauntlet before the man who had made the part his own, "the high water-mark of English Shakespearean acting of our time," in the critic James Agate's words.

Before staging the play with Vivien, Larry had tackled it at the Vic, the very theater where Gielgud's *Hamlet* had been a sensation, giving up the thousands of pounds he could have made in the movies for all of £5 per week. His work drew extensively on ideas articulated by Britain's leading psychoanalyst, Ernest Jones; but it was also a monument to showmanship, a flamboyant, preening, emotional roller-coaster ride aimed not just at Larry's critics but at the most important person in the audience: Vivien. "With all its physical virility and acrobatic flash, it was his way of wooing her," believed Kenneth Tynan. "She told me later on that she went to see at least half the performances, just so that she could be near Larry during a time when she was supposed to be staying away from him."

Supposed to be staying away from him? At whose demand?

Tynan never elaborated, and neither Vivien nor Olivier ever said any more. The line implies they had tried to resist their forbidden love, but that was out of the question once Larry committed to Elsinore and asked Vivien to go with him.

They were granted a week's leave by Korda, who had just cast them in the melodrama *21 Days*, and at the end of May 1937 they left for Denmark, only for it to pour.

"On the opening night," recalled Quayle, who played Laertes, "the rain fell in cataracts. Tony [director Tyrone Guthrie] made one of his Immediate Decisions: rather than abandon the performance, we would present *Hamlet* in the centre of the great Marienlyst Hotel where we were staying. It was a brave move, for there was no time to rehearse; entrances, exits, positions, all would have to be improvised as we went along. Younger members of the audience were provided with cushions and instructed by Tony in his most governess-like manner to sit on the floor— and like it; members of the Diplomatic Corps and elderly, distinguished guests were perched on slender ballroom chairs; everyone else had to stand, climb on benches and tables, or otherwise fend for themselves."

The event, of course, was a stupendous success. Vivien was "enchanting—as lovely and delicate as a violet," noted Quayle. (He was less charitable when he told the writer Alan Dent, "I remember how beautiful Vivien looked; and I remember how far her talent fell short of her beauty.") And then came Vivien's change of mood.

It was the first sign that something was amiss, and nothing in her previous behavior could have prepared Larry for the explosion. He was so shaken that he subsequently asked the Hartleys if they had any family history of mental illness, only for "Ernest, nearly splitting a gut with outrage [to shout], 'Good God, *no!*'"

Still, Larry never wavered. Instead of pulling apart, he drew closer; instead of breaking with Vivien, he bound himself even tighter to her. By the end of the week in Denmark, as he wrote later, "This welding closeness tripped the obvious decision, and two marriages were severed."

CHAPTER 3

———◆———

The shock Holman felt was profound. When Vivien confessed what had happened, revealing the truth in the sanctity of their bijou home, this placid and seemingly passionless man—this cuckold who had never imagined his wife could have an affair, or else was so blinkered to the dark gullies and murky undercurrents of human relationships that it was beyond his comprehension—refused to believe she would leave.

Hadn't he done everything one could expect of a man in his position? Hadn't he gone to his office each day, toiled at his desk, put up with demanding clients, found a lovely house in Mayfair and provided every domestic comfort for his wife and child? True, he'd been somewhat strict, insisting Vivien ask permission if she wished to go out; and true, he'd overindulged his taste for yachting, leaving her alone for days on end—but even then, he knew she got seasick, which explained why he'd go off on his own. He was a lawyer, not an artist; a man of erudition more than emotion. Yes, he knew "the heart has its reasons of which reason knows nothing"; but reason would win out, as it always did, as it always must.

Vivien hesitated. She was still a Catholic, after all, imbued with a nonnegotiable sense of good and bad, and knew this would affect her daughter, now three years old—just three years short of Vivien's age when her life had been turned upside down. Challenging as she had found motherhood, she wasn't blind to her responsibilities, and a sliver of doubt slipped into her thinking. She was in love with Larry; she knew that beyond question. But would he really abandon Jill ten months after she'd given birth? Would he risk society's disapproval? And his father's? And God's? He was in many ways more conventional than Vivien: he loved tradition, respected the establishment, and longed for the day when he could join its ranks, when he would be a Great Man, like his Uncle Sydney. All this would be jeopardized by scandal and possibly destroyed by divorce. Then, too, he had strayed, as Vivien knew: along with his brief flings, there were rumors he had gone off to Paris on wild jaunts with his friend Tony Bushell, another bad boy, surely intent on seeing more than the sights. If he had been unfaithful to Jill, why on earth should Vivien think he'd be faithful to her? And if she had been unfaithful, too (it was said she had cheated with her friend John Buckmaster), could anyone be faithful at all?

"She torments herself with the thought," a friend told Olivier later. "I suppose that when a girl has fucked a bit herself she finds it difficult to understand constancy."

There was another matter, too: the nature of Larry's sexuality. Some believed he was bisexual, and Vivien in later years wasn't above teasing him about it. The actress Sarah Miles claimed Olivier told her he had had affairs with men, including Coward. But his closest friends had no doubts: John and Mary Mills dismissed the notion out of hand, as did Larry's third wife, Joan Plowright.

So did Bushell, who knew him as well as anyone. "David Niven, Milord Olivier, and [another actor] were nattering to each other at some [dinner] or other, + conversation veered as it often did to Mr. Coward," he wrote in a private letter. "It transpired on discussion that each of them at some time or another had been homosexually propocitioned [sic] by Noël. David + Laurence, of course, both laughed him out of it, but [the other actor] said, 'Oh I took it—I needed the part!' "

One of Olivier's biographers, Donald Spoto, author of the controversial 1991 account *Laurence Olivier: The Biography*, alleges that Olivier had an affair with the actor and comedian Danny Kaye, an assertion that drew widespread publicity when his book came out and has lingered in the public imagination ever since. Writing that the two met at a party in 1940 and that Kaye nicknamed Olivier "Lally," Spoto argues that they "were lovers. At first Vivien had merely thought Kaye rude, since he arrived at their house unannounced at odd hours, without invitation or permission. But Olivier was also spending long, late hours with him, and the affair—at first rampant gossip and then a widespread belief in Hollywood, New York and in the Caribbean (where the relationship continued irregularly for several years)—was no secret to Vivien, nor did Olivier deny it." He continues: "For Olivier, the affair with Kaye revealed what the earlier relationship with Coward had—more about his need for affection from those he admired than for sex itself, about which he was, for most of his life, remarkably diffident."

That is vehemently rejected by Victoria Tennant, among others. "My mother was spitting angry [about it]," she says. "She said that was a complete lie and she hated it." Equally adamant is Gawn Grainger, the actor who cowrote Olivier's second book, *On Acting*, and got to know him well. "I think I would have known, because Larry used to tell me anything," he says.

Still, Olivier's sexuality was complicated, and in his memoirs he used a strange choice of words to describe "the homosexual act," which he called "darkly destructive to my soul." He also acknowledged some sort of relationship with an older man when he was young—probably the actor Henry Ainley. By his late twenties, he wrote in *Confessions of an Actor*, "I had got over like a spendthrift sigh my nearly passionate involvement with the one male with whom some sexual dalliance had not been loathsome for me to contemplate. I had felt it desperately necessary to warn him that, dustily old-fashioned as it must seem, I had ideals which must not be trodden underfoot and destroyed or I would not be able to answer for the consequences and neither would he."

Olivier's authorized biographer, Terry Coleman, believes something occurred between the two. "Their probable fling was obviously brief, from December 1936 to early January 1937," he concludes (notably citing the very period when Larry was falling for Vivien). His evidence: a string of letters between Olivier and Ainley. "Christ!" Ainley writes in one of them. "You are a lousy Pansy. Don't you ever dare write to me again." In another, he tells Olivier: "Yes I am a *psod*. And what is more *so are you*. Now summons me! I'd counter claim for worse! Well, you know what you did. I can't walk. I've been in bed ever since. And the child has your eyes. Dear. Shall we call her Olivette? You strumpet, that's you."

Is this evidence of an affair? Tarquin Olivier scoffs at the idea, calling the letters "extravagantly camp" and dismissing Ainley as a terminal alcoholic, "broke, unemployable, washed up and living in exile in Broadstairs, Kent." When he asked his father if he was gay, Olivier was categorical. "Christ no," he said. "I've never been queer."

If Vivien had doubts about Larry's commitment, Jill had none. Shrewder than Holman, and worldlier despite his apparent sophistication, she had long sensed something was wrong, felt the kinetic sparks between her husband and his exquisite friend. But she came from the theater, which had its own particular ecosystem, its own manners and mores, in many ways unlike those of society at large. Sex and sexuality were elastic concepts here, notions that could be bent and stretched to fit different people and different occasions. Only one thing was sacred: marriage. Whatever men and women might do in private, they must follow the golden rule and return to their spouses. Now Larry had gone and broken it.

Still bloated from her pregnancy, Jill waddled around her house, tired and depressed, struggling to feed a baby that refused to be suckled, that seemed to want her no more than her husband. She had returned from Hollywood physically as well as psychically scarred, her skin covered with "a myriad purple veinlets which she ever after had to cloud over with pancake make-up," recalled Tarquin; Los Angeles hadn't just stamped her marriage, it had left a virtual street map on her face. Once, she had held all the cards; now she was ugly and undesired, not just by men but by the movies and the stage, where her career had once outshone his. At rock bottom, forced to give up all semblance of pride, she left her house and crossed the two miles to the Holmans', ready to throw herself on her rival's mercy, a strategy that had worked with Ashcroft.

Arriving at the Holman home in Little Stanhope Street, she was ushered into the living room, where she found Vivien swaddled amid cushions and chintz-covered chairs she adored, enveloped in the scent of fresh flowers, reigning supreme in her own private court. Her taste was, as ever, immaculate, if ultrafeminine, and this overpoweringly pretty place might have made Jill smile if she weren't too upset to notice. The moment her guest arrived, Vivien was on the alert and told her maid to hold any calls. Then Jill begged for crumbs: Have the affair if you must, she pleaded, but let me keep my husband. Vivien sat, revealing nothing. Whatever turmoil she felt inside never spilled out; instead, she parried and tried to divert the attack with housekeeping talk: How did Larry like his eggs?

Jill knew the battle was lost. All she could do was return home and sit out the clock, listening to the ticktock of the seconds going by, with nothing to distract her but the screaming child.

A terrible stillness fell on the couples' homes, "two households, both alike in dignity," an awful period of calm when all four players knew the inevitable must happen but didn't know when. Then, late at night in the middle of June, eight days after Vivien and Larry had returned from Denmark, during a break from *21 Days*, they chose their moment to slink off. Holman was still sleeping and so was the toddler Suzanne when Vivien disappeared without a word, terrified her husband might persuade her to remain if she dared to tell him the truth.

What went through her mind as she passed through the door, not knowing if or when she would see her family again? Did desire outweigh remorse? Did lust prove more powerful than familial love? Later, guilt would wash over her in waves, though never enough to capsize her love for Larry, nor did it ever equal the torment that rippled through him. Surprisingly for a young woman with her religious education—one who had once prided herself on her devotion to God—Vivien was able to rationalize away her bad conscience. "To do it once is forgivable," she confided to a friend, "but never again."

Larry was different: guilt ravaged him. He had done the unthinkable—walked out on his wife and son, abandoned his baby in a way that his father would never have abandoned him. From that night on, remorse tugged at him, tortured him, welded him to the sorrier aspects of a past he longed to escape; it would tarnish his relations with Tarquin, whom he could never again see without an inner tug-of-war. Guilt became his companion, a sentiment that haunted him so much as to be almost pathological: he would even open his memoir with the line "Bless me, Reader, for I have sinned."

Now, in the early hours of the morning, he and Vivien drove through the silent streets, empty and deserted, illuminated only by the electric lamps that had replaced the city's gaslights, removing the soft layer of soot that had once coated every street. The lovers were alone, in every sense, forced for the first time to depend entirely on themselves.

Dawn broke in the Holman home and with it came the discovery that Vivien had left. Arriving at the house early that morning, the maid was surprised to find her master alone with the three-year-old Suzanne, his spirits crushed. "I couldn't believe it," she recalled later, when told that Vivien had gone. "I thought he meant she had gone early to the studio. Later she asked me to stay and look after him. Mr. Holman was very good about it. He never bore her any grudge. But it was a long time before I came to like Sir Laurence Olivier. We were such a happy house until he came along."

Gloom settled in and, as the hours turned to days, the pain sank only deeper, leaving Holman pale and almost unrecognizable from his usual healthy self. He didn't know what to do, didn't even know where his wife had gone, and only later discovered that she and Larry had moved into Bushell's country home, where they were certain nobody would find them. When Holman learned about it later, he felt profoundly betrayed. Before that, "we got on v. well together," wrote Bushell, "but since Laurence + Vivien came to where I lived + stayed there the night they bolted, Leigh never spoke to me again."

Was Holman unable to forgive him? Or was he, in fact, unable to forgive himself? The signs had all been there, and only a form of blindness, or blind trust, had prevented him from seeing more. Now he paid the price in full. When Frewen came to check on him, he found his friend spectral, clinging to the belief that Vivien would return, while struggling to maintain some semblance of normality for their child.

As for Suzanne, she and her mother had never been close, even in an age when children were meant to be "seen and not heard." Vivien, ripped from her parents, seemed unable to connect with her daughter and "had no feeling for the child," one friend observed, as if "the maternal glands [weren't] working." But that meant nothing to the lost child, who couldn't fathom why her mother had disappeared and wouldn't return. With Holman steeped in grief, she turned to her grandmother, Gertrude, who stepped in when Vivien stepped out.

Holman was adamant Vivien would return. "He still hopes to get her back, so powerfully that when you are with him you begin to believe that he may," noted Frewen. Even he half-believed it, and was convinced Vivien's flight was just a "wave of promiscuity." Why else would she abandon a man like Holman, a barrister, an Oxford graduate, for a popinjay, a man of straw? With foolish optimism, Frewen attempted a form of shuttle diplomacy, trekking back and forth between Holman and Vivien, and between Larry and Jill, with the misguided idea that he could bring the runaways to their senses. They weren't villains, he assured Jill, just good people who had erred after doing everything in their power to stand firm. But she would have none of it. "She said flatly they hadn't," Frewen recalled.

Privately, he blamed Larry and shared Holman's low opinion of him. "I'm terribly afraid that *he* is inconstant & unballasted & that it won't last 10 years—perhaps not 5," he confided in his diary. "Once cast loose from dear steady old Leigh's helmsmanship I have awful doubts for [Vivien] too....She *has* brain & a heart, but no ethical upbringing"—a remarkable verdict on a woman who had grown up in a convent—"& instead an overdose of temperament. Can she remain unsubmerged?"

Vivien was already submerged. Didn't he know that? Living with Larry, traveling each day from Bushell's home to the nearby Denham Studios, where the couple were finishing their film, she pivoted between exultation and distress, wrestling with the competing demands of love and money. Romance couldn't exist in a vacuum; without funding, it would die—and Vivien quickly discovered how bad their finances were. Just because they were stars didn't mean they were rich, and Olivier alone owed back taxes that would plague him for years.

Vivien knew, just as crucially, that leaving her daughter meant giving up all hope of custody. Anthony Quayle, the actor who had accompanied her to Denmark, recalled how his mother had been forced to cut off her lover when her husband refused to divorce, knowing she would otherwise lose her son; after she refused to live in adultery (choosing instead to move into a bedsit with young Tony), her lover killed himself. Vivien may not have felt a strong link to Suzanne; still, she wasn't immune to the damage she had wrought. She and Larry "appear to be as much in love as ever, but are not having an easy time, even in *their* milieu," observed Frewen. "Only those who know them both intimately know that they *did* struggle against it for a long time, & were not, & are not, callous."

This was the beginning of a period "of nightmares for us and torture for the others," Vivien acknowledged, as some members of their circle stuck with them, while others dropped them altogether. One friend alone transcended expectations. Drink-sodden and disgraced, banished from the theaters where he had once been a leading light, the fifty-eight-year-old Ainley, Larry's alleged lover, now wrote to his young friend. There were no smutty jokes, no prurient references to sex; instead, the aging actor was touching in his devotion. "And now, please, may I be serious, just for a tick," he wrote. "Allow an old friend just a word. Both of you. Be happy. Let not a second of your united lives be thrown away, and wasted on the past. You have both been so brave, and done the right thing. Forget what has been and thank God for what is, and what will come [and] shine like the angels you both are."

* * *

Divorce dominated Vivien's thinking. But that was a cataclysmic step for anyone who wished to remain on the respectable side of society, which Larry, in particular, emphatically did. Fewer than five thousand British couples divorced in 1937, compared to 165,000 in 1993, when divorce reached its peak. Before the Matrimonial Causes Act was passed in the year Vivien and Larry absconded, men could only divorce their wives for adultery, while women couldn't even divorce their husbands for that: they had to prove them guilty of incest, sodomy or domestic violence. The difficulty of obtaining a divorce had wreaked havoc on people's lives—above all those of women, who earned a fraction of men's salaries, with only one in ten holding a job. It was not until now that the liberalized law expanded the grounds for divorce to include desertion, changing the rules so that men and women would be free to remarry after three years apart.

Holman, however, refused to discuss it. "Leigh says, in essence, that he will never let you go *really* (in spite of divorce etc), that you can never be rid of him, can never be *released* from him," lamented Larry. Instead of searching for a compromise— and what kind of compromise could there be?—Holman refused to see Vivien and issued an ultimatum: she had four weeks to change her mind and then he would move on. She never did. "When she left me for Larry," he informed Gertrude, "she told me that after a month she would write me to say whether it was final. I got that letter & it was the only one from her I have ever destroyed. I felt utterly hopeless."

In fact, the letter still exists. "Leigh," Vivien told her husband of four and a half years, "you will know how hard it is to write this letter, but you asked me to write after a month had passed. Although I am very very happy, I do want to know, Leigh, if you are well & feeling happier, as I do wish & hope with all my heart you are.... However painful it may seem at the moment, Leigh,

I do feel that this is the right thing to have happened for you & me, & I hope that perhaps later we can still be friends, in spite of whatever has come between us."

She was not indifferent to this man who had given her so much. Over and over, in the following months and years, she tried to make amends and acknowledged her errors. "I can never be sure of myself again," she admitted, "or trust myself completely, having behaved and hurt you in a way I thought inconceivable after your great understanding, goodness and kindness to me always."

And yet, even as she begged for forgiveness, she also pushed for the divorce, leaving a question as to her sincerity. "I'm asking you," she wrote Holman, "if you think you possibly can, to divorce me." When he refused, Vivien consulted an attorney, only to be told nothing could be done. Furious, she blamed that "ridiculous little man," who told her she would have to wait three years, according to the law, and even then would need her husband to file for "desertion."

Meanwhile, Holman kept writing, his letters toggling between condescension and concern. "My poor darling Viv," he wrote, "I do feel deeply and sincerely sorry for you. I know very well that it is not me you have run away from, but yourself. If I had known you did not realize you can get nothing from marriage or any other personal contact except through what you put into it, I think I would have helped you. But you did not tell me what was happening, and I did not guess. You put nothing into it, darling, when it was most necessary, and by letting yourself fail you have made yourself weaker for the next trial of strength. . . . Don't put your trust in sand."

Jill had done just that and, in the days following the rupture, her misery was extreme. Almost overnight, her hair turned white and, along with her map of purple veins, a red rash now covered her face, so frightening that a pharmacist drew back in horror. Friends were shocked at this alteration in a woman who had once radiated well-being, who had always seemed so calm and composed. Later, she would have nightmares in which Vivien was almost run over by a steamroller, only to be saved by Jill herself, dreams of wish fulfillment in which she could never allow herself to be the villain. "She couldn't bear any kind of tenderness," writes Tarquin. "The only records she could listen to were Stravinsky, cruel music. Sweet sounds made her break down completely."

All she could do was wait in the hope that Olivier would return. But he never did. And as the weeks turned to months, and the emotion began to settle, little by little she acknowledged the futility of hanging on, until rage gave way to a measured calm, anger to a grudging acceptance.

Vivien and Larry found a temporary home in Iver, a few miles west of London and a short drive from Denham Studios, where they tried to concentrate on their movie until they could move into a more permanent abode, Durham Cottage, a charming house in Chelsea that they'd bought with their earnings from 21 Days.

They were too distracted to focus on their film, and Basil Dean, its martinet director, blamed them for turning his picture into a fiasco, though in all likelihood it would have been that regardless. Originally titled The First and the Last and adapted from a John Galsworthy story by the novelist Graham Greene, 21 Days told the story of a ne'er-do-well who kills his lover's husband, only to see another man take the blame. The source material "was peculiarly unsuited for film adaptation," noted Greene, "as its whole point lay in a double suicide (forbidden by the censor), a burned confession and an innocent man's conviction for murder (forbidden by the great public)." This dark matter, said Dean, was made worse by the actors' "laughter and giggling on the set." Their lack of seriousness made him wonder why Korda had ever cast them, only for him to realize the producer had his eye on the future. "It was not until long afterwards," he wrote, "that I realized that both Galsworthy's story and myself had been pawns in this larger game."

For Larry and Vivien, there was no larger game. One friend, running into Olivier, was surprised to find him so tired. It was Vivien, he insisted, with her constant demand for sex. But sex had to be squeezed in between a host of obligations, what with their movie, their stage work (Larry was about to take on three major Shakespeares—*Macbeth*, *Othello* and *Coriolanus*—while Vivien would soon debut at the Old Vic in *A Midsummer Night's Dream*) and the complicated task of decorating a house, especially after its choicest room was all but destroyed by Larry's friend, actor Ralph Richardson.

"The first night he was asked to dinner at Laurence + Vivien's subsequently celebrated little house in Chelsea—just decorated to the nines by Vivien—he brought a parcel of fireworks which exploded en masse from a dropped taper, + wrecked the living room," recalled Bushell. "Vivien, who had always mistrusted Ralph on account of feminine-whispered reports of up-to-no-good Parisian weekends with Laurence or me, never really forgave him."

Larry, in turn, had to accommodate himself to Vivien's circle, which was fine for now but became tricky when she drew close to the dancer-choreographer Robert Helpmann, a man many found vile. He had "a sting," writes the biographer Alexander Walker. He was "a mimic, a gossip, a wit, a man of transfiguring ambitiousness who had trained himself up to leading roles on the ballet stage, but, being unsuited by temperament and looks for *jeune premier* roles, had made the rare transition to the theatre and was ultimately to turn director. Vivien found his bitchiness amusing, Olivier less so."

Vivien's entanglement with Helpmann found a symbolic representation one evening when the young princesses Elizabeth and Margaret came to see them in *A Midsummer Night's Dream* a few months after Vivien had eloped. Afterward, when the royals were introduced, "Vivien curtsied; Helpmann bowed very low," notes Walker. "Then, on attempting to straighten up, they discovered their sylvan headdresses of gilded twigs and ferns (hers) and silver antlers (his) had become interlocked. They were obliged to do a sort of slow-motion pas de deux backwards until out of sight of Royalty, when they collapsed amidst laughter."

These were days of laughter and mirth. Actress Hayley Mills describes the time they invited her parents, John and Mary, for dinner with the actor Stewart Granger and his then wife Elspeth March. "It was a very dressed-up evening," she notes. "People used to get dressed up to go out to dinner in those days. And when my parents arrived, they were all dressed up and shown into the living room—and Vivien and Larry and 'Jimmy' [Granger] and Elspeth were arranged around the sofa, all of them stark naked, except for wearing a tie."

Laughter helped the new couple get over guilt and regret, and even gave Larry the strength to ask for his father's blessing, of critical importance to a young man who (though he claimed to have lost his religious beliefs) had never escaped Fahv's sway.

Summoning his courage, Larry drove to see him, leaving Vivien with his sister. He found the Reverend Olivier "dreadfully upset at the turn his domestic affairs had taken," wrote Sybille, who added that he was "bitterly shocked [about] the whole affair." He had already betrayed his own moral code by taking a second wife, but this was worse: adultery.

It would be some time before he modified his feelings. And yet, bit by bit he did, and began to thaw until, many months later, he agreed to meet Vivien, when, like almost everyone who knew her, he "melted at last under her fascination."

*   *   *

Leaving their Iver rental, Larry and Vivien settled into Durham Cottage. Each was busy, ambitious and desperately in love. Larry was just beginning to grasp his potential, packing his daylight hours with filming and his nights with the stage, while Vivien was there to support him when she wasn't performing. She had not yet soared to a place where her career threatened his, nor had he climbed to the mountaintop, where his skill would dwarf hers.

She adored her new home and spent much of her spare time decorating, knocking down walls to create a new layout and packing the place with art. She covered their kitchen with blue-and-white-striped paper; painted their dining room gold and cream; and started building her own art collection, with a Walter Sickert landscape given pride of place above the hearth. Later, she gave a Sydney newspaper a glimpse into her taste. "I have chosen no particular period in furnishing, although in the dining and drawing room it is nearly all Regency," she said. "Do I consult [Larry] on furnishing? Well, not exactly; I always tell him what I intend doing so that he has the opportunity of disagreeing—he never does." In fact, Larry caused his friends much amusement in this froufrou abode, where he resembled "an unfortunate bull in a china shop," as one recalled.

The photographer Angus McBean remembered the house as having "two rooms upstairs that were surprisingly big for so small a house [and] a bedroom with the biggest double bed I have ever seen."

The home meant so much to Vivien that she commissioned a painting of it, which she kept until her death. In time, it would become a command post for the most creative minds of the British stage—the writers, directors, actors and others who flocked to the sides of the most glamorous couple in town. Gielgud, Richardson and Tyrone Guthrie were frequent guests, along with writers such as Coward, Terence Rattigan and Graham Greene, and eminent Americans including the directors William Wyler and Orson Welles. They were met with warmth and a touch of theatricality by Vivien and Larry, who would descend an open staircase to greet their guests, and then remain talking, eating and drinking into the wee hours.

While Larry got down to work on a new romantic comedy, *The Divorce of Lady X*, with Merle Oberon (Korda's lover and later wife), Vivien started shooting her first Hollywood feature, *A Yank at Oxford*.

It should have been a joyful experience, reuniting her with that other Sacred Heart alumna, Maureen O'Sullivan, in a comedy about a brash young American trying to succeed at the British university. But Vivien was trapped between two vocal and opposing forces: Michael Balcon, the smooth head of MGM's London division; and Louis B. Mayer, the pugnacious studio chief, who had traveled to England expressly to keep an eye on this picture—men whose mutual dislike intensified as shooting progressed, their antipathy toward each other equaled only by Vivien's toward both. Mayer was an ogre, a hungry, rapacious, sexist and self-pitying former scrap-metal salesman who by sheer force of will had built a giant enterprise, first as the owner of a string of nickelodeons and later as the head of Hollywood's most prestigious studio, where he now held sway as the highest-paid executive in the land. As for Balcon, a major British producer, Vivien felt he couldn't hold a candle to Korda; why, she complained, even his suits seemed shabby in comparison.

She knew the studio hadn't wanted her for the role and that Mayer would have preferred a bigger name. Perhaps unfairly, she also felt judged by O'Sullivan, a good Catholic girl whose virtue highlighted Vivien's apparent lack of it. And so, for the first time in her life, she made herself unpopular, while O'Sullivan did the opposite. "She was the adored of all us bad boys in our girl-chasing days," recalled Bushell, "for a long time a solitary virgin among the riff-raff we chased, + as it were an affectionate sister-girl-friend to us all."

Jealous and stressed, Vivien began to act up. She bemoaned the girdle she had to wear, her sore feet, the long hours. Her shoes hurt her so much, she maintained, that she had to cut holes in the soles, and when MGM insisted she replace them, she refused, furious at her representative, John Gliddon, for having the temerity not to take her side.

Rather than explain herself quietly, she unleashed a tirade the likes of which Gliddon had never seen. It was a shocking moment for the affable agent, but Vivien's rage was nothing compared to what followed, when she went from irate to ice-cold. This was only the second known instance of her flying out of control, but it terrified Gliddon as much as it had Larry, and even more so when Vivien's initial anger subsided, to be replaced by something else. "She wasn't shouting now," he remembered. "But it was far more frightening than if she had bawled me out. Her voice turned suddenly hard...rasping...contemptuous. But the worst thing was her eyes—the look in them. They had completely changed from the smiling eyes I was accustomed to seeing. They were the eyes of a stranger."

Mysteriously, Vivien then fell ill. Frewen believed the cause was "an axillary swelling in the nature of a choked follicle or subcutaneous cyst," though he noted that "the doctors don't know really what." Was her illness real or psychosomatic? She never found out. But there were reasons for her to feel run-down: She was sparring with MGM, tussling with Holman, attempting to be a mother and trying to prove she was a legitimate actress rather than just a beauty. Enraptured as she was with Larry, she was also watching him soar creatively, while she was treading water. She had dreamed they would triumph as a pair, the British version of Broadway's royal couple, Alfred Lunt and Lynn

Fontanne; but that meant they would have to be equals and right now there was nothing equal about them.

Resisting the lure of the commercial theater, Larry had joined the Old Vic repertory company and was in the midst of a stunning transformation, engaged in a handful of plays that would lift him from being a mere matinee idol to a leading Shakespearean. Bushell remembered the effort that went into this—how his friend would go into the fields, bending and buckling words, shouting and screaming to make his voice richer and fuller. "Laurence worked on his voice all his life—hour upon hour," he observed, "+ as + when a great role was coming up he would rehearse in the open air—in the fields around his house....He always said cows were the best audience....Laurence of course eventually developed his voice to a quality + volume unequalled in our time."

The voice was just one aspect of his work, revealing a level of devotion that he had rarely shown earlier on. After strong performances in *Hamlet*, *Twelfth Night* and *Henry V* (and less successful ones in *Macbeth* and *Othello*), everything paid off with the last of Olivier's prewar Shakespeares, *Coriolanus*. His work as the ambitious Roman leader, who turns against the populace and is assassinated for his betrayal, was a tour de force, capped by a spectacular death scene in which he hurled himself from the top of a staircase, did a complete somersault, rolled over three times and crash-landed at the edge of the stage. Critics were nearly unanimous in comparing him to the finest actors of the past, and even James Agate, often a contrarian, conceded that Olivier was "the nearest thing we have to the heroic tradition."

Vivien had nothing to match this. True, she was charming in *A Midsummer Night's Dream*, but she still had to define herself as a major stage actress, and Larry's attempts to guide her may have hurt as much as they helped; such was the impression of Stewart Granger when Vivien began rehearsing *Serena Blandish*, a new play about a poor girl in search of a husband. Her performance suffered, the actor believed, because her line-readings sounded just like her lover's, and "when Vivien spoke, you could hear Larry."

In June 1938, the couple set off on a two-month road trip to France, with Vivien taking an enforced break from *Serena* due to her illness. Driving an old Ford, they crossed the Channel to Boulogne and headed to Paris before veering south to Nice, stopping off to see Gielgud, who was vacationing in St. Paul de Vence with the producer Hugh "Binkie" Beaumont.

It was their first time alone for an extended period and the first time they weren't distracted by work. Together they tooled across the south, as Larry recalled, "straying across the Rhône at Condrieu of the delicious wine" and discovering "a rapturous little bay" with a hotel where they conversed with a charming "monsieur" who would later, to Olivier's shock, be executed as a Nazi collaborator. From there, they continued to Grenoble and then on toward the Spanish border and the village of Nay, where Larry's ancestors had their roots—Huguenots who later fled religious persecution and found their way to England, where they would spawn a long line of soldiers and priests. Lost in his thoughts of the past, Larry was interrupted by a cable from his agent:

ARE YOU INTERESTED GOLDWYN IDEA FOR SEP-
TEMBER FIRST STOP FOR VIVIEN YOURSELF AND
[MERLE] OBERON IN WUTHERING HEIGHTS
STOP ANSWER AS SOON AS POSSIBLE.

Wuthering Heights was the least likely of Hollywood movies. Based on Emily Brontë's 1847 novel, it told the multigenerational tale of Heathcliff, an *enfant sauvage*, and his doomed love for

Catherine Earnshaw, his benefactor's daughter, forbidden to him by money and class. The book, published a year before Brontë's death at age thirty, not only killed off its heroine early in the story but also made Heathcliff's desire for revenge its driving force; it was, in other words, as much about hate as love. But that was exactly what appealed to the screenwriters Ben Hecht and Charles MacArthur.

The duo had had a huge hit with their 1928 Broadway comedy *The Front Page*, after which Hecht had written 1927's *Underworld* and 1932's *Scarface*; he and MacArthur had also collaborated on 1934's *Twentieth Century*—all motion picture classics. Those scripts had nothing in common with the novel, but their authors did: they jabbed at the Hollywood establishment just as fervently as Brontë had jabbed at England's. Visiting their friend Alexander Woollcott on his private island in Vermont, they completed their adaptation in little over a week, jettisoning eighteen of the book's thirty-four chapters, losing the children that Heathcliff and Cathy have with other spouses and focusing entirely on the lovers.

Nobody showed much interest until one of Hollywood's more flamboyant producers, Walter Wanger, bought the script for the stars Charles Boyer and Sylvia Sidney. Wanger knew something of passion: a decade later, he would serve four months in prison for shooting his wife's lover in the groin. His enthusiasm, however, fizzled amid conflict with Sidney; and when his second choice, Katharine Hepburn, was labeled "box office poison" in a notorious exhibitor poll, he dropped the project altogether.

Samuel Goldwyn stepped in. A hawkeyed immigrant from Warsaw, he hid his shrewdness behind malapropisms. A verbal contract wasn't worth the paper it was written on, he reportedly said, and an autobiography shouldn't be written until its subject was dead. None of this was enough to disguise his canniness, despite occasional lapses of taste. "Goldwyn had immense presence and a great dignity," recalled David Niven, who would play Edgar Linton, the man Cathy marries. He was also stubbornly set on doing the film his way, as director William Wyler found out.

Wyler had grown up in Alsace, the son of a haberdasher who had wanted him to take over the family business. But when the young man proved a hell-raiser, his parents reevaluated and packed him off to America, where his cousin Carl Laemmle, the founder of Universal, helped land him a job, thereby setting him on a path to becoming one of the world's most admired filmmakers. Now, however, he and Goldwyn fought all the time. Whereas Goldwyn wanted to brighten the story (he even considered changing its title to *Dark Laughter, The Wild Heart* or *Bring Me the World*), Wyler insisted it should retain its essential darkness and hired Gregg Toland, arguably the screen's most gifted cinematographer, for that purpose. With its pitch-black hues and subtle shades of gray, Toland's lighting is one of the finished film's singular achievements, and he would teach Larry much about his craft when they eventually worked together.

With Oberon on board for Cathy, Hecht cabled Goldwyn about "Lawrence" Olivier after seeing *21 Days*:

THOUGHT HIM ONE OF THE MOST MAGNIFICENT ACTORS I HAVE EVER SEEN HE COULD RECITE HEATHCLIFF SITTING ON A BARREL OF HERRING AND BREAK YOUR HEART.

Five years had passed since Larry's last visit to Los Angeles and he had no desire to return. He had gone there with Jill in 1931, hoping to become a movie star, a hot commodity after *Private Lives*, when RKO had signed him to a multi-picture deal.

At first, he was beside himself with joy. But then his luck

changed. After being cast opposite Erich von Stroheim in the disappointing *Friends and Lovers* of 1931, he had two outright flops with *The Yellow Ticket* and *Westward Passage.* Somehow this most vital of actors—this man who would become such a charismatic presence onstage—was blank on-screen. He was "hollow," he admitted, and had all but given up on film when he was offered the lead opposite Greta Garbo in her passion project, *Queen Christina.*

Only, the movie was a disaster and, from the start, Garbo treated him like ice. Approaching her one morning just before the shoot, he "found her sitting on an old chest on the set," he recalled. "I went boldly up to her and said the three or four sentences that I had made up and practiced; but no utterance came from her. I began to flounder and grab at anything that came into my head; some sayings of Will Rogers, of Noël—anybody—anything at all, until I came to a wretched end and stopped, pale and panting. After a breathless pause, she slid herself off the chest sideways saying, 'Oh vell, live'sh a pain, anyway.'"

Days later, during their first love scene, the actress froze. "I went into the role giving it everything I had," Olivier told *Photoplay.* "But at the touch of my hand Garbo became frigid. I could feel the sudden tautness of her; her eyes as stony and expressionless as if she were a woman of marble." The more nervous he became, the more he hammed things up; the more he hammed things up, the more frosty was Garbo. "In Heaven's name," Olivier asked in desperation, "is there any man this woman *will* warm up to?"

There was one: John Gilbert. On the second day of filming, the studio cabled the silent-screen lover to say the job was his. Years later, Larry blamed himself. "You say she was in love with John Gilbert, who took the part?" he asked the *Los Angeles Times.* "I think that was only a story they made up to salve my pride."

Now, five years after his humiliation, he had come to despise films and the industry behind them. Nor was he excited about *Wuthering Heights*, which "smelled of Goldwyn corn," he wrote, "with a pinch of Merle Oberon tartness."

Wyler tried to convince him, flying to London to do so. "I had seen him in a play in New York, and I agreed he was the best choice," he explained. "We met several times at Larry's house where he and Vivian [sic] Leigh lived together. I presented what I considered a 'plum' for any actor, particularly one relatively unknown in America at the time. But Mr. Olivier was less than enthusiastic, though he agreed that it was a good script, and that Heathcliff was a good role."

Wyler, who was only thirty-seven years old but already a master of his trade, kept on the offensive. "I assumed his reluctance was due to a previous unpleasant experience in Hollywood," he noted, "until he took me one night to see a film in which Vivian [sic] appeared [*St. Martin's Lane*, her follow-up to *A Yank at Oxford*]. This, I thought, was a subtle suggestion that I might use her in the film as well. She was excellent in what I saw. Fortunately, there was Isabella, a secondary role, not yet cast, and later played by Geraldine Fitzgerald, which I immediately offered her."

Vivien dismissed the role out of hand. "I will play Cathy or nothing," she told him.

Without her, Olivier continued to resist—until he learned that Wyler was considering other actors, including one of his friends. "HAVE FOUND HEATHCLIFF AMAZING YOUNG ENGLISH ACTOR [ROBERT NEWTON]," the director cabled Goldwyn, "MUCH BETTER THAN OLIVIER WHO REFUSED PART ANY WAY." Goldwyn wouldn't budge. "NEWTON OUT OF QUESTION," he cabled back. "PLEASE DO EVERYTHING POSSIBLE SELL OLIVIER PART AND PERSUADE HIM COME HERE WITH LEIGH ACT PROMPTLY."

Larry would have liked another shot at stardom, despite his

obsession with the theater; but he also wished to remain with Vivien and knew it was unrealistic, given the potential publicity, for her to travel to Los Angeles. Still, even she was pushing him to take the role. Torn, he turned to Richardson and asked whether he should make the film. "Yes," answered his friend. "Bit of fame. Good."

In November 1938, Olivier set out for America on the SS *Normandie*, leaving Vivien in London, where she had returned to the stage with *Serena*. "Blind with misery" on board the ship, Larry drowned his sorrows in drink, consuming three vodkas and four champagne cocktails one morning alone. Each day he phoned Vivien at an exorbitant cost, sometimes spending a hair-raising £50 on a call, ten times his weekly salary at the Old Vic. And when he wasn't calling, he was thinking about her, writing endless missives that galloped across twenty or thirty pages.

"Darling have just received your darling cable," he wrote on November 15. "I keep weeping a little this morning. I do worship you my love....Please stop wanting to cry my beloved it makes me want to too." She was adorable, he told her, and original, even if she did occasionally become enraged. "I hope you've noticed what a healthy regard I have for your anger!" he wrote after one thunderstorm. "I've spent thousands of pounds in the last few minutes assuring myself that you're not displeased with me."

These were the first of some two hundred letters Larry wrote over the following months, many sprinkled with charming and funny hand-drawn sketches of stick people, with bubbles of dialogue popping out of their heads, designed to make her laugh—all of which Vivien kept in her bedside table, bound in a red ribbon. They can be found today, perfectly preserved, in her archive at the Victoria and Albert Museum; but only Larry's side of the correspondence remains, and what has happened to most of her letters to him is unknown.

These are the scribblings of a young and unformed man, obsessed with his love when he isn't obsessed with himself; rarely in any of them does he mention graver matters, and indeed the absence of such commentary—less than a year before the world would go to war—shows how removed the couple was from the events of the day. In one rather naive letter, written during the voyage out, Larry tells Vivien how much he has gleaned about politics from his shipmates, Coward and the hotelier Victor Sassoon. "I am learning a great deal about politics—very interesting," he wrote. "I never realized that everyone was so het up against [Neville] Chamberlain," the British prime minister who would be forced out of office in 1940, a year and a half after promising peace, following the Munich Agreement with Hitler.

Arriving in Los Angeles, Larry settled into the Beverly Hills Hotel, where his letter-writing resumed, the best way to communicate in an age when long-distance calls were astronomically expensive. "I awoke at 20 to 8 and felt so unhappy + longed for you so," he told Vivien. "I must stop this drivle [sic] as it seems to be wandering a bit—I love you love you my dear dove, how lovely it was to hear your sweet voice darling....LOVE REAL LOVE TRUE LOVE BURNING HEARTS BLOOD PASSIONATE ADORATION."

Vivien was an emotional wreck, terrified her fears might come true and that Larry would cheat on her, as their friend Helen Spencer relayed. "She spent the whole time [during a visit] simply torn with the anxiety of whether she could go to you or not, or whether you were fucking someone else or not! *You*!!"

Larry begged for a short break to meet Vivien in New York. But Wyler shot him down. "My dear dear darling I must try not to make this too much of a tale of woe," wrote Larry, "but I am so very miserable. My beautiful idea was killed stone dead by Willie, I was expecting trouble from Sam, but Willie I thought would be alright....I asked [producer David O.] Selznick the best way to approach this idea + they [sic] said get Willie on your side first, but he wouldn't hear of it, simply wouldn't *hear* of it, said that now that I'm here I must put everything out of my mind but the picture, that he needs me for tests and advice and trials of costumes make ups, rehearsals, that we have a great responsibility to this picture + I must realize it, and I'm showing a very poor state of mind about it by *thinking* of going away."

Reluctantly, he agreed to stay in Los Angeles, but always he had "the sort of hope, the self-deceiving 'telling myself' that I would see you again soon, that *somehow* you would come out here, *some*how *I* could get to New York—even if we had to meet in space, we would and *could* do it, but now I really am in hell my love—the valley of the shadow. I've never felt such a grim feeling…nobody can realize what we've been through for each other and quite how much even a day together would mean—O my sweet loveling this is a very unmanly letter, I am so sorry my angel, I only hope you're not ashamed of me, your Larry does adore you so, and I have to pour my heart out to you my love—I am a selfish slut, and I don't suppose its a *bit* helpful to you either."

He kept praying that Oberon would drop out so that Vivien could drop in, and when he discovered she still hadn't signed her contract, his heart leaped. "Jimmy Townsend [a colleague] told me that Sam wanted to get Merle to play the picture for nothing! as the other picture [*The Cowboy and the Lady*] had gone on for so long," he wrote, "and she had refused and he was holding you up as a lever to force her into it, which was a filthy trick on Merle….Anyway, I saw Sam, and he reiterated how crazy he was about you and then said there was trouble with Merle, and then said how much he owed her, and preached quite a homily about loyalty, which made me laugh, + said that he would like to have you, but still loyalty etc. and wouldn't you come out on the off chance, + I said NO….I was going *mad*!"

Two days later, he wrote again: "I went in to see Sam and said what news? + he said he was afraid he'd settled with Merle. I nearly died—it was so near my loveling, so very near."

In mid-November, Larry began extensive makeup tests, critical for a role in which he would have to age ten years, a process complicated by the fact that the script would not be shot in chronological order. "They're going to fix tapes onto my face!" he told Vivien. "I've got to the John Barrymore stage! I shall have to have it lifted soon!"

Filming got underway in December, when Olivier's relationship with Oberon—which had been fine on their earlier *The Divorce of Lady X*—went from bad to worse. Larry had never thought much of her as an actress, but now she became the target of his pent-up frustration, which spilled over at its ugliest. When she asked Larry to stop spitting in her face during one scene, he pounced. "What's a little spit for Chrissake between actors?" he told her. "You bloody little idiot. How dare you speak to me?" Then, brutally, he disparaged her "pockmarked face," about as wounding an insult as he could muster, given that Oberon still had traces of a childhood bout with smallpox. She stormed off the set.

Wyler knew how to turn this fury to his advantage, knew that real-life loathing would read differently on film. After one row "in which we were both trembling and tears were streaming down, and we were absolutely trembling with rage," wrote Olivier, "Willy said, 'Roll them,' and it was the most heavy-making love scene we'd done and we did it hating each other, but it was one of the top love scenes in the film as it turned out."

Problems mounted. Oberon caught a bad cold, which threatened to turn into pneumonia; she sprained her ankle, causing a delay of several days; and she blamed Wyler for not paying as much attention to her as Larry. Meanwhile, Olivier developed what he believed was an excruciating case of athlete's foot, though it was more likely a vesicular infection, given how extreme it became. One reporter observed that he couldn't even get into his shoes, that he needed crutches and his foot had swollen to twice its size.

When Goldwyn visited the set, Larry hobbled over to greet him, expecting "at least a pat on the shoulder for his courage" in continuing to work, as Oberon remembered. He got the opposite response.

"Goldwyn would regularly let fly at Laurence and Willy Wyler," wrote Bushell. "It would start with, 'Will you look at this UGLY actor! Why that's the ugliest actor I ever see in all my life. I tell you Willy—if this actor goes on acting the way he is—I CLOSE UP THE PICTURE.'"

Larry was convinced Goldwyn wanted to get rid of him, but Wyler denied it. "Sam Goldwyn never seriously considered firing Larry," he said. "It was just a momentary outburst on his part because he was impatient with Larry's appearance as the early unkempt stable boy."

Not that Wyler was thrilled with Larry either. He was a screamer, a perfectionist who asked for take after take without explaining why. "Whereas Garbo was cold, Wyler was vicious: a Hollywood version of the nasty Basil Dean," noted Olivier. Asked to shoot the same scene over and over, without a hint as to how his acting could improve, he exploded. "Look, I've done it thirty times," he yelled. "What the hell is it you want me to do?" Wyler thought and then answered: "Just be *better*!"

On another occasion, during one of Larry's more over-the-top moments, the director scoffed: "For Christ sake what are you doing now? Come off the clouds. Come down to earth." His star shot back: "I suppose this anaemic little medium can't stand anything great in size like that."

He had nothing but contempt for this philistine, this man who apparently understood the craft of acting so little, who seemed as wrongheaded as all those other Hollywood nabobs, each contemptuous of anything resembling art. And yet it was Wyler who educated him, taught him that film registered the tiniest blip, the faintest feeling—told him it was an actor's inner life that registered in this medium, no matter how many layers of putty and makeup he might plaster on his face. It was he who advised Larry, during his love scenes, that he should "*think* of Vivien and *act* with Merle." And it was he who explained that the key to acting in films was for Larry to look deep within himself, to find the character he was playing on the inside rather than the outside, the opposite of his strategy.

For now, all that was wasted on him. "Well, really," he told Vivien, "I stayed as patient as I could + explained, that an actors job is pretending to be someone *else*, at least that is *my* reading of an actors job, and it always has been + always will be." Righteously, he added of Wyler: "I suspect he must have good instinct with no brains."

Their conflict lasted throughout the miserable shoot. And when filming ended four months later, they were barely on speaking terms—though by then, Larry had somewhat calmed down, his stress reduced to a simmer, because he was at last beginning to recognize that what Wyler had told him was the truth—and because Vivien was finally at his side.

Serena Blandish had ended earlier than expected, in late November, after audiences had responded unenthusiastically, perhaps what Vivien had secretly wished. Now she was eager to join Larry, not to mention get the chance to audition for a new movie, already the most-talked-about in Hollywood history: *Gone with the Wind.*

CHAPTER 4

———◆———

Vivien arrived in Los Angeles in early December 1938 to find Larry "crouched in the back of a car a few feet beyond the airport entrance," as he recalled later.

It wasn't his finest hour; he was terrified of being spotted by the press, all the more since Vivien had blithely told reporters, during a stopover in New York, that she was on her way to see him, which caused no end of concern for Goldwyn as he carried *Wuthering Heights* toward the finish line. Larry was still shaken by "a long interview with the publicity [team]," he told Vivien, "whose main anxiety was how did I wish my *romance* angle to be treated?! They all felt very strongly that discretion was essential etc etc, that if you came over *different* addresses would be the thing etc. etc."

The Hollywood gossip machine, which would reach its apogee with the 1950s tell-all magazine *Confidential*, had still not peaked; but two columnists, rivals Hedda Hopper and Louella Parsons, were experts in the form and together reached much of the American population, terrorizing their celebrity quarry. The studios had developed sophisticated systems to placate them with gifts and tidbits, often providing one morsel of news if a columnist held back another; still, they wielded exceptional power, as

Larry's friend Orson Welles would learn when Parsons alerted her employer, William Randolph Hearst, about the dangers of his upcoming *Citizen Kane*. News of Larry's liaison had not yet reached the broad public, but it had made its way to the studio chiefs and their henchmen, who bluntly informed him of the risks.

Did his fearfulness turn Vivien against Hollywood? Or did she come prejudiced against the place, based on everything Larry had told her about its people who had "no soul"? Either way, her reaction was visceral and intense. Taking the scenic route from Cloverfield Airport to the Beverly Hills Hotel, she "regarded the view in absolute silence behind a frozen face," wrote Bushell, "until Laurence hopefully started to point out the possible beauties of Bev. Hills. She suddenly, explosively, + en plein voix, bellowed 'I HATE IT!'"

On the evening of December 10, she pressed the mute button on her hatred when she and Larry joined Myron Selznick, the most powerful agent in Los Angeles and the brother of *Gone with the Wind*'s producer, David O. Selznick, at the Brown Derby, the famed restaurant built by Gloria Swanson's second husband, Herbert Somborn. Their dinner, like every other Hollywood meal, was part fun, part catch-up and all business: Myron was their Virgil, guiding them through the industry's byzantine and labyrinthine ways and, above all, teaching Vivien how to win the role she craved: Scarlett O'Hara.

She had read Margaret Mitchell's 1936 best seller as soon as it came out and longed to play its heroine, a fiery Southerner who thinks she's in love with one man only to discover she's in love with another, while enduring the defining horror of the American experiment, the Civil War. As far back as Vivien's friends could remember, she had been telling them the part would be hers, an extreme unlikelihood for a woman with next to no credits and a minimal reputation outside her country. When one colleague had mentioned in passing that Larry would make an excellent Rhett Butler, the cynical but charming smuggler whom Scarlett eventually marries, Vivien answered whip-fast: no, but she would make a magnificent Scarlett.

Now, eight miles from Culver City, where the picture was set to start shooting that very night—where the cameras were about to roll after two years of chaotic preparation, even though no leading lady had yet been found, and where stand-ins were already getting ready for the first shot to be filmed: a horse and buggy fleeing the burning Atlanta—she tried to tamp down her nerves as the others chitchatted, as Larry entertained and Myron drank and kept drinking, a victim of the alcoholism that would soon take his life.

Across town, David Selznick had taken his place in the backlot of the Selznick Studios, on a watchtower high above his troops, nails bitten to the quick as he huddled with his crew, overlooking a sea of extras and assistants, cameramen and grips, firemen and police officers, all waiting for the signal to start.

As large as he was larger-than-life, as frenzied as he was frenetic, David wasn't yet the mogul he would become, wasn't the producer whose name would become synonymous with obsessive perfectionism; he was no more "David O. Selznick" than Larry was "Laurence Olivier." He was, in fact, the son of a has-been, Lewis Selznick, one of the forgotten footnotes of Hollywood history, a pioneer in the business who had failed where the Louis B. Mayers and Sam Goldwyns had succeeded, and whom they resented for his failure as much as he resented them for their success. Like Myron, David burned to avenge his father.

After years in which he had toiled as an executive in the studio trenches—most recently and humiliatingly as a hatchet man for his father-in-law, Mayer ("the son-in-law also rises," his enemies quipped), he finally had his own company, with a blockbuster in the works as big as his ego. He'd bet everything on this film, the biggest motion picture ever made and the one, he kept telling everyone, destined to be the best.

Since buying the rights to Mitchell's novel in July 1936 for a then record $50,000, he had been buffeted by every challenge a filmmaker could face: humongous expenses that would eventually top $3.9 million; meddling investors, including Mayer, whose studio had a big stake in the project; and a parade of needy and needling stars—among them Bette Davis, Katharine Hepburn and Norma Shearer—who'd used every arrow in their well-stocked quivers to land the lead, though Selznick didn't feel any of them were quite right: Davis was too tough, Hepburn too polarizing, Shearer too old. Somehow, he had dodged them all, and yet he knew he would soon have to make a choice, and his inability to settle on an actress was ruining his already-fractured sleep. Now here he was, about to film the most spectacular scene in his picture, with seven Technicolor cameras ready to capture Atlanta in flames—or rather an ersatz Atlanta, as make-believe as everything else in this citadel of illusion, a construction built from old sets that had been left lying around the Selznick lot, newly painted, with false fronts to make them resemble a Californian's idea of the Southern city.

Eddie Mannix, one of Mayer's subordinates, had tried to dissuade Selznick from staging the fire, pushing him to use models rather than real buildings. But the producer was adamant that they would lack authenticity, and so he forged on, no matter how risky the fire might be. He was surrounded by an army of experts like Ernest Grey, the local fire chief, who'd been having nightmares about this for weeks, terrified that Selznick would not just burn "Atlanta" but Los Angeles itself.

Two hundred extras gathered around while the horse-drawn buggy carrying the stand-ins for Scarlett, Rhett and Melanie Hamilton—the fake ones, in this fake Atlanta—was poised to bolt as soon as the producer gave the word. Only, he kept waiting, hoping against hope that Myron would be there to see his moment of triumph, as if he didn't know his beloved brother was as pathologically late as himself.

The shoot had been kept secret, though "secret" was a relative term in Hollywood, where information was a commodity to be traded like everything else. And on this Saturday night, as the journalist Roland Flamini reported in his book *Scarlett, Rhett, and a Cast of Thousands: The Filming of "Gone with the Wind,"* "Los Angeles city desks, the wire service news desks, and a handful of leading Hollywood correspondents began receiving anonymous telephone tips that the Selznick back lot was in flames"—tips provided, of course, by Selznick himself via his head of public relations, Russell Birdwell. After waiting as long as he could, the producer at last gave the green light and at midnight art director and second-unit director William Cameron Menzies (who was in charge of this nondialogue scene while the real director, George Cukor, looked on) yelled, "Action!"

Orange, blue and yellow flames spurted into life, and suddenly the set erupted, with smoke billowing hundreds of feet in the air, visible for miles around, ready to be extinguished by water gushing from hidden pipes laid under the wooden flats. Eight times the fire was started and eight times it was stopped on this memorable night; eight times the horse-drawn buggy charged and eight times it was sent back to its starting spot, before Vivien and Larry arrived. "The last burning structure had come crashing down and the flames were fighting a losing battle with the water now pouring out of the sprinklers," writes Flamini. "A light wind from the sea carried the black clouds east toward Beverly Hills, where they dissolved over the mansions of Hollywood's aristocracy as they sat playing gin rummy and probably discussing David's folly."

The embers of the fire were all that remained when Myron

showed up with his clients, and there was little trace of the sets that had been burned, those relics of Hollywood's grandeur, from the gates of 1933's *King Kong* to the mansions of 1936's *Little Lord Fauntleroy*; all were gone, never to reappear, objects as disposable as many of the artists who wove in and out of the studios. The past was fungible in this least sentimental of cities. Later, even the footage shot on this historic night would be repurposed, grist for Selznick's *Rebecca*, where it can still be seen in the burning of Manderley.

As the fire died down, Myron led Vivien to the observation deck where his brother was standing. David was on the point of complaining about their lateness when Myron cut him off. "Here, genius," he said. "I want you to meet Scarlett O'Hara."

Selznick was "rocked by her looks," recalled his wife, Irene Mayer Selznick, to whom he wrote the next day while she was in New York, telling her that Vivien was "the Scarlett dark horse and looks damned good." Later, he claimed that he "took one look [at Vivien] and knew that she was right."

In fact, he had had several chances to hire her and dismissed her each time—first, when he could have put her under contract after *The Mask of Virtue*, but chose not to, allowing Korda to slip in instead; and then when an employee suggested her for Scarlett early in the search, only for David to pay him no heed. Now he was desperate. Each of the other candidates brought baggage from too many roles. Did he really want Davis, who had the requisite fieriness but not the looks, and was known to be impossible to work with, in any case? Or Hepburn, who had the acting chops but as much sex appeal as Larry's lemur? Or any of the myriad other contenders, from the eccentric Tallulah Bankhead (daughter of House Speaker William Bankhead) to a flotilla of Southerners, not hundreds but thousands, who had come forward in a casting tour of the South, offering themselves mind, body and soul to Cukor, hopelessly unaware that he was gay? Vivien outshone them all; she was beautiful, spirited, and, perhaps best of all, unknown. As the flames faded, a newly enthused Selznick asked Cukor to put her through her paces.

"I remember my office was nearby where I had these endless test scenes [printed out]," Cukor recalled. "I gave her one and said quite simply 'read it.' She read it in a piping English voice and I was rather rude and funny about it." He added: "I don't think she had ever heard a Southern accent at all, and she began reading this thing very sweetly, and very, very clipped. I said to myself, 'Here is a very precious, affected—I can't say the word I really mean—little English girl.' And so I struck her across the face with the rudest thing I could say. She screamed with laughter."

The two were a natural fit. Vivien was comfortable with gay men, especially those as enamored of the theater as Cukor, who had cut his teeth on the New York stage and arrived in Hollywood as a dialogue coach; she liked him as much as he liked her. "She had the same well-bred, arrogant beauty with a touch of the hell-cat that few men could resist," he observed. Together they rehearsed deep into the night, exploring scenes and each other until just before dawn, when Vivien and Larry retreated to the Beverly Hills Hotel, where they were staying (still anonymous enough not to worry) until Larry could move into a house with Leslie Howard, who would play the courtly Ashley Wilkes.

"Vivien slept very little of what was left of the night," writes Gwen Robyns, one of her early biographers. "She and Laurence Olivier went over and over the possibilities of her getting the part and its implication. She had not been too pleased with her own reading of the part, but Olivier was sure that no woman had ever looked more like Scarlett O'Hara and was backing his own hunch that she would get the part."

Selznick was tempted to cast her at once, but Irene begged

him to wait until she returned from New York. She knew him
well, just like all the men of his ilk, these titans who were as
impetuous as they were impassioned, as liable to be swayed by
desire as deliberation, by lust rather than logic. They had to be
reined in like the children they were, told what to do by adults
like herself who didn't need endless mollycoddling, didn't need to
be tucked in at night as David had been—literally—by his father,
until well into his twenties. For heaven's sake, she implored,
"don't Scarlettize until I get there—please oh please don't decide
even to yourself."

One last time, the finalists were summoned to go through
their rounds, to face one more miserable, humiliating, dispiriting
series of auditions. Four women remained in the running: Joan
Bennett, Jean Arthur, Paulette Goddard and Vivien. The pres-
sure was colossal, their longing a distillation of the longing that
drove Hollywood itself.

"You will never guess what has happened & no one is more
surprised than me," Vivien wrote Holman, doing everything she
could to remain friends. "You know that I only came out here for
a week. Well just two days before I was supposed to leave, the
people who are making *Gone with the Wind* saw me & said
would I make a test—so what could I *do* & so now I am working frantically hard & rehearsing, & studying a Southern accent
which I don't find difficult anyway." She continued: "They seem
to be very pleased with me—& I don't know what I think or
what I hope—I am so afraid it will mean me staying here (IF I
get it) for a long time, & that I don't want to do. The part has
now become the biggest responsibility one can imagine & yet it
would be absurd not to do it given the chance."

Three days after meeting Selznick, Vivien returned to Cukor's
office, where she rehearsed with Hattie McDaniel, the Black
actress who was one of two contenders for Mammy (Scarlett's
maid), along with Hattie Noel. Three days later, she returned

for more tests, with Douglass Montgomery standing in as Ashley. And six days after that, there were still further tests: Vivien shot the paddock sequence in which Scarlett and Ashley embrace, along with two versions of her dressing room scene, when Mammy tugs her into the tightest of girdles, one test featuring McDaniel and the other Noel.

"George is busily engaged on the Scarlett tests," Selznick wrote Irene. "All day today with Jean Arthur, who has been no end of trouble (I look at her as though I had never known her before!), but who looks on the set as though she may be wonderful—although I have seen only a small part of one scene rehearsed. The tests of each of the four girls will consist of three scenes—and we'll then intercut them so that we'll see each of the four girls consecutively playing each of the three scenes...you'll be back in time for the final knockout blow."

Vivien never played anything as well as she played this. There was a fierceness to her, a defiance of sentimentality and convention, a mixture of the sensitive and sensual that transcended anything she had done before and anything she would do again, except for her finest moments in the finished film and in *A Streetcar Named Desire*. Did Cukor draw her out? Or was it her own ferocious need to win the role, to achieve everything she had dreamed of, to fill the gaping hole that had been hollowed out when she was wrenched from her home?

"In the next five days," writes Flamini, Selznick "screened Vivien's Scarlett test over thirty times on its own, and in conjunction with the other three; he had blow-ups made of each of the four actresses from close-ups in the tests and would gaze at them for hours; he held lengthy staff conferences to discuss the relative merits of each performance; the tests were shipped to [his financial partner, John Hay "Jock"] Whitney in New York and his opinion sought. But Whitney replied that the choice was up to Selznick."

By December 24, he still hadn't made up his mind. It was Christmas Eve and Vivien was steadying herself for rejection as Hollywood began to wind down for the holidays. She was due to return to London for *A Midsummer Night's Dream* but begged Tyrone Guthrie, the director, to grant her more time.

On Christmas Day, she and Larry left their hotel for Cukor's lavish party, the kind of event she would have relished any other time: a gathering of Hollywood's crème de la crème, wined and dined by a maestro of modern elegance. But she was sick with nerves. "Vivien was exactly the opposite of Scarlett O'Hara, who said something like, 'I'll worry about it tomorrow,'" recalled Olivier, slightly misquoting her last line in *GWTW* ("After all, tomorrow is another day"). "She worried about everything— yesterday, today, and tomorrow."

Reaching Cukor's magnificent home in the hills, with its deep blue pool and quaint guesthouses set amid acres of rolling green, the couple found their way inside. For a while, they stood drinking and making small talk, until Cukor pulled Vivien aside and said teasingly: "Oh, by the way, we have made our choice: I guess we are stuck with you."

Vivien had won the most coveted part of the century, the most desired since the invention of film. But that was only half the battle. Contracts had to be negotiated, earlier ones annulled, agents informed, angry stars propitiated. Above all, Korda had to be persuaded this was a good idea.

The mogul, now in Los Angeles with Oberon, had signed Vivien to a long-term deal and wasn't certain he should let her go. She was wrong for the role, he insisted, and Selznick was even more wrong to demand that she sign a seven-year contract with him—standard Hollywood fare. For days, the tyrants thumb-wrestled, each wanting to win, each savoring his potential triumph over the other just as much as whether Vivien got what she desired—until finally, like the great powers that had carved up the world in the wake of World War I, they agreed to divide the spoils: Vivien would make one movie per year for Korda and one for Selznick, keeping her in their grip well into the 1940s. These were onerous terms, but not atypical, and Vivien was in no position to say no.

Larry posed a bigger problem. He and Selznick had never seen eye-to-eye; he looked on Selznick as an oversized, underappreciative bully whose occasional flashes of brilliance—visible in the fusillade of cables he shot off, as frequent as emails today—were drowned by his arrogance. Their conflict had climaxed during Larry's previous stint in Hollywood, when David was heading production at RKO: the young actor had found himself in his office at the very time Jill was being considered for a new comedy, *A Bill of Divorcement*. Selznick stepped out, and Larry claimed he glimpsed something on the executive's desk. "[My] attention was caught and held, by God, by a document on his blotter," he recalled in his memoirs. "This turned out to be the agreement for a contract" to hire the unknown Katharine Hepburn at $1,500 per week, twice what Jill was being paid. In that instant, said Larry, he realized Hepburn was the real star in the making, Jill a mere afterthought. Armed with this slender evidence, he convinced her they should return home—or so he explained later, overlooking a key fact: that Hepburn's deal would not be signed until months after his exit from Hollywood.

Now, in the midst of the *GWTW* negotiations, Larry burst into Selznick's office and insisted Vivien would never make his film. "Larry tried in every way possible to kill the casting of Vivien as Scarlett O'Hara," the producer alleged years after *GWTW* had been filmed, when his memory was clouded by time and his distaste for Olivier. "He advanced every argument conceivable against it, and...said that I wouldn't dream of going through with the idea of an English girl as a famous southern heroine; that Vivien...would be ridiculed in the role."

Olivier's version was different: he simply wanted to get Vivien more money, while Selznick countered that he would become a "laughingstock" if he paid her too much. In the end, she received $1,250 per week for sixteen weeks on *GWTW*, with a contract climbing as high as $6,250 per week for future films. This was a fraction of her costar Clark Gable's salary; but the actor (who had been cast as Rhett) was a major star. After taxes and commission, Vivien would earn a total of $25,032.33 for *Wind*, almost half a million dollars in today's terms.

On January 16, 1938, she joined Olivia de Havilland (as the saintly Melanie), writer Sidney Howard and Cukor at a press conference where Selznick announced he had at last found his Scarlett.

The reaction was decidedly mixed. Margaret Mitchell was one of the few to embrace Vivien, whose films she admittedly had not seen. "She certainly is pretty," wrote the novelist, "with the word 'Devil' in her eye."

Carole Lombard, Gable's wife, also told Selznick that Vivien was "THE MOST INTERESTING GIRL TO REACH THE SCREEN IN FIVE YEARS." And even Speaker Bankhead, whose daughter Tallulah had lost out, cabled: "CONGRATULATIONS ON SUCCESSFUL CASTING OF SCARLETT GONE WITH THE WIND O'HARA STOP NOW THAT THAT IS OVER I GUESS WE CAN PROCEED WITH OTHER MATTERS OF STATE."

Others were incensed. A Mrs. Raymond B. Bullock, president of the Dickinson Chapter of the United Daughters of the Confederacy, shot off a warning that, if anyone other than a true Southerner were cast, "WE RESOLVE TO WITHHOLD OUR PATRONAGE." And Hopper, the Anglophobic gossip columnist whose syndicated column warned its readers to avoid anything that smacked of England, especially if it smelled like war, said she was outraged by "the almost unbelievable news that David Selznick has chosen a (practically) unknown ENGLISH actress to do Scarlett O'Hara, the most AMERICAN role of modern times. I'm sure millions of Americans will stay away from the picture in a gesture of protest."

Gertrude followed this from afar, her letters revealing her kindness as she attempted to make good for the past. She had never blamed her daughter for running off with Larry, despite her closeness to Holman, and had not even chastised her for leaving Suzanne, who was effectively placed in her care. "The papers are full of you, it is very thrilling," she wrote Vivien. "I am sure your sense of humour will compete with the jealousy and sentiment of the girls in Hollywood if what the papers say is true, they are quite cross!!" She added: "I do so hope Larry can stay with you. I shan't know a moment's peace if he goes away, & you are by yourself....Don't go out with any one actor—you know all about them, the more charming they are the more careful you must be, [and] that goes for the women as well, they are worse than men."

Vivien was too busy to worry about such things. She was spending three hours a day rehearsing with Cukor while undergoing hair and makeup tests, along with dialect lessons from Susan Myrick, one of Mitchell's friends, whose rose-tinted account of the picture's progress appeared daily in the *Macon Telegraph*. Selznick insisted his star maintain a natural look, avoiding the glossy lips and excessively plucked eyebrows then in fashion. But his quest for naturalism did not extend to her breasts. "Tape them up [to make them look bigger]," he demanded, before embarking on a back-and-forth with the Breen office, the industry's censorship organ, over whether Scarlett should have one button or two undone at the top of her blouse, possibly exposing her cleavage.

On January 26, 1939, principal photography got underway with the opening scene in which Scarlett toys with the Tarleton twins in front of Tara, her family home. That sequence would be reshot multiple times because Selznick kept changing his mind about Scarlett's outfit. (Even after numerous reshoots, he wasn't satisfied and implored Vivien unsuccessfully to film it once again.) Half-blinded by the hulking lights, she stood outside the house and told the twins (Fred Crane and George Reeves): "If you boys say 'war' just once again, I'll walk into the house and slam the door....All this war talk's just ruining every party I go to. There isn't going to be any war."

She knew the dialogue by heart, had an unparalleled ease when it came to memorizing her lines and an equal skill at falling in and out of character the moment the camera started or stopped rolling. De Havilland was astonished at her "ability to snap on and off as if by flicking a switch; when 'action' was called, she would continue her conversation in whispers on the set for a few seconds longer and then turn into the scene, completely in character."

A few days into the shoot came a flash of unexpected drama when Vivien had to slap Prissy, her teenage maid, and did it so hard that actress Butterfly McQueen stormed off, crying: "I can't do it, she's hurting me, she's hurting me." McQueen looked back on the film with no pleasure years later and said, "I hated that role. I thought the movie was going to show the progress black people had made, but Prissy was lazy and stupid and backward."

The generally positive atmosphere quickly degenerated. At the end of the second week, on February 4, "a large mobile dressing room was towed onto the Selznick lot, heralding the arrival of Clark Gable," writes Flamini. "It was uncompromisingly masculine—the captain's cabin or the big game hunter's lodge. It had knotted-pine walls, and a knotted-pine dressing table; the only other articles of furniture were a deep club sofa and arm chair in red leather. Two heavy brass ashtrays and two English hunting prints of men in pink coats with baying hounds were fastened to the wall. There was a built-in clothes closet and a bookshelf containing five or six books, including…a well-thumbed copy of *Gone With the Wind*. Gable always did his homework."

To his fans, the actor may have been "the King," but in truth he was a blue-collar contract player who had been given no say about the role, for which he had been lent out like chattel by the studio that owned him. Others, including Gary Cooper and Errol Flynn, had been considered but rejected, and Gable had long topped the polls for Rhett—even though he questioned his ability to master the Southern accent. He arrived on-set with thoughts of gloom and doom, his mood only slightly improved when he found a gift waiting from Lombard, his new wife—a knitted sock to warm his genitals, with a note: "Don't let it get cold. Bring it home hot for me." (That was generous, given how she'd pooh-poohed his bedroom skills to a friend: "If you want to know the truth, I've had better.")

Gable's late start was a strategic mistake. It left him feeling like an outsider among a group that was more tightly knit than his sock, and his resentment toward his costars and director would soon lead to a split. He'd had doubts about Vivien from the start, believing she wasn't right for the part (she "seemed too demure to me"); and he was furious when she kept him waiting for two hours at a photo shoot before filming began. Fed up, he'd turned to an assistant and muttered, "I'll walk out of this picture with a dame like that!" just as Vivien arrived. "I quite agree, Mr. Gable," she declared. "If I were a man, I'd tell that Vivien Leigh to go straight back to England and fuck herself."

Her language appalled him (though Lombard's wasn't much better), but her sophistication was even more offensive, a daily reminder that at heart he was a rube. On-set, he and Vivien would make a show of closeness, playing card games and beaming whenever a journalist wandered by, part of the well-oiled studio publicity machine that turned ordinary men and women into symbols of perfection and never allowed reality to ruffle fans' dreams. But the actor's dislike of what he saw rapidly turned to disdain.

Gable was never Vivien's type; he was the sort of macho male who represented an America of the frontier, a nation of action rather than intellect, with his coarse humor readily apparent in his new toy, a gun whose shaft was shaped like a penis. Nor did it help that he and Cukor clashed from the start. Gable had "great intolerances," said Selznick's secretary, Marcella Rabwin. "One of the intolerances was for gays, and one was for Jews." Cukor fell into both categories, and Gable counseled the producer to get rid of "that fag," just as Selznick was beginning to contemplate doing so himself.

Before filming had even begun, there'd been reports of tension between the two men. In December, the *New York Times* had reported that "a closely guarded battle" was taking place between Selznick and Mayer over who should direct, with the meddling Mayer telling Selznick to hire a bolder and more visual filmmaker, while Selznick countered that he could get everything he needed from Cukor. By February, their differences had become glaring. The director was bothered by the lack of rehearsal time and by a script he insisted needed major revisions, while Selznick was aggravated by the slow pace of each scene. "We couldn't see eye to eye on anything," he said later. He began to make his presence felt on-set, micromanaging his employees and even chiming in on the correct emotion Ashley should reveal upon seeing Scarlett. "Ashley, at that moment, would be scared to meet her," he argued. "I disagree wholeheartedly," replied Cukor.

Irene begged her husband to be prudent, knowing he was on the verge of firing her friend. "I couldn't accept the fact that he was actually going to change directors," she recalled. "His dissatisfaction was born with the first rushes, and his dissatisfaction grew. I pleaded George's case and won him a couple of days' respite at a time—I thought things would get better when everyone got less nervous. They didn't."

Two weeks into the shoot, Selznick had enough. "George was coming to the house that evening after dinner and David was going to have to break the news," remembered Irene, in one of several conflicting versions of the story. "It was awful. David and I sat upstairs waiting in loud silence. [When Cukor arrived] I ran down and flung myself on him, weeping." It was then, she said, that her husband told Cukor he had to go. On the other hand, Flamini (writing when memories were fresh) believed Selznick didn't have the courage to tell Cukor himself and dispatched his general manager, Henry Ginsberg, to do so. "The efficient Ginsberg made a quick, clean job of it," writes Flamini. "His meeting with Cukor, in a small office adjoining the set, lasted less than half an hour."

On the morning of February 15, word spread that Cukor was out. Vivien and de Havilland, waiting to shoot the scene in which they mourn the deaths of Melanie's brother and Scarlett's husband, were dressed in black. "We got this news and we immediately left the set and we went to see David Selznick," recalled de Havilland. "We spent three hours in his office beseeching him. We cried, we pulled out our handkerchiefs—they had black borders—and you should have seen the poor man. He went over to his window seat, he had a marvelous window seat, and he sat there. The windows were open and when those handkerchiefs came out I thought he was going to go straight over the sill. But he was strong. I don't think he ever had a tougher test than the one he received that day in his office with these two women in black beseeching him to keep George Cukor."

Outraged when Selznick refused, Vivien contacted her agents. She had not yet learned Hollywood's bottom line, that he who controlled the money controlled the art—that the studio controlled the producer, who controlled the director, who controlled the stars. Writers were an afterthought here, the opposite of the theater, where everything began with the text, and with the men and women who brought that text to life. It was understandable, then, that Vivien thought she had influence, and equally understandable that she was told she had none.

"Miss Leigh called me to tell me she was very disheartened and very discouraged with her job in 'GONE WITH THE WIND,'" noted one of her agents, Sig Marcus, adding she'd complained that "David had her working until 7:00 or 7:30 every night and then had her try on gowns all evening—that she had called David earlier in the day, but he had not had the courtesy to return her call—that at this rate the picture would take forever—that [the] script was being sent to her piecemeal every day—to sum it all up, she wanted to be released."

Myron was incensed, not with his brother but with his client. "If you quit this film," he told Vivien, "you will be in court till your last day on earth. You will never work again on stage or screen. You will never be free. David will see to that. And so, too, Miss Leigh, will I."

By now Larry had wrapped *Wuthering Heights* and conveniently departed for the East Coast, where he was rehearsing S. N. Behrman's *No Time for Comedy*. Much as he loved Vivien, he had no desire to play second fiddle, let alone sit at home waiting for her to return, knitting socks like Gable's wife. Hearing about Cukor, he tried vainly to calm her down. "I'm sure that no one can teach you anything about Scarlett," he wrote, "and tho' you may miss George's actual direction + his *talking* things out I'm sure that the fact of your tests being so much better than your first few days of performance shows that *no*-one [can] add much of any great *value*."

Despite Vivien's tearful pleading, he rejected her requests that he return, arguing that this was the devil's candy, to be resisted at all costs. "You know I would give anything but *anything* to have an excuse to work with you, + *be* with you—even in Hollywood," he wrote, "but *because* I am so very inclined to it, it takes the form of a temptation, and needs therefore double consideration."

In truth, he was still worried about the optics, still afraid of the fallout from an industry that was all about image. And yet he couldn't put Vivien aside and wrote to her daily, sometimes even more often, scribbling impassioned letters with the zeal of any young man head over heels for the first time. "If we loved each other only with our bodies I suppose it would be alright," he told her. "I love you with much more than that. I love you with, oh everything somehow, with a special kind of soul." Sex and spirituality bounced back and forth in these letters; when Larry wasn't comparing himself and Vivien to celestial beings, he was asking her to send him her underwear. "I am sitting naked with just my parts wrapped in your panties," he told her.

Vivien was still capable of jealous tirades, and Larry constantly had to reassure her, which he did imperfectly at best. "I love and worship you with my whole being as you know O you know," he insisted, after tactlessly admitting that he was attracted to other women. "But ones [sic] primary reflexes are simply beyond ones control, before they enter the conscious, they just belong to the realm of fundamentals and primitive instincts, and animal reactions, and proto-pleasure urges that one can simply do nothing about.... One can trust temptation to be inconceivable, but to claim it to be impossible is a wee bit head strong to say the least. Real genuine purity of thought is a gift, not a virtue."

As the couple's separation stretched from days to weeks, the tension between them increased. "Darling," wrote Larry on June 10, almost two months after leaving Los Angeles, "I underwent such a wave of dejection after our phone call.... When I get these really murderous hits of depression, I rather feel like crawling into a hole by myself anyway—oh darling I don't know whats [sic] the matter with me, but when things aren't going quite right I go nearly mad—oh darling—things have simply got to go right when we're together—after all this dreadful misery. We *will* be alright won't we? We *must* find peace together and not allow *any*thing to *spite* us."

With Cukor gone, filming on *GWTW* came to an abrupt halt while Selznick searched for a new director. At first, he thought of King Vidor, who had made the silent classic *The Crowd* but was past his peak; then there was D. W. Griffith, the legendary director of 1915's *The Birth of a Nation*, who had fallen from grace but might add magic to some of the second-unit work. Finally, he offered the job to Victor Fleming, Gable's good friend and the filmmaker Mayer had wanted from the start.

At fifty-six, Fleming was the anti-Cukor, a gun-toting, game-hunting, girl-chasing man's man on whom Gable's screen persona was said to be based. He was part of an "extremely masculine breed" of directors, said Selznick, and "the most attractive man, in my opinion, who ever came to Hollywood. Physically and in personality. He had a kind of Indian quality. American Indian, that is. Women were crazy about him, and understandably so."

Fleming was still working on *The Wizard of Oz*, a salvage job like so many of his recent endeavors, that he had taken over when Richard Thorpe was fired. He complained endlessly about his vast load, which had left him exhausted long before *GWTW*. The gossip columnist Sheilah Graham (whose lover, F. Scott Fitzgerald, had contributed to *Wind*'s screenplay) said he was "nervous as a thoroughbred horse," and even Fleming admitted: "I've been working too hard"—not just on *Oz* but on a host of other movies for which he didn't receive credit. An aide to Selznick found him on the *Wizard* set, struggling with 124 munchkins, many allegedly so intoxicated that they had just ruined a sequence by replacing the word "witch" with "bitch," singing, "Ding, dong, the bitch is dead."

Undeterred, Selznick and writer John Lee Mahin (one of several the producer had engaged for rewrites) arrived drunk at his house in the middle of the night and threw pebbles at his window to wake him, pleading for him to join their team. Given that MGM now considered *GWTW* even more important than *Oz*, the director agreed and, while Vivien waited to resume work, he, Selznick, Mahin and Ben Hecht retreated to Palm Springs, that sun-soaked desert outpost a hundred miles east of Los Angeles, to revamp the screenplay. They were already at the breaking point and shooting had barely begun. On the fourth day, remembered Hecht, "a blood vessel in Fleming's right eye broke, while "on the fifth day, Selznick toppled into a torpor while chewing on a banana."

"Everyone is *hysterical* about this film," Vivien wrote Gertrude, "with the consequence that everything is disorganised—after *two* years they are still writing the script which means I don't know where I am. They have changed the director, which has upset me a lot, as I loved George Cukor (who was here before). I like this man [Victor Fleming] alright, but the poor wretch is *exhausted* as he hasn't stopped working for ages, & he did not really want to do this film, as he was so tired, & has not even had time to read the book!!"

Like Fleming as she did at this early stage, she had little confidence in his ability with actors and continued to meet privately with Cukor, as did de Havilland, each arriving at his house separately for coaching, unaware that the other was also stopping by. "I had to keep this a secret because it was the most unorthodox thing to be doing, but of course I felt sort of guilty toward Vivien," recalled de Havilland. "Then, when the film was over, I found out that Vivien had been doing exactly the same thing."

Vivien's relationship with Fleming soon deteriorated. By the time they'd been working together a week, she considered him "a mere workaday hack," while he nicknamed her "Fiddle-de-dee," a play on Scarlett's favorite exclamation. Whereas Cukor had spent hours rehearsing, Fleming's notion of acting boiled down to "Ham it, baby, just ham it!" Nor did it help when he declared loudly, in front of Vivien, "For Christ's sake, let's get a good look at the girl's boobs." And when Vivien had the temerity to challenge him on the screenplay, he exploded: "Miss Leigh, you can take this script and stick it up your royal British ass."

Tired and overwhelmed, Vivien succumbed to the dark moods Olivier had witnessed in Denmark. She would collapse into bed, exhausted, but "couldn't sleep," as she acknowledged later. "Every nerve in my body was pounding. I had to take tonics to keep going. At the end I was quite raving mad—ready for a lunatic asylum."

Her secretary, Sunny Alexander, cautioned Larry that Vivien seemed unwell. "Several times," said Alexander, "I thought she really was going mad. She warned me once that someday she would and I was beginning to believe that time had come." Still, neither fully recognized the extent of her problems or how much stress and a lack of sleep contributed to them, even when she cracked.

"As rehearsals [for *No Time for Comedy*] drew to an end," remembered Olivier, "worrisome news was coming from Hollywood; exhaustion coupled with hysteria owing to our harshly testing separation was producing dangerous symptoms, and David got me on the phone and implored me to get out there somehow to use my influence to calm things down, 'if only for a *day*.'"

In March, Larry took a break from his play's out-of-town preparations and made the long flight to Los Angeles, hoping to restore Vivien's spirits, even if that meant missing his dress rehearsal. He must have been successful, because Selznick's anxiety abated and there were no further memos begging for his help. He returned to Indianapolis in time for the opening night and found he had a hit on his hands, big enough to carry the show to Broadway.

But that was his only good news, coming immediately after he got word that his father had died on March 13, 1939.

Gerard had been living with his wife in Worthing, where he had retired. Was he happy? As much as he could be. He was an unsettled soul, a zealot who had dreamed of changing the world but couldn't change himself; and yet the locals adored him, certainly compared to the slum dwellers in Notting Dale: after his death, a newspaper described him as "a scholarly and devoted priest, of a charming personality [who was] much beloved."

His life was made easier by Ibo, though their marriage was complicated by her postmenopausal lack of desire, a "withdrawal of tender intimacies [that] was distressingly saddening to him," wrote Olivier. "He never upbraided or reproached her; he just dumbly accepted what was undoubtedly a scar across his life."

Difficult as the father-and-son relationship had been, and little as the two men had seen of each other once Larry left home, the older man haunted him. Years later, noted Bushell, Olivier still wore "a heavy gold Albert watchchain he had inherited from his parson Dad." If Larry consciously rejected his father's teaching, it nonetheless shaped his notions of good and bad and stamped him with an eternal sense of guilt and shame. That would only increase when he was unable to get back to England for the funeral; he would devote paragraphs of his memoir to explaining why, while also exploring his unexpected sensation of loss following Gerard's demise, of having "no protective influence between oneself and death."

Gerard had grown inordinately proud of his son as he reached the pinnacle of fame; but Larry never readjusted his feelings about Fahv. Even when he was no longer a black sheep but had become his father's favorite, he could not help flinching at the man's flaws—like the time stinginess made him hesitate before offering Dickie a whisky, though Larry's older brother had just returned from India. "Once [Larry] became famous, his dad didn't really know how to talk to him," says Olivier's younger son, Richard. "There was a kind of awkwardness between them; there may have been all along—it just took a different form."

Still, things had mellowed between them over the years and Ibo later told Larry: "I don't think you can ever know, what a joy you have been to us both, and I am so thankful to Him that he has given me a little of what Mums would have had, if HE had not taken her away when He did."

The day after Gerard's death—from a stroke that had left him incapacitated for months—Sybille went into his room, full of daffodils, and found her father looking like "a marble effigy of a medieval bishop." "Personally, Kim, love," she wrote her brother, "I can feel no sorrow whatever at Fahv's dying. I'm thankful for his sake and everybody else's....I am quite sure the greater part of him had really been gone for quite some time past. Do you remember walking with me across those gardens at Worthing early last August (or was it October?) and asking me how long I thought the old man would last and I replied gloomily that he might taggle [sic] on for 20 years? I've almost prayed for him to go, and now he has, and except for the initial shock of it, and v. acute sympathy for Ibo, all I can feel is sheer relief."

After the funeral, Gerard's flock gathered in his church and sang in his honor:

> God be with you till we meet again,
> Keep love's banner floating o'er you,

Smite death's threat'ning wave before you,
God be with you till we meet again.

In Los Angeles, Vivien was having a harder and harder time and the script was changing so fast she could barely keep up. "Sometimes we were only given our lines for the following day late at night," she said, "and I never seemed to know more than twenty-four hours ahead even what age I would be playing next day."

She got little support from Howard, her costar, an otherwise imperturbable performer who had never troubled to read the book and found Ashley "a dreadful milk-sop, totally spineless and negative." "He scarcely bothered to look at his lines," conceded his daughter, Leslie Ruth Howard, "on the basis that they might be changed and anyway were rehearsed and shot so many times that a halfwit could remember them." Once, when his indifference proved too much, Vivien flew at him for failing to memorize the words. The next day, he gloated when she forgot hers, too.

"Before a scene, she would be muttering deprecations under her breath and making small moans," recalled Selznick. "According to Vivien, the situation was stupid, the dialogue was silly, nobody could possibly believe the whole scene. And then, at a word from Victor Fleming, who was not merely a very fine director but a man who had the ability to conceal the iron hand in the velvet glove, she would walk into the scene and do such a magnificent job that everybody on the set would be cheering."

The days were getting longer, the nights shorter; sleep was something to be envied rather than enjoyed. "The hours were the most punishing," wrote Irene. "They were insane and only made possible [for Selznick] by Benzedrine, in increasing amounts... it was like being under siege." Sidney Howard, the screenwriter, noted "the miasma of fatigue" all around. "Fleming takes four shots of something a day to keep him going and another shot or so to fix him so he can sleep after the day's stimulation. Selznick is bent double with permanent, and, I should think, chronic indigestion. Half the staff look, talk and behave as though they were on the verge of a breakdown."

And then Fleming had one. Six weeks after starting work, he collapsed and was confined to bed. It was a crack in his manly facade, a revelation that he was more fragile than he liked to let on. In fact, macho as he appeared, he had serious issues of mental health and suffered from acute depression, as he admitted to de Havilland, alone among the cast. Vivien had no idea that, during their battles, he was thinking of killing himself. "He gravely told me that on the previous Saturday night [before his collapse] he had driven to the top of a cliff and had contemplated leaping from its edge," recalled de Havilland. "But on the film, despite his melancholy, he was unfailingly professional, capable, courteous, and considerate. I would never have guessed that he was a deeply suffering man."

Selznick tried in the most brazen way to persuade him to come back, offering him a share of his profits, as if money could speed his recovery. "What do you take me for, a chump?" Fleming lashed out.

Unwilling to suspend shooting again, Selznick turned to one of the few directors willing to board this modern-day *Titanic*, Sam Wood. He may not have been quite the worst filmmaker around, but he was far from the best. Vivien dismissed him as "the realtor" (his former profession) and kept him waiting for hours on his first day, May 1, while she, Selznick and de Havilland conferred in her dressing room.

Two weeks later, Fleming was back to direct Vivien in one of her most memorable scenes: walking among the dead and the dying as the camera rose on an eighty-five-foot construction crane, climbing up and up until it paused above the crowds, above the blue and the red of a waving Confederate flag, above the bodies bent and broken. Extras and even amputees from a local veterans' hospital had been recruited for the gargantuan sequence, along with a number of dummies, and they surrounded Vivien as she threaded her way through a living graveyard. She was "exhausted and impatient," said Cukor, her eyes itching, her skin peeling from an allergy to the ninety-seven tons of red dirt that had been imported from Georgia, her mind preoccupied with a false pregnancy scare as she spent several days waiting for her overdue period, terrified she might need an abortion.

She had begun taking sedatives to calm her down and on May 18 she overdosed, though the dosage was small and it appears not to have been a suicide attempt.

Olivier learned the news from her assistant, Sunny. "Urrrrrggh! Urrrrrgh!" he wrote Vivien. "How *dare* you take *four* pills like that you hysterical little ninny (and I know perfectly well you knew people would get alarmed and ring me up and put the fear of God into your poor old Larry at five in the morning). Urrgh! Bend over—Yes, take your drawers down—no, lift your skirt up—*now* then: Smack! Smack! Smack!"

A nastier side of Vivien emerged, most evident in a new game she concocted, which she added to her repertoire of cards, crosswords and charades. Its name was "Ways to Kill a Baby." Friends and colleagues would gather around and invent dastardly schemes to murder a child. Vivien's favorite: pretending she was driving, she would lift the invisible infant on her lap, cooing sweetly, then hurl it out the window.

Black rings of fatigue appeared beneath her eyes, which cinematographer Ernest Haller tried to hide with a diffusion disc. Off-camera, her moods "veered erratically between tantrums and weeping fits," writes Flamini, "and the crew gave her a wide berth. Once, as she stood on the set in the green velvet dress made from the curtains at Tara, Lydia Schiller, the continuity girl, adjusted the fringe of her hat and [she] jumped back, shouting, 'For God's sake, leave me alone.'"

She had lost so much weight that de Havilland, returning after an absence, almost didn't recognize her. Even Selznick was shocked.

"My God, you look so old," he blurted out.

"And so would you if you had been working eighteen hours a day for weeks on end," Vivien shot back.

Desperate, Selznick granted her a weekend's leave, allowing her once again to spend time with Larry, despite the producer's terror that news of the affair would damage his priceless picture. Vivien was no longer in the cosseted and tolerant British theater; she was in America—and the New World was riddled with old ideologies, hemmed in by puritan groups that could bring down an actress, and thereby a film, at the least hint of a moral lapse. Aware of the danger, Vivien and Larry rendezvoused in Kansas City, correctly guessing that nobody would recognize them there. It was only their second time together since filming had begun. "Oh David," Vivien told Selznick when she returned. "I'm so grateful to you. Larry met me in the hotel lobby, and we went upstairs, and we fucked, and we fucked, and we fucked the whole weekend."

Wuthering Heights opened to enormous success on April 13, though Larry wasn't in Los Angeles for the premiere.

The film had seemed like a surefire flop. It had wrapped thirteen days behind schedule and $100,000 over budget, and when it previewed with the tragic ending Wyler had wanted, in which both Heathcliff and Cathy die, the questionnaires completed by the audience "were among the worst responses to a motion picture [Goldwyn] had ever read," writes his biographer, A. Scott Berg. "They found the story hard to follow and seemed to concur with Goldwyn's initial instincts to the material. He said, 'People don't want to look at a corpse at the end of a picture.'"

With Larry in New York, there was no way to reshoot. But Goldwyn remembered something he'd seen in another film, MGM's *Three Comrades*, whose characters reappear as ghosts. That was the way to do it, he said: using doubles seen from a distance, he'd show Heathcliff and Cathy romping amid the clouds. Wyler was horrified, but the producer went ahead regardless. A second preview in Santa Barbara was met with resounding applause, after which the premiere (attended by Eleanor Roosevelt) was a sensation, even if the movie ultimately did less well than expected at the box office.

"It is Goldwyn at his best, and better still, Emily Brontë at hers," wrote Frank S. Nugent in the *New York Times*. "Out of her strange tale of a tortured romance Mr. Goldwyn and his troupe have fashioned a strong and somber film, poetically written as the novel not always was, sinister and wild as it was meant to be, far more compact dramatically than Miss Brontë had made it.... [Olivier] has Heathcliff's broad lowering brow, his scowl, the churlishness, the wild tenderness, the bearing, speech and manner of the demon-possessed [and] Merle Oberon, as Cathy, has matched the brilliance of his characterization with hers."

Overnight, Larry became a major star. His name was now "a synonym for the fiery, impetuous lover," noted the fan magazine *Silver Screen*. In New York, he was virtually assaulted by fans, who at one point almost stripped him of his clothes. But away from Vivien, he was as morose as the character he had played, "mercurial as the month of March," in the publication's words, his smile only rarely dispelling "his habitual somberness [and] steel-trap dourness."

"Life is very dull for Laurence Olivier," wrote a reporter for the *World-Telegram*. "Being a matinee idol is very dull. Having a couple of dozen adoring women waiting in the alley at the

Ethel Barrymore Theater is very dull. Giving interviews is ditto, and playing opposite Katharine Cornell in the hit *No Time for Comedy* is very dull. . . . 'Really I'm just a dull fellow,' Mr. Olivier repeated. 'Really I am. I don't ever know what to say to you reporter fellows. I suppose it's because I don't have a viewpoint about anything. One should have viewpoints about things, I suppose, but I just don't. I just sit here and realize I am becoming more and more boring.' "

This was not Larry at his best and brightest, but all he could think of was Vivien. At times, he confessed, he would sit staring into space, "absolutely transfixed . . . [I] am thinking angrily or indignantly or sulking, quite often, but I am *never* not thinking of you."

He worried not only about Vivien but also her film, which ground on beyond human endurance. Like her, he was convinced it would be a disaster, and so he urged her to find ways to salvage her career. "You have got to justify yourself in the next two or 3 films (or even 2 or 3 years) by proving that the presumable failure of 'Gone W.T.W.' was not your fault and you can only do that by being really good in the following parts," he wrote. "To make a success of your career in pictures [is] ESSENTIAL for your self respect, and our ultimate happiness therefore." If she failed, he warned, "I am afraid you may become just—well boring. Never to me my own you know, but to yourself + because of that to others, and that is a part that simply won't suit my Vivling."

His Vivling was rising at 3:30 a.m. day after day as the shoot entered the homestretch and she had to tackle one of her most emotional scenes: when a starving Scarlett digs up radishes in the dirt and vows, "As God is my witness, I'll never be hungry again." On location just north of Los Angeles, with the sun beating down mercilessly and the red soil staining everything, Vivien's dress changed color and so did her hair. But even that "was not a thing to what the wind was doing to me," she wrote later. "The tears made great crimson rivers down my cheeks! My face was washed twelve times that day." After a long night of shooting, by dawn she was so drained that she fell to her knees and hammered her hands on the ground in sheer frustration. But at last her torture was over. On June 27, principal photography came to an end.

"SOUND THE SIREN," Selznick cabled his partner, Whitney. "SCARLETT O'HARA COMPLETED HER PERFORMANCE AT NOON TODAY. GABLE FINISHES TONIGHT OR IN THE MORNING AND WE WILL BE SHOOTING UNTIL FRIDAY WITH BIT PEOPLE. I AM GOING ON THE BOAT FRIDAY NIGHT AND YOU CAN ALL GO TO THE DEVIL....PLEASE TELL MARGARET MITCHELL WHAT SHE CAN DO TO HERSELF."

CHAPTER 5

———◦◉◦———

Larry and Vivien thought they were done with Hollywood, but Hollywood wasn't done with them. Vivien was not just a star; she was on the threshold of becoming a superstar—which meant she was chained to Selznick, and not only to him but also to a city she abhorred. The sun that had burned Jill's face seemed to have burned its inhabitants' brains; they never read, never thought, never spoke about anything but the movies, and not the art of the movies but the money they made. Where was the cultured conversation of the theater, the talk of books and plays and performances? Intellect meant nothing here, only one's salary, all of it lavished on cars as big as boats and mansions as immense as palaces, among which Hollywood's magnates would shuttle back and forth, mimicking friendship with the rivals they secretly despised.

Vivien hated these men, just as she hated their business— because it *was* a business, even if it occasionally spat out an accidental work of art. If she had arrived a few years earlier or had more time to explore, she might have discovered a colony of migrants fleeing the Nazis, an ecosystem within an ecosystem of exiles who had found an improbable refuge in this spiritual wasteland—the Brechts, the Schönbergs, the Alma

Mahlers—people who were in some ways more like-minded. She spoke excellent German, after all, along with French and Italian; she knew history and literature, and devoured novels as readily as her contemporaries did the daily papers. But that meant nothing to the princes of this town, the men who'd built an empire of their own, their studios solemn temples to their grandeur—the moguls who surrounded themselves with sycophants in a community, as one observer has noted, "that was partly an industry, partly a technology, partly just a hunger for money and success."

Now, in the brief interregnum between *Gone with the Wind*'s wrap date and its December premiere, Vivien longed to escape and be with Olivier, and so the moment filming was over, she flew to New York and refused to come back for yet another retake, despite Selznick's demands. There she remained with Larry until the completion of *No Time for Comedy*; and then in late July, eight months after she had left England on what had seemed like a whim—in the mere hope of auditioning for the grandest of all motion pictures, unaware that it would change her life forever—the couple sailed home.

Even as they were planning their next ventures, Selznick was finding ways to bring them back. The producer had been developing another picture in tandem with *Wind*, one similarly based on a best-selling novel and one that would again place Vivien and Larry at his mercy.

Rebecca told the story of an innocent and naive young woman (never named in the book or the film) who marries the aristocratic Max de Winter and moves to his British estate, Manderley, only to find it haunted by the presence of his late wife, the Rebecca of the title. Daphne du Maurier's novella was brought to Selznick by his invaluable East Coast representative, Kay Brown, who had discovered *GWTW*, a shrewd, sharp judge of material and character who would later become one of the Oliviers' agents.

Her boss was not alone in circling the waters. Alfred Hitchcock, who had yet to leave his native England and settle in America, wanted to buy the rights, too, but was intimidated by the hefty price Selznick was willing to pay when he landed the book: $50,000, the same sum he had paid for *Gone with the Wind*. He guarded it with the same ferocity, doing everything to prevent the young Orson Welles from staging a radio adaptation weeks after his notorious *War of the Worlds* broadcast, which had convinced millions that aliens were invading Earth.

Having lost the rights, Hitchcock nonetheless agreed to direct the film for Selznick and relocated to Los Angeles, where his acerbic wit and portly frame made him an odd addition to its sunbaked citizens. There he began work on a script with writers Joan Harrison and Michael Hogan, while the producer focused on casting.

There were few satisfactory candidates for de Winter, a man of mystery, a criminal hiding an unknown crime; even so, at least prior to *Wuthering Heights*, Olivier was by no means the frontrunner. Instead, Selznick favored the elegant British expatriate Ronald Colman, who, in pictures such as 1935's *A Tale of Two Cities* and 1937's *The Prisoner of Zenda*, had come to personify everything suave and sophisticated—and everything that Larry, at the beginning of his film career, chose to imitate. It was all an illusion, of course: the actor was a former bank clerk made good, who protected his new image with the ferocity of any mad dog or Englishman still out in the midday sun. Worried that playing a murderer (the killer of his own wife, no less) would make him look bad, and knowing he'd inevitably play second fiddle to the female lead, he passed, and Selznick reached out to Larry.

"Called Olivier in Baltimore [during the out-of-town run of *No Time for Comedy*]," reported one of his agents, "and advised him of David Selznick's great interest in him for REBECCA, as well as for two other stories; namely, FLASHING STREAM and

THE CONSTANT NYMPH. Olivier appreciated hearing about David's great desire to have him, but stated he would never make a commitment to do three pictures for anyone. And would not want to make a commitment for REBECCA until he had read a script."

Never an avid reader, Larry had yet to familiarize himself with du Maurier's tale. ("He was not au fond a witty man, nor was he even reasonably well educated," noted Bushell, "+ he NEVER read books.") Consumed with his Broadway play, he hesitated and kept on hesitating, just as he had with *Wuthering Heights*, prompting Selznick to consider others, including Leslie Howard, William Powell and David Niven. How seriously the producer took them isn't clear; they are barely mentioned in his voluminous memos because in all likelihood he preferred to wait Larry out. He knew stars, knew their follies and foibles, knew that a categorical "no" one day might mean an enthusiastic "yes" the next. And so he kept on pushing, remembering something Deverich had relayed from his brief telephone call with Larry: that the actor might reconsider "if he were able to spend a few weeks in England"—and if Vivien were cast as the female lead.

Olivier had done this dance before. He had fought for her on *Wuthering Heights* and then unleashed his resentment on Oberon when Vivien didn't get the part. But he had political capital now and planned to use it: in the weeks since *Wuthering* had opened, he had become the most wanted star alive and, with Colman out of the running, no one else could believably play de Winter. As for Vivien, she wanted the role almost as much as she had wanted Scarlett.

And yet Selznick was unpersuaded. True, there were strong arguments for casting the actress, whose fame was about to explode with the opening of *Gone with the Wind* and who was now contractually part of his stable of stars, a collection he had built with the assiduousness of a brilliant agent, just like his brother. But there was another argument more overpowering: Vivien was nothing like du Maurier's frail and insecure girl. That girl, in fact, was Vivien's opposite: innocent but not ignorant, soft but not supine, attractive but not beautiful—none of which sounded remotely like the woman Selznick knew and certainly not the one who was at her most magnificent when angry, when clutching the red earth of Georgia and vowing she would never be hungry again.

Instead of giving his verdict, he kept on searching while dangling her as bait for Larry. At the same time, he auditioned anyone he could—using that opportunity for personal as well as professional gratification, like so many men in his position, seeking women who were either right for the role or right for him. "He talked all the big stars in town into doing tests for *Rebecca*," said Hitchcock. "I found it a little embarrassing, myself, testing women who I knew in advance were unsuitable for the part."

Anne Baxter, Bette Davis, Danielle Darrieux and Loretta Young were all in contention. Some could act but couldn't convey innocence; others could convey innocence but couldn't act. Only de Havilland's older sister, Joan Fontaine, seemed like a vague "possibility," said Hitchcock, although he and Selznick feared she didn't have the requisite skill—perhaps didn't have any skill at all. When Selznick decided to audition her, the "audition" quickly became something else and Fontaine told friends he had tried to force himself on her. Still, this was the woman he ultimately bet on, his choice reflecting his belief that an actress, above all else, had to be right for the part.

Jock Whitney was aghast. Fontaine wasn't simply inadequate, he said; she was as wooden as a plank. "The last test of Joan Fontaine was so bad," he wrote Selznick, "that I cannot see her playing the role otherwise than as a dithering idiot, or as her other version—a talking magazine cover." His advice: take Vivien.

Vivien believed in herself, was convinced she could become someone wholly different from Scarlett. She was still under Larry's influence, still unaware that acting and stardom were two separate and discrete things—especially when it came to film. And so she kept chasing the role, even enlisting him on her side. "Miss Leigh told me this morning that Laurence Olivier has told her that he will definitely do *Rebecca* if she does it," noted Selznick.

Larry, in fact, had guaranteed no such thing. He didn't even know if he wanted to play de Winter and, privately, wasn't at all sure Vivien should be his costar. And so he vacillated, as his correspondence with Selznick testifies. A rush in Vivien's favor would be followed by a hasty retreat. "I didn't like having to plead Vivien's case," he said later. "But I couldn't say no."

By early June, Selznick had had enough. The picture couldn't be delayed any more; it was due to start shooting in less than three months. He therefore instructed his staff to "inform Mr. Olivier that unless we get an answer from him immediately we are going to have to negotiate with others for the lead." Once again, the fear of losing a meaty role tipped the balance. Larry capitulated and on July 1 signed a contract for a twelve-week shoot that would pay $4,166.66 per week or $50,000 in total. With overages, his final payment would be $54,861, more than $1 million in today's dollars.

That left Vivien dangling. She was the most-watched, most-envied and most-talked-about young actress alive, but she was also a movie star without a movie, a performer in search of a part. Determined to hook *Rebecca*, she had agreed to do a screen test, only to realize it wasn't her best work, when she begged to do another, this time with Larry rather than the actor who had fed her lines. If she was too aggressive in the first test (she was "Scarlett in a cardigan," one critic quipped), she was too passive in the next. She simply couldn't button up her essential vitality, the dynamic and even volcanic emotional register that made her so distinct. She would have been perfect as Mrs. De Winter, quipped Hitchcock—only, the dead one, not the living one. "[Writer Robert E.] Sherwood and Cukor respectively, and without any prompting whatsoever, made the same comments that Hitchcock and I made," Selznick assured Whitney, "that she doesn't seem at all right as to sincerity or age or innocence or any of the other factors which are essential to the story coming off at all....I am convinced that we would be better off making this picture with a girl who had no personality whatever and who was a bad actress [that is, Fontaine] but was right in type than we would be to cast it with Vivien."

Whitney threw up his hands. "My first choice has been and always will be Vivien for this part," he replied, "but since mental, as well as ocular ophthalmia seems to have descended upon Culver City as a plague, I will attempt to vote on a second choice with as much enthusiasm as I can muster."

Vivien and Larry were traveling back to America after their vacation, ready to start work on the film and fully expecting good news when Selznick cabled them on board their ship in August 1939. His nervousness was obvious: he sent two telegrams, one for Vivien and another for Larry. To the latter, he cabled:

DEAR LARRY PLEASE SEE MY WIRE TO VIVIEN STOP. I KNOW YOU MUST BE DISAPPOINTED BUT VIVIENS ANXIETY TO PLAY ROLE HAS IN MY OPINION BEEN LARGELY IF NOT ENTIRELY DUE TO HER DESIRE TO DO A PICTURE WITH YOU WHICH WAS BEST DEMONSTRATED BY HER COMPLETE DISINTEREST IN PART WHEN I FIRST MENTIONED IT TO HER AS POSSIBILITY AND UNTIL SHE KNEW YOU WERE PLAYING MAXIM.

Vivien was furious. And all Larry could do was assuage her as she read, over and over, the condescending wording of Selznick's message to her:

DEAR VIVIEN WE HAVE TRIED TO SELL OURSELVES RIGHT UP UNTIL TODAY TO CAST YOU IN REBECCA BUT I REGRET NECESSITY TELLING YOU WE ARE FINALLY CONVINCED YOU ARE AS WRONG FOR ROLE AS ROLE WOULD BE FOR YOU STOP YOU MUST REALIZE IT IS THIS SAME PATIENCE CARE AND STUBBORNNESS ABOUT ACCURATE CASTING THAT RESULTED IN PUTTING YOU IN MOST TALKED OF ROLE OF ALL TIME IN WHAT EVERYONE WHO HAS SEEN IT AGREES IS GREATEST PICTURE EVER MADE.

It would have appalled Selznick, if he could ever have aimed his periscope at the outside world, to know that he wasn't alone in deeming *Wind* the greatest picture ever made. On the other side of the ocean, in the Old World that was now bracing for a seemingly inevitable war, Hitler was almost as impressed by the movie as its producer. "Now that, that is something our own people should also be able to do," he told his propagandist, Joseph Goebbels, after viewing an illicit print, nominally forbidden by the Reich, which had banned Hollywood products in Germany. Weeks later, Hitler sent his juggernaut army into Poland, violating the peace agreement he had signed with Chamberlain. And two days after that, on September 3, 1939, England declared war.

"At 1115 BST [British Standard Time] the Prime Minister, Neville Chamberlain, announced the British deadline for the withdrawal of German troops from Poland had expired," reported the BBC. "He said the British ambassador to Berlin had handed a final note to the German government this morning saying unless it announced plans to withdraw from Poland by 1100, a state of war would exist between the two countries. Mr. Chamberlain continued: 'I have to tell you now that no such undertaking has been received and consequently this country is at war with Germany.' "

War had been rolling forward implacably, and Europe's citizens had been waiting, caught between fear and hope, terrified that bloodshed was unavoidable and yet praying it would never occur. Even Vivien and Larry, who rarely expressed an interest in politics, had been swept up, along with everyone else, and had spent their time in London glued to the radio. News that war had been declared broke two weeks after their arrival in America, when they were sailing on a yacht near Catalina, an island off the Southern California coast. Larry felt "blighted" and proceeded to get "smashed as a hoot-owl," recalled the actor Douglas Fairbanks Jr., one of his close friends. After pronouncing multiple toasts to Allied victory, he took off in a small boat and sped from one moored vessel to another, bellowing the news to all and sundry, prompting the harbor authorities to report that a man who looked suspiciously like Ronald Colman was making a fool of himself. "This is the end! You're all washed up!" he screamed. "Enjoy your last moments. You're done for..."

Vivien, more subdued, was in tears. It was "one of the few times I ever saw her cry," observed David Niven.

Deeply patriotic, the couple vowed to go back to England, which would have meant breaking their contracts. But the authorities in London and Washington told them, like all the other Hollywood expatriates, to remain where they were, explaining that they would be more useful lending their talents to pro-British propaganda. And so they waited, living an American idyll as their friends back home lived through hell, or at least through the so-called "Phony War" from September 1939 to May 1940, during which Britain geared up for conflict without firing a single bullet. In the blistering Los Angeles heat, Vivien and Larry commiserated with their fellow expats—men like Charles Laughton (who had suffered from PTSD after the gas attacks of World War I) and Cedric Hardwicke (the last British officer to leave France at the end of that war). They even occasionally dined with "Huns," including Erich von Stroheim, Larry's costar in *Friends and Lovers* (one of his flops before *Wuthering Heights*) and the son of a Jewish hatmaker, who had added the "von" to his name and reinvented himself as an aristocrat.

Back home, Larry was vilified for staying away. True, he could have followed Niven's lead and enlisted at once, defying Hollywood; but Niven was a Sandhurst graduate, and besides, no less a figure than the British ambassador to Washington, Philip Kerr, had told Larry to remain where he was. He would come to regret his decision, especially when he was so severely attacked back home. "People felt strongly about what were called the 'homing pigeons' who came back later—particularly in the film industry and theater—because so many had stayed [away]," says Michael Korda, the producer's nephew. "There was a lot of bad feeling about that. [In England] people were bombed, people had terrible things happen. [Upon her return, Vivien] felt a deep shame at having been out of England during the Battle of Britain and the Blitz."

Olivier's misery was apparent on-set when he started shooting *Rebecca* in September. Assailed by guilt, torn between his loyalty to Vivien and his movie, and troubled about the fate of the child he had left behind, he was appallingly mean-spirited. His costar, forced to shoot eleven hours each day, would have struggled in the best of circumstances; with both Larry and Hitchcock against her, she buckled and almost broke. It was clear to everyone, including Selznick's secretary, that "she was not a good enough actress" for the role and they let her know it.

"Hitch" had no more patience with her than any other amateur, though his loathing for actors has been exaggerated and Olivier, for one, held him in high regard. When Fontaine struggled to muster tears, the director asked what she needed to make her cry. "Well, maybe if you slapped me," she replied. He did so, he said, "and she instantly started bawling."

"His technique was 'Divide and conquer,'" recalled the young woman. "He wanted total loyalty, but only to him. The very first week of shooting, he confided to me that Olivier really wanted his fiancée, Vivien Leigh, in my role."

Another time, Hitchcock told her that "Larry had just come to him, saying Fontaine was awful and that Vivien was the only one who should play opposite him. As was Hitch's intention, I believe, I could hardly be friends with Laurence Olivier after that, though I hope I didn't show it."

She was afraid of Larry, terrified of Hitchcock and desperately insecure. ("I have an inferiority complex," she explained later.) She was thus ready to have her buttons pushed, which Larry did adroitly. When he learned she was about to marry the actor Brian Aherne, a former colleague and rival, he sniffed: "Couldn't you do better than that?" Fontaine was "shattered," as she remembered. "Arriving home that evening, I gazed upon my Prince Charming with new eyes. Try as I would to forget his remark, Larry had rudely awakened me from my pillow dream." The couple divorced five years later.

Two camps emerged on-set. There were the expatriates who bonded with Olivier—George Sanders, Judith Anderson and C. Aubrey Smith—the very types he had previously avoided. ("Hollywood was full of phony Englishmen," notes Michael Korda, "people who would walk down Santa Monica Blvd. in a Sherlock Holmes hat and cape. Larry was much too smart and too classy a personality to do anything like that.") On the other side was the inexperienced actress they shunned. None of them showed up for her twenty-second birthday party, a terrible slight given that Hitchcock was the host. Vivien, almost always well-mannered (at least when she had self-control), made up for it by inviting Fontaine and Aherne to dinner, only to leave them waiting for an hour until she and Larry appeared.

Olivier's acting skill dwarfed Fontaine's, but he had taken to underplaying, either to compensate for his excesses in *Wuthering Heights* or because his heart wasn't in the work. "Acting for films is about as satisfying as looking at a Michelangelo fresco with a microscope," he sniffed. Selznick urged Hitchcock to draw more emotion from him, to "be a little more Yiddish Art Theatre, in these moments, a little less English Repertory Theatre." He disliked Olivier's sullenness, his clipped dialogue and his "habit of throwing away lines too much," he said. "I know that this is the modern style of acting, but it's also a modern style of losing points!" He even objected to Larry's appearance, demanding the actor grow his hair and sideburns and trim his mustache, while also pointing out that he wasn't "going to be nearly as attractive as he was in WUTHERING HEIGHTS if he doesn't build himself up somewhat, both in height and the width of his shoulders." As a result, Olivier wore three-inch lifts in his boots, making him seem taller than his real-life five-foot-ten. Selznick also urged him to absorb the "moods and descriptions in the book that we are not bothering to put into the script on the assumption that each of the players is studying the book. I don't mean this at all as a criticism, but rather as a defense, and as a suggestion to make your own job easier and more thorough." Disingenuously, he added: "As I have told you, I am delighted by your charming performance."

In truth, he found it anything but charming and his disappointment turned to rage when Olivier got a stand-in to speak his lines during Fontaine's close-ups. The producer knew full well that she wouldn't stand a chance if Larry didn't help her, and that meant he had to be present for her close-ups, as well as his own. Selznick further ridiculed the languorous pace of each scene. "Larry's silent action and reactions become slower as the dialogue becomes faster, each day," he complained. "His pauses and spacing on the scene with the girl in which she tells him about the ball are the most ungodly slow and deliberate reactions I have ever seen. It is played as though he were deciding whether or not to run for President instead of whether or not to give a ball....For God's sake speed up Larry."

After weeks of frustration, Selznick was so exasperated that he considered pulling the plug, an almost inconceivable notion halfway through filming. "He seemed uncertain about the *Rebecca* rushes and didn't know what was wrong," recalled his wife, Irene. "When the picture had been shooting some weeks, he phoned in the middle of the day to say that he needed me and to come right over to the studio. There was a vital decision to be made; I was to decide whether the picture should be scrapped.... He showed me a couple of reels that had been roughly assembled and awaited my verdict. When the lights went on in the projection room, I told him the footage was superb."

While Larry filmed *Rebecca*, Vivien began a new feature, *Waterloo Bridge*, a romantic drama about a ballet dancer and an army colonel, directed by *The Wizard of Oz*'s producer, Mervyn LeRoy. At first, she had little enthusiasm for the picture. Disappointed in her costar, Robert Taylor (who had worked with her quite amicably on *A Yank in Oxford*); livid that Selznick had the power to loan her out at will, per the terms of their contract; and wishing that Larry could play the lead, she tried to persuade Louis B. Mayer to replace her with Joan Crawford, but failed.

"The story we do is so dreary, that I cannot look forward to it," she wrote Holman, continuing the correspondence that kept them close. "It is a very sad affair which starts in this war & goes back to the Great War! & altho' I'm a good girl to start with I turn into a prostitute thereby ruining my chances with my fiancé (who is believed killed, but who of course isn't!). Eventually I either go mad or commit suicide, or am just plain blown up!—it's gay isn't it?"

Later, she came to love the picture, and would consider it one of her finest. "Hate Hollywood though she did," observes Alexander Walker, "it was the 'company town' that taught Vivien her screen craft. Compared to the films she made there, her early British ones look amateurish. Hollywood and its tough corps of no-nonsense directors... knocked technical craftsmanship into Vivien without bruising her beauty. The experience annealed her: the porcelain emerged finished."

In December 1939, precisely a year after she had won the role of Scarlett, Vivien joined Larry, Selznick and de Havilland on a plane to Atlanta for the premiere to end all premieres: *Gone with the Wind*.

Selznick was still smarting from his star's apparent indifference to his film, which she'd seen in its near-completed form in October, when she had failed to give it the praise he felt it deserved. Perhaps seeing herself on the big screen was too overwhelming or perhaps she was still influenced by Larry's conviction that the picture was destined to fail. Either way, she scrambled to make amends. "I am awfully distressed to hear that David was hurt by my seeming lack of enthusiasm the other night after the picture," she wrote Irene. "I assure you this was not at all the case, as I was immeasurably thrilled by it."

The actress and producer were fighting over everything, right down to Vivien's reimbursement for the outfits she would have to wear during three days of festivities in Georgia. At one point, she told Selznick she was planning to leave town in the middle of the premiere. "She wanted to take the first plane that left during the intermission," he said. "I explained to her that Atlanta didn't have planes leaving the city every ten minutes."

If Selznick had brought his insight to Vivien—the same insight he brought to his scripts—he might have realized she was terrified. She was about to experience a public unveiling of the biggest film of all time, knowing it could make or break her career. And so she lashed out, as she always did when she was scared, usually to back down. Only on one thing did she remain adamant: that Larry must be there for the premiere. If he didn't go, she said, "Then I won't be going either." Reluctantly, Selznick gave in.

On December 12, the party arrived in Atlanta, many for the first time in their lives. Emerging from the airport, they were serenaded by a military band performing "Dixie." ("Oh, they're playing the song from our picture," exclaimed Vivien.) A motorcade flanked by state police drove her into the city, while Larry sat in another car, as if to create the illusion that he was there with someone else. Vivien's picture was everywhere—in storefronts, on posters and in the photos that fans clutched in their hands—as confetti rained down by the ton, all orchestrated by city officials guided by Selznick's publicist. De Havilland believed a million people lined the streets, though that was likely an exaggeration in a town of only three hundred thousand. Vivien couldn't help but be caught up in the excitement; later, she cut out newspaper clippings about the event and kept them in her scrapbook.

Among the movie's notable names, three were conspicuously absent: Hattie McDaniel, Leslie Howard and Victor Fleming. McDaniel had chosen not to come rather than face the rampant racism of the South, which was still thirty years away from desegregation; Howard had no interest in the hoopla and had returned to England, while Fleming was smarting from a ferocious, but unexplained, falling-out with Selznick. The locals, however, were in a frenzy, whipped up by a mayor who saw this as the city's best promotion in years. "[William] Hartsfield urged every Atlanta woman and maid to put on hoop skirts and pantalets, appealed to every Atlanta male to don tight trousers and a beaver, sprout a goatee, sideburns and Kentucky colonel whiskers," reported *Time* magazine. "He also requested citizens not to tear off the clothes of visiting movie stars, as happened in Kansas at the premiere of *Dodge City*"—and as had also happened to Larry in the wake of *Wuthering Heights*.

Here at last Vivien met Scarlett's creator, Margaret Mitchell, who had kept a studious distance from the film, declining to consult on either the adaptation or the cast. At a private dinner, she gave Vivien a copy of her novel, inscribed, "Life's pattern pricked with a scarlet thread / where once we were with a gray / To remind us all how we played our parts / In the shock of an epic day."

The night before the premiere, six thousand movie stars, executives and dignitaries, along with five state governors and any locals lucky enough to obtain a ticket, attended a costume gala, with Vivien as the belle of the ball and Gable at his charming best. "Lord," one young woman gasped before fainting, "I can't stand this any longer." An eleven-year-old girl, kissed by the actor, wondered, "Now am I a woman?"

At a critics' screening, the response was rapturous. The picture was "the greatest motion mural we have seen and the most ambitious film-making venture in Hollywood's spectacular history," trumpeted the *New York Times*. Added the *Hollywood Reporter*: "This is more than the greatest motion picture which ever was made. It is the ultimate realization of the dreams of what might be done in every phase of film wizardry."

That night, when the movie unspooled before a packed house at the Loews Grand, "there was a hush [in the intermission]," recalled Evelyn Keyes, who played Scarlett's sister, Suellen.

"Nobody breathed, nobody moved for a moment. And when they did it was in slow motion. I felt almost that I'd never seen a movie before—and I haven't seen one since."

Gone with the Wind remains one of the most beloved of all Hollywood films, if no longer an undiluted triumph. True, Selznick managed to adapt a long and rambling novel; made it clear and cogent; found perfect actors for iconic roles; gave his picture drama, scope and even depth. But he failed to eliminate the book's most vexing problem, its romanticized view of slavery. He couldn't claim ignorance as a defense: well before the start of production, the head of the National Association for the Advancement of Colored People had written to him, sounding an alarm, and Selznick had been conscious enough of the matter to express concern. He knew he ran the risk of adding racial stereotypes to an industry that had been replete with them and was old enough to remember firsthand the fallout from the racially inflammatory *Birth of a Nation*, a picture then hailed as the greatest ever made, but also a celebration of the Ku Klux Klan. Regardless, he had gone ahead with his film, while making modest concessions such as eliminating a black-on-white rape and removing the word "nigger."

His short-term success was his long-term failure. He created a world so enchanting, so enticing, that it became the definitive portrait of the antebellum era, the very incarnation of plantation life as millions would perceive it for generations to come. He didn't just redefine history; he reinvented it. More than any other movie, *Gone with the Wind* set a false image in stone.

Nor is this simply revisionist history, written from the perspective of the modern era, eighty years after *GWTW*'s release: even at the time, amid all the hosannas, a backlash was gathering steam. "While responses to the finished film in the black press were mixed, the criticism was harsh," noted the *New York Times* in a recent analysis of contemporary responses. "*The Chicago Defender* initially published a column calling it inoffensive and the performances of Hattie McDaniel (Mammy) and Butterfly McQueen (Prissy) examples of 'Negro artistry.' But a week later, it ran a scathing review calling it 'a weapon of terror against black America,' a sentiment echoed in other black papers like the *Pittsburgh Courier*, which denounced the depiction of all blacks as 'happy house servants and unthinking, helpless clods.' "

Vivien, who never showed any personal prejudice, was sadly silent. True, she was English and knew little of the South; still, there were others in her orbit who proved far more sensitive to the plight of Black Americans. When McDaniel was forbidden to stay in the stars' Atlanta hotel, it was Gable, the redneck, the blue-collar hick, who threatened not to attend the premiere unless she came too. McDaniel persuaded him to go, while she stayed away.

Vivien was curiously ambivalent about *Wind*. She had longed for the role with such vehemence that it overshadowed everything in her life except Larry. But now that it was done, she showed little interest in the film. Perhaps the nightmare of production had soured her; perhaps she was unpersuaded about the quality of her acting; or perhaps she was afraid her star might outshine Larry's. Never as ambitious as he, she told Selznick's team that she wouldn't leave him again, no matter what the professional cost; years later, she advised the actress Jean Simmons, "If you're happy, don't give up anything because of your career." Whatever the cause, Vivien turned against the picture. "I knew it was a marvellous part," she said, "but I never cared for Scarlett. I couldn't find anything of myself in her."

That was an odd assertion for a woman who had identified with Scarlett so completely, let alone for an actress who had created one of the most compelling characters in twentieth-century cinema—and, paradoxically, one of its most modern: a heroine who evolves from weakness to strength, from dependence to independence, from selfishness to selflessness, from girlhood to womanhood. She's a forward-looking figure in a backward-looking film. If Rhett and Scarlett are right for each other, it's not simply because they're opposites (and the law of all drama is that opposites attract); it's because both are iconoclasts, challenging a system that seeks to confine them, hammering at the walls that hem them in, even if they never reach the point of consciously knocking them down.

David Thomson gives kudos to Fleming, the director Vivien despised, and indeed his scenes seem more authentic, more fully alive, than the early ones helmed by Cukor. "Victor Fleming came on the picture like Cagney sneering at rookie cops," writes the Selznick biographer. "So Leigh's Scarlett became embittered, tougher, bitchier, and more dangerous—all to the benefit of the performance."

Others credit her illness with adding a new dimension to her work. The mania she was beginning to experience, the incipient madness that her secretary so feared, was fanned by her exhaustion and peaked in tandem with her biggest scenes, introducing to some sequences "a note of near panic," as Walker puts it, "like someone teetering on the edge of imperious hysteria."

By the time of the premiere, gossip about Vivien's romance was trickling out of Hollywood and into the world at large. Selznick reacted with alarm when the *New York Daily News* ran a picture of her and Larry, prompting one of his employees to cable: "I HAVE CAUTIONED VIVIEN AND LAURENCE AGAINST LEAVING THEMSELVES OPEN TO THIS SORT OF THING, BUT YOU CAN BELIEVE ME THAT THEY NEED WATCHING EVERY MINUTE." He attached "CLIPPINGS WHICH MAKE MY HEART FAIL AND PROBABLY WILL YOURS TOO." This was an overreaction, given that fan publications such as *Silver Screen* had done little to cover up the truth. "There is no longer any secret of their interest in each other," the magazine noted in August 1939, while another wrote in April: "It's an accepted conclusion by those who know them that, when both are free, they will marry each other."

One New York journalist gloated about "breaking" the news of the couple's affair, apparently unaware that others had outscooped him. "It took the naïve question of an ingenuous young newspaper reporter at the Newark Airport to reveal the greatest love story to come out of Hollywood in a decade," wrote Cedric Chalmers in a syndicated article. The Olivier-Leigh romance, he said, was "a love story so sizzling that, for one of the few times in its history, it found Hollywood going full steam into reverse in frantic efforts to suppress the facts."

To Selznick's surprise, the gossip didn't tarnish Vivien's image and may even have helped. Rather than turn women against her (and women were *Wind*'s core audience), it drew them to her side. Maybe, deep in America, couples were unhappier than the producer had realized; maybe they were longing for second chances and wishing for their own illicit affairs. Knowing she was capable of a deep and searing love enhanced her performance for them and fed an audience starving for the same.

Times were changing. Divorce, which had once been unthinkable, an assault not just on society but on God, was starting to be a fact of life. Gable had divorced his first wife nine years earlier; while Bette Davis, who had so longed to play Scarlett, had just left her husband and would be married four times, none of her breakups bad enough to derail her career. Marriage and love were no longer seen as one and the same.

All this seeped into the coverage Vivien and Larry received. But no article shifted perception as much as a December 1939 profile in the fan magazine *Photoplay*, titled "A Love Worth Fighting For." Ruth Waterbury's eighteen-hundred-word encomium celebrated a couple that had captured the public's imagination.

Outlining a "tumultuous romance that laughs at careers, hurdles the conventions, loses its head along with its heart, and laughs for the exhilarating joy of such wildness," Waterbury asked her readers to sympathize with the lovers' plight. "They each have a child which perhaps they will never be permitted to see again. They may have to listen to some pretty severe things said about them, the English not being inclined to mince [their words about] such matters. Larry and Vivien care terribly about all that. There is a passion and a vitality that touches both of them, that makes them care terribly about all things. But they care more for each other. They care more for each other than they do for money or careers or friends or harsh words or even life itself."

Gauzy as the piece was, it ended on a note of caution. "As for what will happen to them after they wed," Waterbury concluded, "well, we were talking of romance—and matrimony is quite a different story."

CHAPTER 6

⸻

Two months after the *Gone with the Wind* premiere, on February 29, 1940, Larry and Vivien arrived at the Cocoanut Grove, the industry mecca where the twelfth Academy Awards were about to take place. They were anxious, like everyone else in this elegant mosh pit where friend battled friend and career wrestled with career, and where an actor's stock could sink or soar in the space of minutes. The Oscars weren't yet the blood sport they would become, but they were far from the all-smiling celebrations that outsiders believed.

The couple didn't travel together, of course; how could they, with Selznick at the helm? Instead, after meeting at his house, Vivien left on his arm, while Larry accompanied de Havilland—a nod to decorum, though of somewhat less importance than it might have been, now that the truth was leaking out. The actors were living together in Beverly Hills while pretending to reside apart, and the whole of Hollywood was in on their secret, even if the rest of the world was not.

For once, Selznick was too preoccupied to worry, so much so that he forgot his wife when he left home for the gala. Irene came running out, too slow to catch the car, though not the symbolism of what had taken place: David may have waxed eloquently about her importance to his movie, about how her judgment and insight had saved the day, but this was how he really felt. "I'd been forgotten," wrote Irene. "I was dumbfounded. Perhaps 'the real heroine' of *GWTW* had better go upstairs and go to bed." Instead, she found her way to the ceremony, where, she claimed, she sat at a different table from her husband's, the first public sign of a crack in the Selznicks' union, which would split wide open five years later when David left his wife for Jennifer Jones.

It was in this simmering state that Vivien and Larry arrived at the Grove—a nightclub in the storied Ambassador Hotel, where Robert F. Kennedy would be assassinated four decades later—and took their seats amid the faux Moroccan decor, the papier-mâché palm trees and dangling metal monkeys, their eyes glinting malevolently from the red bulbs in their sockets. Once at their table, the couple could relax, or come as close to relaxing as possible given the stress. Word had already filtered out about the winners after the *Los Angeles Times* had spilled the results earlier that day; but who knew if the *Times* was correct? Doubt piled upon doubt, worry on top of worry, creating a fetid atmosphere that corroded whatever pleasure Vivien and Larry might have had as they sat among the 270 industry nabobs who had come for the presentation, all fifteen minutes of it, once the ceremony got underway.

Olivier, a Best Actor contender for *Wuthering Heights*, fully expected James Stewart to win for Frank Capra's moralizing drama *Mr. Smith Goes to Washington*, the kind of message movie Hollywood most admired. Nor did the other nominees (including Gable for *Gone with the Wind* and Mickey Rooney for *Babes in Arms*) think much of their chances. Robert Donat (*Goodbye, Mr. Chips*) was so certain he'd lose that he didn't show up—which, of course, made him the fitting winner when Spencer Tracy announced the verdict and the film's producer accepted the award on his behalf.

As to Vivien, she was in a tight competition with Bette Davis, who was still smarting over her loss of Scarlett. Five years older than her rival, Davis was decades wiser in Hollywood's ways: she had fought hard for the role and even harder with her studio's tyrannical chief, Jack Warner—so hard, indeed, that she had finally fled to England in search of better parts, only to be dragged back against her will. Now was her night for revenge, or so she hoped. Bettors favored her for playing the terminally ill young socialite in *Dark Victory*, over nominees who also included Irene Dunne (*Love Affair*), Greta Garbo (*Ninotchka*), and Greer Garson (*Goodbye, Mr. Chips*). Then Tracy, who had remained onstage after Donat's award, announced the Best Actress winner, and it was Vivien.

Reaching the podium, dressed in a flowing chiffon robe decorated with a profusion of poppies, she spoke in her most dulcet tones, while neglecting to mention any of her costars, let alone her assorted directors, the various screenwriters, technicians, agents and a flotilla of support staff, none of whom then figured into Oscar-winners' speeches. "If I were to mention all those who have shown me such wonderful generosity through *Gone with the Wind*," she said, using the sort of florid language that bore Olivier's fingerprints, "I should have to entertain you with an oration as long as *Gone with the Wind* itself." Instead, she singled out one person alone, her producer, "that composite figure of energy, courage and very great kindness, in whom all points of *Gone with the Wind* meet, Mr. David Selznick."

Vivien then took her seat next to Selznick, who would collect the Oscar for "outstanding production," along with the treasured Irving G. Thalberg Memorial Award. De Havilland, who had reportedly fled in tears when she lost as supporting actress to McDaniel (the first Black woman to win an Oscar), returned from the kitchen where she had been crying and sat with the rest of them, trying to look composed, while McDaniel was consigned to a lesser table.

Commentators have cited a widely seen photograph of Olivier, his expression sour, as proof of his jealousy; but many photos taken that night also show him mugging for the camera and poking out his tongue as he sat with Vivien and her Oscar, half a century before it sold at Sotheby's for a then record $510,000. Still, he acknowledged later, "It was all I could do to restrain myself from hitting her with it. I was insane with jealousy."

This was the right time, Cukor advised the couple, to cash in. They were universally admired, even held on a pedestal, despite their illicit union. Around the country, hordes of people would surely flock to anything they did onstage. And so they made their biggest error to date with a nationwide tour.

Rather than choose something simple or even a manageable contemporary work, Larry selected the one play in which he had most conspicuously failed: *Romeo and Juliet*. The last time he had tackled Shakespeare's tragedy, in his joint production with Gielgud, he had been slammed for mangling its language, for essaying a Romeo who was all fire and no finesse. And yet he was determined to do it again. Call it foolish (as many did), the effort nonetheless revealed a side of Olivier that was only now beginning to flower: a willingness to try and try again, no matter how great the odds—not simply to sidestep his past mistakes but to confront them head-on. That intellectual and artistic courage became one of his defining traits, most apparent when he returned to the title roles in *Othello* and *Macbeth*, two notable flops at the Old Vic that he would make memorable hits.

As he began a new film of *Pride and Prejudice*, costarring his former lover, Greer Garson, he used every spare minute to study the text, reading and rereading the play during his breaks. He turned to his director, Cukor, for counsel, perhaps not the wisest move given that Cukor had shot a lumbering 1936 adaptation of *Romeo and Juliet* that Larry had turned down. At the same time, he immersed himself in every detail of lighting and staging, planning to direct this production as well as play the lead.

But when the show opened in April 1940 at San Francisco's cavernous Geary Theater, it was a flop. His Romeo was hardly any different from the Romeo he had played before—a "roaring boy," as cast member Jack Merivale described him (though at thirty-three years old, he was a little old to play a boy). Vivien's Juliet fared somewhat better, conceived with Larry's guidance as a young girl barely into her teens, but she lacked the vocal projection to reach the back of the theater.

On opening night, Larry was so exhausted that when he attempted to vault up a wall to Juliet's balcony, he fell short and was left clinging by his fingertips, provoking peals of laughter.

From San Francisco, the company traveled to Chicago and then to New York's Fifty-First Street Theatre, where any hope of success was killed by the sweltering heat. Audiences in the unair-conditioned auditorium dripped with sweat, just like the actors, and Olivier, wrapped in thick clothes and squeezed into a tight corset meant to contain an incipient paunch, was horrified when his putty nose began to melt. "The stage was like an oven," he wrote. "I was drenched." The production, wrote *Time* magazine, was "not merely weak or spotty, but calamitous. [The audience] saw a Juliet who looked like a poem, but had no sense of poetry, a Romeo who made a handsome lover, but talked as though he was brushing his teeth, conducted his courtship as though he was D'Artagnan. They saw fear and grief portrayed by belly-writhings and animal howls. They saw Olivier, in the first balcony scene, rush around like a dazed fireman trying to save a trapped maiden from the flames."

When a crowd gathered to demand its money back, Larry stormed outside, where he proceeded to distribute wads of cash, promising a refund for anyone who wanted it. Too many did and the show ground to a halt in June, a month after its Broadway premiere, costing the couple all their savings: $96,000. "For sheer, savage, merciless cruelty," he said later, exaggerating the disapprobation he felt on all sides, "I have never seen any judgments to approach those that faced me at breakfast in our New York hotel." He had lost everything: his money, his pride and his reputation. Even worse, he had lost his supremacy in Vivien's judgment, at least in his own mind.

Always more sensitive to slights than Vivien (she had a gift for turning enemies into friends and making her harshest critics her allies), he began to perceive adversaries all around, nitpickers finding fault with everything he did. This was more paranoia than reality, but it was also deflection, designed to disguise the truth he couldn't bear: that he had let Vivien down.

Vivien herself was sick with disappointment and begged her castmate, Merivale, to come over and restore her and Larry's spirits. He found them "drowning themselves in lethally strong Martinis" and in a foul mood, writes one of Olivier's biographers, Anthony Holden. When Merivale beat Vivien at checkers, "she threw a tantrum and accused him of cheating, screaming for Olivier to come and intervene." Her words were revealing: "Don't you try to come between us," she yelled. "We've been together for years. Nobody's coming between us. Don't you try!"

The day after *Romeo* opened in New York, on May 10, 1940, an ascendant Germany attacked Belgium, France and the Netherlands in a massive land and air assault that overwhelmed its flabbergasted enemies. As Allied forces tried to repel the invasion, 136 divisions stormed their frontiers, backed by twenty-five hundred planes and sixteen thousand airborne troops, dropping in swarms from the fighter-thickened skies. German tanks quickly penetrated the French defense and continued to the Atlantic coast, where within a month the "Boche" had trapped three hundred thousand French and British soldiers on the beaches of Dunkirk.

It was against this backdrop, as the Nazi threat drew ever closer to their homeland, with no guarantee the country would survive, that Vivien and Larry decided to get married.

Holman and Esmond had finally conceded and the divorce papers had come through, freeing their former partners. And so, back in Los Angeles after their tour, late on August 31, 1940, they set out for Santa Barbara, joined by their friends Katharine Hepburn and Garson Kanin, the writer of *Born Yesterday*. They could not have picked a more idyllic venue—one of the prettiest parts of the state, overlooking the untarnished Pacific coastline, among gentle bluffs covered with ancient pines, where the sound of waves was broken only by the cries of gulls. But the wedding was a shambles, if one is to believe Kanin, who described it gleefully, though quite waspishly, in his 1971 book *Tracy and Hepburn: An Intimate Memoir*.

According to Kanin, he had just left the Beverly Hills house he was nominally sharing with Olivier to visit Hepburn, hoping she would agree to star in a new movie about the wife of Ulysses S. Grant (in which Grant would never appear), when Larry called him in a panic. He was getting married that night, he revealed, and wanted Kanin to be his best man. Enlisting Hepburn as the maid of honor, the group set off on the long and winding ninety-mile road to Santa Barbara, with Larry at the wheel and Vivien at his side. The lovebirds quarreled incessantly. "It was absolutely hilarious," writes Kanin. "She was sharp-tongued, Larry was tough as hell. They were scrapping all the way to the banns."

Hepburn recalled things rather differently. "At that time, I really didn't know Vivien or Larry well," she said. "Vivien led the social whirl kind of life that was anathema to me. But Gar Kanin and I sat in the back seat of Larry's Packard and Larry drove and, of course, Vivien sat close to him in the front seat. I remember feeling the conversation she and Larry were having as we drove along was, well, rather racy. But this was probably the prudish reaction of a girl like myself who had been sheltered from the great world."

The prude, the filmmaker and the lovers arrived that evening at the San Ysidro Ranch, a hotel partly owned by Ronald Colman, who was waiting with his wife, Benita, and a justice of the peace. The justice had been cooling his heels for an hour and a half, recalled Kanin, and had to be plied with drink just to stay and wait; by the time the couple arrived, he was so drunk that he kept calling Larry "Oliver" and Vivien "Lay." "Larry was asked if he took this woman to be his lawful-wedded wife," writes Kanin, "but [the official] forgot to ask Vivien for her vow, and me for the ring, although I kept waving it under his nose." (With mischievous humor, Larry had gotten the ring inscribed, "The last one you'll get, I hope." Vivien had chosen something more earnest: "La fidélité ma guide"—faithfulness is my guide—a less-than-subtle hint.) "Finally," continues Kanin, "there was a long pause and a silence, broken only by a few chirping crickets and my continuing sneezes [from allergies]. The justice of the peace, weaving slightly, looked up and shouted, 'Bingo!'" That account puzzled Hepburn, who later had "no recollection of anyone calling out 'Bingo!' It would seem to me a very odd thing to do."

Afterward, the married couple drove back to Los Angeles and on to the port of San Pedro, where they took Colman's yacht to Catalina and stayed glued to the radio, waiting for word to leak about their "secret" wedding, only to be sorely disappointed when it didn't. At ten o'clock the news broke.

"Too bad it got out," said a joyful Olivier.

"Yes," sighed a happy Vivien.

As England entered its gravest crisis, Vivien and Larry knew they had to do more, but what? Attacks on them were growing daily; no longer mere actors but megastars whose every utterance was dissected by a hungry public, both were prime targets for criticism and yet were shocked by its intensity. Sir Seymour Hicks, an actor-manager who was in charge of the British arts organization ENSA (the Entertainments National Service Association), said he would start a "roll of dishonor" and ban such exiles from ever setting foot in their native land. And Michael Balcon, Vivien's former employer as producer of *A Yank at Oxford*, condemned the pair as "deserters" and "isolationists" who were "being allowed to accumulate fortunes without sharing in any way the hardships their fellow Britons gladly endure for our cause."

Korda came to the rescue. The producer had been a voice in the wilderness, warning everyone he knew (and he knew everyone) about the Nazis. Now he proposed a new film, designed to boost British morale.

"Larry, you know Lady Hamilton?" he asked.

"Not intimately," replied Olivier. "Wasn't she Admiral Nelson's piece?"

This was the beginning of *Lady Hamilton* (*That Hamilton Woman* in the US), the third and last of the couple's joint movies. Its subject was the much-maligned Emma Hamilton, allegedly a former prostitute (or at least a rich man's mistress) before she married Sir William Hamilton, the British envoy to Naples, when she was only twenty-six and he was sixty. Witty, artistic and beautiful, she was known for her charm and humor, all of which appealed to Britain's preeminent naval hero, Horatio Nelson, when they met in 1793, two years into Emma's marriage. Their affair-proper began five years later, after Nelson's return from his victory in the Battle of the Nile, minus an arm and many teeth. Hiring Emma as his private secretary, he moved in with her and Sir William, who not only tolerated their affair but also the child Emma bore her lover. Hamilton was heartbroken when Nelson died in 1805 at the Battle of Trafalgar, cementing his place in history, as well as her own. She described with indelible pain how an officer came to her home and told her of the admiral's death.

"Captain Whitby was unable to speak—tears in his eyes and a deathly paleness over his face made me comprehend him," she wrote. "I believe I gave a scream and fell back, and for ten hours I could neither speak nor shed a tear."

This was the story Korda wanted to tell, not merely because of its romantic appeal but because of its obvious call to duty. Just as England had stood firm against Napoleon, so it must stand against Hitler, a message the film successfully conveyed in ways more sensational than subtle. "Look out, Bonaparte," Nelson shouts at one point, "by gad we shall lick you now!"

This fictionalized Nelson paid lip service to historical fact, with his perfect teeth and arm amputated on the wrong side. He was nothing like "the neurotic I discovered in my researches," Olivier observed later. As to Vivien, she was gorgeous and grace-ful, though Korda found she lacked an essential ingredient of her real-life counterpart.

"My dear Vivien," he chided, "Emma was vulgar."

"My dear Alex," she shot back, "you wouldn't have given me a contract if I had been vulgar!"

Neither she nor Larry had any great hopes for the picture. "I am extremely dubious about it," Vivien confided to Holman, their relations growing ever friendlier with distance and time. "But now one does not plan a career much as it seems futile & we are certainly only doing this for financial purposes which are useful in these days. Hollywood is more odious each time and I loathe it heartily & wish I could come home."

Shooting began in October 1940 without a finished script, breaking one of the industry's cardinal rules. Screenwriters Wal-ter Reisch and R. C. Sherriff (the author of *Journey's End*, one of Larry's first and most notable stage hits) raced to keep up with Korda's brother, the set designer Vincent, who prepared a fleet of miniature ships for the Battle of Trafalgar, manned by technicians hiding under the boats. Vivien spent her spare time knitting for the British soldiers, accompanied by a new pet, a sheepdog named Jupiter, while Larry did everything to make her laugh, especially when shooting—though her on-screen composure never cracked. During their scenes, "he started popping into weird makeups and costumes—artfully timing his entrance so that she couldn't see him until the scene had begun," reported *Hollywood* magazine. "But nary a twinkle from Vivien, once she had started her scene. Afterwards, of course, she would go into gales of laughter."

"We made *Lady Hamilton* in six weeks," she recalled. "It proved that if need be, Alex could work in a hurry—though he hated it—and still turn out a fine job. Yet there was some skimping and ingenious saving on the production. When, as the ageing Emma, I had to wear a rubber mask, we could only afford to cover the upper half of my face so that I was always photographed at a certain angle." Olivier used extensive makeup too. "Nelson had the most extraordinary girlish mouth," he noted, "so I wore rose lips because I was now becoming relatively at ease in the medium, didn't have a star's face that couldn't be changed from one film to the next, and wanted to practice my craft of acting."

He took the whole thing with a pinch of salt, joshing with Michael Powell when the *Red Shoes* director visited the set. "Saturday I did my big scene with Viv: 'Goodbye, my darling. I go to win Trafalgar and come back to you on my shield,'" he told his friend. "I was terrible. I dried up twice and had to fling myself about to cover up, got my scabbard caught in my cloak." When Korda tried to hurry him, "I went off the deep end. I really exploded."

The filmmaker's haste almost wrecked his movie, as he had neglected to run the script past Hollywood's censors. "You cannot possibly make this picture," the head censor, Joseph Breen, told him when he finally read the screenplay well into the shoot. "Here is a man living in sin with another man's wife. His own wife is still alive, and her husband is alive, and she has a baby by him, yet neither of them shows the slightest remorse or even consciousness of wrongdoing. Impossible!" Worse, he said, "in your script you condone the offence. You glorify it, make it exciting and romantic. And you let them get away with it." Breen had the power to kill the film's release, and for a while it seemed doomed, until Sherriff came to the rescue, adding a simple scene in which Nelson's father, a country vicar like Larry's, reprimands his son for doing "an evil thing that all right-minded people will condemn."

Hamilton earned a gigantic $1 million when it opened the following year, at a time when isolationists were warning America against any involvement in a European war—a time when eight hundred thousand citizens had joined the America First Committee, urged by aviator Charles Lindbergh to favor "peace and preparedness" rather than fight. The movie justified the British government's rationale for keeping the Oliviers and others like them in Los Angeles, where they were free to make such propaganda, which could influence the still-neutral United States. Of equal importance to Vivien and Larry, it helped cement their legend: they were doomed lovers, like Emma and Horatio, as heroic as both and as important to their nation's fate.

Critics largely embraced the movie. The *New York Times*' Bosley Crowther singled out "the admirable fidelity of the scriptwriters, Walter Reisch and R.C. Sherriff, to the basic facts of [Nelson's and Hamilton's] troubled lives"—clearly unaware of the film's manifold inaccuracies. "In real life," notes one modern commentator, "Nelson didn't wear an eyepatch. He may have worn a less glamorous eye shade on his hat when it was sunny on deck. In fact, this film is largely responsible for spreading the myth that he wore a pirate-style patch. [And in] the film, Nelson has to wait for Sir William to die before he can shack up with the lady. Worst of all, Emma's performance career [she was an actress at one time] is almost entirely ripped out and replaced with dreary domesticity. Not only is watching Vivien Leigh play goody-goody wifelet a lot less fun than watching her play crazy freewheeling nympho, it's also wrong."

None of this bothered the picture's fans, least of all the most eminent, Winston Churchill. While there's no evidence that he gave Korda the idea for the movie, as some have suggested, he would screen it again and again for his guests, and rewarded Korda with a knighthood. The prime minister idolized Vivien and sent her and Larry a signed copy of his book, *The Second World War, Vol. 4, The Hinge of Fate*. More touchingly still, he gave Vivien a rare gift: one of his paintings, *Study of Roses*, which she kept in her bedroom from then on.

With *Hamilton* completed and no other immediate commitments, the Oliviers had no reason to remain in America. They were mortified to be sitting in the sun, living a life of comfort when their friends and families were suffering. Larry had begun to pave the way for his return by taking private flying lessons, while Vivien had raised funds for the Red Cross, though American neutrality made it illegal for her to solicit money for much-needed armaments.

At the end of December 1940, the pair set out for London, first flying to New York and then sailing to Lisbon, since they were unable to fly back directly. There were only twenty-three passengers on the ship, which usually carried four hundred, and all were risking their lives. A year and a half earlier, they could have made the voyage without danger; but now it was perilous. Selznick for one thought the Oliviers were insane. "It sounds like a suicide pact to me," he confided.

Even on a neutral vessel, the potential for death was all around: German U-boats filled the seas, and the travelers were petrified of being torpedoed, their fear fanned by a shipmate who three months earlier had watched a U-boat sink the SS *City of Benares*, killing 87 children and 175 adults. "Hitler's secret weapon was already gaining a reputation," wrote Olivier, "and sailings were not the gay sprees that they had been. If every ship was jam-packed from bilges to crow's nest sailing from Europe to America, it certainly was not the case in the other direction."

He was shaken to discover that the ship's captain and many of his crew were German, and on New Year's Eve, after four days at sea, the sailors broke into a resounding chorus of "Deutschland über Alles," followed by a toast to Hitler. Vivien understood enough to be terrified of an imminent abduction. "Overdramatic as it may well seem now," Olivier continued, "this constant nightmare was a very real one to us. Sometime during the day or night, went our nightmare, we would be aware of an ominous scraping sound against the side of the ship, followed by a sharp rap on our cabin door, through which we would be unceremoniously pulled onto the outside deck, thrust down a rope ladder, to disappear as prisoners of war into the waiting U-boat."

The couple docked in Lisbon, where they waited in limbo for three days, unable to secure tickets back home and convinced they were being watched at all times, which may well have been the case, given that this was one of the major spy centers of Europe. Then, on the plane carrying them from Lisbon to Bristol, their cockpit burst into flames, eerily echoing a dream Larry had had in America, when he fell "from an aeroplane in the dark between England + France." In real life, "about halfway home a fat little uniformed man came bustling out of the pilot's compartment, leaving the door open in his hurry, rewarding us with the sight of the cockpit on fire."

He and Vivien finally landed in England unharmed and spent the night in Bristol, shivering and shaking in an ice-cold hotel, one side of which had been blown away by a bomb. The next day, home at last, they collapsed into bed, overjoyed that their beloved Durham Cottage had survived the Blitz with nothing worse than a cracked wall.

CHAPTER 7

━━━◆━━━

London was under siege. Streets that had glowed bright with phosphorescent lights were now pitch-black at night; squares that had bustled with life and love were deserted as soon as the sun went down. A stench filled the air from the barrels of tar that burned steadily, creating a smoke screen for incoming enemy bombers—those that weren't deterred by the "barrage" balloons, zeppelin-like monsters that pockmarked the sky, fourteen hundred of them in London alone, each tethered to the ground by chains of steel.

This was the reality Larry and Vivien encountered and it was almost unrecognizable from the reality they had left behind. After living in luxury, after spending weeks amid the neon of Broadway and then months in the California sun, they now struggled to survive. Their home was damaged, but habitable—functional, but hardly ideal—while the house Vivien had shared with Holman on Little Stanhope Street had been wiped out, leaving "just a hole in the ground," as her friend Oswald Frewen noted, "with a bonfire burning gaily behind it."

"It is most strange to find oneself in the middle of an entirely different life, without having seen the change come about," Vivien wrote Selznick.

Like Scarlett, at twenty-seven years old she had suddenly and unimaginably found herself stripped of her past, or at least the recent past of privilege and pampering and wealth; she had been plopped out of one world and into another, far graver than she had conceived. War was the great leveler, and this war more than any in living memory. Food was rationed—at first butter, bacon, sugar and ham, and then meat, milk and eggs. Clothes would soon be doled out by the item; even King George VI had to use vouchers, just like his desperate subjects. "The only topic of conversation for us girls today is the clothes ration," Vivien wrote Daniel O'Shea, one of Selznick's aides. "A fine thing, isn't it?—I'll have to inveigle Larry into giving me all his coupons—What'll we all do about the glamour now?"

Despite her bravado, she was surrounded by death. Friends died and were dying, and so were friends of friends, and relatives and acquaintances; nobody could escape the pain. Four hundred and fifty-five thousand British soldiers and civilians would perish over the six years of war, or one out of every hundred citizens. Already the losses were mounting: Vivien's former brother-in-law, Alwyn, had lost his life in an air raid, along with his eighteen-year-old daughter; that was Holman's second sibling to die, following another in the Great War, and Vivien was heartbroken. She had learned the news, to her shock, on the set of *Lady Hamilton*, where a reporter watched her tear open an envelope before she "rushed to her dressing-room...in tears."

"I don't suppose living on the verge of such things makes it any less shocking when they occur," she told Holman.

Everywhere came news of the distressed. Two million Englishmen between the ages of nineteen and twenty-seven had been called to service as the country attempted to transform its underequipped armed forces into a weapon of war, guided by a prime minister whose bold rhetoric barely disguised the thin line that separated England from defeat. With neither the requisite men nor matériel, he had to depend on his friendship with Franklin D. Roosevelt, who only just managed to finagle the ships, planes and tanks without which England would almost certainly have lost the fight against the Nazis.

The Oliviers had missed the first air raids in September 1940, when the sirens wailed, their pitch rising and falling and then rising again as the Luftwaffe sent 350 bombers toward London, dropping three hundred tonnes of bombs and killing two thousand people in one night alone, each bomb emitting a horrifying screech as it fell, growing louder and louder as it came closer, only for silence to kick in seconds before it exploded. That was accompanied by similar attacks on such cities as Liverpool, Birmingham and Coventry, ones Larry knew well from his early touring. But it was the capital he loved best, and by the end of the Blitz, a third of it had been destroyed.

On occasion, the Oliviers joined their fellow Londoners in the warren of subway tunnels that extended fifteen miles beneath the ground, now used as provisional bomb shelters. "Families from the East End with scraps of bedding jostled West End folk with luncheon baskets and expensive travelling rugs in underground stations in the Metropolitan area last night," noted one reporter, describing "bearded Bohemians, dignified dowagers, typical Cockneys [and] a young woman in black," all crowded into a London "tube" station. Thousands of men, women and children, their residences crumbling, their incomes collapsing, found a haven here—some permanently, as the number of homeless living underground swelled to almost two hundred thousand, spread across seventy-nine stations, by the end of the first year of war. Once, Larry had believed he could distance himself from ordinary suffering; but now it was everywhere, above land and below.

"We had our first really bad raid the other night," wrote Vivien to a Selznick aide, putting on a cheerful front, "and it's no use saying, it isn't a lot of fun and games. When one wakes up in the morning now, with the blossom trees coming out, and the carpets of blue crocuses in the parks, you simply cannot realise the night before wasn't just a nightmare." She volunteered to be a nurse but was unable to secure a position, perhaps because she inexplicably asked for a posting in Egypt; while Larry joined the propaganda effort with a small role in Michael Powell's *49th Parallel*, playing a Canadian trapper murdered by Nazi invaders.

The Oliviers had only themselves to rely on and only themselves to worry about. Gertrude had left for Vancouver with seven-year-old Suzanne, knowing the girl would be safer with Ernest's sister (though she would later be forced to leave her convent school when the nuns learned her mother, Vivien Leigh, was an adulteress). She was going into exile at almost the same age Vivien had been exiled from Calcutta, with this difference: her grandmother was at her side.

If Gertrude had erred twenty years earlier, she would never do so again—though her move was not entirely selfless. She had recently lost Tommy Thomson, the friend of Ernest's who had followed the couple from India to England. He had died in 1938, bequeathing "Mrs. Hartley" his stocks and shares. For the next five years, Gertrude and Ernest would live apart, before reuniting. As for Ernest, he remained in England, volunteering as a grenade expert in the Home Guard. It was his second world war—he had served as a cavalry officer in the first, carting his family from one Indian posting to another, losing two stillborn babies along the way, siblings Vivien would never know.

By early 1941, a miasma had settled over the British Isles. There were no longer the haves and have-nots; nobody had anything. Many of Larry's closest friends had enlisted: Noël Coward to run the British propaganda office in Paris, where he remained until the city collapsed; and Ralph Richardson to become an officer in the Fleet Air Arm, a division of the Royal Navy. Larry was eager to join him and soon got his chance.

"I heard from the Admiralty...that I was to be given a commission," he noted later, neglecting to mention that he had at first been rejected after failing a medical. Larry "did not quite pass the medical exam because of a tiny trouble with his ear (ever since our lovely Atlantic trip)," Vivien wrote Selznick. But "in everything else he flabergasted [sic] the doctors, and they thought he was the healthiest chap they'd ever seen. He broke all records for blowing out a lot of breath for a very long time."

In April 1941, Acting Sub-Lieutenant (A) Olivier RN reported to his base in Lee-on-Solent, sixty miles from London, a much better location than the one he had feared: Trinidad, more than four thousand miles from England and Vivien. He found a bare-bones airfield that, as he remembered, "consisted of a large hill, sloping away downwards so that much of one side of the field could not be seen from the other, and consequently only a skillful pilot could make a decent three-point landing by putting the machine into a double stall at the last moment before the actual touchdown." He added, "I think I may describe myself as a decent pilot."

He was, in fact, a pilot "of notorious incompetence," says Michael Korda. As Bushell noted: "Having gained [his pilot's wings] to his vast credit, he was rapidly disgraced for twice crashing a plane on landing it + was demoted to the v. boring duty of towing a target for learner-gunners to shoot at. Boring + dangerous—for the learners were often dozy Poles or drunk Frogs who shot at the plane + not the target."

Larry wasn't averse to a bit of tomfoolery himself. On one occasion, he decided to "shoot up a friend," flying dangerously close to the coastal home of actress Jeanne de Casalis. As he swooped down, de Casalis came running out, waving frantically; then a British Spitfire appeared out of the blue, waggling its wings—as if to say hello, Larry thought. He didn't realize the pilot was desperately signaling for him to return to base, given that a German attack was said to be imminent. He made it back just in time.

Vivien joined Larry, moving into a cottage a few miles from his headquarters, where they would spend much of the war. It was an extraordinary interlude, with none of the frenzied activity that had marked their Hollywood existence or the frenetic period when they began their affair. Here, for the first time since becoming famous, they experienced the ebb and flow of ordinary life, the life every other Englishman was enduring, with nothing to do outside work but read, garden and tool around in an old Invicta that Larry had bought from Richardson. "It was an amazingly different home from the one [they] had known in California," the magazine *Screenland* reported. "There was just one living-room, with old-fashioned heavy oak furniture and an open fireplace which Vivien had to feed with logs she bought from a local farmer. She sewed and hung some pretty blue chintz curtains. She pinned up photographs of Hollywood friends on the plain white-washed walls. She cooked and she laundered and she tended the vegetables and the fruit-trees in the garden herself because the war had made it impossible to hire any help in the district."

Writing to Douglas Fairbanks Jr. (in a letter designed for public consumption), Larry described his new life, poking gentle fun at the omnipresent use of naval terminology even on land: "One gets 'shore leave' to go down the street to the post office," he noted. " 'Signals' instead of letters—and a little party of men waiting just inside the gate with their bicycles held stiffly behind them, is called a 'liberty boat.' [But] it's a good job and feels useful. I'm a pilot in an Air Gunmen Training Squardron [sic] and it's very good experience. I gto [sic] my wings quite soon, which was a blessing and I hope to be promoted in a week or two...."

Viv, praise God, is with me and we live by the sea quite a few miles from work, to which I dash at a most ungodly hour (worse than pictures!) on a motor-bike! It's all so different as you may imagine! I worry very much for Viv the nights when I have to be away tho' God knows we've been lucky lately (famous last words!) and she's a model of tact with the officers' wives!"

Larry "couldn't ever remember such contentment," he said. Vivien would wave goodbye each morning as he took off on his motorbike and then tinker around in the house and garden, filling the place with elegant furniture and paintings she had brought from London. Once or twice a month, they would visit the city, discovering anew the pleasures they had taken for granted. "It sounds an odd thing to say," reflected Larry, "but life really feels more *peaceful* than it ever did before!" Still, he admitted: "*Anything that might bring about a separation is our constant dread.*"

"Anything" included Selznick. Always obstreperous, he had become altogether impossible since his unprecedented success with two back-to-back Oscar winners, *Gone with the Wind* and *Rebecca*. Another man might have rested on his laurels, but he was incapable of it; his dual victories, if anything, seemed to ratchet up his drive and deepen his neuroses, pushing him to accomplish more and adding a new and nagging fear: that he might never do so. He had been taking drugs for some time and now was medicating himself to get to sleep, and then further medicating himself to stay awake. At the same time, he gambled untold sums, as if testing his good fortune: he lost almost as much at the poker table—more than $1 million in the years 1945 to 1947—as he made from selling *Wind*, which his partner, Whitney, bought in 1942 for just over $700,000.

Irene struggled to bring him down to earth, but her husband was getting worse. Once, he had contented himself with flings, like his fellow moguls in this empire of machismo; but now he desired far more—to be like the characters in his movies, experiencing life on a thrilling plane that he could no longer just enjoy vicariously. A humdrum relationship wasn't enough; he craved romance with the sort of feminine ideal that he alone could create. A Pygmalion of the silver screen, he now embarked on a full-fledged affair with his discovery, Jennifer Jones, whom he molded to meet his dreams, just as he tried to mold every other actress he kept under contract, including Vivien.

Safe in his Palladian mansion, far removed from the horrors of Europe, Selznick was oblivious to her struggles. He understood everything about war as he had discovered it in books, knew better than anyone how to capture it on film; but the misery of war, the daily toll, the sparring to survive, the endless deprivations and depredations—all this was foreign to him. So was Vivien's quandary: even if she had wished to return to Hollywood, an overseas voyage would have been out of the question. Everywhere, there was threat, from the strafing of overhead planes to the surveillance of U-boats that glided *Nautilus*-like under the Atlantic. When Selznick demanded she fulfill her contract, she tried to explain. "CLIPPER IMPOSSIBLE VOYAGE ALARMING PERSONAL FEELINGS FRANTIC," she cabled.

Back and forth they went without resolution. "This is a very difficult letter to write as I am afraid it will annoy you," Vivien told Selznick in February 1941. "David I cannot collect myself sufficiently to feel I can come back, the idea just seems impossible, and I can't somehow make it punctuate [puncture] my mind. As I said in my wire the journey is frankly frightening alone, and *then* leaving Larry!—One does really rather feel here that we are living on the edge of a cataclysm, and that every moment is precious."

Selznick persisted. He was genetically programmed to oppress, just as Vivien was genetically programmed to wriggle free, and so he kept tossing projects her way, insisting she choose among them: a Yugoslavian war drama; an adaptation of W. Somerset Maugham's *The Letter* (later to be filmed with Bette Davis); the melodrama *Portrait of Jennie* (eventually to star Jennifer Jones). Vivien refused them all and instead pressed for a vehicle she could shoot in England, though that was almost as difficult as crossing the Atlantic, given the dire shortage of materials.

In March 1941, she responded to Selznick's latest request: that she and Larry top-line an adaptation of *Jane Eyre*, in which David planned to cast Suzanne as the young Jane. Her letter was a masterpiece of evasion. First, she appeared to embrace the idea: "I think it would be a lovely picture and was at one time going to do the play, so have been interested in it for some time," she wrote. Then she introduced a note of doubt: "Do you think there is any danger of it being too similar to *Rebecca*? *Rebecca* always seemed to me to be a rather frank crib of *Jane Eyre*—but it is a beautiful story." Finally, she demolished the notion, observing that Larry "would not want to play it in any case even if it were remotely possible that he could, which it isn't. So that seems to settle that."

Still, Vivien was restless. Without work, she fretted, and her fretting weighed heavily on Larry. She was idle, and idleness was never a good recipe for someone with her agile and agitated mind. Worried that boredom would lead to depression, a pattern Olivier was beginning to recognize, he tried to find her a job in the theater. She would have been content to join a repertory company, subsuming her stardom to the group's greater good; but when Larry approached Tyrone Guthrie and asked if Vivien could join his newly reconstituted Old Vic Company, the director bluntly told him she wasn't a good enough actress.

Larry was concerned to see his sparkling wife sink into gloom and knew she must work again soon, even at the cost of his domestic joy. Aware that his friend Katharine Cornell had had a

Broadway smash with a revival of Bernard Shaw's 1906 comedy
The Doctor's Dilemma, he pitched the idea of a London production to the producer Binkie Beaumont, who agreed to back it,
with Vivien assuming Cornell's role as the wife of a scoundrel
artist in a play about medical ethics.

Legally, she was wading into troubled waters. Her Hollywood contract forbade her to do anything without Selznick's permission, and the play was no short-term venture but a yearlong
endeavor that would include a six-month tour of the provinces,
followed by another six months in the West End. Ignoring the
risks, in September 1941, Vivien left Larry to go on tour, stopping off for weeks at a time in war-ravaged cities like Manchester
and Liverpool during "one of the coldest winters on record," as
Alexander Walker notes. "Vivien spent hours making long journeys in unheated trains, packed with troops on leave or returning
to camp, hardly able to read the works of Dickens by the dim
lightbulbs conforming to wartime blackout orders. She lugged
the books everywhere, as well as a copy of the greatest Victorian
writer's letters which [humorist] Alexander Woollcott had sent
her as a wedding present."

Vivien's travels came as a sharp shock for the once-cosseted
star. "The war meant interminable train journeys, late to start,
late to arrive and endless unexplained stoppages in draughty
underheated carriages," writes Richard Huggett in his biography
of Beaumont. "It meant chilly hotel bedrooms without service
or hot water, it meant restaurants closing early with no meals
available after the theatre, it meant discomfort, little sleep, living
out of suitcases and a slowly accumulating exhaustion; it meant
that every night it was a little bit more difficult to give a good
performance." Vivien nonetheless kept working, trekking home
each weekend to see Larry, no matter how exhausted she was.
On Saturday nights, he would meet her at the local train station, and for a few brief hours they would be together, before

being wrenched apart. Each separation was agony, each reunion all the more pressured because of the clock that started ticking the moment they embraced. Distance fueled desire but also magnified tensions, adding a new element of stress to the heightened state everyone was experiencing as a function of war.

Once, two cadets recognized Vivien in her train compartment. "One of them asked me, 'Is that Vivien Leigh?' " recalled the actor Cyril Cusack, who was in the play. "And I said 'No.' 'Just as well,' he said truculently, 'that husband of hers, Larry Olivier, is our training officer and he couldn't fly his way out of a fucking paper bag.' " Luckily, Vivien was dozing and didn't hear a word.

Cusack himself caused trouble when he got into a brawl after *Dilemma*'s London opening in March 1942. "It was believed that he had taken his understudy, Geoffrey Edwards, on a pub crawl to celebrate St Patrick's Day," writes Huggett, "that they had both become hopelessly drunk, that he had forced his way on to the stage, insulted and even assaulted Vivien Leigh, that he had vomited on the carpet, scandalised the audience, reduced the play to a shambles, had been forcibly carried off to his dressing-room, had been instantly sacked and compelled to leave the theatre."

Vivien forgave him and, two weeks later, invited him to the best restaurant in town. "She was charming, witty, and she sparkled as only she could when she was in a happy, relaxed mood," continues Huggett. "The events of St Patrick's Day were never mentioned. She took him to the station in a taxi, saw him off, kissed him and wished him good luck. They never met again."

This was Vivien at her best, a woman who seemed more mature, more considerate and more thoughtful than she ever had in her early days of stardom, let alone during the *GWTW* shoot. War softened her and a different Vivien emerged from the crucible of conflict. If Hollywood had remade her as an actress, war remade her as a human being.

So did personal tragedy, which she experienced for the first time when she lost a baby in the early stages of pregnancy. Information about her miscarriage is elusive, complicated by the fact that neither Vivien nor Larry mentioned it in public; nor have any of their biographers written about it. And yet one can glean what took place from two contemporary references that confirm her pregnancy, though each places it at a different time.

In January 1942, *Photoplay* reported that a movie had to be rescheduled. "The production proposal most eagerly awaited by fans, 'This Above All,' co-starring Vivien Leigh and her husband Laurence Olivier, had to be abandoned as an English project and transferred to Hollywood where Tyrone Power and Joan Fontaine will do the starring roles," noted the magazine. "This was not because of wartime emergencies but because of Vivien's impending motherhood. By the time leave could be arranged for Olivier, it was too near January, when Vivien expects her baby." Later, the journalist Alan Dent implied the baby was expected not in January but the fall: describing Vivien's appearance in September 1942, he explained that she was "fragile because she had had one of her miscarriages not many days before and was wearing an invalid's long shawl of the purest and whitest and softest wool."

Pregnancy, the miscarriage and the endless, grueling travel contributed to make 1942 even more daunting than it would otherwise have been, and the success of *Doctor's Dilemma* didn't proceed without a hitch. Costars came and went (Cusack was replaced by Peter Glenville, who in turn was replaced by Gielgud), and the demands of the show, along with Vivien's profound need to satisfy her entertainment-starved audience, began to wear her down. In this harshest of winters, where the sunshine never broke through the gray, cloudy skies and where the drizzle and the damp penetrated even the hardiest of bones, a cold turned into a constant cough. Soon, Vivien's cough became a rasp, exacerbated by her heavy smoking. Months into the London run, much to Larry's concern, Vivien was on the edge of collapse—a risky state for anybody, let alone someone with her underlying mental condition. She looked "older & more tired," noted the designer Cecil Beaton, though she was still "completely unspoilt [and] almost incredibly lovely."

At age twenty-eight, she had a new sense of life's evanescence. When the young Richard Attenborough auditioned to be an understudy, she advised him to look for a better role, telling him, "Time is very precious to us all."

Time, for Larry, dragged on. His latest assignment, managing a parachute-packing unit, was infinitely less glamorous than the military career he had envisioned, largely modeled on his heroic *Beau Geste*, a 1929 flop about a young man who joins the Foreign Legion rather than face dishonor.

Instead of sacrificing his all for king and country, Larry was giving it up for a dark and dusty warehouse, persecuted by a conscript who at one point shared his room and "could hardly believe he was sleeping next to the man he knew on the silver screen as Heathcliff in *Wuthering Heights* and Maxim de Winter in *Rebecca*," as Olivier later told the actor Robert Stephens. At first, the fellow was delighted to invite him home; but once he was promoted, he "started treating him abominably, sneering at his acting and narking him at every opportunity. Larry was determined to get his own back. Iago-like, he thought of the bloke's wife who had been so impressed at meeting him. He got himself invited over to the house again and took the wife out for an extremely long walk...popping into pubs and into every shop, buying stationery, cigarettes and flowers. When he returned, laden with these purchases, he kissed her hand in front of her husband—she had, of course, been utterly bedazzled by his charm—and did everything to imply to his host and superior officer that he and the lady had been out in the fields having a splendid fuck." The rival never bothered him again.

Larry was flying less and less—and, even then, only the sort of battered old planes that were the Edsels of aeronautics. He may have impressed Richardson ("His manner was naval, it was quiet, alert, businesslike, with the air of there being a joke somewhere around"), but his friend was in a distinct minority, as the mocking cadets on Vivien's train made clear. After parachute-packing, Larry was relegated to an even humbler task: doing demonstrations for the locals, sad little attempts to fan enthusiasm among teenagers who might wish to sign up, the few who still harbored the same illusions as him. His pride suffered its greatest blow when a local woman decided he was just the man to help with her newest mission: driving around, using a loudspeaker to urge villagers to contribute to the wartime cause.

Lonely and bored, Larry found solace in his rare getaways, often accompanied by Richardson and equally often by alcohol. When the friends heard that a fellow actor, Frank Duncan, was appearing at a nearby theater, they showed up drunk and attempted to climb onstage, only to be repelled by a vigilant stagehand.

Olivier may have loathed his military experiences, but he, too, was maturing, which became clear when he met up with Leigh Holman for the first time since he and Vivien had fled. Holman had at last begun to date other women (though none ever led to a second marriage), but he was dealing with terminal boredom as a lieutenant in the coastal town of Ramsgate, where he was nominally involved in top secret work, though in reality all he did was interrogate the passengers on visiting ships. Larry was surprised how much he liked his former friend. "I found him quite changed—greatly grown in stature & personality," he wrote. He might well have been speaking of himself.

Joining Vivien for a week's leave in Wales, he rediscovered the pleasure of her company in a place where they were free of obligations. Here they went on long walks, picked blackberries, and talked and talked, for a few brief days able to live "the sort of life one had forgotten existed."

Larry's spirits rose when he got time off for another propaganda picture, *The Demi-Paradise*, in which he played a Russian inventor who travels to England, hoping to build a revolutionary new propeller. In the movie, he delivers a not-entirely-convincing Eastern European accent. "I had, at first, a Russian lady to teach me the accent until I began to find my consonants becoming alarmingly, not to say suspiciously, effeminate," he explained. "I turned to a male Russian, who immediately declared, 'Avreesink see huss told yu iss alll wrongg,' at which point I decided I might do worse than invent my own Russian accent."

He followed this with a series of pep talks and speeches to men and women across the country, all demoralized by the war, and turned them into mini-performances, often climaxing with that most inspiring of Shakespearean rallying cries:

Once more unto the breach, dear friends, once more;
[And] when the blast of war blows in our ears,
Then imitate the action of the tiger;
Stiffen the sinews, summon up the blood....
Follow your spirit, and upon this charge
Cry "God for Harry, England, and Saint George!"

This was the inspiration for Larry's new movie, the first he would direct: *Henry V.*

Olivier had played England's fifteenth-century warrior king at the Vic, where he had slowly gotten over his initial doubts about the "scoutmaster" and embraced a full-throated heroism. Still, he had never thought of bringing *Henry* to the screen until a

BBC producer, Dallas Bower, reached out. The two men had worked together on a 1936 movie adaptation of *As You Like It* that Larry had particularly disliked, crystallizing his conviction that even the worthiest Shakespeare would disappoint on-screen. If Cukor had failed with *Romeo and Juliet* and if the great Austrian director Max Reinhardt had flopped with *A Midsummer Night's Dream*, he wondered, why should he do better? Then he reread the play and, urged on by Vivien, his doubts melted away.

At first, he wanted Wyler to direct and pursued him without success—an astonishing reversal and a recognition (after much resistance) that Wyler had been right all along. Nor did he have any better luck with a host of other filmmakers, from Carol Reed (*The Third Man*) to John Ford (*The Searchers*). Michael Powell was intrigued, but skeptical. "We pulled up a couple of chairs and Larry opened a big folder with sketches by [art director] Paul Sherrif [sic] and [costume designer] Roger Furse, and started to explain how he saw the film," Powell recalled. "I pulled him up short. 'Why don't you direct the film yourself?'"

Olivier was secretly itching to do so but lacked faith in his talent following the disastrous *Romeo*. Still wavering, he tried to hire Terence Young, a fledgling filmmaker later to become known for the James Bond thrillers *Dr. No* and *From Russia with Love*. When Young's employer, the British Army Council, refused to let him go, Olivier and another of his producers, Filippo Del Giudice (who would be pivotal to the movie's success), took Minister of Information Brendan Bracken to dinner. "They got him drunk as a skunk," said Young, "and wheedled from him the promise that I could have just ten weeks' leave to direct *Henry V*."

Ten weeks came and went, and the movie was nowhere near ready to shoot, and so Young returned to duty, leaving Olivier with only one option: to direct it himself. With Vivien back home, recuperating from the loss of their baby and the end of her play, Larry buried himself in Shakespeare's text, discussing each line with her, drawing on her wide reading and knowledge of history as well as his own instincts. The more they spoke, the more enthusiastic he became, and one can still feel his passion tearing across the nine pages he devoted to *Henry* in his memoir, compared to a few paragraphs for *Wuthering Heights* and a few lines for *Rebecca*. "I could think of the play sideways, upwards and outwards, because I knew it backwards," he remembered. "I saw its nuances of rhythm and movement in my mind's eye, and then heard its dialogue."

This man who had once despised motion pictures was now their most zealous advocate, steeping himself in "the old masters like [Sergei] Eisenstein and D. W. Griffith" and discovering a fervor for filmmaking he had never known before. "I was amazed how easily I thought in the language of film: panorama shots, tracking shots, dolly shots, medium shots, close-ups, and the movement and prying of the camera," he wrote. "Flash upon flash came the problems. Flash upon—no, perhaps a little longer—came the solutions. How I loved the problems! How I loved the medium's ingenuity! How I loved the medium! Wyler's medium, mine, William Shakespeare's."

He didn't say "Vivien's," though her influence was crucial: she understood film in many ways better than he did, followed the work of the great European auteurs and shrewdly observed how their innovations often preceded Hollywood's. Through their conversations and with the help of his team, Olivier developed some of his most brilliant scenes. He took Shakespeare's very limitations—the boundaries of a tiny stage—and turned them to his advantage, made them his movie's most inspired conceit. Opening in the playwright's theater, the Globe, his film introduces the actors as they begin to perform the story of Henry V, only gradually to leave the theater for the "real" world where the rest of the drama will unfold, a real world whose painted backdrops are never entirely removed from the stage where the story began. This breathtaking idea allowed audiences to adjust to Shakespeare's heightened language, suspend their disbelief and enter a stylized environment. Plundering lines and characters from other plays, Larry not only added new material but even found room for Shakespeare's beloved Falstaff, who was plucked from *Henry IV* and plopped down in *Henry V*. "To hell with the purists," he argued.

For the first time, he began to think of film as having its own rules and grammar. If Shakespearean adaptations had gone wrong in the past, he theorized, it was because filmmakers had hammered in the close-ups for the big moments, when the playwright's speeches were powerful enough to stand alone—more than that, needed room to breathe. "I felt there was a quarrel between the eye and the ear, between the behavior of the camera and Shakespeare's verse," he explained. "If Shakespeare has a flourish and a big speech, bring the camera back; if he has moments of humor and poignancy, bring it forward." Later, some critics would carp about the absence of close-ups in his films; but this was intention rather than ignorance, strategy rather than mishandling.

With a start date set for spring 1943, Olivier worked on the script with Alan Dent while exploring the movie's color scheme and its depiction of the medieval world with Sheriff and Furse. "The elusive animal that we were all chasing was, of course, the Style," he noted. "Paul [Sheriff] had drawn some color sketches of two or three of the sets that would obviously be required. Bless his heart, it was wonderfully helpful that these sketches were so thoroughly wrong."

Initially, Larry had planned to cast Vivien in the small role of Henry's inamorata, Princess Katherine. But as the start date approached, Selznick forbade it, partly out of pique and partly out of conviction that a minor part would diminish her luster. The Oliviers were devastated, while the Selznick cabal secretly gloated. "[Olivier] very foolishly *guaranteed* the producers—Two Cities Films—that she would appear, despite my statement to the contrary," noted Jenia Reissar, the head of Selznick's London office, in one of her many letters to Hollywood. "They chose to believe him and Larry appeared something of a fool."

In May 1943, filming began in Ireland's County Wicklow with the picture's most challenging sequence, the Battle of Agincourt. Vivien, knowing Larry would be absent for months, chose to leave England and visit the troops in Africa—an act of generosity that Selznick would have been churlish to block—and thereby missed one of the most impressive chapters of her husband's life. "I remember the tremendous vigour and confidence he exuded to all around him," noted Furse. "There were hundreds of people to be fed and housed, as well as costumes, makeup, props, horses, dressing rooms, and first aid to be seen to. Olivier himself commanded all."

"[I] had never been in command of anything like seven hundred men before, and here they were, marshaled in serried ranks before me as I stood on a beer crate about to address them for the first time," recalled Olivier. Then and there he made a promise he would later regret. "I may sometimes be asking some things of you which might be difficult, perhaps even dangerous," he said, "but I want you to know that I shall not be asking anything of you that I shall not be willing at least to try to do myself." The warmth that greeted "this mighty line" should have served as a warning, which Larry realized when he told an extra to shinny up a tree and jump on a passing rider. The day player asked to be shown how, and so Larry scuttled up, took his position and leaped down on the galloping horse. "Somehow I scraped both feet off backwards, hung for a second and let go," he remembered. "On landing, a telltale stab of sharp pain in my right ankle made me clutch desperately to the tree trunk. 'There, you see?' I gasped out through clenched teeth. 'Easy, really.'"

He had twisted his foot and had to hobble through the rest of the shoot—one of many mini-disasters that provided an endless source of amusement to gossips. "Larry nearly went mad," Reissar wrote. "I am told the extra refused to jump from the trees, so, nothing daunted, Larry decided to do it himself. He changed into twenty different costumes and did twenty different jumps...only to discover at the end there was no film in the camera!"

She was conflating that incident with a graver one described by Olivier's friend, the screenwriter Charles Bennett (*The 39 Steps*). "Larry had a railroad track laid across the mile or so of the scene of battle, from which the camera, mounted on a traveling flat car, could shoot the entire length of the famous charge of French knights, adjusting its speed and gathering momentum as the action advanced," he explained. "The knights started their steeds at a walk, which increased to a trot, becoming a canter, merging into a gallop...finally becoming the full, thundering charge. Masses of heavily armored assailants hurtled toward a meager army that seemed about to be overwhelmed. Then came director-Larry's magic moment. A direct cut to the long, thin line of waiting English longbowmen. *ZING!* Off went the arrows, arching, hitting the advancing horde. Down went the knights, horses screaming, dying...and in effect, as history relates, the battle was won." Alas, he added, "when the negative was examined it was found to be badly scratched, all of it—hundreds of feet from one end to the other!"

Much to Larry's relief, Del Giudice, his producer, allowed him to reshoot the sequence at considerable cost.

Another time, Larry was looking through his viewfinder as an actor on horseback charged toward him. Fully expecting the man to veer aside, Larry stayed where he was, only for the horse and rider to collide with the camera, knocking his viewfinder into his mouth. "The finder hit my upper lip and pierced right through into the gum," he recalled. "The operator had had the sense to dart out of the way, and I got the weight of the camera directly on my right shoulder, fortunately just missing my collarbone, before it fell down to the ground on its side, where it lay still grinding. I turned to see the boy, still mounted, quite close to me. Had I felt inclined to tears then, it would not have been on account of my own pain but at the sight of the twelve-inch gash straight along the horse's flank, right through its coat and layers of tissue, the lower lip of the wound hanging down a good three inches."

All of this Larry relayed to Vivien as she set off for Africa, describing the ins and outs of each day's work in a series of long letters, many of them written late at night, when he was so worn out that he should have slept. This second collection of letters was very different in tone from those sent during the making of *Gone with the Wind*—calmer, steadier, packed with information, far from the gushing and rather jejune epistles he had written before, when all he could do was search for ways to tell Vivien how magnificent she was. These letters, by contrast, conveyed a mutual affinity and soft care, a tenderness rather than a sexual hunger, and yet were no less loving. The Oliviers were older now: Larry was about to turn thirty-seven, while Vivien was approaching thirty; they were settled in their relationship and more settled in themselves.

"Things, I suppose have gone fairly well," wrote Larry on June 7, 1943, "but sometimes it seems that they are not going at all, + I feel things closing in on me + I get panicky + very very nervous. My back is much better my darling tho' I still feel it a bit especially when tired at the end of the day but it is improving all the time. My arm however is another matter which is quite maddening because I don't remember doing it at the time, but... I must have clutched at an overhanging branch during the fateful pursuit of Duffy + wrenched my elbow."

A day before the anniversary of their elopement, Larry wrote again: "I shall think of you so hard all tomorrow. Six years, it seems quite timeless altogether, just as it should.... My Vivling I do thank you with all my heart for the undreamt prize you have brought to me. You have sown such a harvest in my heart my beloved."

In Africa, soldiers were everywhere. Sailors and airmen filled the streets and haunted the brothels, despite the military warning that "Pox does more than Rommel can / To bugger Monty's battle-plan." Street children scurried around, offering shoeshines and black-market goods at startlingly low prices. Just as in India, there was a strict separation of races, and Caucasians were "warned against 'close contact with the native population' on the ground of 'vermin' (fleas) carrying the typhus bacillus, though we had been inoculated against this," an officer wrote. "Fleas, those Olympic jumpers, might make an inter-racial leap."

Vivien missed Larry terribly, but her spirits soared when a naval vessel carrying Coward happened to dock in Libya, where she was performing in the historic Leptis Magna amphitheater. Leaving the ship, the playwright was charmed by her rendition of Lewis Carroll's "You Are Old, Father William," taken from *Alice's Adventures in Wonderland*:

> "You are old, father William," the young man said,
> "And your hair has become very white;
> And yet you incessantly stand on your head—
> Do you think, at your age, it is right?"

"The sight of this small, beautiful woman, by herself, in that vast Arena, speaking the most perfect English was breathtaking," wrote an audience member. "There was dead silence for each piece, followed by a great roar of applause and acclaim.

The soldiers, sailors, airmen, all of us there, and there were many nationalities, were spellbound."

The amphitheater was just one of the sites that astounded Vivien as she traveled from Algiers to Tripoli, from Tripoli to Cairo; and yet each discovery made her feel the pain of Larry's absence all the sharper. "I am so miserable," she wrote to him. "To think I am having all these excitements + seeing so many places without you—I can never really enjoy any of it, or anything that I don't share with you my darling love—my only life."

Voyaging across the continent, through torrid heat and torrential rain, moving in and out of makeshift auditoriums and provisional camps, Vivien visited hospitals where thousands of soldiers lay sick and sometimes terminally ill. This was carnage on an epic scale, the sort of horror she had seen fictionalized in *Gone with the Wind* but never expected to witness in real life. "One's emotions are continually swayed by all sorts of things— playing in hospitals for instance where the wounded are brought in in their beds is so terribly moving that one can hardly get on with one's job," she wrote. "One meets very young pilots who are either just off to the front or home, or rather on leave, after having had a gruelling time. They seem so completely fatalistic its [sic] difficult to talk to them."

Unable to communicate by telephone and forced to be apart from his wife for months—their longest separation since *GWTW*—Larry could only guess at the effect Africa was having on her. She still had not fully recuperated from *The Doctor's Dilemma* and, despite her protestations that all was well, was so taxed that she lost thirteen pounds, making her seem almost skeletal at five-foot-three and less than a hundred pounds. "I get more + more anxious about you as time goes on," Larry wrote from his shoot. "I only pray that you are enjoying it or some of it, but its [sic] horrid that you might be miserable + anxious +

worried + scared or anything. As for me, I have my ups + downs, very much to myself in a sort of purgatory."

Vivien was in purgatory, too, especially when she didn't hear from Larry, whose letters would arrive intermittently, some carried to far-off places, some lost in the uncertain journey overseas. She was ecstatic when the producer Beaumont arrived with a sheaf of correspondence. "My sweet sweet Larry boy," she wrote, "when I saw Binkie coming out of a shed with a layer of envelopes, [I] charged him like a bull, sand flying behind me, and there they were." Describing her tiny room with its huge bed, she told Larry it "only makes me cry dearest heart how I long for you and think of you so strongly that I am sure you must feel my heart + my thoughts....I couldn't believe that one of the most exciting experiences of my life [dinner with the Moroccan king] was going to be without you."

Then a note of her old insecurity crept in. "But we'll have many wonderful times together," she insisted. "Won't we?"

CHAPTER 8

————◆————

In August 1943, Vivien returned to a nation stripped to the bare essentials, a salvage yard of human endeavor and emotion. Four years into the war, the tide had turned: Allied forces had declared victory in North Africa; Germany had suffered its first major defeat at the Battle of Stalingrad; and Italy had capitulated, essentially signaling that the end was in sight. Still, in London, the toll of the conflagration was all around, visible in everything from a hundred thousand destroyed homes to an even greater number of heartsickening headlines, one of which noted that thirty-eight schoolchildren had just died in an enemy attack.

Now came the latest horrible news: Leslie Howard, Vivien's costar in *Gone with the Wind*, had been shot down while flying back from Spain, possibly because a German fighter believed his plane was carrying Winston Churchill. He and Vivien had tangled on *GWTW*, but they had had a long and cherished history: Howard had wanted her for his stage production of *Hamlet* way before Hollywood called, and he had helped Larry disguise his affair by serving as his roommate in Los Angeles. Later, the Oliviers would learn that their friend was as noble as Ashley Wilkes and had taken great risks to spy for the British government in an operation reputedly organized by Korda, though that has never been proved. Now he was gone, another among so many.

Compared to his sacrifice, Vivien's and Larry's seemed slight; but nobody was criticizing them anymore. Both were part of the war effort and had given up much in the form of money, liberty and human loss. The cost of Vivien's own contribution was obvious when she landed in Portsmouth, where, after undergoing a somewhat humiliating inspection for lice, she saw Larry for the first time since June, so thin she appeared almost emaciated. She was equally concerned about her "little bag of bones," as she called her husband, though their physical decline did nothing to diminish their hunger for each other.

Renting a small house not far from Denham Studios, Vivien did her best to care for Larry as he continued to shoot *Henry V*, wrapping the rest of the film at the studio now that his location work was completed; he would remain there day and night until early January 1944, so drained that he was "like to have a nervous breakdown," said Frewen. Vivien was also at the studio almost every day, as one journalist observed, "[taking] up her chair on the studio floor, to assist and advise and encourage and relieve Larry of every possibly routine detail she could [and serving as] mentor, critic and adviser." Another visitor acknowledged her contribution to everything "from choosing costumes to doing research."

When she wasn't at her husband's side, Vivien dabbled in domesticity, chatting to friends on the phone, reading copiously as always, and tackling her beloved word games and crossword puzzles, at which she was a master. Reuniting with some colleagues from the African tour to stage a revue, she performed "meticulously to the best of her ability and with the minimum of fuss," noted a fellow performer, John Clements.

And yet there were hints of malaise that would bob up and break through Vivien's surface composure. She had been relatively untroubled by her illness in the five years since her outburst during *GWTW*, but now she was more changeable. When she went backstage after a performance of Coward's *This Happy Breed*, the actress Judy Campbell was surprised to realize Vivien had been crying. "She sat in front of my dressing table, dabbing away, blowing her nose, borrowing my face powder, while I was getting out of my clothes," remembered Campbell. Then came another revelation: after their backstage visit, Vivien was like a different person, suddenly distant, politely saying goodbye and how it was "*so* nice to have met you." This was hypocrisy, Campbell believed, and she registered Vivien's "little pussycat smile."

They ran into each other again at a concert for the troops. This time, Vivien joined Campbell in her hotel room, where she began to drink—and kept on drinking late into the night. Soon she had lost all self-control and unleashed a string of four-letter words that astounded her fellow actress, who claimed she had never heard anything like it. By now "it was after midnight," recalled Campbell. Vivien "was rapidly getting stoned [drunk] out of her mind. She was flinging it back and I won't say that I felt my idols had feet of clay but I thought 'this is the other side of the coin.'" Once again, Campbell noted a blink-of-an-eye personality shift and, like everyone else, failed to connect it to Vivien's graver issues. "In my dressing room she was in tears and therefore somehow had a nakedness," said Campbell, "and then later on became very exquisite and formal and here it was the other way round."

None of these incidents, in isolation, was extreme enough to indicate something was profoundly wrong. But they were tremors running beneath the surface, signals of a temblor to come.

In the early hours of June 6, 1944, the Allies launched an unprecedented aerial and naval attack on the beaches of Normandy. More than twenty-two hundred bombers swooped down on German targets as thirteen thousand paratroopers dropped behind enemy lines. This was the beginning of Operation Neptune, better known as D-day. While Olivier was completing postproduction on *Henry V*, 6,939 ships, 2,395 planes and 156,000 troops launched their amphibious drive, the culmination of almost a year's planning that at times had pitted Stalin and Roosevelt against Churchill, who remembered only too well the slaughter at Gallipoli under his aegis in World War I and hesitated before committing to an attack.

British forces would battle on for another year in Europe and even longer in the Far East, but victory was now apparent. Soldiers were being demobilized every day, and Larry quickly joined them. He had been given leave to make *Henry*; he would never return to active duty. "Before the work on the picture had been finalized," he wrote, "the dear old Walrus flying-boat [a plane he had flown] had been withdrawn from service in the Fleet Air Arm. There was now no branch of operations for which I was eligible, and to pursue my idea of returning to the Navy to take up taxi-driving trainee air-gunners round the sky again seemed to be really a bit cranky."

Free to move on, he began to explore a return to the stage. Although he doubted that England was ready for a proper national theater—a concept that would become his most-cherished dream in the latter part of his life—he agreed to join Ralph Richardson and John Burrell, a BBC drama producer, as joint heads of the Old Vic Company, given that Guthrie was stepping down and the British government had promised to cover half its losses through subsidies. Larry resigned his commission, faux-modestly telling the press that "I am a man who does what he is told."

The repertory group would present some of the world's greatest plays (mostly at the New Theatre, rather than the Vic, which had been badly bombed), supported by luminaries including Sybil Thorndike, Harcourt Williams and George Relph. Only Vivien was conspicuously absent. In a blow to her self-esteem, Larry and his partners had not asked her to join their company, an exclusion she couldn't ignore.

She was fragile, as she knew, and still not quite able to cope with a repertoire this taxing, where she would have to appear back to back in productions of Ibsen's *Peer Gynt*, Shaw's *Arms and the Man* and Shakespeare's *Richard III*. Still, the slight hurt. For the first time Larry was hurtling ahead without her, taking a great leap forward in which she had no part. And so she began to look elsewhere, searching for a way to work—alone if need be—and if not onstage, then in a film.

She had always wished to play the Egyptian queen in Shaw's 1898 comedy drama *Caesar and Cleopatra*; indeed, one of her prime motives for doing *The Doctor's Dilemma* was the hope that Shaw would come to see her—which he never did, averse as he was to watching his work onstage. Long before Vivien entered his life, the master had grown bitter toward the actors who made his characters flesh, and so loathed Sir Herbert Beerbohm Tree's Henry Higgins that he refused to see any production of *Pygmalion* beyond its initial renditions. Now, two years after Vivien had learned that a feature version of *Caesar and Cleopatra* was in the works, she was offered the leading role.

She took it against Larry's advice. "It was Vivien's desire to play Cleopatra that finally made her fight against Larry," noted Jenia Reissar, the Selznick staffer. Olivier "kept on saying she might as well give up acting for the duration [of the war] and be spared the worry and anxiety which a picture deal in the present circumstances brought in its wake." Vivien deemed otherwise.

The movie's existence was something of a miracle. Nobody could quite explain how its producer, Gabriel Pascal, had convinced Shaw to give him the rights after decades in which he had refused to part with them, let alone how Pascal had found enough money and equipment to mount such an ambitious project in the midst of war. "Despite anything the trade press says," added Reissar, "there is a terrific muddle inside the industry and the shortage of directors, writers and stars does not help. Pictures are made spasmodically.... Usually [there is] no time for preparation and the script is being written during production.... [Producers] make a film, and then for months—and sometimes years!—no more is heard of them."

Vivien had to get Shaw's approval before shooting could begin, and so she went to see him at his home in the village of Ayot St. Lawrence, where she was at her most charming and seductive. By the end of their meeting, Shaw was so impressed that it was he who suggested she take the role, not the other way around. "Do you think so?" Vivien asked coyly. "Would I be good enough?" Holding her hand, the eighty-seven-year-old summoned the name of the legendary actress who had created *Pygmalion*'s Eliza Doolittle, and told her: "You are the Mrs. Pat Campbell of the age."

This was the high point of a relationship that quickly turned sour, just like the film. Leading actors declined to take part; expenses spiraled out of control; the man Pascal had hired to direct was fired halfway through the shoot; and Vivien soon found herself living the sort of nightmare that made *Gone with the Wind* look like a dream. Gielgud, everyone's first choice for Julius Caesar, couldn't stand Pascal, a bumptious egomaniac; instead, Caesar went to *Casablanca*'s Claude Rains, an exceptional actor who had no chemistry with Vivien.

Production began on June 12, six days after D-day. "Never had there been such a colossal or so splendiferous a sight as Pascal's Egypt," writes Shaw's biographer, Michael Holroyd. "The interior of the Memphis Palace with its pseudo-granite columns each weighing two tons, its carvings of men with wings, hawks' heads, black marble cats, was to cover 28,000 square feet; while the palace steps and quayside were immense exterior sets constructed for the thousands of extras he had hired. All their costumes, the hieroglyphs and statues were copied from originals—even the formation of the stars behind the mighty Sphinx was designed by an astronomer. 'The film promises to be a wonder,' Shaw told Pascal."

The opposite was true. Vivien, who had so captivated the playwright, alienated him by delivering her dialogue in a flat staccato he couldn't understand. He complained about her "gabbling tonelessly such sounds as *cuminecho* and *oaljentlemin* (rather than 'The Romans will come and eat you' and 'old gentleman')! Does she always go on like that or should I have had her here to drill her in the diction of the part?"

Vivien was thirty years old and struggling to play sixteen in her first major movie role since *Lady Hamilton*. She had hoped for help from Larry, who was editing his picture at the very studio where she was filming, but he was too exhausted, too absorbed with editing, along with his Old Vic duties. Nor was Vivien supported by Pascal, who soon replaced director Brian Desmond Hurst with himself and then laboriously pondered each shot, redoing take after take until the budget soared to £1.3 million, three times the cost of *Henry V*. Production was further complicated by the flying bombs that kept exploding near Denham, along with icy weather that made a mockery of attempts to simulate an Egyptian summer. (When Pascal insisted on shooting some sequences in Egypt, while Vivien remained behind, rains washed out the set and 1,200 famished extras ate their edible shields.)

"No film—not even the £800,000 *Gone With the Wind*, which took 26 weeks to film in Hollywood—has ever accumulated so many legends, true and apocryphal, as *Caesar and Cleopatra*," noted one reporter seriously underestimating the cost of *GWTW*. "There is the story of the small-part player who got £30 [the equivalent of today's £1,300 or $1,800] a day for 15 days' work on a job which eventually took only a few minutes in the studio....It is a fact [that] Miss Leigh's black wigs had to be plaited into 80 strands each night so that they were properly crinkled the next day; that 2,000 costumes were made; that one scene had 1,500 people in it; that they used a hundredweight of dyes in addition to those used outside the studio; that an Egyptian god in one scene was 22 feet high and weighed 25 cwt. [hundredweight]; that more than 500 pieces of jewellery were used and that thieves stole a lot of them one day; and that the whole job was done with the studio staff 50 percent under strength. *Caesar and Cleopatra* has made Gabriel Pascal the most-criticized film producer of all time."

Vivien detested him even more than Selznick, who was still pressuring her to return to Los Angeles even as he took a hefty cut of her fee. By late summer, she and Pascal were no longer speaking, "except when he actually directed her on the set," reported Reissar. "Nor is she too happy with Claude Rains, who not only acts Caesar in front of the camera but also in life."

While Vivien was struggling to finish her film, Larry was reevaluating his craft, and at the age of thirty-seven he had a revelation. When his second performance in *Arms and the Man* tanked, "he remained moodily in his dressing room, waiting for the arrival of Guthrie, who had not been able to make the first night," writes the biographer Anthony Holden. "It did not cheer him much to bump into Guthrie and Richardson emerging from the Number One dressing-room—Thorndike's—in high spirits." Olivier trailed behind his friends, despondent, until Guthrie brought up the play.

"Don't you love Sergius?" he asked.

"Are you out of your mind?" replied Larry. "How can you love a ridiculous fool of a man like that?"

"Well, of course," retorted Guthrie, "if you can't love him, you'll never be any good as him, will you?"

Guthrie's comment came like a bolt from the blue, the sort of epiphany that is a staple of drama but rarely real life, and it would transform Olivier's approach to his work. From then on, he said—from that moment in August 1944, when Guthrie confronted him—he aimed not just to like his characters but to love them, and not just love them but be in love with them, too. And once he was in love with a character, it was harder for him to remain in love with Vivien—which came at a striking moment, given that she had just discovered she was again pregnant.

The news of her pregnancy seemed to have a greater impact on the Oliviers than before. Perhaps Vivien's earlier miscarriage had affected them more than they let on; or perhaps their long separation while Larry was shooting and Vivien was touring Africa had made them reconsider their relationship and indeed their lives. A baby would help repair strains and redeem previous failures: neither had been a good parent, after all—Larry had barely seen Tarquin and, whenever he did, the boy's presence only reminded him of his mistakes, while Vivien had essentially absolved herself of her maternal duties, leaving them to Gertrude. Given this reprieve, both were ecstatic.

"*What* do you suppose has happened," Vivien gushed to Holman. "I'm to have a baby. Everyone is *very, very* cross & keeps asking me how I suppose they are going to make me look like the 16 year Cleopatra & I keep saying I can't help it, that it's an act of God."

Then two weeks after writing that letter, Vivien slipped and fell on the hard floor of the soundstage, injuring herself so badly that a doctor had to be summoned. While no bones were broken, the doctor insisted she stop shooting for several days. Two days later, she lost her baby.

In public, Vivien made light of the miscarriage and even joked that there were "plenty more where that one came from." Privately, however, she was devastated. "She never forgave Pascal," noted her costar, Stewart Granger, who blamed the producer for not hiring a stand-in.

Losing one baby was hard; losing two was excruciating. She and Larry "were both terribly disappointed about the loss of the child," confided Reissar, "and when I spoke to Vivien on the phone (she was still at home in the country), she was crying bitterly." Back at her house after a brief hospitalization, her mood turned somber. Exhaustion gave way to depression, exacerbated by the bitter weather and Larry's growing inaccessibility as he raced to finish his film, while immersing himself in the theater. And with Vivien's depression came a flood of worry, a gnawing anxiety that is "very much a feature of the depressive phase of bipolar disorder," says Guy Goodwin, a professor of psychiatry at Oxford University.

Vivien was in despair when she returned to the set of *Cleopatra*. She walked as if weighed down by misery and sometimes her mind was so clouded that she failed to hear Pascal call "Action!" Then, in the middle of shooting the film's big banquet scene, her mood suddenly switched. "She stopped dead," writes Walker. "As the other players faltered, they saw her features transfigured. Her face sharpened. She broke away from Shaw's dialogue and began berating her dresser for some small sin of omission she discerned in her costuming. Her voice was now high and harsh. Her brows had hardened into an angry line. Bystanders saw her eyes take on a piercing glare." Pascal called for a break, but that only aggravated things and triggered an explosion. "She suffered a hysterical fit," continues Walker, "but it was short-lived and ceased as suddenly as it had come on her."

The producer called a halt to that day's work and ordered a car to take Vivien home; and yet, even as she agreed to leave the studio, she seemed unaware of how over-the-top her behavior had been and insisted nothing out of order had taken place, telling everyone she simply had to learn her lines. Nor did she acknowledge the gravity of the incident when she saw Larry, which might explain why he didn't take it too seriously. He initially "attributed her collapse to delayed depression following the miscarriage," writes Walker, a sort of postpartum depression, though that term had not yet come into usage.

Then Vivien's mood altered again, not once but multiple times. She was cycling rapidly between exaltation and dejection, unlike anything Larry had seen, a horrific experience for both and all the more because it seemed to continue without end. As the poet Robert Lowell noted of his own extreme episodes of mental illness, "The light at the end of the tunnel is just the light of an oncoming train."

Larry failed to understand this, like so many others in an era when the line between sanity and insanity appeared crystal clear, and to fall on the wrong side of it could have terrifying consequences.

To declare Vivien "mad" would have meant taking her to a psychiatrist or, worse, locking her up. The term "mental illness" had yet to enter the lexicon; another term, "mental defectives," was used for those beyond the pale, the very language revealing its stigma—especially for women, who were liable to be dubbed "hysterics" and confined for months, if not years. Few people asked for psychiatric help unless forced to do so; indeed, the number of patients who did was one-sixth what it would be by the end of the century. Besides, in England, erratic behavior was par for the course, especially in the arts, where eccentricity was a given. Was Vivien's turbulence any different?

With this in his mind, Larry hid his fears, channeled his

energy even further into his work and, when Vivien returned to *Cleopatra* after an absence of five weeks, he mistakenly pronounced her better.

"She appeared to make a good recovery and he found it unthinkable that the gentle, loving woman he was with had been the person with the glowering looks and abusive temper," continues Walker. "She seemed not to believe it herself, or to remember how she had behaved. She asked what she had done and to whom she owed apologies. She refused to go into hospital, assuring Olivier that she had recovered. The disturbance seemed so localized, almost a social *faux pas*, that the idea of mental impairment didn't seriously suggest itself to Olivier. His pity and relief at her return to her normal self were immense—and dissuaded him from insisting that she be examined further against her will."

Larry thought the worst was over. He didn't realize it had just begun.

CHAPTER 9

⎯⎯◈⎯⎯

On the southeastern edge of central Kolkata, just a short distance from the imposing Fort William, sits a squat brick edifice, all but ignored by the stream of pedestrians surging down the busy road. This is ground zero for anyone who wants to understand Vivien's illness.

For decades this two-story retreat was the local asylum, filled with the shunned and the shamed, men and women whose screams would waft over the walls and terrify passersby. Horrific as it might seem, the European Lunatic Asylum was one of India's most advanced institutions for the mentally ill, founded as a response to the dens of iniquity then prevalent. An enlightened hospital superintendent had authorized its construction next to the local jail, where the government erected a clean and airy complex, made up of a central house, as he wrote, "surrounded by several ranges of barracks, which were thrown together in no very definite plan but were added from time to time to suit the needs of the public."

It was here that one Gabriel Yackjee came in August 1867, diagnosed with "mania chronic, cause unknown." What led him to this place and who brought him are unknown, but this much appears certain: he was Vivien's great-uncle. Institutionalized at the age of thirty, he remained locked up for nine months before being discharged on June 3, 1868, either because his condition had improved or because the asylums had begun shipping long-term inmates to England, a profitable enterprise for all—except, perhaps, the inmates themselves.

Yackjee was well treated by the standards of his day. "Cruel as the natives of India naturally are both to man and to beast," wrote a European visitor, "cruelty to lunatics is not one of their characteristics." This was especially true in the asylums for foreigners (as opposed to the indigenous ones), whose welfare was of prime importance to the British Empire; after all, if the empire's sons were treated no better than the natives, what claim could they have to moral and intellectual superiority? In the Europeans' asylum, "the gardens were beautiful and had a pleasing and refreshing appearance," notes one scholar. "Patients looked happy, cheerful and comfortable. The asylum was managed by a European superintendent and a steward. There was an Apothecary to look after the male patients and a Matron to watch the female patients. Restraint was in use but it was in extreme moderation."

Yackjee's presence may signal a genetic element in Vivien's illness, a common characteristic of bipolar disorder—or manic depression, the label eventually given to her condition. If so, he is the only member of her family known to have suffered similar episodes, and a doctor who treated Vivien noted in 1964 that "there is no history of nervous or mental illness on either side of her family."

There was, however, a history in Vivien's own life. As a child, she had been unusually moody and as a baby she had had such trouble sleeping that her mother had felt compelled to take her to a doctor, only for the doctor to allay her fears. Bipolar symptoms do not usually emerge until the late teens or even twenties; but recent studies indicate the illness may appear earlier than previously thought. "If you look at those kids, they tend to have symptoms," says Po Wang, the director of Stanford University's Bipolar Disorders Clinic. "They'll have sleep abnormalities or irritability or a hodgepodge of symptoms that aren't specific."

There were further hints of trouble when Vivien was at the convent, where she could swing from being the light, bright girl her friends knew and loved to an altogether darker creature—though Maureen O'Sullivan, later, was shocked to learn of Vivien's depresson. Her diaries are also revealing: For decades, she kept a record of her activities in tiny volumes with wafer-thin blue pages. These are far from extensive journals, but one period stands out: In July 1930, she describes feeling "terribly miserable," the first of a host of entries where she records "feeling blue + down." That fits a classic pattern, says Wang. Bipolar disorder "often happens within a year of menstrual cycles starting. The onset is usually with depression in one's teens."

A manic phase quickly followed Vivien's first obvious bout with depression. In March 1931, when she was thirteen, her handwriting suddenly shifts and neat penmanship gives way to a molten scrawl, the letters so large that they bump against each other in a chaotic mess that's almost impossible to decipher. (Years later, the producer Binkie Beaumont said he could always tell when Vivien was entering a manic phase from the abrupt change in her handwriting.) But is this evidence of illness or just the usual teenage *Sturm und Drang*?

There are two forms of bipolar disorder, as described in the psychiatric manual *DSM-5*. Those who have had at least one episode of mania, sometimes with psychotic features—meaning they are unable to separate the real from the unreal—are bipolar I, the category that best fits Vivien, though a break with reality would not come until much later. Those who have had episodes of hypomania (that is, "less than" mania) but never a full-blown manic experience, and show no signs of clinical depression, are bipolar II. Still, this simplifies an enormously complex illness that seems different in each patient, and many psychiatrists now argue that bipolar disorder is a "spectrum" disease rather than one that can so easily be categorized. "It may be that over time, when we get more research results, we'll have to completely redefine our classification systems, based more on an understanding of the mechanisms that are actually involved," says John Geddes, head of the department of psychiatry at Oxford University.

"Bipolar disorder is the chameleon of psychiatric disorders, changing its symptom presentation from one patient to the next, and from one episode to the next even in the same patient," writes Francis Mark Mondimore, a psychiatrist at Johns Hopkins University. "It is a phantom that can sneak up on its victim cloaked in the darkness of melancholy but then disappear for years at a time—only to return in the resplendent but fiery robes of mania.... The depressed phase can be merely gloomy or profoundly despairing; torpid and lethargic, or agitated and churning. The manic phase can be no more than an enthusiastic glow, or it can be an exultant, transcendental fervor, frenzied panic, or delirious, crashing, raving psychosis."

In both kinds of bipolar, periods of mania alternate with depression, along with a third "mixed" state in which these extremes occur simultaneously, the most worrisome aspect of the illness and the hardest for a layman to understand. "Sometimes," adds Mondimore, "opposite moods seem to be combined, as inseparable as smoke and fire."

This mixed state leads some psychiatrists, like Kay Redfield Jamison, to question the very idea of mania and depression as strict opposites. "[That] perpetuates the notion that depression exists rather tidily segregated on its own pole, while mania clusters off neatly and discreetly on another," she writes in a memoir of her own battle with bipolar disorder, *An Unquiet Mind.* "This polarization of two clinical states flies in the face of everything we know about the cauldronous, fluctuating nature of manic-depressive illness."

For centuries, there was no treatment for BP. Its victims were written off as deranged—or, as Lady Caroline Lamb described her lover Lord Byron, "mad, bad and dangerous to know." Then in 1948, John Cade, an Australian researcher, made a surprising discovery: that lithium carbonate, a mineral used to treat illnesses such as gout, had a calming effect on guinea pigs, eventually leading to its modern-day utilization in BP. Today, lithium is mined in great salt flats in countries from Argentina to Australia, from Mexico to Bolivia, where holes are drilled deep into the ground to suck it out. But its commercialization came too late for Vivien, who lived at a time when there was no proper treatment and when others blamed her for behavior they thought she could control.

"What has driven her round the bend again is the demon alcohol," wrote Coward, in a typical response. "This is what it has always been. I suspect there is far less genuine mental instability about it than most people seem to think....I have a dreadful suspicion that all this disgraceful carry-on is really a *vino veritas* condition! She has always been spoilt and when she fails to get her own way she takes to the bottle and goes berserk." He added, "Personally, I think that if Larry had turned sharply on Vivien years ago and given her a clip in the chops, he would have been spared a mint of trouble."

Olivier's sister, Sybille, had conditioned him to erratic behavior. Always an eccentric, she was an outlier from the start, rejecting social norms and flouting the very conventions her brother held so dear. When she was in her twenties, a moralizing judge condemned her and her first husband as "a pair of fools" and noted it was obvious that "the wife is a woman who has the feeblest hold upon the virtue of chastity, either in herself or in her husband." Then, in 1929, she had some sort of breakdown, leading to the first of several hospitalizations. Her symptoms, according to some of the psychiatrists consulted for this book, were consistent with bipolar, though it would be rash to diagnose her from a distance. At one point, she experienced a psychotic break, which her second husband, Gerald Day, described in his memoir, *Rivers of Damascus*, recalling "how my young wife became suddenly insane." Using the pseudonym "Sylvia," he explained that "a terrible change had come over her.... She was violently excited and incoherent, and had lost practically all self-control." At times she "babbled fantastically like a child," while at others she became "subdued and listless" and even began to hallucinate, hearing voices that told her what to do. "Was this fey creature really Sylvia?" he asked.

Such was the reality Larry had grown up with, which may have primed him for what the psychiatrist Terence Ketter calls "assortative mating, in which people whose relatives have mental illness are more likely to hook up with those who also have mental illness." Still, he was unprepared for the chaos that enveloped him, unaware of what to do or whom to approach for advice. Instead of tackling Vivien's illness directly, he turned away; instead of facing it directly, he shifted his gaze toward work. He was busy all the time, finishing his film, running the Old Vic Company with Richardson and Burrell, and—above all— embracing a new role: Richard III.

It is impossible to separate Olivier's most brilliant creation from the drama that permeated his domestic life. The more angelic he was with Vivien, the more demonic he became onstage, as if his conscious and unconscious selves were at war—living proof, it seemed, of Jung's notion that "once the unconscious gets into active opposition to consciousness, it simply refuses to be suppressed." At home, Larry was caring and compassionate. But when he stared in the mirror as he developed his Richard, he wrote later, "the monster stared back at me and smiled."

Initially, he had been reluctant to take on the hunchbacked king, Britain's last Plantagenet monarch, who had ruled for two terrible years from 1483 to 1485. But in the wake of Hitler's dictatorship, Richard seemed newly relevant. The deeper he delved, the more excited he became. "An actor," he reflected, "when he begins to sense that he is on to something, is a bit like a stoat coming out of its hole and smelling the morning air: the nose twitches and the body starts to tingle. The flash of lightning away in the distance, the thunder still muted, but coming, slowly coming."

He drew on real life for inspiration, taking his limp from his colleague Burrell (who had had polio as a child) and his loathsomeness from Jed Harris, a brilliant but reviled Broadway eminence who had directed him onstage in 1933's *The Green Bay Tree* and whose reptilian manner, facial warts and malevolent glee all fed Larry's creation. So did Harris's undeniable sexuality, which led him to make his Richard "one of the most sexually attractive characters ever to disgrace the stage," as the playwright Terence Rattigan observed—a quality that seemed more evident onstage as it receded at home.

And yet, even as he reached for new heights, something was chipping away at his psychic foundations. Vivien's turmoil had a clear impact and "for the first time in his career," writes Holden, "[he] had great trouble memorizing his lines. He laughed it off as 'wartime rust,' but the real reasons were clearly more deep-seated." Larry's castmates began to worry and their anxiety spread beyond the confines of the theater to the world at large, where they blended with rumors of an impending disaster. "Stories had been circulating about Larry's characterisation and make-up and the extra rehearsals that he had demanded," recalled Powell, the *Red Shoes* director. "There were ear-witness tales that he hadn't found the Voice yet. There were eye-witness tales that Richard's crouchback was to be presented with two humps; or none."

Vivien tried to reassure Larry—even came to rehearsals and helped him go over his lines—but that didn't help. On the eve of his first performance, says Hayley Mills, "Larry called my parents [John and Mary Mills] and said, 'You must come around [before the show].' Otherwise, they wouldn't have dreamed of going to his dressing room. He said, 'I've got to speak to you.' So they went around very nervously, and he was in a terrible state. He said, 'I don't know what to do. It's going to be a disaster. I just need to tell you.' So they went back to their seats, absolutely shaking with fear and gripping each other's hands. And the curtain went up—and, of course, he was absolutely, devastatingly brilliant."

Bushell marveled at what he saw, how Larry "rushed to the throne + delivered the lines 'Is the chair empty? Is the sword unswayed?' in an appalling double fortissimo. And the steel girders in the roof rang as if they had been struck with a hammer."

"Nothing prepared us for what we saw on the stage, when the curtain went up on that memorable night," wrote Powell. " 'Now is the winter of our discontent / Made glorious summer by this sun of York.' The voice is cultured, the tone venomous. The figure is rich and noble, but twisted out of shape. The eyes are enormous, but as observant as a cat's and filled with sleeping cruelty. The nose—ah! that nose!—is long and pendulous. His pale face is shadowed by long dank hair which hangs to his shoulders. He stands alone upon the stage—not, if I remember right, in the centre, but on the prompt side and downstage where he can dominate the house and mark the slightest inattention, or movement. We return his look, terrified. Somehow he conveys the effect of a beautiful body and a brilliant mind, diseased and gone to the bad. He speaks. We shudder. His words drip like vitriol....Ah! What a night that was! I thought we would never stop clapping."

The next day, when Larry resumed his role, he could almost sniff the approval. "There it was," he recalled, "that sweet smell (it's like seaweed) of success. The audience had come in response to some sixth sense; it was in the air, though by no means uniformly expressed by the morning newspapers, that people should come and see—me. It was the first time in my twenty-year-old career that I had ever felt anything like it."

Two months later, on November 22, 1944, *Henry V* premiered at London's Carlton Cinema. "Nothing could [have been] more gentle, more quietly wistful than his 'Upon the King' soliloquy," recalled Charles Bennett, the screenwriter. "Larry's performance was so compelling that when a V-2 bomb fell less than a quarter mile away, seemingly tilting the theater upside down, Larry's quiet delivery had the shaken audience hushed and listening again for his whispered words even before the shock of the bomb had subsided."

Despite this, the critics were lukewarm. The film was, at best, "an indication of what could be done with Shakespeare on the screen," wrote the *News Chronicle*'s Richard Winnington, while Ernest Betts of the *People* called it "the most difficult, annoying, beautiful, boring, exciting, wordy, baffling picture yet made." Admissions lagged when *Henry* screened across the country, not helped by the distributor's decision to include it in a double bill with utterly different pictures: a Betty Grable musical or a George Raft film noir. Such double bills were routine but, after watching gangsters and dancers, audiences had little appetite for Shakespeare. And then something changed: teachers began to bring their schoolchildren; the schoolchildren told their parents;

and ticket sales climbed. The movie became a hit and used its domestic success as a launching pad for its US release, eventually earning four Oscar nominations and a "special award" for Larry.

Henry V marked the beginning of a magnificent decade in which Olivier believed he could do no wrong. But rather than slake his ambition, the double-triumph of that film and *Richard III* made him yearn for more. Actor-director Peter Glenville was awed (or was it appalled?) by his enormous appetite for success, his mono-maniacal desire to conquer the sacred beasts of the stage. He was "a sea monster [who] thought about nothing but the great classical roles. He wanted to appear with Vivien Leigh because he was very much in love with her. But his love was second to his obsession with acting."

A shift took place, not just in his raw drive but in his person-ality. As so often, Larry seemed to take on aspects of his roles—the ruthlessness of Richard and the grandeur of Henry. Many of his peers noted the former, while Charles Laughton singled out the latter. "Do you know, Larry, why you're so good in this part?" he once asked Olivier. "Because you *are* England!" And for a while, Olivier seemed to believe it. He was no longer the parson's son scrambling to make good: at thirty-seven years old, he was theater aristocracy, if not quite the real thing, and his altered sense of self became evident in his search for a country home.

In February 1945, he and Vivien took everything they'd saved, all £18,000 (more than $1 million today), and used it to buy a crumbling country estate that would be the terrestrial hub of their marriage. Notley Abbey was an enormous stone edifice a few miles outside Oxford, a religious abode founded in the mid-twelfth century that Henry VIII later gave to John London, a key figure in his dissolution of the monasteries and "a stout and filthy prebendary," as one contemporary called him, who was tasked with ferreting out heretics, many of them burned at the stake. Turned into a farmhouse, it later became a private home, but had long since fallen into ruin.

"Olivier has just bought a house for £15,000," Reissar reported to Selznick, getting the price slightly wrong but striking at the heart of the matter. "How he is going to meet that obligation unless he makes pictures, remains to be seen.... Meantime, the Oliviers are so short of money that the [Myron] Selznick agency has had to make them an advance against monies due to Vivien on May 1st."

Larry was obsessed with his new abode. If Vivien seemed less so at first, she was unwilling to go against him and came to love it as much as he did. Here Larry was able to indulge his baronial fantasies, walking through acres of land, overseeing cattle and sheep, and planting orchards of trees, helped by his brother Dickie, whom he hired as a live-in estate manager. The Oliviers would make the house the focus of their social lives, hosting soirees that would often kick off at midnight, when guests would arrive after seeing a show in London and settle down for a late supper, then stay up half the night, eating, drinking and playing the games Vivien adored.

"At Notley I had an affair with the past," wrote Larry. "For me it had mesmeric power; I could easily drown in its atmosphere. I could not let it alone; I was a child lost in its history. Perhaps I loved it too much, if that is possible."

Eventually he would love it more than Vivien.

On May 7, 1945, Germany surrendered, and men, women and children took to the streets to celebrate. "Many people in Britain didn't wait for the official day of celebration and began as soon as they heard the news on May 7," notes one historian. "After years of wartime restrictions and dangers—from food and clothes rationing to blackouts and bombing raids—it was understandable how eager they were to finally be able to let loose and enjoy themselves. Colourful bunting and flags soon lined the streets of villages, towns and cities across Britain. On the eve of VE day, bonfires were lit, people danced and the pubs were full of revellers."

"All the shops had got their rosettes and tri-coloured button-holes in the windows and men putting up lengths of little pennants and flags," noted the diarist Nella Last. "Till at three o'clock, the Germans announced it was all over. As if by magic, long ladders appeared, for putting up flags and streamers. A complete stranger to the situation could have felt the tenseness and feeling of expectation."

Churchill appeared on a balcony beside the royal family and addressed the nation. "We came back after long months from the jaws of death, out of the mouth of hell, while all the world wondered," he told the country. "When shall the reputation and faith of this generation of English men and women fail? I say that in the long years to come not only will the people of this island but of the world, wherever the bird of freedom chirps in human hearts, look back to what we've done and they will say 'do not despair, do not yield to violence and tyranny, march straight-forward and die if need be—unconquered.' "

Afterward, Vivien returned to the London stage for the first time in three years with Thornton Wilder's *The Skin of Our Teeth*. It was a risky choice: Tallulah Bankhead had played the lead, a woman who has been married twenty thousand years, with great success on Broadway; but Vivien at least had Larry as director. The play gave them a chance to be fully together after *Henry V* and *Richard III* had pulled them apart; it reminded them of everything they so admired in each other.

Skin opened on May 16, a week after Churchill's victory speech, and was an instant success. But Selznick was livid. "It is high time we stopped falling in with every whim of Vivien's, and catering to her caprices," he wrote Reissar. To another colleague, he emphasized: "You may think I am nuts, but we are dealing in nutty subjects."

Reissar fed his fury, describing the couple as the worst kind of prima donnas. "We talk of actors," she wrote after one meeting. " 'Can I have Robert [Donat] to play with me?' [Vivien] enquires, and I explain why it is impossible. She retorts: 'But there's nobody else here,' and I mention James Mason [not yet a big name]. She turns him down because she says she can't co-star with him. I agree co-starring is out of the question, and then she tells me she will not star alone. When I ask why, she says 'I just won't.' [After all this] she tells me she is dreadfully tired and must take a rest."

As to Olivier, he was "a far deeper person and with a much more tricky mind than Vivien. She is just inconsistent: she says what happens to be her opinion at that moment." Larry, Reissar noted, "is an extremely difficult and unreasonable person, and now that he has had his head somewhat turned by the production of *Henry V* he is even more difficult. He is a terrific highbrow and has got it into his head that only classics are worth bothering about."

After years of resistance, Selznick had had enough. A few weeks before *Skin* opened, he sued to block it from reaching the stage, claiming the contract he had signed with Vivien gave him "her exclusive services (apart from her obligations to Korda)," as his lawyer argued. "She has no right to appear in stage plays, on the radio, television, etc. *unless* Mr. Selznick's permission is obtained."

The case was legitimate, except for one thing: a California court had recently ruled in favor of de Havilland, who had fought Warners for extending her contract ad infinitum, resulting in a verdict that no such bond could continue beyond seven years. This was the grounds Vivien's lawyer used to claim she was legally exempt. He also claimed something else, more shocking: that his client was close to going broke—not entirely wrong, given the endless drain of Notley. If Vivien were held to the Selznick contract, the lawyer maintained, she would be unable to act and would be forced to do menial work, like thousands of others. The British tabloids went to town, dubbing her "Char lady Vivien."

Vivien won the case; but, in a horrible irony, she still had to leave the play. She had begun to cough again, and the cough was getting worse. At first she attributed this to the thick smog of London, which would lead to countless deaths (indeed, the Great Smog of 1952 killed four thousand people), as well as her own excessive smoking. Then, in the middle of the play, she collapsed and, after consulting two doctors, she discovered she had tuberculosis.

It was a harsh blow—not the death sentence it would once have been, but a terrible illness that would cast a pall over Vivien's life. Most of her friends believed she had contracted TB (or consumption, as it was once known) in Africa; but she may have had a bout during childhood. An extremely contagious, bacteria-borne disease, TB primarily affects the lungs, though it can also attack other parts of the body, causing pain as well as the coughing-up of blood. It spreads through coughing, spitting and speaking, passing from one person to another, often remaining latent and without symptoms; indeed, only about ten percent of those who have it develop an active case of the disease—though when they do, if untreated, it can be fatal. Getting TB in the 1940s was almost as troubling a prognosis as being told one was HIV-positive in the early years of AIDS. And there was nothing Vivien could do.

Romanticized by the Victorians, tuberculosis was a horrifically painful illness that led to a constant, racking cough, which would cause blood vessels to hemorrhage, leading to the bright red blood that tuberculars would spit out, staining their handkerchiefs and clothes. Prior to the Great War, one in four deaths around the world came from TB and, before the discovery of the antibiotics streptomycin and isoniazid (and their introduction to the public in the early 1950s), the only way to treat it was with sleep, fresh air and good food.

"In the decades before the introduction of chemotherapeutic interventions in the 1950s, treatment of tuberculous patients in Britain consisted of stays in regional sanatoria," note historians Sue Bowden and Alex Sadler. "Some sanatoria offered 'light treatment,' but the majority of centres were used to facilitate natural convalescence rather than offer curative treatment. They were also, and crucially, seen as a way of isolating an infected person from close family members—notably in homes where overcrowding was such that the infected person did not have use of a separate bedroom."

Vivien, who already had one disease, now carried another, equally serious and even deadlier. The combination of the two in an actress so young—she was thirty-one when she received her diagnosis—was devastating, not just to her professional life but also to her marriage.

She left *Skin* in July, after only seventy-eight performances, too weak to do anything but rest. "An ambulance took Vivien swiftly away to a private clinic in the rugged Scottish Highlands," a magazine reported, "where she lay before a great window opening on to the lonely mountainside, breathing the keen pure air, just sleeping or eating her special diet, not even permitted to read or listen to the radio."

Larry was on tour in Germany when he heard the news, and his letters home reveal his concern. Before her collapse, he had worried about her state of mind and told her how troubled he was "to feel that you are sad all the time [which] can't be good for you." Now he asked repeatedly about the doctor's reports and feared Vivien wasn't taking proper care. There's a tenderness in this correspondence, a sweetness that he rarely showed the outside world; still, he was forced into the role of caretaker just as he was entering his most challenging period creatively. He never complained, any more than Vivien did, no matter how bad her illness; but quietly, unconsciously, a resentment was building up, a slow drip of pain that would eventually undermine the foundations of the relationship.

Vivien was obliged to reassess her career. She was no longer in the full bloom of youth but the victim of a terminal disease. From this point forth, tuberculosis "was a spectre which never left her side," observed the Broadway director Chester Erskine. "Death was her partner from then on, although she cleverly and successfully concealed it. It ravaged her body, her mind, her spirit sometimes and, in my personal opinion, her marriage as well."

That summer, Vivien was admitted to University College Hospital, where she remained for six weeks, visited by Larry each morning, "although he was only admitted to her bedside for a few moments," noted one reporter. Returning to Notley, she was ordered to rest completely in the empty, echoing mansion that had yet to be fully furnished, where she was often alone while Larry was performing in London. As his vitality was surging, hers was shrinking. She had "a worm in the blood," said one of their colleagues, Esmond Knight. "It probably began to eat away something in her and this extraordinary deterioration began."

CHAPTER 10

While Vivien recuperated, Olivier embarked on a series of theatrical productions, dazzling in breadth and scope. Reenergized by *Henry V* and *Richard III,* he seemed to be further catalyzed by Vivien's illness, as if her very weakness fed his strength.

From *Richard* he went to *Henry IV* (parts I and 2), *Uncle Vanya, Oedipus Rex* and *King Lear*—all within a year, all for the Old Vic Company and all for a fraction of the salary he could have earned elsewhere. That puzzled Selznick to no end; he could never fathom why money mattered so little to this maddening man, even though he went through it like fish. He didn't understand that Larry was an obsessive like himself, that acting was as intoxicating for him as sex, an audience's applause as thrilling as "the miraculously soft warmth of a rapturous first night of love."

Vivien loved the stage, too, but it was only part of her life, not its raison d'être. She was content to spend time with her friends; to sit for long stretches reading Dickens, Confucius and Montaigne, her latest loves; to enrich her intellect while Larry enriched his craft. The writer-director Garson Kanin spoke of her "tremendous erudition, her wide reading," which seemed, if anything, to become even broader with her illness, while Larry's interests narrowed along a deep tunnel carved out by the needs of his characters. They resembled Isaiah Berlin's hedgehog and fox, to borrow his analogy: Vivien (the fox) had a knowledge of many things; Larry (the hedgehog) had a knowledge of only one.

A reporter, visiting them in London, gave a glimpse of what they were like at home, where "Tchee, the dainty little cream and brown Siamese cat, is usually running around Larry's legs or sitting in the tiny paved garden where Vivien grows scarlet geraniums and scented wallflowers. Inside the cottage itself there's a mixture of period furniture, mainly walnut pieces, which the Oliviers have picked up all over the world during their professional travels. Vivien's antique china has been collected in half a dozen different countries and Larry bought the two Mexican rugs when he first visited Hollywood in 1933." Here in Durham Cottage (which they retained along with Notley Abbey), the Oliviers would spend Sundays attending to correspondence, "working through it together. Larry squats at his green portable typewriter, puts on the heavy spectacles which always make Vivien laugh, and assumes the noisy quick-fire manner of the super-efficient Big Business Man dictating to his dumb secretary."

"Asked about their private life," she wrote, "both Larry and Vivien smile vaguely and turn the conversation to other channels. Nothing can make them self-communicative. They have been called aloof and unfriendly and even stand-offish, but that is not really true. They are two people seriously and sincerely dedicated to their work."

Increasingly, Olivier picked up the jagged parts of that private life and turned them into art. Blood didn't just seep from the blinded Oedipus's eyes; it gushed forth, as if flowing from Larry's inner wounds. And the gut-wrenching scream he famously let loose when Sophocles's hero discovers he has killed his father wasn't solely drawn from the screeching howl of an ermine

trapped in the Arctic wilds, as Larry claimed; it was also a pri-
mal scream, his own.

Work of this order lifted him into a different league from
his main rivals, Gielgud and Richardson. But the higher Larry
climbed, the more he feared a fall. Dreams of falling began to
puncture his sleep, nightmares of pitching from the "flies" or
tumbling from the sky. He had already had one such dream in
Hollywood, when he saw himself hurtling into the sea (a dream
that had almost come true when the plane's cockpit burst into
fire). Now images of that sort interrupted his nights, and the
more they did, the more they also pervaded his work. Plunging
and plummeting, diving and dropping became the visual tropes
of so many Olivier performances, it is hard not to view them as
emanations of his subconscious. Only by confronting his terrors
onstage, it seemed, could he defeat them—and then, twice, in
real life they came close to defeating him.

One evening, during a performance of Sheridan's comedy *The
Critic* (part of a jaw-dropping double bill with the ultimate tragedy, *Oedipus Rex*), Larry was hoisted high above the stage on a
cutout cloud, when he reached for a rope ladder and missed. He
would have crashed to the ground and been injured or killed if
he hadn't managed to clutch a dangling wire.

Then in June 1946, when he and Vivien were returning from
New York, where Larry had taken his Old Vic productions, the
couple looked out their plane window and saw one of the engines
in flames. It was the second time they'd flown on a plane that
caught fire and Vivien was petrified. "At 5:35 p.m., half an hour
into the flight, a shaft from one of the starboard engines to the
cabin pressurizer broke and thrashed around, setting fire to the
plane's hydraulic fluid," writes Terry Coleman, Olivier's authorized biographer. "The engine caught fire, and the plane's car-
bon dioxide extinguishers failed to put out the blaze. The pilot
turned back. The flames melted the engine mounting, and over

Plainfield, New Jersey, the flaming engine fell off the wing." Olivier, a trained pilot, knew just how much skill it took for the captain to land the plane, which hit the ground so hard it skidded three thousand feet. "It was the most magnificent piece of airmanship I've ever seen," he told the *Hartford Times*.

Forever after, Vivien would remember the passengers' frozen features. They looked like specters, she thought—only to realize: so did she.

She had accompanied Larry to New York as a wife, not an actress—a consort, not a queen—with little to do but bask in her husband's glory, just as he had had to bask in hers on the night of the Oscars. It was a sad reversal for a woman of such talent, which couldn't help but add to her insecurity. Perhaps she remembered what Larry had said during *Gone with the Wind*: that if she didn't put work first, she risked being "boring." Was she boring now?

Anxious to work, in September 1946 Vivien returned to *The Skin of Our Teeth*. It was a terrible mistake: she was still recuperating from TB and her illness had left her depressed. Weeks after resuming the role, she dropped out and returned to Notley Abbey, where she succumbed to an all-engulfing lassitude, a heaviness so great it felt as if she were being crushed under an invisible boulder, stripping her of her joie de vivre.

Much has been written about Vivien's mania; far less about her depression. And yet one was inextricable from the other. This was the nature of BP: a high was inevitably followed by a low and then another high, each liable to be triggered by an outside event such as stress or physical illness. There were times when these cycles would last for months and others when they would alternate in the blink of an eye. But the shifts were speeding up; after years in which Vivien had been relatively untroubled by her illness, it was coming back stronger than ever.

Vivian's mother, Gertrude Yackjee (right, with Vivian, as her name was then spelled), was born and brought up in Calcutta. Later, she tried to conceal her origins, telling MGM publicists she was Irish and her maiden name was Robinson. *(Courtesy of Victoria and Albert Museum, London)*

Vivian Hartley was ecstatic following her December 20, 1932, wedding to Leigh Holman. But her mother was distraught. "Terribly sad," she confided, after fleeing to the comfort of a wafer-thin musical. *(Courtesy of Victoria and Albert Museum, London)*

With a new name (Vivien Leigh) and a new daughter (Suzanne Holman, seen here in 1935), Vivien had every reason to look happy. But she chafed at motherhood and had already started to be unfaithful to her husband. *(Courtesy of Everett Collection)*

At age eight, Laurence Olivier was four years away from the death of his beloved mother. "There was undoubtedly a paradise in my childhood, and it lasted until my mother died," he said. "I've been looking for her ever since." *(Courtesy of Everett Collection)*

Both Larry and Jill Esmond were virgins on their wedding day. The next morning, in an act that would have made Freud proud, the groom accidentally shaved off half his mustache. *(Sasha/ Hulton, Archive/Getty Images)*

Vivien and Larry were making love "every day, two, three times" while shooting their first film together, 1937's *Fire Over England*. *(Courtesy of Everett Collection)*

Olivier had a decent rapport with Merle Oberon, seen here while making the 1938 romantic comedy *The Divorce of Lady X*. But their relationship soured on 1939's *Wuthering Heights*. Left to right: Oberon, producer Alexander Korda, costar Robert Taylor, Olivier, and director Tim Whelan. *(London-Denham/United, Artists/Kobal/Shutterstock)*

A few months after this 1935 photo of Vivien was taken at her London home, she saw Olivier for the first time and declared, "That's the man I'm going to marry." There was only one problem: she was already married—and so was he. *(Sasha/Hulton, Archive/ Getty Images)*

Vivien could barely hide her contempt for *Gone with the Wind* costar Clark Gable, whose coarse humor was visible in his latest toy: a gun shaped like a penis. *(MGM/ Photofest)*

No matter how exquisite Vivien seemed as Scarlett O'Hara, she and Larry were convinced the film would be a flop. "You have got to justify yourself by proving that the presumable failure of *Gone with the Wind* was not your fault," he warned. *(Courtesy of Everett Collection)*

Despite David O. Selznick's fears that the Olivier-Leigh affair would doom *Gone with the Wind*, the couple did little to disguise their romance. *(Snap/Shutterstock)*

Olivia de Havilland (third from left) believed more than a million people turned out for the 1939 premiere of *Gone with the Wind*. Among them were Selznick's partner, John Hay Whitney (left), Irene Mayer Selznick and her husband, David, and Vivien and Larry. *(Keystone-France/Gamma-Keystone via Getty Images)*

Larry and Vivien hoped to make a fortune from their 1940 stage production of *Hamlet*. Instead, they lost all their savings and one reviewer called Larry "the worst Romeo ever." *(Courtesy of Everett Collection)*

Larry admired director Alfred Hitchcock (sitting, center) but loathed his *Rebecca* costar, Joan Fontaine (in bonnet), partly because she had cost Vivien the role. *(Courtesy of Everett Collection)*

Marlon Brando believed Vivien's "sense of herself became vague" on 1951's *A Streetcar Named Desire*. "She began to dissolve and fray at the ends," he recalled. *(Warner Bros. Pictures/Photofest)*

"She had a small talent, but the greatest determination to excel of any actress I've ever known," said director Elia Kazan (center), seen here with Vivien at the *Streetcar* wrap party. *(Courtesy of Everett Collection)*

"Larry nearly went mad," one of Selznick's aides reported of Olivier's time as director and star of *Henry V*. *(Courtesy of Everett Collection)*

Actor Danny Kaye (top) was falsely alleged to be involved with Larry. He's seen here at a party he threw for the Oliviers, along with Vivien's daughter, Suzanne (top right), then age fifteen. *(Hart/ANL/Shutterstock)*

Vivien went through her worst manic episode while filming *Elephant Walk* in Ceylon with her lover, Peter Finch (center). She would be replaced by Elizabeth Taylor. *(Uncredited/AP/Shutterstock)*

After flying from Los Angeles to New York with his desperately sick wife, Olivier had to drag her onto a plane to London, with the help of Danny Kaye, while she started "screaming appalling abuse at both of us, with particular attention to my erotic impulses." *(Bettmann via Getty Images)*

Olivier lost patience with Marilyn Monroe on *The Prince and the Showgirl*. "Why can't you get here on time for fuck sake!" he demanded. "Oh," said Marilyn, "do you have that word in English, too?" *(Courtesy of Everett Collection)*

"At Notley I had an affair with the past," wrote Olivier of his country home, a twelfth-century monastery. "Perhaps I loved it too much, if that is possible." *(ANL/Shutterstock)*

Noël Coward remained close friends with the Oliviers, despite a shocking insensitivity to their problems. "If Larry had turned sharply on Vivien years ago and given her a clip in the chops," he wrote, "he would have been spared a mint of trouble." *(AGIP/ RDA/Everett Collection)*

Vivien found solace with actor Jack Merivale, who remained her companion until her death. *(Daily Mail/Shutterstock)*

Warren Beatty has never revealed whether he had an affair with Vivien on *The Roman Spring of Mrs. Stone. (Courtesy of Everett Collection)*

Vivien is seen here circa 1965, two years before her death. *(Photofest)*

In March 1961, Olivier and Joan Plowright were married outside New York, where Plowright was starring in *A Taste of Honey* and Olivier was appearing in *Becket*. *(Paul Slade/ Paris Match via Getty Images)*

The eighteen-year-old Sarah Miles began an affair with Olivier on 1962's *Term of Trial*. "He loved living on the edge," she said. "He loved that feeling of naughtiness, and he did like danger." *(Mary Evans/ AF Archive/Everett Collection)*

Vivien is pictured here on the lake at Tickerage Mill, her last home. *(Popperfoto via Getty Images)*

"You go on living," said Olivier, years after he and Vivien had split, "and there you are, knowing what has happened, remembering its details. Yet what else is there to do?" *(Courtesy of Victoria and Albert Museum, London)*

"In depression, a kind of biochemical meltdown, it is the brain as well as the mind that becomes ill—as ill as any other besieged organ," wrote the novelist William Styron in an influential 1988 account of his own psychic battles for the *New York Times*. "The sick brain plays evil tricks on its inhabiting spirit. Slowly overwhelmed by the struggle, the intellect blurs into stupidity. All capacity for pleasure disappears, and despair maintains a merciless daily drumming. The smallest commonplace of domestic life, so amiable to the healthy mind, lacerates like a blade. Thus, mysteriously, in ways difficult to accept by those who have never suffered it, depression comes to resemble physical anguish."

Try as Larry might, he could not raise Vivien's spirits, and with every rebuffed attempt he was reminded of his inadequacy. Then, when she emerged from her bleak state, the opposite condition kicked in. "Throughout his heaviest season ever—the immense physical strain on him increased by the need to commute—Olivier still had to find a way of responding to his wife's intense, if less frequent, spells of hysteria," writes Anthony Holden. "He could sense the worst when she became unusually agitated for a few days: her voice, her laughter, her nervous gestures all took on an obsessive edge. Above all her eyes could never settle. Once the objects of his worship, they would now find it hard to focus on him, on anyone or anything, darting hither and thither nervously. Soon would come an uncontrolled outburst of abuse and violence lasting hours, followed invariably by a long period of quiet, intense depression, then one of abject remorse."

Vivien did her best and even gave up smoking and drinking for a while in the hope that would help. But nothing worked. Nor did Gertrude's attempts to offer solace, to prove she was not "that horrible mother," as she put it, now that she and Suzanne were back from Canada. Once, Vivien lashed out at her in a rage, "gave way to a fit of fury with poor Gertrude and tore her breast, hurting her badly," Olivier recalled. "Gertrude forgave her at once and never mentioned it again."

Vivien's illness "made her behave in all sorts of very extreme and uncharacteristic ways," recalls Hayley Mills. She would have "sudden bouts of extraordinary generosity, when she would give people jewelry and [other valuable gifts]. Radie Harris, the gossip columnist, was a great friend of hers, and one day Vivien pulled off her mink coat and gave it to her."

She began to stay up all night, surrounding herself with aco-lytes and acquaintances who would descend on Notley and turn it upside down. Actor Godfrey Winn remembered making the fifty-mile drive from London with Orson Welles, Rex Harrison and Harrison's wife, Lilli Palmer, in tow. Arriving at 1:00 a.m., he was escorted inside. "Just as he was wondering if he dared ask for a biscuit," writes Hugo Vickers, "a lavish candlelit dinner was served. The evening ended in broad daylight, at which point Vivien took him on a tour of the garden." The visitor had barely gone to bed when a maid knocked on his door to say Vivien "would like you to join her for a game of bowls."

"An attitude circulated that these weekend parties were in some way exclusive gatherings of a small and somewhat supe-rior theatrical clique," observed one regular. "It was never like that. Vivien adored her home and she was never happier than when she could share the peace and beauty of Notley. I think Larry would have appreciated their being on their own a little more. But Vivien was one of those people who must have people around her. They were not wild parties nor in any way particu-larly unusual—except possibly that they gave us a chance to relax and be ourselves far removed from the artificiality that surrounds much of the life of the theatre."

At first Larry embraced this social whirl, content in his patri-cian role; but increasingly he dreaded the next influx. Time and

again, he begged Vivien to slow down, to no avail: she had energy
to burn—sometimes literally, says Juliet Mills: "I remember when
we were staying over at Notley, and they had some terrible row
that I was hearing through the walls, and [Larry] slammed out
of the room, and about half an hour later there was smoke and
Vivien had set the bed on fire."

Olivier won a temporary reprieve from all this in April 1947
when Vivien began work on a new film, *Anna Karenina*. It
seemed like perfect casting: she was as charismatic and compelling as Tolstoy's heroine and loved the novel so much she had
even convinced playwright Thornton Wilder to give it a second
read. But tackling one of fiction's greatest heroines was a double-
edged sword, especially since it meant taking a role Greta Garbo
had made her own.

The two had met briefly at a Hollywood party, where Vivien
had felt pangs of misplaced jealousy as Larry reconnected with
the star who had him fired. Talented as she was, she could not
compete with one of the screen's most remarkable actresses. But
Garbo aside, there were red flags that should have warned her to
steer clear. For one thing, director Julien Duvivier was an odd
choice, best known for his 1937 gangster film, *Pépé le moko*,
and his vision quickly collided with Vivien's. Whereas Vivien saw
Anna as a woman possessed by lust as well as love, Duvivier
considered her an angel untarnished by such base urges. Nor did
Jean Anouilh's script make things easier; the French playwright,
whose modern rendering of *Antigone* had been a wartime sensation, preferred to keep his characters at a distance and was the
last person Korda, the producer, should have hired for a romantic
tragedy.

Once filming began, matters went from bad to worse when
Vivien was forced into an unbearably tight corset and struggled to breathe—a problem that continued for days, until she

realized she was wearing it upside down. Then she had to deal with her costar, Kieron Moore, a good-looking newcomer who had stepped into the role when Michael Redgrave stepped out, but who had none of his talent. If Vivien had been on form, she might have made this work, just as she had with Clark Gable. But she was still depressed, and the result was an exquisite but disappointing performance in an exquisite but disappointing film.

"Leigh dominates the picture, as she rightly should, with her beauty, charm and skill," noted *Daily Variety*. "It isn't her fault that eyes remain dry and hearts unwrung."

There was something else, too, as Vivien's friend, the art historian Kenneth Clark, observed—something that kept Vivien from engaging with her character. "For some reason she couldn't convey the feeling of love," he said. "She could act it very skilfully, but one never felt it was really true. She was a passionate, but totally unsentimental character."

Vivien had hoped to go from *Anna Karenina* to playing Ophelia in Larry's new film, a version of *Hamlet* in which he would star as well as direct. But J. Arthur Rank, the financier, insisted on a younger woman, and after token resistance, Larry capitulated. Once, he would have fought on the ramparts for Vivien, just as he had with *Wuthering Heights* and *Rebecca*. But not now.

His own commitment to the role was shaky. Before filming, he had tried to find someone else to play the prince, aware that he was old for the part and mistakenly thinking another man would willingly perform it as he wanted. "I would have liked to have found an actor of sufficient standing to carry the role on whom I could have impressed my interpretation of the character of Hamlet without the actor resenting it," he explained. But that was impossible, of course; no actor "of sufficient standing" would have agreed to copy Larry.

With nobody else available, he took the lead himself and then became consumed by it to the exclusion of all else. On Vivien's advice, he cut out such minor figures as Rosencrantz and Guildenstern; gave Fortinbras's closing speech to Horatio; reworked the order of the scenes; and eliminated several soliloquies including Hamlet's "Oh, what a rogue and peasant slave am I," while "How all occasions do inform against me" was left on the cutting-room floor.

Ninety-three actresses auditioned for Ophelia and twenty-two were given screen tests before Larry opted for Jean Simmons, a newcomer with a passing resemblance to Vivien. He was willing to bet that the eighteen-year-old—who had impressed him in David Lean's *Great Expectations*—could handle the challenge of playing a young woman who goes mad. But signing her was no simple thing, and to get her, Larry tussled with Michael Powell, who had booked her as the Indian lead in *Black Narcissus*, which he planned to shoot at the same time as *Hamlet*.

"Dear Larry, anybody can play Ophelia. I can play Ophelia," he joked.

"Dear Micky," Olivier shot back, "how you could imagine that a typical English teenager, straight from the vicarage, can play a piece of Indian tail, beats me. I enclose a book of erotic Indian pictures to help your casting director. Love, Larry."

Rank intervened, rearranging the movies' schedules so that Simmons could appear in both, and Vivien alone lost out. Still without work, she fretted that Olivier would trade her in for the younger woman, and perhaps because of that, as one reporter observed, "when Vivien wasn't in front of the cameras herself, she was on the *Hamlet* set with Larry. She was the only visitor he permitted to enter that closely sealed and constantly guarded corner of the Denham studio. [Her] name doesn't appear on the credit lists but it should for she has discussed all Larry's ideas of *Hamlet* with him and helped him rehearse for hours on end."

She was more vulnerable than before, more aware that he was pulling away from her professionally and personally. Nor were her instincts wrong: he was attracted to this teenager and would perhaps have made a move if she hadn't been in love with Stewart Granger, with only thirty days to work on his film before leaving for *Narcissus*. Larry took out his resentment on Simmons once shooting began in May 1947. During Ophelia's drowning scene, he insisted on dunking her over and over again. "We had a perfect double for her," recalled Bushell, the film's associate producer, "but she would lie down in the bloody stream again + again, with Laurence at his bloodiest-minded + paying more attention to the precise fall of the 'willow [that grows] aslant a brook / That shows his hoar leaves in the glassy stream.'"

Larry chose another young actress, Eileen Herlie (thirteen years his junior), as Hamlet's mother, Gertrude, because he wished to highlight the sexual tension among her, Claudius and Hamlet, an idea that soon imploded. "Laurence's first + v. strong intention," wrote Bushell, "was to cast Claudius and Gertrude so that he could project a dual image he always regretted not to have seen in other productions ie:—that King and Queen were still sexually obsessed with each other—to the exclusion of virtually all else around them—including Hamlet. And to get this he was determined to get Godfrey Tearle and Diana Wynyard to play the parts. Alas and alack, the dread cancer had already hit Godfrey and Diana couldn't get out of a West End hit she was adorning. And we were stuck with Herlie and Basil Sydney [as Claudius]—who further mucked any such possible interpretation up by taking a cordial dislike to each other during rehearsals."

Olivier complained frequently about Sydney, whom he called "constipated." "This latter was a favourite, and vivid, description of certain actors by Milord Olivier," added Bushell. "I remember as if yesterday when we finally got Basil Sydney through Claudius's prayer ending 'Help angels, all may yet be well,' Laurence saying 'it's no good going on—he'll still be constipated after twenty takes. Print it.'"

No longer a neophyte, Larry was now a forty-year-old who celebrated his birthday a few days before filming. To many who worked with him here, he seemed grander and more remote than he had on *Henry V*, a patriarch who was beginning to resemble his father. Flickers of humor alternated with flashes of anger; traces of the younger Larry remained, but the man who had once seemed like "one of the lads" was rarely that way again. He controlled everything with a guardedness he had never shown before.

"Larry forbade everybody except the players and technicians actually engaged in the scene," reported *Screenland*. "Even the artists waiting to be called were not allowed to go on the set while other scenes were being shot. They sat out in the corridor, as ignorant of what was happening as all the studio staff. Press reporters and photographers never reached the threshold. Once an enterprising cameraman who climbed up to the roof seeing a private peephole found his ladder had been quietly removed and spent several hours aloft in the rain before he was rescued. Larry was completely adamant that nobody should see sufficient of the film to make any criticisms until *Hamlet* was officially shown on the screen. 'I'm trying out something completely different in technique,' he explained to his intimate friends. 'I haven't even got a complete script. I'm altering and improving and experimenting as I go along.'"

To those on-set, Vivien seemed lighter than her husband. "Handsome mobile-faced Larry tends to be conservative and cautious, always thorough and careful and sometimes slow, with a fierce streak of obstinacy when it's aroused," wrote another reporter, unaware of the currents crisscrossing their marriage. "Vivien balances him because she is essentially light and quick and incisive. She encourages him out of those moods of introspective depression which sometimes overwhelm him, because he is never satisfied in his constant search for perfection in his work."

Whereas Larry had begun *Henry V* with its most challenging scene—the Battle of Agincourt—here he left the hardest to last, a jump from fifteen feet high at the climactic moment of the play, when Hamlet stabs Claudius with his sword. It was another leap, another fall; but this time Larry had to perform with a broken ankle, which he had damaged earlier on. He was intensely aware of the risks. "I could kill myself," he reflected. "I could damage myself for life; I could hurt myself badly enough to make recovery a lengthy business; I could hurt myself only slightly; or I could get away with it without harm." When he finally mustered the courage to leap, he did it so hard he knocked Basil Sydney out cold, along with two of the poor man's teeth. It was "the one brave moment of my life," Larry observed later, blissfully indifferent to his victim.

On July 8, 1947, halfway through the shoot (which would earn Larry his first and only Oscar as best actor), he was knighted at Buckingham Palace. He borrowed his tails from Bushell, hair still close-cropped and dyed blond (in fact, almost yellow) for *Hamlet*. Vivien, accompanying him, was dressed elegantly, with small earrings and a perfect pearl necklace. She was exquisite in her black dress, but oddly sad. Kneeling before King George VI, Olivier was nervous, he told journalists. "I like to have a dummy run before I do anything, but there wasn't any rehearsal." Later, he made fun of the occasion, gently mocking the king for his well-known stutter.

None of this was funny to Vivien. Her husband may have achieved one of his dreams, becoming Sir Laurence at last—and she may have had the glory of being Lady Olivier; but their new rank also separated them from their simpler past. As the ceremony took place, "Vivien, sitting nearby on a golden chair, was deeply moved," noted a reporter. "Her lovely eyes filled with tears of emotion, though she quickly brushed them aside and gave her radiant smile."

CHAPTER 11

O nce, Vivien and Larry had dreamed of becoming the royal couple of the stage and now they tried to revive that idea with a six-month tour of Australia in which they would be together, onstage and off, all the time. But in the weeks before they left, they bickered constantly. Watching them rehearse *Richard III*, *The Skin of Our Teeth* and Sheridan's eighteenth-century comedy *The School for Scandal*, their friend Mercia Swinburne believed Vivien was experiencing "a great struggle theatrically against the overpowering thing of Larry."

She seemed to find fault with everything he did. One of the designer Cecil Beaton's assistants found her "entirely destructive" in her critiques and remembered watching as she and Olivier glared "daggers at each other [after lunch], having obviously argued like mad all the way through the meal." Another time, when Larry asked Vivien to fall off a chair, the actress, "who never lets a chance slip by of contradicting him piped up 'Larry, she wouldn't do anything of the sort—it's right out of character...' and so on for some time. L.O. bore it for a while and then said through clenched teeth 'The Lady Anne will fall off her chair if I have to bloody well push her off myself!'"

Australia gave the couple a chance to reset. A scouting

expedition had paved the way, reporting back that large, spacious theaters were just waiting to be filled and, if culture was wanting, enthusiasm was not: the locals were eager to embrace these demigods, the subject of wild speculation Down Under. Larry alone, it was said, had a fortune "between a quarter and half a million pounds," a figure that made mockery of the truth: he owed back taxes all the way to 1939.

In February 1948, the Oliviers joined the rest of the cast and crew onboard the SS *Corinthic* and set off for Perth. As the ship eased out of its Liverpool dock, chugged down the Mersey estuary and into the Irish Sea, before embarking on its monthlong voyage, Larry, despite searing pain from gout (like "white hot needles in my right toe," he said), a symptom of his increasing drinking, got straight to work, calling rehearsals each morning and spending the afternoons alone, gazing at the hammerhead sharks and flying fish before returning to rehearsals in the evening. He was a man obsessed, while Vivien was more relaxed: she read, played cards and spent time with her new friends.

The company loved them and nicknamed them God and the Angel. One of the cast, Peter Cushing, remained forever grateful to Larry for letting him bring his wife on the tour and making her useful with small roles and backstage chores. But Vivien was even more popular, as almost always during her nonmanic spells. "The cast were devoted to her," recalled Swinburne, who nonetheless failed to spot warnings of trouble: a longtime cat lover, Vivien spent hours writing home, not to a human being but to her favorite feline, New Boy, ominously signing her letters "Clara the alley cat."

Having left England in the midst of a bitter winter, the ship docked in Fremantle, Perth's port, on March 15 during a summer heat wave. Temperatures soared above a hundred degrees with no place to find relief, least of all the unair-conditioned hotels where most of the company stayed, while Vivien and Larry were lodged in an apartment overlooking the Swan River. They found themselves in a rough-and-ready city of 250,000, where ancient trams squeaked up and down the streets from four in the morning until late at night; where strange birds—buff-banded rails, black-shouldered kites and squadrons of ring-necked parrots—squawked from dawn to dusk; and where sleep was next to nonexistent as they battled the stifling conditions. Rivers of sweat ran down their faces and arms, forcing them to launder their shirts over and over. They gasped for air, flopped in any body of water they could find, while still giving their all during rehearsals.

At least there was food and drink: sixteen-ounce steaks, mountains of butter, and as much beer as the cast could consume. This was extravagance itself for men and women who had considered a half dozen eggs the definition of luxury in a country where food was still rationed, and it was almost enough to compensate for the city's aggravations, like the mosquitoes as big as "flying elephants," one visitor recalled.

With the British government partly funding their trip, the Oliviers were cultural emissaries and had endless obligations besides their plays. Vivien was a model of discretion, ignoring the locals' sometimes-comic blunders, including her favorite: addressing her as "Sir Lady." But the interminable meetings with dignitaries and VIPs were exhausting, and the couple was bombarded with social requests—asked to attend everything from a tour of the Shakespeare Room in the New South Wales state library to a student production of *Oedipus Rex*—while being showered with more than a thousand fan letters per week. "One is always on one's feet 'saying a few words' & you know how that terrifies me," Vivien wrote Ralph Richardson's wife, Meriel. "Larry is getting wonderful at it though."

Backstage, the Oliviers were equally gracious and agreed to share their private dressing room with the other actors, while

Vivien helped sew and iron costumes. "Vivien Leigh came into the wardrobe at three this afternoon and stayed till 10.30," marveled one cast member the night before they opened. "Sir Laurence has been in the theatre all the time since he arrived. I cannot tell you what it is to work with them, nothing is too much trouble, they are both so full of energy."

The morning tickets went on sale, a 120-yard line formed at the box office, and an hour before the premiere some 2,280 Australians had gathered inside the Capitol Theatre, dressed to the nines in suits and furs despite the broiling weather. Their excitement was at fever pitch as they took their seats and then stood to sing "God Save the King," their voices rising against the rackety air-conditioning. Then they watched, rapt, as two liveried servants emerged from the darkness to "light" the footlights, while Handel's music swelled and the curtain rose to reveal Lady Sneerwell (Swinburne) plotting with her malevolent aide, Snake (Oliver Hunter). Ten minutes later, Olivier made his entrance as the doddering Sir Peter Teazle, looking so old that most of the crowd didn't recognize him.

" 'Tis now six months since Lady Teazle made me the happiest of men," he declared, "and I have been the most miserable dog ever since that ever committed wedlock! We tiffed a little going to church and came to a quarrel before the bells had done ringing. I was more than once nearly choked with gall during the honeymoon and had lost all comfort in life before my friends had done wishing me joy."

Then Vivien appeared as his wife, her hair a blond mass of curls and flowers, gorgeous and utterly in her element. "Sir Peter," she complained, "you may scold or smile, according to your humor, but I ought to have my way in everything, and what's more I will, too!"

The production was a smash hit. "We were the first company to play there for 12 years," noted Larry. "And do you know what everybody said to us? They said, 'In the second act you began to speak up.' But in reality it was they who by the second act had learned to listen."

When the players left Perth in early April, the entire country was on fire with excitement. "They [had] expected a certain amount of adulation," noted an assistant, "but nothing like what they received." Flying to Adelaide, Vivien shrieked with joy as the sun rose over the infinite vistas of the Nullarbor Plain and insisted on waking the others to see it too.

In Adelaide, a hurricane tore through the city on April 11, uprooting trees, ripping off roofs, yanking a jetty from its mooring and hurling a ship onto the beach, but Larry insisted they carry on and delivered such an explosive performance as Richard that one critic "felt almost a physical weariness when the curtain fell at the finale."

He was thrilled when Vivien won plaudits for *Skin of Our Teeth*. She was "better than ever," he noted in his diary. And yet, deep down, she was not. The reporters who followed her all the time dubbed her "Miss Vitamin B," astonished at her energy and unaware that vitamins had nothing to do with it. Then something started to shift, within both the troupe and the country at large. A tour that had begun so well faltered, either because the actors were growing tired or because the excess of expectation could only be met with disappointment.

As Vivien's mood changed, so did others' perception of her and the group. She was "a strange woman," writes Garry O'Connor, who interviewed many of the cast and crew for his book *Darlings of the Gods* and felt that Vivien's personality seemed to "smother" Olivier's. A wonderful hostess, she would invite members of the troupe to dinner, but she would also display flashes of fury, often directed at her husband. Their fighting was even noticed by passersby, who could hear them yelling from the apartments they had rented. Away from Vivien, Larry bemoaned her "damned awful fuss."

Needing a break after weeks on the road, the Oliviers left for a few days' vacation at a seaside resort, Surfers Paradise, only to find five hundred people waiting for them outside the airport and a fleet of journalists ready to pounce.

By the time they reached Melbourne, their enthusiasm had plummeted, along with the crowds'. Larry wrote his Old Vic partner John Burrell that audiences here were "piss-elegant and nervously smug at first. There's a great feeling of tense humourless fear that one is getting at them all the time." One reporter complained, "We have better *Richard III*s here in Melbourne." Another carped that *Skin* was so weak, the company might as well have performed that old chestnut *Charley's Aunt*.

For the first time, Larry was beginning to feel his age. At forty-one, his looks were changing: his upper lip had grown thin and, if it wasn't yet the harsh line he would use to such villainous effect in 1960's *Spartacus* and 1976's *Marathon Man*, it was enough to subtly diminish his looks. Self-conscious about his appearance, he felt naked without his mustache, which also covered the scar from his collision with the horse in *Henry V*. As for Vivien, whenever her disorder flared up she would lose weight, and she now looked so frail that a university student feared "she was going to float away."

She was only too aware of the younger women muscling for her husband's attention and was visibly slighted when Larry waxed on about Jean Simmons when asked to speak to some students—though he was only describing the trouble he had had in coaxing a performance. Ever so slightly, as he spoke, Vivien pulled away her chair.

Arriving in Sydney in mid-June, the pair became prey for the world's most bloodthirsty tabloids. "I once thought I'd like to be

Sir Laurence Olivier," a reporter mused after a press conference, "but not after the time the press boys and press girls gave him at Usher's [a downtown bar] last night: they did everything but play football with him. They knew they had the best of him once they got him in the corner. I don't know whether someone pushed Sir Laurence, but he sat down on the lowest couch I've ever seen. The rest was easy.... Just when we'd reached some high cultural plane one fellow at the back yelled: 'Break it up; let's have a go at him!'"

Despite this, Larry delivered his finest *Richard III*. Spurred by his jealousy toward Dan Cunningham, a fellow cast member who had flirted with Vivien, he flew at the hapless man, who was still recuperating from five years as a prisoner of war and still getting over his wife's desertion. But that didn't mitigate Larry's anger. Onstage, he unleashed the full force of his anger—his "splendid fury," as Ralph Richardson described it—and flung his sword at the actor, who "just managed to shield [it] off him," as a colleague recalled. "Sir Laurence remembered [Edmund] Kean had done that; [but] he had never rehearsed it or anything."

Olivier paid the price for his attack when a burning pain ripped through his leg. It wasn't his gout: he had torn the cartilage in his knee. A morphine shot helped, but he then ignored his doctor's advice to rest. "Next day," writes O'Connor, "he found a period crutch which he put to brilliant use, integrating it into his performance just as if Shakespeare had written the part for an actor using a crutch. So expert did he become in its employment that on Monday night he broke it in rage on the back of George Cooper, playing Brackenbury, and stage-hands had to work frantically to make it a new end."

In the midst of all this, Larry was astonished to receive a letter from Lord Esher, the chairman of the Old Vic board, informing him that he was being dropped as artistic director, along with the others in the Vic triumvirate, Richardson and Burrell. The organization, Esher argued, could not be run "by men, however able, who have other calls upon their time and talent," a judgment that may have been true but quite overlooked the reason for the Australian tour: to raise money for the theater. The letter stung all the more given that Olivier had just written to congratulate Esher on the passage of the National Theatre Bill, which set aside £1 million for a new building in London, ultimately to be run by Larry himself. "O ME," he cabled Burrell. "I SEE THE ENDING OF OUR HOUSE."

Later, he claimed all he could do was laugh. But in truth, he was badly hurt and blamed Tyrone Guthrie, his former friend—the man who had put this leadership team in place—for turning against him. He was "the rogue elephant who kicked the whole thing down," said Burrell's wife, Margaret, who believed the director was bitter at not receiving a knighthood in the same year as Olivier and Richardson.

Leaving Sydney for Brisbane, and then Brisbane for New Zealand, Larry saw Vivien trembling. On the plane to Auckland, a flight attendant, Anne Chandler, noted her paleness "and attributed it to too much party-going and to her dislike of flying"—rather understandable, given the Oliviers' previous misadventures. "But Anne found herself in no way prepared for what happened halfway through the journey when they were flying over the water at 11,000 feet," writes O'Connor. "Suddenly Vivien became breathless and started fighting for air. The pilot quickly brought the plane down to 4,000 feet, and fortunately on board they had a portable oxygen mask which Anne applied to Vivien's face."

Upon landing, she was rushed to the hospital and seemed to recover. But both she and Larry had reached their limits. "Somehow, somewhere on this tour," Olivier wrote later, "I knew that Vivien was lost to me."

Forced to rehearse in a freezing Christchurch theater as

winter brought an end to the Indian summer they had encountered on their arrival, the Oliviers broke into "a blazing row during which they made little attempt to restrain their language,"
notes O'Connor. "The cause was Lady Teazle's red shoes, which
could not be found anywhere: instead of gracefully accepting a
substitute, Vivien stormed at the staff who cowered before her
brilliant green eyes flashing at them from below stage eyelashes.
Before the girls could escape, Olivier himself appeared, telling
Vivien she was late and to grab any shoes and get up on stage.
Only moments later, after her refusal, and calling her a bitch, he
slapped her face and at once she hit him back, referring to him
as a 'bastard' for hitting her."

He was fighting her even as his leg was getting worse. When
more morphine failed to help, he agreed to an operation and in
Wellington a doctor sliced open his leg, removing the ruptured
cartilage. That repaired Larry's knee but left him unable to walk.

On October 18, 1948, the Oliviers boarded the *Corinthic* for
the long voyage home. Rain was spattering down, turning the
water gray and the sky leaden, a sad contrast to the cloudless
blue firmament that had met them upon their arrival. Larry's leg
was in plaster—not that anybody seemed to care except a young
girl, who held an umbrella above his prostrate body as he was
laid on a stretcher and hoisted to his cabin.

Vivien boarded the ship alone. She was doing everything to
make him suffer: dressing provocatively, openly disparaging him,
dancing with any eligible young man and showing no interest in
his pain. The most glamorous couple in the world left Australia
bedraggled, dog-tired and barely talking. Once, they had been so
full of life; but now, in Larry's words, they were little more than
"walking corpses."

CHAPTER 12

————◆————

Weeks later, in early 1949, the Oliviers were sitting at home when Vivien spoke up. "It came like a small bolt from the blue, like a drop of water," Larry recalled. "I almost thought my ears had deceived me: 'I don't love you any more....There's no one else or anything like that; I mean, I still love you but in a different way, sort of, well, like a brother.' "

The shock was profound, despite the rift that had deepened in Australia. He "felt as if I had been told that I had been condemned to death. The central force of my life, my heart in fact, as if by the world's most skillful surgeon, had been removed. It left me agasp but not gasping; it was as if I had been rendered forever still inside, like a fish in a refrigerator."

Did Vivien mean what she said? Kay Redfield Jamison, the psychiatrist, notes the bipolar person's uncanny gift for twisting the knife where it hurts. To expect graciousness would be folly, she says: "There's no nice way of putting it. People are foul-mouthed, they're abusive, they're violent, they're just dreadful. There's nothing nice about [their behavior]."

The couple continued to have sex—as Larry ruefully observed, despite their new, nominally fraternal relationship, "occasional acts of incest were not discouraged." But Vivien was entering a dark and frightening period of her life; she was coping with moods she couldn't fathom, let alone control, even if she was beginning to recognize something was wrong.

"When she had the breakdowns and behaved very, very violently," said Gielgud, "she would always, afterwards, write letters and go and see the people, the nurses who had looked after her, and apologize for having upset them. It must have been a dreadful thing to know [that] was coming on."

Vivien returned to the stage with two hits—a resumption of *School for Scandal* and Anouilh's *Antigone*—performed in repertoire with Larry's continuing *Richard III*. But no matter how well she did, she was constantly reminded that her talent paled beside his. To compensate for their struggles, the Oliviers kept living beyond their means, accumulating ever-more ferociously: furniture; trees for their garden; paintings by Renoir, Degas and Bonnard; and even a new Bentley fitted with the "best quality twill upholstery covers to the four seats and squabs in the same materials as used for the Daimler cars we recently supplied to His Majesty," according to the dealer. Their problems persisted, regardless. Vivien needed something more than a Bentley to validate her. But what?

After eighteen years of marriage, Irene Mayer Selznick had had enough. She was sick of men, fed up with their bullying, brazen ways, done with her father's enormous ego and her husband's bottomless needs. Why couldn't people see that, without her, David would have been just another Hollywood hustler chasing after power and girls, like the one he was planning to marry now, Jennifer Jones? He and Irene had finally broken up and she was reimagining her life on the brink of turning forty. She was a dominant if soft-spoken woman, one with "the most extraordinary powers of will, or drive, or vitality—or whatever you call it—that I've ever seen," said the playwright Tennessee Williams.

And yet now she was adrift, cut loose from one magic kingdom, Hollywood, and trying to drop anchor in another, Broadway.

Moving to New York, she decided to become a producer, not in the movies but the theater, where it was her cash rather than her intelligence that initially appealed to Audrey Wood, Williams's agent. The writer had tangled with his previous backers and knew that Irene was a "Female Moneybags," "supposed to have 16 million dollars *and* good taste. I am dubious."

He was wrong. Unlike many of her contemporaries, Irene recognized a masterpiece when she saw it and knew just how good Williams's latest work was, when Wood sent it over. That night, reading the play after canceling a date, she was "overwhelmed by its power and beauty," brokenhearted by its story of a former schoolteacher with a mysterious past who leaves Mississippi to move in with her sister, only to disintegrate in her New Orleans home, amid revelations of sexual promiscuity. "I was speechless, dazed with disbelief," Irene recalled. "Finally I managed to get a few words out [to Wood]: 'What would your author say?' He already knew; anyway, he always left it up to her. I was beside myself with panic. I repeated, 'Why me? Why me?' "

Vivien had no such doubts when she read *A Streetcar Named Desire*—though by then it was a year later, after it had become a Broadway legend with Jessica Tandy as Blanche DuBois and Marlon Brando as Stanley Kowalski. She could barely control her excitement at the thought of playing Blanche in the West End, under Larry's direction, of course.

Larry was less convinced. The play was seamy, he thought, and its subjects—homosexuality, prostitution, nymphomania—were all but unmentionable on the British stage, where they would surely draw the wrath of the Lord Chamberlain, Britain's censor. He knew too well that the Chamberlain and his "examiners of plays" (all based in Buckingham Palace, the very place where he had been knighted) had almost killed Coward's brilliant early comedy, *The Vortex*, and that they had insisted on major changes to *Private Lives*, the first giant hit of Larry's career. Back then, he was too myopically focused on his own role to consider anything else; but now he was wiser and worldlier and therefore more wary. He was Sir Laurence Olivier, after all, a pillar of the establishment, with a reputation to maintain and a knighthood to cherish, an honor he held sacred.

British theater was still gliding in the slipstream of its pre-war masters, men like Coward and Terence Rattigan, whose elegant comedies and effete characters filled plays that had not fundamentally changed in style or intent, despite the upheavals of World War II. Had these writers wished to break their mold, they would have had trouble: the censor's strict limits all but stifled avant-garde creativity—even improvisation was forbidden, as the actor Richard Harris would find out a few years later when he was fined for impersonating Churchill at the mock-unveiling of a public toilet.

England had always been ambivalent about message-driven theater and Larry shared that sentiment. He wanted to create spectacles rather than become one himself, and he therefore played safe in his choice of material. No matter how bold his acting, he had largely confined himself to the canon; indeed, from the mid-1940s to the mid-1950s, he would only direct or star in six contemporary works: Wilder's *The Skin of Our Teeth*, Garson Kanin's *Born Yesterday*, Anouilh's *Antigone*, Christopher Fry's *Venus Observed*, Denis Cannan's *Captain Carvallo* and Rattigan's *The Sleeping Prince*. None of these works—not one—addressed the political upheavals that were rocking the country: the introduction of the "welfare state," the creation of a national health system and the nationalization of vast portions of the economy. Success, for Olivier, had become all about reinventing the past, not revolutionizing the present.

Still, driven to support Vivien despite their troubles, he told

Irene he was keen to direct *Streetcar* in England, with Vivien as Blanche. "TREMENDOUSLY ENTHUSIASTIC ABOUT PROSPECT AND HOPE IT WILL FRUCTIFY," he told the producer, his ornate choice of language revealing his ambivalence. Fructify? That sounded "pretty exotic," she noted.

Like her ex-husband, she had never cared for Larry, any more than his wife. She remembered all too well the difficulties they had caused David, and had followed the ins and outs of his lawsuit against Vivien, the one he had lost. Besides, other directors were hot on *Streetcar*'s trail, including Olivier's friend-turned-rival Guthrie (whom Irene had almost hired for the Broadway production when she was at loggerheads with Elia Kazan). But now she had to be careful: In England she would have far less clout than in New York, where producers held ultimate power, not directors or stars—and that made it crucial for her to find the right partner. Could it be Olivier? *Should* it be?

She turned to impresario Binkie Beaumont for advice. "Apparently in London 'Binkie' was a magic name,. a password," she recalled. "Not to know its meaning was to be illiterate."

Seeking to be literate, in 1948 she traveled to London to sound him out and found him waiting at Waterloo Station in his chauffeured Rolls-Royce. Effortlessly charming, invisibly manipulative, silken and smooth, he was the perfect counterweight to the intense Irene and quickly tipped the scales in the Oliviers' favor. "By the time we reached Claridge's [Hotel]," marveled the neophyte, "I was swept with admiration....He was unprepared for so quick a victory. It was almost an anticlimax....I mentioned Vivien. Oh, a great friend! He happened to know she adored the play....Larry? Well, that might be managed. I detected less enthusiasm and no intimacy."

Olivier was her priority, however, as he was Williams's. The writer was in Rome, working on a short story, *The Roman Spring of Mrs. Stone* (later to be filmed with Vivien in the title role), and developing the Italian version of *Streetcar* with director Luchino Visconti. Absorbed in this work, he kept a distance, favoring Larry while remaining skeptical about his wife. "The prestige of his name, and his great gifts as a showman, must certainly be considered," he granted, "although I have yet to see Vivian [sic] give a striking performance."

Irene convinced him otherwise—at least partially. "You have evidently given the matter a great deal of consideration, and I am glad to see that you have included in your consideration that Mme. Olivier has not yet given us a ghost of an idea of her latent dramatic powers," Williams told her. "But I believe, as you do, that Mr. Olivier is a smart cookie who would not want Vivien to lay anything bigger than [an] ostrich egg on the London stage even in a play by an American author." He added: "If only we could be devastatingly frank with Sir Laurence, and say, Honey, we want *you* but could do without *her*!"

Vivien could not do without Williams. She had "fastened her hopes" on Blanche, Larry believed, ignoring his warning that to play a woman on the edge of insanity could trigger a return of her own. Despite friends' fears that the production would prove too taxing, Larry listened to what Vivien wanted and kept fighting to obtain the rights. "I thought, if her critics have one grain of fairness," he explained, "they will give her credit now for being an actress and not go on forever letting their judgments be distorted by her great beauty and her Hollywood stardom."

In May 1949, Williams came to London to see Vivien in her three revolving plays: *School for Scandal*, *Richard III* and *Antigone*. He found the city choked with traffic and smog, but his trip paid off. "Vivien in essence did an audition for three nights running, and she was all too aware of it," wrote Irene. "By the third evening the matter was settled, so we all had a quiet supper at Binkie's."

Now that the deal was done, Larry invited Irene and Williams to Durham Cottage. Only, when they showed up for dinner, he was nowhere to be seen. They were left to spend the evening with Vivien, listening to their host pacing around upstairs and refusing to come down. Had he and Vivien fought? Irene wondered. Or was he having second thoughts about the play? She never found out. "We heard his footsteps back and forth, back and forth, throughout the evening," she wrote. "Tennessee was not the only one disconcerted."

There was nothing Irene could do except worry. And worry she did, unleashing her fears in a fusillade of letters to Williams as work commenced on the London production and Larry began to impose his will. Soon, he was playing fast and loose with the text; next, he was casting it with a casualness Irene couldn't comprehend. "There were no auditions, even for accents," she complained. "Larry summoned whom he chose and interviewed them in Binkie's own office, while Binkie and I sat in the next room. Binkie didn't bat an eye. Nor was there any kind of preproduction meeting. I didn't think anyone's position in the theatre was that high and mighty"—except her own, of course.

Larry started pushing for cuts. Try as Irene did to remind him that they had an ironclad deal forbidding changes, he waved her away. "Oh, the old boy won't mind," he insisted of Williams. "Why should he? Surely it is a director's prerogative to take out anything he wants to and rearrange as he sees fit."

He wasn't alone in wanting changes. The Lord Chamberlain had a whole list, particularly relating to Blanche's shocking revelation that her ex-husband was gay, the one thing Williams insisted "cannot be altered." And yet it was and he was forced to capitulate to the Chamberlain's rules, leaving British audiences under the impression that Blanche's husband had cheated on her with a woman, rather than a man, and not only a woman but "a Negress."

Desperate to maintain authority after Larry refused to let her attend rehearsals, Irene went to Beaumont in tears. Wasn't she the one who had discovered the play? Hadn't she found Brando and persuaded Kazan to cast him, too (an assertion others questioned)? Now here was Larry, banning her from the production altogether. No one would have dared to do that in Hollywood. "You are absolutely in the right," said Binkie, but "the Oliviers are the king and queen of the English theatre." Yes, replied Irene, but "I am the daughter of an emperor."

In an attempt to heal the rift, Beaumont called a meeting between the parties, and miraculously, as Irene remembered it, Larry came "willing to listen....Scene by scene, I outlined the play's intentions as opposed to what I had seen that morning. Larry protested just once; he got to his feet and waved a letter from Tennessee, claiming it gave him carte blanche (which, incidentally, was wishful thinking)....It was a bruising experience for one and all."

To Irene's surprise, Vivien sided with her and not only resisted Olivier's changes but stayed up arguing about them until six in the morning, when he finally conceded. And yet when rehearsals started in Manchester (where an out-of-town run was due to begin in September 1949), Larry reverted to his original blueprint. In an impassioned, sixteen-page letter to Williams, scrawled late at night in his suite at the Midland Hotel, when he was too tired to be tactful and too stressed to tone down his wording, he heaped scorn on some of the writing, while paying lip service to the writer.

"You must *know* that I think *Streetcar* is a really great play," he told Williams before insisting on an hour's worth of cuts. "I honestly think the play is a little long. I also *hear* from every single person I have spoken to who has seen it in America that this is not only theirs but a general feeling. 'Repititious' [sic] and 'Over-written' (horrid isn't it?) are fairly usual expressions of critical comment. Among even the most enraptured praise and wonder, these reservations of opinion are usual."

Dismissing "Dame Irene's" objections (he was borrowing Williams's nickname for the producer), he singled out two scenes for cutting: one between Stella and Blanche (act 1, scene 4) and another between Blanche and Mitch (act 2, scene 2). He also accused Williams of "capriciousness" "when you insist on 'Butterfly wings' (the phrase I mean) and allow the whole implication of *Blanche's attempt at confession to Stella* to go by the board, letting the whole purpose of the speech be dissolved to a sort of moan about her looks with a 'lovely piece of writing' about Butterfly wings to fancy it up. Surely to God, these tremulous hints, these pathetic attempts to *confess*, these anguished little half disclosures to her sister are not only *vital* to her character, [but] establish the farthest point *ever* reached in the Stella-Blanche relationship theme. God damn it, Colonel, I don't understand you, how you can [object to] a single thing I've done when you submitted (I suppose you submitted) to this vandalism in N.Y."

Olivier's outburst had as much to do with Vivien as the play. Locked in rehearsals, fighting to capture the precise Southern accent, as well as the essence of a character who goes out of her mind, she was tackling the most challenging role of her life, one that made even Scarlett look easy. Her voice was flagging and preview audiences complained that they couldn't hear what she said; the play was too long for her to manage; and she was still uncertain of her interpretation, worried that it would never equal Tandy's. Larry knew all this and perhaps knew, too, that he didn't connect with Williams. Cutting made things simpler, for both him and Vivien. And when the cuts were made, things began to go better.

The production was well received in Manchester and on October 1, when it debuted in the West End, it was a sensation. "Advance booking started six months in advance," notes Beaumont's biographer, Richard Huggett, "and by the week of the opening over 10,000 applications for first-night tickets had been received for a theatre which held only 1,200. The queue for the 200 seats in the gallery started three days in advance." A stampede took place on opening night, when the crowds waiting for spare tickets discovered five more were on sale. In the frenzy to reach the box office, "women fainted, clothes were torn, faces scratched. The police were called, ambulances arrived, the wounded were carried to hospital."

Even critics who denounced the play as seedy (one compared it to wading through a garbage heap) gave Vivien and Larry their due. "It is only Olivier, I should say, who can bring out the pathos in that hard lovely beauty of Vivien Leigh," noted the journalist David Lewin, who found "a coldness in her acting. Something remote. Tonight she has had to give a warmth of the heart as well." Added the *Illustrated London News*' J. C. Trewin, "If the play lasts in London, its good angel will be Vivien Leigh. She has never developed more power and authority, and she controls the stage finely in those last 'strong' theatrics when Blanche, her mind shivered, is on the way to the asylum."

At first, Vivien relished this attention. But as she settled into her role, she began to dread the smut-seeking audiences, the ones who had heard she was playing a "nymphomaniac" and came to ogle her and the play "like apes," as she confided to Gielgud. Her confidence was further shaken by a negative review from Kenneth Tynan, London's sharpest and shrewdest critic, whose pen dripped acid, particularly when he wrote about his revered Olivier and Olivier's less-revered wife. This was a fine "illustration of the way in which a good play can be scarred by unsympathetic and clumsy direction," he began, before homing in on Vivien's Blanche, crushingly calling her "a posturing butterfly, with no depth, no sorrow, no room for development, and above all, no trace of Blanche's crushed ideals. Miss Leigh's Blanche is a bored nymphomaniac with a frenziedly affected tremolo, a Hedda Gabler of the gin-palaces; and in the love-scene with Mitch, which should be inexpressibly moving, she becomes almost comic. This cardinal error in casting did what I should never, having read the play, have thought possible: it made the whole action shallow and salacious."

Vivien felt "bulldozed" by Tynan's review, as one of her friends recalled. A role she had once coveted began to seem overwhelming. She couldn't believe she had to "go through it" every night. Stress and exhaustion were precisely the tinder to ignite her illness. Only this time, when her mania returned, it seemed to come and go in faster and faster cycles—a phenomenon psychiatrists describe as "kindling," where each occurrence helps "kindle" another, thereby shifting the illness from an episodic state to a chronic one.

With mania came a heightened and indiscriminate sexuality that was part and parcel of her condition, and that even spilled over on Tynan, hardly the kind of man Vivien would normally have desired. The critic, who had managed to finagle his way into the Oliviers' lives despite his harsh critiques, later recalled lying in a guest bed at Notley, trying to take a nap, when Vivien entered his room. "No sooner had I stripped to my Y-fronts and fallen asleep than I felt the sheet slowly turned back and a hand placed on my genitals," he wrote. "It was Vivien, naked under a peignoir. I began to respond and then suddenly thought how impossible it would be to cuckold a man I venerated under his own roof—a really cock-crinkling thought. I muttered it to Vivien, who pouted a bit, but eventually rose to her feet—and tiptoed across to Elaine's bed [Tynan's then wife, Elaine Dundy]. I hastily dressed: as I left the room, Vivien and Elaine were sleepily embracing."

Soon after, Vivien pointed to a writing desk and told him mischievously: "There's a secret drawer where Larry keeps letters from all his ladies. He doesn't think I know about it. Shall we peek?" Tynan declined.

Vivien began to roam the streets, wandering at night through parts of London that were unsafe for a woman of her class and distinction. She was becoming the "alley cat" of her letters from Australia. "She would dismiss her driver and walk home through the West End's red light district, stopping to chat to the street-girls plying their trade," writes Alexander Walker. "She said she felt an affinity between their flamboyant appeal and Blanche's more pathetic promiscuity. To Bonar Colleano, the play's Stanley Kowalski, she would later repeat the girls' cutting witticisms and laugh over them."

Playing Blanche, Vivien later acknowledged, "tipped me into madness."

And yet when Hollywood came calling, she could not resist.

Williams had hoped Louis B. Mayer and MGM would buy the film rights to *Streetcar* for Irene to produce, but he had over-estimated the father's taste and the daughter's influence. Mayer had seen the play before it came to Broadway and believed it was a sure-fire hit—or would be, if the team made some tiny changes. "He buttonholed Elia Kazan," writes his biographer, Scott Eyman. "It was a great play, he told Kazan, and they were all going to make a fortune, but they had to do one crucial piece of rewriting: after the 'awful woman' who'd broken up that 'fine young couple's happy home' was taken to an institution, there had to be something to indicate that the couple would live happily ever after."

The mogul's judgment was fading, like his clout. He was caught in a turf war with his New York superior, Nick Schenck, who controlled the money and therefore the studio. A few years later, Mayer would be ousted from the company he had founded, effectively ending not only his long reign but also the "dream factory" he had pioneered, with its mass production of movies and stars, unseen before and unrivaled since. Now, in decline, he had neither the authority nor the inclination to film *Streetcar*.

With Mayer out of the picture, so was Irene. Williams and Wood circled other buyers, only to find them unenthusiastic. At 20th Century-Fox, Darryl F. Zanuck wanted to tackle the project, but studio chairman Spyros Skouras called it "a piece of filth." The major studios' appetite for *Streetcar* was "nonexistent," said Wood.

And yet Hollywood was changing to the writer's advantage. As the studio system was crumbling, independent companies were springing up, many of them led by the giants of Hollywood's golden age, cut loose from their former employers. William Wyler was one such, and when he approached Wood, she was tempted to say yes, but that would have meant ditching Kazan. Instead, she eventually sold the rights to Charles K. Feldman, a debonair agent-turned-producer who was an expert at the new art of "packaging," assembling the creative elements and taking them to the very studios that had passed in the first place. With Feldman in charge, Warner Bros. agreed to make the movie.

At first, Kazan was reluctant to direct. He hated "to get it up twice for the same material," he explained. "It's unbearable to me—impossible." But it would have been even more unbearable to let someone else do so and he ultimately signed on. While Brando was attached from the start, Vivien wasn't Kazan's first choice for Blanche: he was afraid she'd be under Olivier's thumb and too bound to his original direction; and so he pushed for Olivia de Havilland, while Feldman kept fighting for Vivien.

Throughout, no one mentioned the most obvious choice, Jessica Tandy, who had created the role on Broadway. She was not a film star, of course; but there may have been another reason she was out of the running: she and Brando had never gotten along. Early in rehearsals, the actress had lashed out at him for being late and forgetting his lines. When he apologized, she wrote an icy, three-page response. "This kind of casualness is bound to hurt you eventually and earn you a reputation for irresponsibility which I don't think managers or directors will tolerate, despite your unusual abilities," she bristled. Then she knocked his acting, asking sardonically: "Do you have a stammer? Or is it just something that happens to you on stage?"

With de Havilland unavailable and Tandy out of contention, Vivien had no serious competition and was able to command $100,000 for the film, compared to Brando's $75,000. But Williams was still dubious and cautioned Kazan: "*Don't* listen to Leigh about script." Blaming her for the changes Larry had imposed, he added: "The Oliviers are as bad as the Lunts in that Dept."

In fact, rather than demand cuts, Vivien asked for some of the excised material to be restored. "I have read the script three times," she wrote Kazan on June 16, 1950. "Extremely attached to 'may I rest my weary head on your shoulder'—to prove how complet [sic] her dream world is—STANLEY's voice should bring her back to reality with a shock and for a second she does not realise what has become of her imagined company of friends."

She went on to discuss the subject she knew so well: madness. "I may be totally wrong," she wrote, "but having tried a number of different things over the last 9 months, I am sure it is desperately important to get as much variety and as little monotony into BLANCHE's sudden flights, fancies, terrors and what have you's as possible. What I'm trying to express very badly is that the running, clutching, brittle, jumpy exposition of BLANCHE's nervosity quickly becomes tedious, and one must find as many different ways as possible of expressing her neurasthenia.... You probably know that playing BLANCHE is not exactly a rest cure, so if I have said anything particularly stooped [stupid], I hope you will forgive and put it down to temporary fatigue."

Kazan said he planned to retain his cuts, while agreeing that most of the play was best left unchanged. He had experimented with "opening it up," and at one point had hired screenwriters to help him do so, only to return to the original because he felt it worked best when reproduced as it was: shot largely in one place and on one stage, thus retaining its inherent theatricality.

"I think we might trim a bit more here and there, perhaps a couple of more pages in toto," he wrote Vivien. "But I don't think we should forget that it is the best talk ever heard from the screen by a modern writer and no matter how we trim, that's our flag and we better hold on to that."

On July 31, 1950, Vivien flew to America, leaving Larry in London, where he had just opened in *Venus Observed*. After spending several days at Kazan's Connecticut home, she accompanied him by train to Los Angeles where, in early August, she met Brando for the first time in the Warner Bros. commissary. It was an uncomfortable encounter.

"Why do you always wear scent?" he asked.

"Because I like to smell nice—don't you?" she replied.

"Me?" he said. "I just wash. In fact, I don't even get in the tub. I just throw a gob of spit in the air and run under it."

After that inauspicious, if comical, beginning, shooting commenced in August on one of the biggest sets ever built at Warners—150 feet wide and 215 feet long—depicting Stella's New Orleans home, the courtyard outside her apartment and a section of the French Quarter. The rooms were life-size, making filming tricky but allowing Kazan to capture their claustrophobia. One part of the stage was "out of limits at all times to members of the troupe," noted a Warner publicist. "It's a rehearsal room on a far corner of the stage where Kazan, upon completion of a scene, takes Miss Leigh, Brando, Kim Hunter [as Stella], Karl Malden [as Mitch] and others of the cast, to go through their lines and action for the next set-up. The room consists of four canvas 'flat' walls and rough rehearsal furniture. Only those invited by Kazan are allowed to enter the room or go near it.

Otherwise everybody is advised to stay clear by at least 200 feet or be considered by the director as unwanted trespassers."

On the first day at work, "Brando, quietly and without ostentation, started his investigation of Stanley's squalid home," wrote the publicist. The actor proceeded to go "through the drawers of every table and cupboard, handling the contents and examining them minutely. He then sat in every chair, tested the bed, turned the water on and off in the sink and bath. He felt the walls, tested the dirty drapes, looked out the window at the dreary view of a bowling alley across the narrow street. Brando then re-hung the clothes in the closet, reassorted the ties and hung them in a clump, too." Rather than socialize with the rest of the cast, he preferred to spend his lunch breaks in the studio gym, often with his friend Burt Lancaster, an actor who had been considered for Stanley before Kazan discovered Brando. "[Brando] candidly admits he's not a fiend for exercise," continued the publicist. " 'But,' he says, 'if you're an actor you've got to keep your body fit and in trim.' "

Vivien kept to herself. She had not made a film since *Anna Karenina* and hadn't been in Los Angeles since the early days of the war. Waiting for Larry to join her, which he had promised to do as soon as his play ended, she spent time alone in her dressing room or was visited by friends like Humphrey Bogart and Lauren Bacall, not to mention the occasional, curious celebrity (including Cary Grant and the future founder of Scientology, L. Ron Hubbard). "Because of the strenuous emotional nature of her role, she seeks as much rest as possible when not before the camera," noted the publicist.

The gossip columnist Louella Parsons asked Vivien how she was doing, aware of her battle with TB but not her issues with mental health. She "opened her big, blue eyes—and they looked even bluer with the blonde wig she was wearing. 'Why, there's nothing wrong with me,' she said, 'I am all right. I don't know how those rumors ever started that I was in such bad health. Friends from America used to telephone and say, "Are you all right, dear?" I had one little breakdown, but I have fully recovered.' "

At first, Vivien rubbed everyone the wrong way. Her fellow cast members had all been in the original production and their roots were in the Actors Studio, whose Method Vivien never understood. "I don't know what that Method is," she said. "I've read Stanislavsky, naturally, and it seems to me that the Method is: if you say something, you've got to mean it, and you've got to say it as interestingly as possible. But that applies to life—and acting is life, to me, and should be."

She was an interloper, an outsider among this band of brothers, who resisted Kazan's attempts to fit her acting style to theirs. Because of that, "For the first three weeks, I was as miserable as I've ever been," the director maintained. "She kept saying, 'Well, Larry and I in England...' and I'd say, 'You're not doing it with Larry now, you're doing it with me, and I don't like it that way.'... She'd get irritated with me, and I'd get plenty angry with her." He urged her to think more deeply about the South, especially as a foreigner who knew little of Southern ways. Southern women, he told her, would float in and out of reality, unaware that Vivien did, too. "Have you ever been with a Southern girl?" he asked. "That's the way they are." More than anything, he wanted her to capture Blanche's essential dilemma: that she loves the thing she hates. "I wanted to show exactly what Williams meant," he explained, "which is that he, as a homosexual, is attracted to the person he thinks is going to destroy him—the attraction you have for someone who's on the other side, supposedly dead against you, but whose violence and force attract you. Now, that's the essence of ambivalence."

Gradually, the relationship between the two improved and they became friends. Vivien teasingly called him "Pasha," referring

both to his Turkish roots and his authoritarian instincts, while he
found her more willing to follow his lead than he had expected.
"As filming continued," he recalled later, "we got to like each
other, mainly because I thought she was such a terrific worker."
He added: "She had a small talent, but the greatest determination to excel of any actress I've known. She'd have crawled over
broken glass if she thought it would help her performance."

Vivien drew closer to Brando, too. When he poked fun at
Olivier, mimicking him with needlepoint accuracy as he recited
his Agincourt speech, Vivien howled with laughter. The actors
would get together outside work, sometimes swimming in one of
their pools.

Kazan did what he could to put her at ease. At one point,
he asked the six-foot-one Malden to remove his shoes so that he
wouldn't tower over her. At another, when Malden was meant
to lift her like a ballerina and Vivien insisted he "pick her up
as though I were lifting her over a threshold," Kazan agreed to
alter his staging, though that meant re-creating the way Olivier
had done it in London. Kazan also allowed a stuntman to take
Vivien's place for a key scene in which Blanche throws a bottle
at a mirror, because she was superstitious; he lobbed the bottle
eleven times, breaking eleven mirrors. "[Kazan] made a point of
wanting us to try to accommodate Vivien since she was the outsider," said Malden.

"Gadg is doing a brilliant job on *Streetcar*," raved Williams,
using Kazan's nickname, an abbreviation of Gadget. "And believe
it or not, Madame Olivier is nothing less than terrific! I was
almost startled out of my 'sissy britches.'"

The publicist was also impressed, especially by Vivien's
unequaled ability to memorize her lines. "While the average
length of a scene is timed to one minute and 15 seconds," he
wrote, "Vivien Leigh yesterday spoke a solid speech...lasting
four minutes and 11 seconds. Miss Leigh went through the vernal

[that is, verbal] ordeal without faltering and Kazan wrapped up the scene in one take." (That was only a slight exaggeration: Vivien's longest speech lasted three and a half minutes.)

The rest of the shoot was "pleasant, unpleasant, tedious, dull, exciting, stimulating, boring," recalled Brando, despite a few mishaps off-camera when he dislocated his shoulder while taking fencing lessons and then sprained his right thumb, incidents that pushed the production nineteen days over schedule and raised its total cost to $1.9 million.

After three weeks on location in New Orleans, principal photography ended in September 1950. At the wrap party, the crew gave Vivien a cigarette case, while Kazan gave her a silver necklace.

Larry's play ended early and he arrived in Los Angeles ten days after Vivien to begin work on another film, an adaptation of Theodore Dreiser's turn-of-the-century novel *Sister Carrie*, which would reunite him with Wyler.

The book was the prototype for one of Hollywood's favorite allegories, about a rising star and her falling lover. It told the story of an unsophisticated young woman, Carrie Meeber, who moves to Chicago with dreams of becoming an actress, only to fall in love with a successful restaurant manager, George Hurstwood; her climb accompanies his descent.

Olivier had hoped to appear in the movie (retitled *Carrie*) with Elizabeth Taylor, then an eighteen-year-old who had graced such films as *National Velvet* and *Little Women*; instead, he ended up with Selznick's wife, Jennifer Jones, which meant he once again had to contend with his former nemesis. Wyler had chosen her after rejecting a long list of names Paramount had suggested when Taylor proved unavailable—among them Lana Turner, Ann Sheridan, Linda Darnell and Ava Gardner. But he then changed his mind. When he tried to replace her just before shooting, Selznick was incensed. This was yet another instance of the "DOUBLE DEALING WHICH HAS MADE ME SO FED UP WITH HOLLYWOOD," he cabled Wyler. "EITHER YOU OR YOUR ASSOCIATES HAD THE CONSUMMATE BAD TASTE AND INGRATITUDE TO USE MY WILLINGNESS TO LET JENNIFER PLAY THE ROLE AND JENNIFER'S WILLINGNESS TO PLAY THE ROLE WITH OLIVIER TO ATTEMPT TO GET ANOTHER STAR.... YOU OR YOUR PEOPLE EVEN WERE DISHONEST ENOUGH TO STATE THAT JENNIFER WAS DYING TO PLAY THE ROLE BUT THAT YOU DID NOT WANT HER."

Inevitably, this tension spilled onto the set, but Larry gave the film his all, impressing Kazan, who was living across the street. "I remember pausing outside a window late one Sunday morning and, undetected, watching Larry go through the pantomime of offering a visitor a chair," he recalled. "He'd try it this way, then that, looking at the guest, then at the chair, doing it with a host's flourish, doing it with a graceless gesture, then thrusting it brusquely forward—more like Hurstwood that way?—never satisfied, always seeking what would be the most revealing way to do what would be a quickly passing bit of stage business for any other actor." He noted: "Some great actors imitate the outside and 'work in' from there, Laurence Olivier, for one. Larry needs to know first of all how the person he's to play walks, stands, sits, dresses."

Despite Olivier's efforts, *Carrie* was not a happy shoot. He adored Wyler this time around, but couldn't bear Jones, who infuriated both men by revealing she was pregnant when filming was already in motion. Writing to Vivien, who was wrapping *Streetcar* with the location work in New Orleans, he mocked his costar's vapidity. "I'm doing the 'Caerey downt DOWNT [sic] make me live through teoo much PAIN to get ut' sequence with Jennifer really being a cunt," he wrote. "'I guess I downt know'—I *guess* she bloody well fucking doesn't know *anything* about *anything.*"

His irritation wasn't entirely due to Jones. He was in frequent pain and suffered agonizing flashes that would shoot up his leg, making it drag as he walked, perhaps a residue of his injury in Australia. "Larry could be warm and entertaining, but there were temperamental outbursts," said actor Eddie Albert. "And that caused some tension. I remember one time we had some visitors on the set. They were off in the background. Maybe there was a slight murmur. All of a sudden, Larry looked up, and you heard that great voice of his: 'Anyone who is not in this picture, would you piss off?'"

His moods were also influenced by his ongoing spats with Vivien. The last time they had been in Los Angeles, they couldn't bear to be apart. But both before and after Vivien's New Orleans hiatus, they fought with a vehemence that shocked the fifteen-year-old Suzanne, who was spending the summer in California. "It was my first real experience of them together—and very uncomfortable it was too," she recalled. "What I remember most about my stay in Hollywood was the fights that went on between them—real theatrically pitched arguments behind closed doors....But in spite of the shouting matches, it never occurred to me that their marriage was breaking up. It was just too precious to Vivien. I put it down to two overwrought people at the end of a long day's work on their separate movies."

Around this time, Vivien began to be unfaithful, or so Brando believed. "Her mind began to wobble and her sense of self became vague," he noted. "Like Blanche, she slept with almost everybody and was beginning to dissolve mentally and to fray at the ends physically." While Brando never witnessed anything inappropriate (he was too busy with his own extracurricular activities, he explained), he was a master of observation and admitted he might have slept with Vivien too. "I might have given her a tumble," he admitted, "if it hadn't been for Larry Olivier. I'm sure he knew she was playing around, but like a lot of husbands I've known, he pretended not to see it."

Among those he pretended not to see, allegedly, was Scotty Bowers, an occasional gas station employee and gigolo renowned for servicing men and women alike. After meeting Vivien at Cukor's home, Bowers claims in his 2012 autobiography *Full Service*, she told him to come to the director's guesthouse, where she occasionally spent the night. "We had to be careful," he writes. "George was a very light sleeper. The slightest noise would wake him. Vivien and I looked at one another, sniggered quietly, and tried to make as few sounds as possible as we began to passionately make out." The next morning, Vivien sat staring at her dressing table mirror, brushing her hair and refusing to make eye contact with him. Then, says Bowers, she barricaded herself in her bathroom and insisted he leave, only to fly out, sobbing: "Oh, darling, darling boy. I'm sorry. Can you come around again tonight?"

The story warrants skepticism, but some members of Vivien's circle believed it—indeed, the agent Irving "Swifty" Lazar once lashed out at her for being two hours late to a dinner party and "accused her of picking up strangers at gas stations," says Michael Korda. "Her behavior certainly raised eyebrows."

Malden thought Vivien "had a more tenuous relationship with reality [than Tandy]" and never cared for her, perhaps because she was rude to his wife at a party. When Mona sat next to her, Vivien ignored her completely and kept talking over her head, chattering on and on with her old friend John Buckmaster, who had recently resurfaced in Los Angeles. "Mona sat there, utterly baffled," recalled Malden. "Never once did they acknowledge that another person was even there, let alone sitting between them."

In December 1950, with both films completed, the Oliviers left for home. Eager to restore their relationship, they made the odd choice to travel on a cargo ship, hoping that the long, crawling journey and relative absence of other passengers would leave them free to rediscover each other.

Their love was no longer the simple, uncomplicated matter it had been thirteen years earlier when they had run away. Resentment, jealousy, workaholism and mental illness had all come between them. But their love was no less real and, strangely, no less intense. Larry had written to Vivien repeatedly when she was in New Orleans—deep, passionate letters, telling her how violently he missed her, just as she missed him; it was only when they were together, it seemed, that hostility got in the way. Vivien told the press they were "counting on the freighter trip as a vacation we've both needed for a long time."

It was a disaster. The crack that had opened in Australia had turned into a crevice. Here on the boat, they didn't so much converse as confer, with nothing to distract them and little company besides the forty thousand boxes of apples, twelve thousand boxes of pears, six hundred tons of flour, five hundred thousand feet of lumber and ten thousand cases of canned sardines.

Out at sea in every sense, with a woman who had once meant everything to him but now seemed like a stranger, Olivier felt more alone than at any time since his mother's death. He had everything in the world: success, acclaim, an Oscar for *Hamlet* and another for *Henry V*, and one of the most beautiful women in the world as his wife; but all he could dwell on was his misery. "It is interesting how seldom life bestows equality of fortune in a man's public and his private life," he reflected. "Ralph [Richardson] has remarked to me once or twice that he never had known a fellow with such extremes of good and bad luck."

A thousand miles from land, and even further from inner peace, he was in despair. "For the first time," he noted bleakly, "the idea of suicide had its attractions."

CHAPTER 13

——◆——

S hortly after returning to England, Vivien chose to vacation alone, leaving Larry to prepare their next venture, alternating productions of Shakespeare's *Antony and Cleopatra* and Shaw's *Caesar and Cleopatra*, while she joined Korda on his yacht, the *Elsewhere*.

She had a prodigious task ahead of her, playing Shakespeare's mature heroine and Shaw's kitten-queen in tandem, a courageous move for anyone but especially for an actress whose previous Cleopatra had failed. Privately, Korda thought the effort "of two such demanding roles, in which Vivien would have to play a young girl, then age twenty years to play the older Cleopatra, would be more than Vivien could bear," recalled his nephew, Michael. Alex also feared "another of Vivien's hysterical episodes, or worse."

She was drinking heavily, even by the standards of the day and when compared to the other heavy drinkers on board the boat as it cruised the Mediterranean, including the novelist Graham Greene and Selznick, who was still hooked on Benzedrine. "They all drank far too much," says Juliet Mills. "They'd start with a sherry or a gin and tonic at lunch, go on to wine with lunch, and then again at night, a lot. And that's not good, especially for bipolar [people]."

Vivien was in emotional pain and Korda was one of the rare men who understood it. Despite the success of *Streetcar*, which would earn her a second Best Actress Oscar, her unhappiness kept spilling out, mystifying the sixteen-year-old Michael, who watched these larger-than-life adults as if they were gods, unable to fathom the currents that swept them up more turbulently than his uncle's yacht. In London, he had seen Vivien down a large vodka and burst into tears, while Alex had warned him obscurely never to mention Larry's name in front of her, because he knew their relationship was at its most delicate. Everybody, it seemed, cut a wide swath around Vivien, as if they realized something Michael didn't.

"People tended to be around Vivien as if they were walking on eggshells," he says. "Alex was very careful. There's a rumor I couldn't track down that they'd been lovers, and that's certainly possible and even probable. But Alex had better control over Vivien than anyone else. He was one of the few people who could talk to her and one of the few she trusted."

Korda had his own share of problems, no matter how much he tried to hide them from his guests. Divorced from Merle Oberon, he had a new woman in his life, the twenty-something Alexandra Boycun, who resented Vivien's presence just as much as Vivien resented hers. At fifty-seven years old, the producer was in poor health and money, once so abundant, was no longer in endless supply, meaning he would soon have to sell his beloved *Elsewhere*. The man who had bragged, "I've been broke many times but I've never been poor"—who had advised Michael, if ever he were on the skids, to rent a Rolls-Royce and take the biggest name he knew out to lunch—was beginning to temper extravagance with caution. But here he spun a sublime vision of the movies he and Vivien would make, stories of distant empires and faraway realms, including a biography of Shah Jahan, the seventeenth-century Mughal emperor who had built the Taj

Mahal as a tribute to his dead wife, a project that promised to take Vivien back to India for the first time since she had left. She, of course, would play the wife, and Larry the shah—which meant, yet again, that in most people's eyes her career was still inextricable from his.

Despite this, she was often in high spirits and "went swimming and fishing with me, played gin rummy with Alex, inspected the engine rooms with the engineer and took the helm at the captain's direction, charming the poor man so effectively that we made our landfall in Corsica at least twenty miles off course," recalls Michael. Charm was Vivien's "secret weapon," used to cast a spell on whomever she desired, "as if the nuns had drummed it into her along with cleanliness and good manners." She was, Alex told his nephew, "the only person in the world who could be charming while she was throwing up," which she did frequently, given her propensity for seasickness.

But Michael saw something more serious than seasickness: a "high-pitched nervous laughter, increasing alarmingly in intensity," that could all too easily give way to tears. Once, when the party went onshore, Vivien laughed so loud that she shocked two elderly ladies, who muttered about these "theatricals." She "began to giggle, then to laugh and finally to cry," remembered Michael. Like an ocean swell presaging a typhoon, "Vivien's laughter had a certain nervous effect on everyone around her, since it was sometimes the first sign of an onslaught of hysteria."

Just as Alex was thinking of selling the *Elsewhere*, Larry was considering whether to keep Notley. He adored it beyond words, loved it almost as much as any woman and associated it with some of his finest times; but the house was a financial drain—an estate fit for a lord, but only one with a lordly income. Whatever Vivien and Larry earned was plowed into it, one row of trees, one gravel driveway, one ornate room at a time. There they had indulged their patrician tastes to the full: in one three-month period alone, they had consumed "forty-two bottles of champagne, sixty bottles of wine and twenty-one bottles of spirits," writes Terry Coleman, while lavishing money on countless bouquets of flowers and even trying (but failing) to obtain a rare white telephone—as if objects could make up for love. Despite Vivien's windfall from *Streetcar*, cash was tight and Larry's attempt to get rich as a producer through Laurence Olivier Productions had failed and kept on failing. It seemed inevitable that Notley must go, and the Oliviers were only spared when Cecil Tennant, their manager and business partner, found a financial loophole, transferring it from the couple's personal ownership to their company.

Notley was just one source of distress. Other actors were beginning to challenge Larry's preeminence when it had seemed most secure. Alec Guinness had recently tackled *Hamlet* at the Old Vic, newly reopened after extensive repairs, while Robert Donat was mulling a *Hamlet* that would take direct aim at Larry's interpretation. Acting did not exist in isolation, it seemed, but in a cauldron of envy and ego that Larry would not escape. Time and again, he would measure himself against others and the same man who could be flamboyantly generous—who would give his makeup artist a gigantic bouquet of flowers with diamond earrings hidden inside—could also throw a fit of jealous pique, as he did when Donald Wolfit was awarded a knighthood. He couldn't believe this old ham merited the same honor that he did. "He was consumed with jealousy," says the actress Rosemary Harris. "He was very jealous of people's success. And he couldn't hide it. It was part of his makeup."

Like a modern-day Mephistopheles, Kenneth Tynan was buzzing in the background, reminding Larry of his gifts while pointing out the danger from others. Later, he would become an inner member of the Olivier tribe and even work for Larry at the National Theatre; but for now he was an irritant on the outside, his columns an endless source of agitation, dripping honey but almost always adding a sting. "Between good and great acting is fixed an inexorable gulf, which may be crossed only by the elect, whose visas are in order," he wrote. "[John] Gielgud, seizing a parasol, crosses by tight-rope; [Michael] Redgrave, with lunatic obstinacy, plunges into the torrent, usually sinking within yards of the opposite shore; Laurence Olivier pole vaults over, hair-raisingly, in a single, animal leap. Great acting comes more easily to him than to any of his colleagues: he need no more than lift his head, neigh, and extend a gauntletted hand to usher us into the presence of tragic matters." Still, he added: "One wonders what will become of him now."

Larry wondered too. He had years ahead, maybe decades, in which to seal his reputation or let it slide, invent new tricks or watch other magicians pull bigger rabbits from their hats. The two *Cleopatra*s were the kind of big idea he loved; and yet he knew how challenging they would be, not just for Vivien but also himself. Caesar, he understood: he was a brilliant leader, a general, a fellow whose ruthless ambition matched Larry's own. But Mark Antony was an altogether different beast, and Larry was nagged by the feeling that he was a milquetoast who had foundered on the rocks of his love. Was Antony all that different from *Carrie*'s Hurstwood? Or, for that matter, from Larry himself?

His uncertainty bubbled up in rehearsals at the St. James Theatre, a grand old venue on Piccadilly that he had rented to stage his plays. There he fought so vehemently with director Michael Benthall that a friend took him to task, telling him either to let the other man direct or take over himself. "If you try to muddle through I think it will be very dangerous and the Company will be confused, nervous and unhappy," warned the friend, Glen Byam Shaw. "You must remember the enormous power of your personality and authority, particularly in your own theater."

Vivien was also worried about playing two versions of

Cleopatra, knowing how often she would have to switch from one to the other as the plays rotated in repertoire. With Larry distracted, her anxiety poured out, literally: she began to sweat during rehearsals and continued to do so in front of an audience. Perspiration soaked her clothes, forcing her to add an extra layer under her diaphanous gown so that it couldn't be seen.

When the productions debuted in April 1951, however, the Oliviers' fears were swept away. Critics raved about Vivien's ability to capture these disparate women. Who else could have pulled off such a coup? they asked. Who else could have delivered Shavian comedy and Shakespearean tragedy, and made these heroines sexy too? Only Tynan took issue, as always, slamming Vivien in his *Observer* review. "She picks at the part with the daintiness of a debutante called upon to dismember a stag," he wrote of her performance in *Antony and Cleopatra*. "Miss Leigh's limitations have wider repercussions than those of most actresses. Sir Laurence, with that curious chivalry which some time or other blights the progress of every great actor, gives me the impression that he subdues his blow-lamp ebullience to match her. Blunting his iron precision, levelling away his towering authority, he meets her halfway. Antony climbs down; and Cleopatra pats him on the head. A cat, in fact, can do more than look at a king: she can hypnotise him."

Never had someone stated so openly what was becoming apparent to one and all: that Larry was lowering his standards for Vivien. To fulfill his ambitions, he would have to strike out on his own.

In November 1951, the Oliviers left for America, bringing the *Cleopatras* with them, as well as their usual supply of luggage, twenty-five tons of scenery and a giant Sphinx.

A residue of fear had settled over the country, which was firmly in the grip of Senator Joseph McCarthy and his witch

hunts. That fear had been present before, certainly after the 1947
hearings of the House Un-American Activities Committee, but
never as pervasively as now. Back then, friends of the Oliviers
such as Danny Kaye, Humphrey Bogart and Lauren Bacall had
felt safe enough to fly to Washington and protest; but the terror was so widespread and the danger of losing one's career so
real that they had been silenced. Some, like Bogie, had recanted;
while others, like Kazan, were thinking of naming names, as he
would do a mere five months hence, maintaining his preeminence
as a director but severing his ties with many friends.

Two plays about politicians and power might have seemed
ripe for metaphor; but the Oliviers were political naïfs and, as
always, it was the personal rather than the political that stamped
their work, particularly when it came to Larry's portrait of Mark
Antony. Unlike Vivien, who would lock into her characterization
and never change, Olivier kept delving deeper, not merely adding nuance but shifting his entire interpretation. In London, he
had stressed the man's greatness, but now he saw another side.
"[Olivier] interprets Antony not so much as the great triple pillar
of the world, the broken colossus whom Cleopatra describes as
her dream of the Emperor Antony," noted one academic, con-
trasting the British and American productions, "but rather as
a man in the process of disintegration," a disintegration that
reflected Larry's own.

Audiences lapped this up. J. D. Salinger, whose *The Catcher
in the Rye* had recently been published to widespread acclaim,
was so taken with the show, he told Larry: "I think you're the
only actor in the world who plays in a Shakespeare play with a
special, tender familiarity—as if you were keeping it in the family. Almost as if you were appearing in a play written by an older
brother whom you understand completely and love to distrac-
tion. It's an almost insupportably beautiful thing to watch."

The *New York Times*' Brooks Atkinson not only considered

these plays "the finest work of this wretched season" but also singled out Vivien as "superb," especially in the Shakespeare, a relief after Tynan's battering. "She is smoldering and sensual, wily and treacherous, but she is also intelligent, audacious and courageous," he wrote. "It is as though *Antony and Cleopatra* never had been played before. Everything about the Olivier production is glowing or crackling with vitality."

Vitality was precisely what Vivien lacked outside the theater. Staying in the actress Gertrude Lawrence's dark and claustrophobic apartment, she succumbed to her old depression, folding in on herself, but also demonstrating a vulnerability she had never shown before. Larry had noticed the change before they left England, when she had seemed almost needy, with a "funny little child-like clinging need for protection." That flattered his masculinity, and he mistakenly took it as a sign that their relationship was on the mend. But halfway through their six months on Broadway, Vivien's depression became crippling; she could hardly get out of bed and only kept working through a stupendous force of will. She began "shivering with weakness," observed cast member Wilfrid Hyde-White; and when *Vogue* magazine editor Diana Vreeland came to visit, she sensed an "exquisite unreality," as if Vivien were neither wholly present nor wholly absent but operating in a fugue state, like Sybille's.

Larry told Coward he was afraid Vivien was having a nervous breakdown, but the playwright swatted it away, like so many others at the time, trapped in a dismissive view of mental illness. "Nonsense," he said. "If anybody's having a nervous breakdown, you are." Soon Vivien was spending each day in bed, sobbing and impervious to her husband's attempts to lift her gloom. Only when Irene Selznick came to visit and found Vivien "in a pitiful state" did Larry fully acknowledge the extent of her illness and insisted she see a psychiatrist.

Vivien had visions of being tossed in a madhouse, just like her great-uncle in India or de Havilland in 1948's *The Snake Pit*, a widely seen movie whose heroine wakes in an asylum and has no clue how she got there. But after much persuasion, she agreed to meet Dr. Lawrence Kubie, a distinguished analyst and president of the New York Psychoanalytic Society.

Kubie has gone down in history as something of a charlatan, tarred by the writer Gore Vidal as "a slick bit of goods on the make among the rich, the famous, the gullible." It was Kubie, the writer claimed, who told Tennessee Williams to "give up both writing and sex so that he could be transformed into a good team player." That account drew heated objections from Kubie's colleagues, including a Yale professor, who wrote: "Dr. Kubie was a leading psychoanalyst and psychoanalysts do not order patients to do anything." No matter how polarizing, Kubie at once recognized the gravity of Vivien's situation and warned Larry it was explosive. And, for the first time, he put a label on her condition: manic depression.

"I am sure that they must have taken some pains to tell me what was wrong with my wife," wrote Olivier, "that her disease was called manic depression and what that meant—a possibly permanent cyclical to-and-fro between the depths of depression and wild, uncontrollable mania. These changes of mood could be irregular, or regular, or increasing in frequency, this last the most dreaded as it invariably led to schizophrenia, which was thus far regarded as being incurable."

Schizophrenia, in fact, was unconnected to Vivien's illness; but the Kubie analysis made the Oliviers confront a truth they had resisted: that Vivien was not simply a victim of moods or alcohol, but a woman in desperate need of help. She was dangerously ill and, worse, entering a phase in which her episodes would cycle ever more frequently and extremely. She should have sought further help, but didn't; should have taken medication, but there was none to be had. She needed more sustenance than Larry could offer—and was therefore perfectly primed for another man.

At thirty-two years old, Peter Finch was as sensual as he was sensitive, an actor whose rugged looks matched his robust talent. He had something of Larry's originality and something more of Vivien's turbulence, and in real life simmered with a sexuality that Olivier only ever seemed to muster onstage.

Born in London and brought up partly in India, like Vivien, he had been a pawn in his parents' breakup, wrenched from his mother and ditched in one temporary home after another, including a Buddhist monastery where, he later claimed, a monk had sought to make him a priest. Some of this was true, some false; some possible, some preposterous—even those who knew him best could never tease the real from the fake. "Finchie," as his friends called him, was comfortable in ambiguity; he functioned best in the murky zone that existed between truth and lies, and was therefore excellent company for a woman who could no longer always tell them apart.

The Oliviers had met him in Melbourne, where Larry recalled seeing him in *Tartuffe* (though Finch's then wife, Tamara Tchinarova, said it was another Molière, *Le malade imaginaire*), staged in an old factory. "The Oliviers, whether out of interest or duty, went, arriving well before time to see the actors clearing a section of the factory floor, setting the proscenium frame, securing the curtain, putting up the furniture, fixing the spotlights, and being ready when the bell rang for the lunch hour break," Tamara recalled in her 2007 autobiography, *Dancing into the Unknown: My Life in the Ballets Russes and Beyond*. "It looked more like a troupe of strolling players giving a village square performance."

Olivier was nonetheless impressed and urged Finch to move to London, as did Vivien, her interest solely professional—or so Tamara and Larry believed. "You bring that clever husband of yours to London," Vivien told the former ballerina, who had given up her career for Finch and would soon be pregnant with their first child.

Later, Olivier blamed himself for his naïveté in drawing the actor so close. "I suppose I had encouraged it," he wrote, "oh, quite innocently at first." Still, Finch didn't need much prompting: he knew that to make it, he had to conquer either England or America or both, and he would need a patron's support. And so, in November 1948, he and Tamara set sail from Sydney, waving their friends goodbye, unsure if they would ever see them again.

Arriving in the bitter cold of a London winter, they felt "a mixture of elation and sadness," writes Tamara, "elation at how much there was to see, to do and to explore; sadness at the damage done during the war, the devastation around St Paul's Cathedral, and the blocks and blocks in ruins." Living in a freezing flat in Notting Hill, the couple struggled to keep warm by feeding shillings into a tiny gas heater and spending their time "eating whale meat and meatless sausages," while trying to contact the Oliviers. At first, they got nowhere. "When finally an invitation came for a sherry party, it was an appalling anti-climax," recalled Tamara. "It lasted half an hour, and the exchange of conversation was, 'You're all right, dear boy? Good. Do keep in touch.'" They didn't realize that Olivier was sizing Finch up for a new play he was producing, James Bridie's *Daphne Laureola*, about a young man who becomes obsessed with an older woman.

In December, Finch was asked to audition for the role at Wyndham's Theatre. "The stalls were pitch black," writes his friend and biographer, Trader Faulkner. "Peter could see no one, only hear voices. He knew that somewhere down there were Sir Laurence Olivier, Dame Edith Evans, Vivien Leigh, James Bridie, and the play's director, Murray MacDonald. Two bentwood chairs were set on the bare stage, one for [actress] Diana Graves, one for Peter. 'When you're ready,' called a voice from the darkness.

They started reading." A few moments later, Olivier's voice rang out, asking Finch to wait a few moments. He "sat with that hideous feeling of stark, lit exposure, gazing into the pitch blackness of the orchestra stalls, with the sibilant sounds of a decisive conversation going on some twenty feet away....Then, in Peter's own words, 'Suddenly I heard a rich, bell-like, rather mannered but arrestingly beautiful English voice calling me from the darkness. I turned around to see a woman leaning on that balustrade by the orchestra pit at Wyndham's. "My name is Edith Evans and I shall look forward to seeing you at rehearsal on Tuesday." ' "

The play opened on March 23, 1949, and the audience went wild. The *Daily Telegraph*'s W. A. Darlington said Finch had made a name for himself in a single night, like Vivien in *The Mask of Virtue*. He was a star—or, better yet, a young man with the promise to become one.

Success emboldened him, adulation added a new layer of sex appeal, and when Vivien started inviting him to Notley, he quickly became part of the Olivier entourage. Was Larry oblivious to the danger? Did he willfully blind himself? Or did he possess such tunnel vision that he was willing to ignore everything that didn't relate to his work?

In early 1953, Vivien proposed that Finch star with her in a new movie, *Elephant Walk*, and Korda scoffed. "Forgive me, dear Larry," he said, "but I nearly had to laugh when I asked [Vivien] who was to be her leading man and she said, 'Peter Finch,' in that incredibly offhanded way—I mean, really! It was the only truly bad performance I've ever seen her give."

Elephant Walk told the story of a powerful tea planter who builds his house on the path elephants take to reach their watering hole. The movie had been developed for Douglas Fairbanks Jr. and Deborah Kerr, but when bad weather delayed the shoot, it was reassembled with a new cast under the aegis of producer

Irving Asher and director William Dieterle. Larry had turned down the lead (as had Gable and Brando) and advised Vivien to do the same; but she resisted his advice and agreed to star for $150,000. With no one to play the planter and only a few weeks before filming was due to kick off in Ceylon (now Sri Lanka), Asher gave her carte blanche to choose the male lead, an extraordinary concession to a woman who was no longer a box office guarantee.

"On a frosty January night in 1953, when we were warm and snug in bed, the phone rang," writes Tamara. "I glanced at the clock: 2 a.m. Unable to let it ring without answering it, and knowing that Peter never would, I dashed into the living room to do so. A determined voice named herself as Vivien Leigh and announced that she was coming round to [the Finches' new home in] Dolphin Square to see us." Vivien arrived, wearing a mink coat and nothing but a thin slip underneath. Her hair was wet from the snow and she was ravenous. Raiding the fridge, she found "the remains of a roast, shrivelled and close to the bone. She wanted it, then didn't, said it looked disgusting, and proceeded to polish a small round table with her handkerchief, telling me, 'You should be careful and put place mats under your glasses—rings from wet glasses ruin furniture.'"

Vivien had brought the *Elephant Walk* screenplay with her and told Finch she'd like him to be her costar. When he hesitated, not having read the script, she insisted. Never the strongest of men, he agreed.

On January 26, 1953, the two left London for Ceylon, with Vivien blowing Larry "a sad little kiss" as the upstart wrapped his arm protectively around her and disappeared inside the plane. "Great God in heaven," Larry thought, sensing danger, "what was it to be now?"

After a long trip from London to Rome and from Rome to Bombay, the actors arrived in Colombo, which Vivien had last seen as a six-year-old when the ship carrying her from Calcutta had docked there on its way to England, and settled in the Galle Face Hotel. She cabled Larry, begging him to join her: "MY DEAREST PLEASE PLEASE TRY COME FOR ONE WHOLE WEEK FOR LESS THAN THAT JOURNEY DREADFULLY EXHAUSTING ALL MY LOVE." Two days later, she cabled again: "MY LOVE HAVE MET NO ELEPHANTS YET BUT HAD A CHAT WITH A COBRA WHO SAYS WE SHOULD BRING A COMPANY OUT HERE I JUST WISH YOUD BRING YOURSELF CANCEL HORSE WENT TO NIGHT CLUB AFTER ALL."

Was her cable sincere? The couple's longing for each other had always peaked when they were apart, but Vivien also knew that Larry was tied up shooting *The Beggar's Opera* for director Peter Brook and desperately needed a vacation, which he planned to take as soon as the film had wrapped. And so she proceeded with her work, which went smoothly at first. True, she fell off a horse and was temporarily housebound while she recovered, but otherwise nothing seemed amiss, except for her inability to rest. "Tormented by sleeplessness," noted one observer, "she'd wander at night among the ruins or sit still till daybreak watching the natives dance. When she was urged to rest so she would be 'your most beautiful self,' her reproach was, 'I'm no longer young. I shouldn't look like an ingénue.'"

A new friend, Bevis Bawa, a former army major and famed landscape gardener, noticed her superhuman energy, always a bad sign for those who knew her well. "If she did sleep," he wrote later, "it must have been for a few minutes in between going places and doing things. She appeared to be racing with time. She never got tired. She never got tight [whereas] I developed bags under my eyes that looked rather like the udders of two ten bottler cows, and Peter looked like a boxer who enjoyed being knocked out."

Vivien's energy kept growing. She would drive two hours from Anuradhapura to Kurunegala for a "devil-dancing" ceremony or break off dinner to climb Bible Rock, leaving Finch so surprised he "swallowed a chicken bone," wrote Bawa.

Quickly, she began to deteriorate. John von Kotze, a Technicolor technician, was surprised when his sixty-four-year-old Cockney assistant came to him "shaking like a leaf" and swore that Vivien had "tried to *vamp* him." Asked about it the next day, she had no recollection. Soon she was making moves on her handsome, married costar, Dana Andrews, knocking on his door stark naked, only to be turned away. Within days, she was coming and going from the set at all times, her eyes wild, her emotions ready to erupt, making it impossible for the production to stick to its planned schedule. Dieterle, the director, tried to work around her but she was "swinging from being tense and overbright to tears and black depression," reported Elaine Dundy.

Days into the shoot, the producer cabled Olivier and begged him to fly out, just as Selznick had done a decade and a half earlier. He agreed, though he had just left England for Ischia, where he hoped to take a break at the home of his friend William Walton.

Arriving in Colombo two days later, he was crushed to find Vivien wasn't there. Having set out from Kandy, where the production was based, she'd insisted on stopping off for a drink on the way to the airport, then raced to make it on time. "It was a drive I shall never forget," recalled Bawa. "We took all the bends on two wheels, my tyres [sic] melted, my brakes burnt, my chauffeur who up to that day was a perfectly normal person went squint-eyed and he now walks with his feet turned inwards. At Ambepussa we dropped in for a quick gin and then tore on. We had another quick one at the Galle Face, then aimed at Ratmalana and shot off. We arrived just in time to see Larry getting into a taxi and looking very cross indeed."

Over dinner at Kandy's Muslim Hotel, Vivien "suddenly started talking about sex," added Bawa. "As I felt she was skating on rather thin ice I told her that I was homosexual. She laughed and said, 'But isn't everybody? Larry is inclined that way too.'"

Alone with her husband, she told him she and Finch were having an affair. He was shaken but not entirely shocked. "I could find no blame in my heart for Peter," he wrote later. "Was he not simply doing what I had done to her first husband seventeen years ago? I found it pretty old-fashioned to work up any extra feelings of outrage."

That was not how others remembered it. Larry, observed Dundy, was seething and "understandably exhibited a certain chill towards [Finch]. Not so understandably he held him responsible for Vivien's breakdown."

There was nothing he could do, and after a few days he returned home, thinking with regret "of the wretched waste of time, effort and money that I had been a party to."

He unburdened himself to Holman, who stepped in with his usual mix of kindness and obtuseness. "My Darling Vivien," he wrote his ex-wife, "Larry rang up last night after he got back. I did not feel too happy about you from what he said. If you don't sleep properly that film will wear you out.... There can be no alternative to going to bed early when you have to get up early and don't waste all your [good] nature in amusing other people as well as doing your work. If I think you are tired I feel tired myself. Perhaps, get out your paint brushes in the evening, the ones for the canvas rather than the face."

Paintbrushes, whether for the canvas or the face, were no solution. Vivien was showing signs of psychosis, a complete break from reality—the first time she had reached this alarming point. She began running after Finch, calling out "Larry" as if he were her husband and they were newlyweds. "It was apparent to everyone in the company that she was hallucinating and that there was something very wrong with her that was not due just to exhaustion," writes Dundy. "By now her condition was so bad that she was no longer able to work and it was decided to get her off the island as quickly as possible."

Two days before location work was scheduled to end, Vivien was bundled on a plane to Los Angeles, where shooting would resume on a soundstage. Her mind flashed back to her horrific airborne experiences with Larry, as it had when she was on the plane to New Zealand. "[She] suddenly unfastened her safety belt and stood up rigid—exactly as she had done seven years before when the plane she had been in crashed in 1946," continues Dundy. "She began screaming that the wing was on fire—as it had been then. Peter, the steward and the air hostess all tried to calm her but, strong in her panic, she threw them off. She became hysterical. She flew at her window like a trapped bird, beating it with her fists, fighting to get out. Then she tore at the neckline of her dress, ripping it down the middle. She scratched and clawed at everyone trying to restrain her. Finally they managed to sedate her."

Vivien appeared to be in a "mixed state," where mania and depression merge and "a very high physical energy [is] combined with a depressed mood," says Kay Redfield Jamison. "It's the most dangerous of the mood states for suicide. Robert Burns has one of the best descriptions of this incredibly agitated, perturbed sense of being a bird flapping around inside a cage"—the very image Dundy used to describe Vivien in the plane. "It's a horrible, horrible, horrible feeling that's usually accompanied by a fair amount of rage."

One can only imagine Vivien's agony when she realized what she had done. But for now, she was incapable of objectivity. As to Finch, he was shattered; a fleeting romance had become a nightmare, costing him not only his friendship with Olivier but possibly his marriage.

Tamara was still in London, where she had remained with her now-three-year-old girl, Anita. Removed from her husband by a distance of five thousand miles and by the astronomical cost of international phone calls, she was unaware of the turmoil until Finch's agent called with a warning: hurry to Los Angeles. She left as soon as she could.

Arriving in California, Tamara was shocked to discover that her husband was sharing a house with Vivien, each theoretically living in a separate wing of the mansion, which Paramount had rented. Once inside, Tamara began to unpack while the two stars were filming at the studio. Hours later, "the doors flew open and Peter, followed by Vivien, rushed in and embraced me warmly," recalled Tamara.

She was startled when Vivien told her to hurry up and get ready, because guests would be there "in half an hour." Guests? Only now did she learn that Vivien had arranged a welcome party and invited seventy famous friends, including David Niven, Stewart Granger and Kazan, the sort of VIPs designed to intimidate this inexperienced and, in her own mind, unattractive young woman. But when the partygoers arrived, Vivien was nowhere to be found. "The waiters, hovering around the tables, looked stony-faced and unconcerned," wrote Tamara. "Where was Vivien?" There was no answer. And then, as the evening wore on, "shouts and loud sobs pierced the conversation, and all heads turned towards the portico. Peter's panic-stricken running steps reverberated in the stunned silence. He shouted to David Niven to come up, he needed some help. 'Can I do anything?' I asked. No, I was to sit down with my guests. After a while Stewart Granger's help was requested."

Minutes later, "Vivien began to rush down the stairs screaming, crying and fighting, restrained by Niven and Granger, then forcibly taken upstairs again, shouting 'Larry, Larry. I want Larry!'" recalled Tamara. "Peter stopped me rushing upstairs, assuring me that she only wanted the comfort of her old friends. The waiters calmly started to clear the tables, pretending to be deaf and dumb. Although they were used to Hollywood dramas, this one was on a major scale. Finally, the noise appeared to stop."

Tamara collapsed into bed, her limbs entwined with Finch's, when "our bedroom door flew open and a demented-looking Vivien, with her light robe open and disclosing her naked body, rushed to our bed and with tremendous energy and screaming obscenities tore off the bedclothes. On discovering us naked, she threw herself on Peter in great passionate embraces. He pushed her away and she collapsed at the foot of the bed sobbing, shouting, 'You haven't told her, you haven't told her! How could you be sleeping with her, you monster? You're my lover!' "

The news came like a "thunderbolt," remembered Tamara. "I was stunned. Peter, who had quickly grabbed a robe, was shaking with anger—I had never seen him in such a wild rage before. He tried to get Vivien to her feet, but she was clinging to his legs. He got her up, but she still clung to his head and pressed her lips to his. He unfastened himself from her grip, pushed her back, pinned her arms against the wall and shouted, 'We'd agreed to keep Larry and Tamara out of this, last night—we'd agreed to keep it secret, not to hurt anyone, and to finish it all.' " When he released Vivien, she "menacingly, forcefully, pushed him and started fighting, calling him every dirty word, forcing him to make a choice between us. He shouted that it had been agreed that they both would remain married. He yelled at her, overpowered her again, dragged her to her part of the house, then, leaving her there sobbing, shut all the doors between her and us."

Somehow, the next day calm returned, at least for a few hours. Finch drove off to Paramount and so did Vivien. That became their routine: the actors would head to the studio each morning and return at night, still living under the same roof,

Vivien now attended by a parade of nurses. But she was far too ill for this makeshift solution. At first, she fluffed lines, and then threw tantrums, and soon began appearing and disappearing without telling anybody where she went.

"Eyes overbright, she chattered ceaselessly," wrote one reporter. "Obviously weary, she dreaded solitude, refused to be left to herself for five quiet minutes. She shocked people by sitting for hours by a radio with her head pasted against the loud-speaker, the volume turned up to a pitch that deafened all others in the room."

Vivien had lost any semblance of rationality. It was a horrible situation for her, even more than for everyone else. "There's very little that is comparable to losing your mind," reflects Jamison. "You're used to having sanity and you take rational thought for granted. And when you lose the capacity to control your thinking, it's terrifying. Very often people have their thinking speed up so fast that they cannot control it; it may start off pretty rapid and then it goes wildly and completely out of control."

At dawn one morning, Vivien crept into the Finches' bed, tears rolling down her cheeks. Tamara managed to get her back to her room. There, "she cried, imploring my forgiveness for what she had done, begging for my friendship, my affection, my love. She looked distressed and said she needed to be cuddled like a child. It made her unhappy, she said, that I was looking at her coldly. She wrung her hands, tried to arouse my sympathy, told me stories about her childhood: how, when the family lived in India, she had walked into a room when her parents were making love. It had given her the impression that her father was violating her mother." Vivien had never mentioned this before and never did again. But, ever since, she insisted, "she had deeply resented men, their selfishness, their superiority, their authority....Deep down she wanted to avenge all women, wanted men to suffer for what they were doing to women. 'I have found a way,' she said."

She was barely eating, but consuming vast quantities of alcohol and cigarettes, all billed to Paramount. Things looked as bad as they could get, when John Buckmaster, her former lover—the man who had spoken over Mona Malden's head at the *Streetcar* party—showed up at the house, presumably invited by Vivien. This son of actress Gladys Cooper had only just been let out of an asylum, New York's Bellevue Hospital, after groping a stranger and pulling a knife on the police. Moving in, he began an affair with Vivien, to which he brought a mystical twist, with dark lighting, overpowering incense, chants and strange rituals—so strange that the maid, terrified, fled and never returned.

There are three different versions of what happened next, besides Olivier's: Tamara's, Niven's and Granger's. Each one places himself or herself center stage; Peter was nowhere to be found.

In Niven's *Bring on the Empty Horses*, he describes getting a late call from the new maid, hysterical. "Mista David," she screamed, "she's *possessed*—that's what!...You git over here real quick now!" Arriving in the dark, Niven entered the house. "Suddenly all the lights went on, and there stood Missie [his pseudonym for Vivien] at the top of the stairs. Her hair was hanging down in straggly clumps; the mascara and makeup made a ghastly streaked mask down to her chin; one false eyelash was missing; her eyes were staring and wild. She was naked and looked quite, quite mad. I had never seen real hysteria before and didn't know how to cope with it. I tried walking up the stairs toward her, but she backed away, screaming, 'Go away! Go away! I hate you!...Don't touch me!'"

When Niven attempted to reason with her, "she sat on the landing, alternately sobbing like a child and snarling down at me through the bannisters like a caged animal." Then she tried to seduce him. "'Come and get it,' she whispered from the top of the stairs, turning her back in a parody of sexiness. It was not an easy evening for me, to put it mildly, and it ended in a glass- and bottle-throwing scene with Missie ordering me out of the house, an instruction I longed to, but dared not, obey."

Once Vivien had calmed down, Niven led her into the hall, hoping to call a doctor, only for her to resist violently. "Clumsily I spun the poor naked girl around, hooked one leg behind her knees, and flung her to the ground," he writes. "After a first startled gasp she fought with incredible ferocity and strength. She didn't scream; she was spitting like a panther, biting, clawing, and kicking. I finally managed to spread-eagle her on the floor and to pinion her arms by kneeling on the elbow joints. I yelled for the doctor."

Later, he admitted, "I found I had come to hate her."

Niven never mentions Granger, who, according to his own account, was shocked to see "Buckmaster, clad only in a towel, standing on the landing at the head of the stairs leading to Viv's bedroom and proclaiming that he had been sent by a higher power to protect her." After convincing the interloper to leave, Granger tried to give Vivien sedatives while she sat naked by the pool, but she grabbed the pills and hurled them into the water. Only when a doctor arrived with two mammoth-sized aides and an equally outsized hypodermic needle did the drama come to an end.

According to Tamara, however, it was she who took charge and saved the day—and Vivien's life. Twice, she recalled, Vivien tried to kill herself. The first time, Tamara pulled her out of the pool, "choking and gasping....She fought me, crying, 'Let me drown, I want to die!'" The second time, Tamara found her "submerged in an overflowing bath, her head completely under water, her legs rigid, sticking out, her eyes open, her hair flowing. It was like a frightening shot out of the [Roman Polanski] film *Repulsion*. I hurriedly pushed her feet down, lifted her head. She was foaming at the mouth. I saw an empty bottle of pills by the side of the bath and assumed she had swallowed them. I fought to get her out of the bath: she pushing her head back under water, I trying to keep her head out, pulling the plug and emptying the bath."

After forcing Vivien to throw up, the actress started sobbing. "She looked like a poor, miserable, drowning kitten," reflected Tamara, "her beautiful eyes begging for help."

Olivier had returned to Ischia, where Paramount tracked him down. He left at once. Arriving in Los Angeles with Cecil Tennant, his business partner, he found Vivien swaddled in cold wet sheets, a crude but effective means of sedation. Usually stoic, Tennant was so saddened by Vivien's condition that he began to cry; but, sensing Larry's exhaustion and his inflammatory effect on her, he offered to stay in the house and advised his friend to check into a hotel.

Paramount issued a statement: "Vivien Leigh is suffering from an acute nervous breakdown. Following the arrival from Europe of Miss Leigh's husband, Sir Laurence Olivier, and later Olivier's consultations with doctors and studio executives, the studio reports that there is a slim hope that the improvement in Miss Leigh's condition, which already has begun, will be rapid enough to permit her to return to work in *Elephant Walk* in a few weeks. No decision, however, has been made regarding this at the present time and there is the possibility that she will be replaced in the picture." In fact, negotiations were already in process with Elizabeth Taylor, who would begin work a week later.

Helped by Tennant, Larry managed to get a sedated Vivien out of the house and off to the airport, only for more drama to ensue on the plane, where a passenger saw her, unconscious, and started screaming, "She's stopped breathing." Danny Kaye met the Oliviers in New York and tried to help them board a plane to England, only for Vivien to throw a fit at the sight of a nurse with a hypodermic needle. She started "screaming appalling abuse at both of us," wrote Olivier, "with particular attention to my erotic impulses [implying he had had sex with Kaye]. It seemed an eternity before she went limp and Danny and I were able to let go of her, both shattered and exhausted."

The press had a field day. "Actress Vivien Leigh, weeping hysterically, was dragged from an automobile to a transatlantic plane today by her husband, Sir Laurence Olivier, and Comedian Danny Kaye after she delayed the flight for 20 minutes," reported the *Los Angeles Times*. "The British actress, suffering a nervous breakdown and what a physician called a fear of flying, alternately sobbed and shook her fist at her husband until he and Kaye each grabbed one of her arms and pulled her from a limousine and up the ramp to the plane floor."

When the plane landed, four doctors and two ambulances were waiting for Vivien. "Wan but smiling radiantly, Miss Leigh came slowly down the stairs," noted the *Daily Herald*. "She was wearing a mink coat over a pink-beige check skirt and yellow sweater and hugged a bunch of red tulips which had been hidden in the plane for her arrival." She seemed, if anything, less drained than her "tired, jaded husband [who] had deep, dark rings round his eyes [and stood agitatedly]. He kept putting his hand to his forehead, trying to remember the formalities of landing at an airport. He dashed into the Customs Hall and dashed out again. He had forgotten the passports."

Leaving the airport, the Oliviers drove thirty miles to Netherne Hospital, the place that had treated Sybille. There, Vivien was given a sedative to make her sleep. At last, Larry was free to go home, so bone-tired that he slept for twelve hours straight.

"Poor Olivier," wrote Tamara, "nothing could have been worse. Affairs, infidelity, all paled with the ordeal of his responsibility."

CHAPTER 14

High on a hill in once-rural Surrey sits the redbrick shell of what used to be Netherne Hospital. Patients no longer roam its elegant grounds, nor do doctors scurry along its empty hall-ways. Instead, dozens of low-rise buildings have been converted to stylish apartments, a modern-day village spread across leafy parkland for those unwilling or unable to pay London's exorbi-tant prices. It was here that Larry brought Vivien on March 20, 1953, according to the hospital's records. She was unrecogniz-able to those who knew her and, as her friend Oswald Frewen observed, had "gravitated out of normal life."

The hospital was bright, modern and well-equipped, far removed from the madhouses of yore. The man in charge of Vivien's treatment, Dr. Rudolf Freudenberg, had previously cared for Sybille, who was "excellently looked after here, and inwardly more at peace & much happier than for many years," she told her brother then. "I am (in this ward) under a brilliant Austrian, a Dr FREUDENBERG, who, I gather, before the war was one of *the* big shots in Vienna."

The forty-four-year-old psychiatrist had fled Nazi Ger-many for Austria, and then Austria for England, where he had arrived in 1936 and found his way to Netherne, an institution he transformed so thoroughly that Eleanor Roosevelt singled it out for praise. "There are about 1600 patients, 800 of whom are allowed out on the grounds under a parole system," she wrote in her newspaper column, after a visit. "The hospital's own farm provides milk and other necessities which would not be obtainable in any other way. An unusual feature is a cafeteria where patients can bring their friends and wait on themselves. A great amount of freedom is given. The treatment is completely up-to-date, and the percentage of cures this past year was 77.5— a record of which they must be proud."

That record may have been exaggerated (Roosevelt never explained how permanent the cures were), but the patients were indeed treated well, receiving individual and group therapy as well as art classes, a breakthrough in mental health. Freudenberg had pioneered the use of insulin for inducing "comas," a strategy considered beneficial—although it was coming into question and would soon vanish from the medical repertoire. "All sorts of treatments can be given while the patient is kept sleeping," noted a contemporary psychiatrist, adding that one of those treatments was electric shocks, which, he acknowledged, ran the risk of causing "considerable memory loss," at least for a while.

That danger was a genuine issue for anyone, especially an actress; but there's no evidence Vivien suffered long-term damage to her memory when she received electroconvulsive therapy (ECT) for the first time, then a relatively new form of treatment. She "would have had a muscle relaxer and a barbiturate anesthetic beforehand," explains Edward Shorter, a medical historian and the author of *A History of Psychiatry: From the Era of the Asylum to the Age of Prozac.* "Then they would have applied the [ECT] treatment, which would have caused a cerebral convolution lasting about thirty seconds, and she would be sent to the recovery room."

Like most patients, Vivien received several such treatments, the electric current passing through electrodes placed on either side of her head. This was "quite humane," says Shorter. "It isn't painful." Still, because gel was not applied to the electrodes, the treatment could burn the skin. "There was the risk of breaking bones or getting a lot of soreness and trauma," notes Po Wang, the Stanford psychiatrist. "There was a lot of that because the body would be shaking. Now we have muscle paralyzers, but when they first started [ECT], they didn't."

Sybille assured Larry that Vivien would quickly bounce back, just as she had. "When convalescent myself I have helped to give such patients their breakfast," she said. "Usually they were too sleepy to do more than take a few mouthfuls. They are kept heavily drugged, of course, but seem to make an amazing recovery once treatment is over."

Vivien remained unconscious for four days, at times wrapped in ice bags. When she revived, however, another manic episode occurred; she was again sedated and kept in a coma for a fortnight.

"The treatment is progressing very satisfactorily and the prolonged sleep still continues," Freudenberg wrote Olivier on March 29, 1953. "She wakes every four hours, as she should, for meals, etc. and then without difficulty takes her medicines and goes on sleeping. I am greatly relieved that the temperature has gone back to normal, so that if everything goes on well, the sleep treatment may be continued for up to three weeks." He continued: "I have been seeing her during her waking periods several times every day and her condition is still changeable. At times she is very much improved, sweet and charming realising her illness; at other times she has been very aggressive and hostile. This morning I found her quiet and friendly but without a clear recollection of all the happenings since Hollywood, which is not unusual. I have given her your letter yesterday morning and in the evening she told me that she had received a very charming letter from you. It is still too early to say definitely how much time will be needed to get her well but I am very hopeful about the outcome."

Freudenberg would have liked to keep Vivien unconscious longer, but on April 13 she woke fully. Despite her pleasure at receiving Larry's letter, she was horrified by her surroundings. "I'll never forget Netherne," she later told the actress Rachel Kempson. "All those other patients walking around—I thought I was in an asylum." She *was* in an asylum. Did she not understand?

Flowers and chocolates were waiting by her bed, but from Coward, not Larry. Vivien was crushed. Calling the playwright at his home in Jamaica, "she started in floods of tears and then made a gallant effort to be gay and ordinary," he wrote, "but the strain showed through and she didn't make sense every now and then."

Larry was back in Ischia, hoping to find peace on the rugged Mediterranean island. Instead, he was besieged by reporters and only managed to escape when the Waltons wrapped him in a blanket and hid him in the back of their car, before taking him on an improvised tour of southern Italy.

Before flying home, he received a sympathetic letter from Jill, who had returned to England after the war and was trying to revive her career while bringing up her teenage son. She and Larry had had little contact as he went from one success to another while she struggled; since coming back, she had had trouble finding work. She felt isolated among her former friends and never remarried, nor did she find happiness in the land of her birth. "I had never known her comfortable in her own skin," writes Tarquin, "probably the aftermath of Larry, but here in her own country where everyone else had such an unhealthy pallor, and for the most part wore frayed clothes, her nervousness and never-ending cigarettes had changed her."

Despite her problems, she told Larry how much she empathized with his situation. It was a heartfelt gesture, all the more generous given his gripes about paying her alimony, and led to a rapprochement of sorts, though the two would never be truly close. Each was suffering, each alone. "I do most desperately feel the need of friends just now," Larry told her. "It has been a very bad time. Getting [Vivien] home was an incredible nightmare. As you may have gathered she set up the strongest resistance, and of course as naturally follows when things go wrong, I was to her, her worst enemy."

For years, he blamed himself for being away when Vivien regained consciousness, for "not being more alive to my duties, no matter how painful or how mortally sick of them I was." But, in all fairness, Freudenberg had told him she would be sedated for weeks, and that his presence might do more harm than good.

When Larry returned, he found Vivien in London's University College Hospital, where she had transferred of her own volition—at her insistence, in fact, as she refused to remain in a madhouse. There she received five additional ECT treatments, which left her feeling "totally numbed [and] worse than before."

Larry was shocked to find her so lethargic. He didn't seem to understand that her condition was only temporary; instead, he regarded it as another brick pulled out of the rickety edifice of his marriage. "I can only describe [the changes] by saying she was not, now that she had been given the treatment, the same girl that I had fallen in love with," he wrote. "Insofar as she was no longer the person I had loved, I loved her that much less. She was now more of a stranger to me than I could ever have imagined possible."

Rather than return to Notley, when she left the hospital in mid-April, Vivien chose to stay with Holman, sealing a bond of friendship that had grown deeper over the years, though their relationship was entirely platonic. She stayed with him for the next few days, before going home.

Six weeks after her release from the hospital, she and Olivier made their first high-profile appearance on June 2, joining eight thousand guests in Westminster Abbey for the coronation of Queen Elizabeth II. Taking their seats at 8:30 a.m., the Oliviers waited two and a half hours before Elizabeth entered the building to the sounds of "God Save the Queen." They watched the twenty-seven-year-old walk down the central aisle, one year and four months after her father's death, accompanied by the lords of the realm in their ermine capes, all viewed by the biggest television audience ever known. It was the kind of pomp and circumstance the Oliviers would normally have admired; but they were here under duress, sending a message to the world that Vivien was fine and that their relationship was intact.

Rumors were spreading fast and wild that the couple's marriage was a sham, and Olivier knew better than anyone how dire things truly were. He had tried everything, not least "fucking" his marriage back into life, but nothing had worked. Now here he was, doing the British thing, maintaining a stiff upper lip, playing one role in public and another in private, the pattern of his life. This was not so much performance as performance art, hardly what he had had in mind when he embarked on a career as an actor.

Vivien told the press she was suffering from exhaustion and would work less from now on. "I did some hard thinking while I was ill," she said. "I stared myself in the face and mapped out a new way of living."

Her new way of living was all but indistinguishable from the old. Four months after leaving Netherne, in August 1953, she and Larry agreed to star in a new play by Rattigan, *The Sleeping Prince*. It was yet another attempt by Olivier to bring them back together, as if a public success would ensure a private one.

The production had originated with Korda, who had advised

Rattigan to compose "a trifle about Kings and Queens" timed to the coronation. The writer's solution: a featherweight farce about the regent of a tiny fictional kingdom who arrives in London for the ceremony and has a fling with a naive chorus girl, only for her to mistake his lust for love. Even in the 1950s, the story seemed dated, though it was rooted in reality: Rattigan's father had been a diplomat assigned to a visiting dignitary at the crowning of Elizabeth's father, the late George VI.

Binkie Beaumont, the producer, had been hesitant to sign the Oliviers, close to them as he was. Perhaps he thought the material was too slender or perhaps he knew Vivien might relapse. Still, he went ahead and hired Alfred Lunt to direct—only for Lunt to drop out and be replaced by Larry when Vivien's illness forced a delay.

Why would he take on such a trifle, "a quilted cushion," as Tynan called it? He was at the peak of his powers, free to do whatever he wished and itching to take on the great classical roles that had eluded him, keenly aware that other performers were nipping at his heels. Gielgud was directing *Richard II* with a young Paul Scofield, Wolfit was staging the entire *Oedipus* cycle—and here he was, committing to this creaky work. One can only attribute his decision to Vivien and a willingness to put his ambition on hold for his wife. This was his shining moment, proof of an underlying generosity that others sometimes failed to see, and even Rattigan recognized he was "subordinating his career to hers."

While the playwright worried that "my flimsy little fairy tale [might] be burst asunder by the vastness of his talent," the opposite proved true. When rehearsals began that summer, the production was "held firmly in shape by his quietly magisterial performance," wrote Rattigan. "Over the weeks, he built his performance slowly and with immense application from a mass of tiny details, some discarded, some retained. 'Are you going to say it like that, Larry?' Vivien would ask. 'I don't know yet,' Larry would reply: 'Let's go on.'" Looking back, Rattigan remembered torrents of laughter, despite the tensions in the Oliviers' relationship. "Sometimes he would break [Vivien] up into helpless giggles. 'Is it as funny as that?' he would ask anxiously. Vivien, unable to reply, would nod, wiping her eyes. 'Terry, what do you think?' In paroxysms of laughter myself, I would say: 'Yes, marvelous.' Then he might consider, frowning: 'No, I think it's too much. It's out.' And out it would be for no discernible reason except that we had both laughed too much and *we* weren't the audience. His instinct for such things is superb, and he was almost certainly right."

Prince opened in London on November 5, 1953, to warm reviews and solid box office. But it was a footnote in the Oliviers' careers, of negligible importance compared to the project Larry held most dear: his film version of *Richard III*.

Olivier had hesitated when he was approached to shoot the tragedy, afraid that his hunchbacked king had become "ham fat" after the Australian tour and a long run in London. But at Korda's prompting, preparations for the shoot began when *Sleeping Prince* ended in summer 1954.

At first, Olivier hoped someone else would direct—perhaps *The Third Man*'s Carol Reed, an acquaintance from their early acting days, whom Larry had also contacted for *Henry V*. But Reed was adamant Larry should do it himself. And so he committed, bringing in Tony Bushell to help him produce, and they set out across the country, searching for locations and even visiting Bosworth Field, the site of Richard's most famous battle, only to reject it because telephone lines proved an insurmountable obstacle.

Filming began in late 1954, with three weeks on location in Spain, followed by several months at Shepperton Studios. Just as Olivier had slashed *Hamlet* and *Henry V,* so he cut *Richard,* eliminating not only words but scenes and characters, while again adding lines from other Shakespeare plays and even a few of his own. He moved fast, filming and editing his 160-minute movie in seventeen weeks, a third of the time he had needed for *Henry V.* Once more, he commanded an army of hundreds, designed to look like thousands; and once more, he dominated a cast that included Gielgud as the Duke of Clarence, Richardson as the Duke of Buckingham and Cedric Hardwicke as King Edward IV.

But his patience was taxed by some of the actors. "Esmond Knight wanted to make more of a thing of some line when he came into Richard's tent at dawn on the day of the Battle of Bosworth, 'The cock croweth, my Lord' or some such line," recalled Douglas Wilmer (who played Lord Dorset). "He said, 'Larry, suppose I loosen my sword in the scabbard, then look over my shoulder through the flap of the tent towards the horses, and then say it.' And Olivier just sat and looked at him, sucking his teeth, then said: 'No. Just say the line and piss off.'"

Inevitably, he injured himself during the shoot. To underscore his line, "A horse, a horse, my kingdom for a horse," he set up a sequence in which he was shot and lost his horse. As he galloped toward the camera, a master archer unleashed an arrow but the horse moved a fraction of an inch out of place and the arrow pierced Larry's calf. The pain was intense; still, he kept going and only when the camera stopped rolling did he scream for a doctor.

One weakness marred the film: Olivier's reluctance to use close-ups, despite Bushell's pleading. "I well remember one of my surprisingly rare shouting matches with L.O.," he said. Getting him to shoot those shots "was like pulling teeth." Months later, when Bushell showed Olivier a critical review by the *New Yorker*'s Pauline Kael, in which she pointed out the same thing, "he didn't take that well."

Vivien had hoped to play Lady Anne, as she had onstage; but in an echo of *Hamlet*, Korda asked for a younger, more contemporary actress and settled on Claire Bloom, fresh from her big break in Chaplin's *Limelight*. The twenty-three-year-old had previously lost the part of Ophelia to Jean Simmons and was surprised when Olivier called out of the blue to offer her this new role. In person, she recalled, he was "far different in character from either Heathcliff or Maxim de Winter. Extremely pragmatic, with a cool and impersonal sexuality that belied his dark and Italianate good looks, he had little interest in anything outside his own particular sphere of genius, and, unlike his more brilliant wife, Vivien Leigh, could even be somewhat pedestrian and dull."

Vivien was convinced they were having an affair, which Bloom initially denied, only to confirm it in her 1996 memoir, *Leaving a Doll's House*. Looking back, she had little sympathy for Olivier and depicted him as a man who mesmerized her with the same "fatal combination of attractiveness and repulsiveness" as his King Richard. Off-camera, she found "a dryness, a lack of spontaneity. Careful, somewhat plodding, full of theatrical mannerisms, he was brimming with a kind of false charm. But I ignored all the evidence; I saw only what I wanted to see, seeking only to continue a romance that was being enacted, considerably more emphatically, onscreen. It was the fascination of the rabbit to the snake."

One evening, Larry invited her to Notley while Vivien was away. They were joined for dinner by his brother, Dickie, and his wife, Hester, neither of whom seemed fazed, prompting Bloom to conclude there must have been other "guests" like her. But she was convinced, no matter what, that Larry still loved Vivien, that nobody would ever displace her in his heart, that "Notley Abbey was absolutely hers, and so was Laurence Olivier."

*   *   *

She was wrong. Shortly before Vivien embarked on her affair with Finch, Olivier had met another actress on the set of *The Beggar's Opera*.

Dorothy Tutin, then twenty-two, was both charming and disarming, a blend of innocence and intelligence that was the perfect bait for an older man beginning to feel his age. She had been seeing Finch's friend Trader Faulkner when she met Larry and the two began an intense affair; soon, she was caught up in a romance that would continue for five years.

Faulkner was indignant. He had gone to Bermuda that fall and returned to find his girlfriend obsessed with another man. When he discovered that Larry was visiting her regularly late at night on the houseboat where she lived, he arranged to lie in wait and hid in a trash can, where he hunkered down, despite the bitter cold, armed with a bottle, planning to crack him across the head. In the wee hours, Larry stepped out of Tutin's boat, only for Faulkner to spring up, terrifying the young actress, who promptly fled inside and left the two men alone. Then Faulkner looked at his rival and saw him anew. Unshaven and alone, here in the dark by the river, he appeared older and wearier than Faulkner had remembered, not so much a colossus who bestrode the planet as a sad and middle-aged man who looked more like an accountant than a movie star.

"Baby, what are you doing here?" asked Olivier.

"I'm about to play a madman on TV and I'm getting into character," mumbled his assailant.

"Well," said Larry, "let me tell you you're a very convincing madman. You're going to be wonderful in the part. A definitive lunatic, baby."

With that, as Faulkner recalled, Olivier kissed him on both cheeks and then hurried off. Moments later, a car pulled up on the embankment and a woman stepped out. She looked like a common prostitute, with an outfit to match, a leopard-skin coat, and Faulkner wondered who she could be. For a while she watched, and then departed. Years later, he told Vivien about the incident and how jealousy was eating him up. "Oh Trader," she said, "jealousy was eating *both of us*. The leopard-skin whore you saw on the embankment that night was me."

Improbable as that story seems, Vivien's jealousy was not. When she learned about Tutin, she insisted on meeting her face-to-face and threatened to kill herself if the young woman didn't break off the affair. When Tutin's father added his objections, the actress had enough: she refused to continue with Larry, even though he promised to leave Vivien and marry her.

"My new love," he wrote later (without naming her), "was naturally and sensibly coming to the conclusion that the fruition of her love for me was altogether too mixed a blessing.... We parted and remain on the friendliest terms."

He retained a special place in his heart for Tutin and kept her last letter to him in his wallet until it had frayed away. "He was really upset," says Tarquin, and so was she. "She said she didn't think the world would allow them to be happy."

Vivien felt the same way. She and Larry were clinging to the carcass of a romance, to the memory of being in love when real love seemed so far away. Each had long stopped being faithful and, though Vivien could no more blame Larry than herself, it hurt to see him eyeing younger women when she was no longer in the full flower of youth. She was worried about her age, concerned about her appeal and hyper-conscious of her looks, an obsession that had been building for several years. Some time ago, she had insisted on approving Cecil Beaton's photos for *Anna Karenina*, demanding he destroy the ones she didn't select, and had even told him that her face was "not at all what she would like....It has deteriorated and appalls her."

Her anxiety was not entirely without cause. If her youthful beauty was fading, so was Hollywood's interest in the women who had helped build its brand, the great female stars of the 1930s and 1940s. Increasingly, women of that era were supporting players, footnotes in male-written and male-centric scripts— and when a lead came along, all too often they were deemed fungible, quick to be replaced by younger actresses with shorter resumes and fewer demands. Ironically, the studio system that had treated these women like chattel had also given them some marvelous parts; whereas the new, freewheeling industry, with no pipeline of actresses under contract, had no reason to cater to them, no producers to advocate on their behalf.

Still, this only partially justified Vivien's fears. What had been self-consciousness soon blossomed into a full-blown phobia, and she now muffled herself in furs, covering her face and seeking out the dark rather than the light. Nor was her self-regard bolstered when Korda approached her with a new role as a drab housewife in another Rattigan vehicle, a film version of his play *The Deep Blue Sea.*

Sea tells the story of a woman who leaves her husband for a semi-alcoholic pilot, only for him to leave her in turn. It had been a hit onstage with Larry's former drama school classmate (and lover) Peggy Ashcroft, who would have been perfect for the film if her name had meant anything in the movies. But even with Ashcroft out of the running, Vivien was not Korda's top choice: he had first pursued Marlene Dietrich, then Garbo and de Havilland, all of whom passed before he reached out to his old friend.

Filming began in September 1954 on a stage at Shepperton Studios adjoining that of *Richard III*, with Anatole Litvak directing. The Lithuanian-American had drawn excellent performances from other stars, such as Ingrid Bergman (*Anastasia*) and Danielle Darrieux (*Mayerling*), but he was no better suited to this very British material than Duvivier had been to *Karenina*. "He had this theory that you have to destroy somebody first to get a good performance out of them and he used to—systematically—every day—destroy Vivien until he got her to cry," recalled the actress Moira Lister, "and he said 'Right. Now you're in a mood to do the scene. We'll do the scene.' He was really very harsh with her."

So, to some degree, was her costar, Kenneth More. He was shocked, during filming, when "Larry came down to see her. He was so much in love with her in those days. He gave her a beautiful aquamarine ring on the set. He pressed this into her hand. I thought, what a gift for a girl to have. But she hardly looked at it. She just said, 'Oh, darling, how lovely,' and put it into her handbag."

Unaware of her private pain, he felt she was "petulant, spoilt, overpraised, and overloved." She was, in fact, lonely and miserable, feeling older and unwanted by her husband, not to mention the industry in which she had once reigned supreme. She knew, too, that no matter how good she might be in the film, she could never compete with Ashcroft. "Peggy A. was unforgettable in the original, though she cheated on account of her unique power of making you sorry for her," noted Bushell. "Vivien made the film of it + gave one of her most brilliant performances which unhappily went for nothing owing to a surprising + unpredictable failure by Kenny More to convey the sexual pull of the R.A.F. anti-hero."

The movie's poor box office deepened Vivien's insecurities and made her yet more dependent on Larry. Each step she took away from him seemed to result in disappointment, regardless of her success in the film version of *Streetcar*. And so, rather than strike out alone, she bound herself tighter to her husband.

But when they returned to Stratford in April 1955 for three

Shakespeares (*Twelfth Night*, *Titus Andronicus* and *Macbeth*), "she started to go strange," recalled Maxine Audley, who played Olivia in the first of the plays, *Twelfth Night*. "Not only did she behave violently to everybody—probably worse to the people she loved and who were closest to her, but she physically swelled up. It was really weird. Her whole body swelled, particularly round the neck and face and shoulders. That would last two days and then she would be back to normal again." (Medics consulted for this book offered varying explanations for the swelling, possibly including an allergic reaction to medication; doctor's notes show she was taking Libraxin, Serenace, Seconal and Marplan, among other drugs.)

Gielgud, who was directing *Twelfth Night*, remembered the swelling, too, and saw it come and go at the same time as Vivien's manic spells. "She'd lose her looks terribly when she had these attacks," he noted. "Her face used to widen....Sort of blew up."

He was always fond of Vivien and far closer to her than Larry, with whom he had a tense and competitive relationship. Despite their rivalry, he had agreed to direct him as the officious majordomo, Malvolio; but he soon realized it was a mistake. They clashed—and how could they not? Gielgud didn't understand that the higher Larry rose, the more he longed to rise even higher, the greater became his need to crush anyone who might challenge his supremacy. And nobody presented the same sort of challenge as Gielgud, his polar opposite but also his most brilliant contemporary. "The truth is he is a born autocrat, and must always be right," Gielgud wrote a friend in the middle of their rehearsals. "He has little respect for the critical sensitivity of others; on the other hand he is quite brilliant in his criticism of my directing methods and impatient with my hesitance and (I believe) necessary flexibility." He added: "I may still make a good thing of that divine play, especially if he will let me pull her little ladyship (who is brainier than he is but *not* a born actress) out of her timidity and safeness. He dares too confidently (and will always carry an undiscriminating audience with him) while she hardly dares at all."

Days before the production opened on April 12, 1955, Olivier asked Gielgud to leave the show and took over as director. Mortified, he did as he was told but fretted that nobody would now rein Olivier in, that he would continue to play Shakespeare's pompous steward like a "Jewish hairdresser, with a lisp."

Twelfth Night was a success, despite Gielgud's fears; but it didn't come close to the two plays that followed it: *Titus Andronicus* and *Macbeth*.

Titus reunited Olivier with his *Beggar's Opera* director Peter Brook, and neither initially expected the collaboration to go well. Larry had tried to get Brook fired from the film, and so the thirty-year-old wunderkind arrived at the *Titus* rehearsals "armed with a battering ram," as he put it, only to find their relationship infinitely smoother than it had been before. He attributed this to Vivien's diplomacy, at which she was a master, along with a series of polite gestures on either side, feigned acts of friendship and false expressions of warmth.

For Brook, Larry remained "a strangely hidden man," whom he could never quite understand. "Onstage and on the screen," he wrote, Olivier "could give an impression of openness, brilliance, lightness, and speed. In fact, he was the opposite. His great strength was that of an ox. He always reminded me of a countryman, of a shrewd, suspicious peasant taking his time. When he tried to catch up with a new idea, his forehead would seem to shine, as though from determination not to be outwitted. The dazzling virtuosity of his acting came from a painstakingly composed mosaic of tiny details, which when finally assembled could flash by in sequence with breathtaking speed, giving the illusion of glittering thought."

Like Claire Bloom, Brook found Olivier insincere. He was "polite and attentive, [but] even his laughter was acted, as though he never ceased remaking and polishing his mask." Only onstage did the mask come off, as if solely in the midst of illusion could Larry be real.

He was willing to risk everything to get the effect he wanted, even if it meant horrifying his audience, as in the play's most spectacular scene, when Titus's hand is severed onstage. The sequence was made indelible by Brook's decision to have a fraction of a pause between the ax falling and Larry's scream. "Olivier put his hand down and [Anthony] Quayle [chopped] it off and as he lowered the axe I was right beside the stage with a great big awful piece of sort of squashy bone stuff," recalled Colin Clark, one of Larry's assistants (and the son of art historian Kenneth Clark), who was handling the effects. "And it made the most awful, sickening noise."

Bushell remembered how Olivier delivered Titus's celebrated speech "I am the sea!" by moving downstage and uttering his words "at the very summit of what his tongue larynx + lungs could project.... This one line of Laurence's literally rang round + back from the beams, rafters, whatever there were up above in the roof. The effect on the audience was astonishing and unforgettable. They shouted, cried, + cheered."

Vivien had her own powerful moment in the play: when her hands were cut off, she appeared with red streamers flowing from her wrists. But her personal drama overpowered her character's. "Poor Vivien," recalled Quayle, "she was suffering badly from manic depression, and she had turned against the very man she loved most in the world—against Larry. Her behaviour was sometimes quite rational, but sometimes aggressive and desperately hurtful to him—both off stage and on. Standing there beside them while Titus was speaking words of love and comfort to poor mutilated Lavinia, she would be cursing him with the most extreme obscenities imaginable, with a piece of bloody gauze tied over her mouth. The audience could not hear what she was saying or realize that she was speaking at all, but it was perfectly audible to those of us who were there."

None of that was apparent in *Macbeth*, as perfect a vehicle for the Oliviers as any they had performed. The actress Sybil Thorndike had long maintained that the tragedy needed a real-life husband and wife, and here was living proof.

"Most Macbeths and Lady Macbeths don't seem to behave like a married couple," said Maxine Audley. "I never believe they actually lived together. But Larry and Vivien at the banquet scene, when he sees the ghost of Banquo and she's trying to keep control, they were like any married couple with awkward guests."

Larry's Macbeth mirrored his own innermost anguish, not so much through screaming or falling as through a profound weariness he couldn't shrug. His Scottish thane wasn't a young man dominated by youthful ambition but a Macbeth "in his old age," as he explained later, "yearning for the troops of friends he must not look to have, the mind roaming over the past."

His work was so impressive that Albert Camus sent him an inscribed copy of his play *Caligula*, thanking him for "the greatest theatrical emotion of my life." Here Larry "shook hands with greatness," wrote Tynan. Most Macbeths, he observed, "let off their big guns as soon as possible, and have usually shot their bolt by the time the dagger speech is out." But Larry did the opposite. "He begins in a perilously low key, the reason for which is soon revealed. This Macbeth is paralysed with guilt before the curtain rises, having already killed Duncan time and again in his mind. Far from recoiling and popping his eyes, he greets the air-drawn dagger with sad familiarity; it is a fixture in the crooked furniture of his brain." He noted, further, that "instead of growing as the play proceeds, the hero shrinks; complex and many-levelled to begin with, he ends up a cornered thug, lacking even a death scene with which to regain lost stature."

While praising Olivier, Tynan again savaged Vivien, sniping that "Vivien Leigh's Lady Macbeth is more niminy-piminy than thundery-blundery, more viper than anaconda, but still quite competent in its small way." He would later regret his harsh words, but his shaft drew blood and Larry was incensed, blaming him for pushing Vivien over the edge.

She was staying up later and later, inviting friends to visit and then refusing to let Larry rest. Just as Macbeth longs for sleep, so did he, adding a whole new layer to Shakespeare's plaintive lament:

> Methought I heard a voice cry, "Sleep no more!
> Macbeth does murder sleep"—the innocent sleep,
> Sleep, that knits up the ravell'd sleave of care,
> The death of each day's life, sore labor's bath,
> Balm of hurt minds, great nature's second course,
> Chief nourisher in life's feast.

If Lady Macbeth sleepwalks, Vivien herself seemed never to sleep at all and so neither did Larry. "With only two hours of sleep," he moaned during his *Titus* rehearsals, "how in God's name had I any hope of committing to memory the unfamiliar myriad of words in this huge part? I felt a growing sense of desperation, more intense than anything I had yet known."

He begged Vivien to return to Freudenberg. "She was not too difficult to persuade," he acknowledged, "but she had a trick up her sleeve. When we had been ushered in to see the doctor, in whom I had more faith than any other upon this earth, God help me if she didn't put on the most devastatingly convincing performance of a calm, sane, normal woman, not even aggrieved to have been brought all this way: poor Larry, he's overanxious, that's all; it's easy to understand when you think of all the terrible dances I have led him, but, you see, I've never really been or felt better. To my horror, I saw that she had hoodwinked even Freudenberg." The psychiatrist rejected further ECT, warning that "in these circumstances such treatment could be highly dangerous."

Coward, visiting the Oliviers in Stratford, was shocked by what he saw. Vivien "talked at supper wildly," he wrote. "She is obsessed, poor darling, by the persecutions of the Press; her voice became high and shrill and her eyes strange." Larry, he added, "is distraught and deeply unhappy. Apparently this relapse has been on the way for some time. She has begun to lose sleep again and make scenes and invite more and more people to Notley until there is no longer any possibility of peace. Their life together is really hideous and here they are trapped by public acclaim, scrabbling about in the cold ashes of a physical passion that burnt itself out years ago....She, exacerbated by incipient TB, needs more and more sexual satisfaction. They are eminent, successful, envied and adored, and most wretchedly unhappy."

Quayle, who had to deal with them each day, was less sympathetic. "They have made a pact with the devil," he told a friend. "He said 'You can have everything, all the riches, and you will be King and Queen of the theatre but there's only one condition: You must stay together for the rest of your lives.'"

Vivien again found solace with Finch. The actor, astonishingly, had moved into the Oliviers' temporary home in Stratford, where he remained for weeks, and then continued to see them at Notley.

"Vivien, more and more, called for Peter," wrote Tamara. "Invitations for me to visit Notley ceased—in fact, secret arrangements were made so as to exclude me. A car came to collect Peter, and occasionally waited for him for hours. He assured me that he was only helping. Helping, I thought! Helping...I couldn't imagine that with Olivier there Vivien and Peter were still 'carrying on.'"

One night, Trader Faulkner, who had gotten past the houseboat incident and become part of the Olivier circle, was visiting them and "Vivien was on edge as we sat alone in the drawing room, drinking gin and discussing reincarnation," he recalled. "She was convinced Peter was 'an old soul,' full of timeless wisdom, tenderness, understanding—all the qualities that every woman looks for in every man. Larry was 'a brand new soul with a plastic Karma and a marital deficit balance.'" While she was saying this, Faulkner was horrified to notice "Larry's familiar shadow outside the door silhouetted against the wall, listening."

In December, Vivien and Finch ran away. It was their second attempt, after an earlier effort had fizzled when fog grounded their plane. Now they left for Paris, where Vivien asked to stay with Ginette Spanier, only to be turned away by her friend, who refused to betray Larry. The lovers next headed south, where Olivier eventually caught up with them shortly before Christmas. Whatever anger he might once have felt had gone; he was beyond jealousy, rage, self-righteousness, perhaps beyond any emotion at all.

A confrontation took place between him and Finch. "He was invited to Notley where dinner for three was served with impeccable elegance," writes Faulkner. "Vivien departed with the coffee and Larry summoned Peter to the library to chat over the port. Finchie suddenly got the giggles at the idea of being interviewed among the calf leather and the moroccos. Once in the library with the door shut, neither actor knew how to begin the scene, so there was a very long pause. Eventually Larry, the most resourceful and ingenious of men, began to play the rather idiotic lord-of-the-manor, realizing the need to stop embarrassing Peter and put him at ease. Peter, taking his cue instantly, was transformed into Sir Laurence's elderly, rather seedy butler, who had served his lordship from his youth. They continued in this fashion and gradually built up a scene. Both ended up hysterical with laughter at their own wit. Suddenly the door burst open and there stood Lady Macbeth. At her most imperious she demanded, 'Will one of you come to bed with me now?' "

History was repeating itself—just as it always did, just as it always would—first as tragedy and then as farce. "Larry said to Vivien: 'You've got to choose. This isn't OK,'" says Victoria Tennant. "Vivien looked at Peter, and looked at Larry, and said: 'Darling, his fingernails, they're dirty!' And Peter got up, and he went to the station, and he got on the train, and that was the end of it."

And yet it wasn't. Vivien pursued Finch with the same relentlessness she had once applied to Larry, abandoning all pride as she hurled herself at her increasingly disengaged lover, an Anna Karenina in a limousine. "It was impossible to get away from [her]," writes Tamara. "No one ever got away from her. She told me that, when she saw my efforts to rebuild our life, she did her damnedest to continue the affair. [Peter] resisted, but not hard enough." She adds: "How could one resist the charm, the beauty, the sophistication, the wit and the demands of Vivien Leigh? How could one escape being carried away by the tide of her moods and emotions?"

Finch couldn't. Leaving his wife and child, he moved into his mother's Chelsea home, which, with a strange sort of pride, the older Mrs. Finch let him use for his assignations. "Vivien found Betty's cottage convenient for meetings," continues Tamara. "Poor Peter: torn by loyalty to Olivier, fascinated by Vivien and ashamed of his neglect of Anita and me. The more guilty he felt, the worse he became."

In July 1956, Vivien discovered she was pregnant. But was the father Larry or Finch? Without doubting that the child was his,

Olivier was nonetheless torn. On the one hand, this was the last best hope for his marriage; on the other, he was ready to break free and didn't wish to repeat his previous, unfortunate experience with fatherhood. Even as he tried to untangle this thicket of emotions, he found himself swept up in a media frenzy when word of the pregnancy leaked.

"The publicity this attracted now seems incredible," writes Terry Coleman. "[Vivien] and Olivier were the pop stars of their day. The report and a picture covered practically the entire front page of the tabloid *Daily Sketch*. The *Daily Mail* gave half a page to the news. It was to be a baby for Christmas, expected to arrive on 22 December. Vivien, photographed sitting on a love seat, said they would prefer a girl and then looked up at Olivier, 'standing bashfully behind her,' and said: 'Oh, you know men. They like to be comforted in their old age with a daughter.' Olivier was invited to kiss his wife and declined, saying, 'We're too old for that.' "

Vivien had just returned to the stage with a big success, Coward's *South Sea Bubble*, while also performing in a benefit at the Palladium, and had to tell the playwright she was pulling out. "It *saddens* and *saddens* me to have to leave," she wrote. "I *am* sorry my darling for this upheaval—but I do believe and trust the play will go happily, bulgingly, on its way for you without me.... Tell me please at once you're not too angry."

Coward was enraged. *Bubble* was his first bona fide hit in years and here was this spoiled and selfish prima donna, this madwoman, turning down an opportunity for which any other actress would have given her eyeteeth. "The hysterical, disorganized silliness of the whole thing infuriates me," he wrote in his diary. "In the first place, to try to have a baby at her age [forty-two] is fairly foolish; secondly, it is not very bright, if pregnant, to dance about at the Palladium with Larry and Johnny Mills and go out to parties while playing an arduous part eight times a week....Meanwhile, a smash success is destroyed, she is wretched and on her way round the bend again....Altogether I'm sick to death of them both."

Vivien was full of remorse. "I am so terribly distressed to think I have hurt you and I do hope you will really forgive me for my seeming thoughtlessness," she wrote him. "You are such a wonderful dear and wise friend and I am utterly miserable at having pained you in any way....If you *knew* the turmoil poor Larry-boy is going through, darling Noelie, you would understand why you have had no word from him."

Later, when Coward had calmed down, he apologized for his rant. Still, the damage was done; their friendship would continue, but it would never be the same.

A month after leaving *Bubble*, Vivien miscarried, quashing her hopes that the baby would save her marriage. "On August 13th—the pains started," noted a reporter. "In agony, she was rushed to the hospital. The doctor's [sic] worked feverishly. They barely managed to save her. They couldn't save the baby." Adding salt to the wound, Vivien's sister-in-law, Hester, who was living at Notley with Dickie, gave birth the next day.

The Oliviers were at their lowest point in years when a newcomer added her special brand of combustibility to the mix: Marilyn Monroe.

In February 1956, Larry, Rattigan and Cecil Tennant flew to New York to discuss filming *The Sleeping Prince* with Monroe after her company had bought the rights. Arriving at Marilyn's Sutton Place apartment, they found her business partner, Milton Greene, sitting in the living room, where he plied them with drinks while they waited for the star.

At twenty-nine years old, the former Norma Jeane Baker was at the pinnacle of her fame and the nadir of her personal problems. She had long given in to a cocktail of drugs and alcohol, which helped mask her bottomless insecurity, the residue of a disastrous childhood in which she had been kidnapped by her stepfather, dumped in a foster home and molested by a boarder. The hole left behind was as big as America. But Olivier was blind to all this when Marilyn made her entrance from an adjoining room, two hours late, dressed in a simple outfit and no makeup. "I'm sorry," she said in her girlish whisper of a voice. "I just didn't know what to wear. Should I be casual or formal? I went twice through my entire wardrobe, but everything I tried on wasn't kinda right."

She seemed so nervous about meeting Larry that his pride swelled, his ego kicked in and his sex drive shifted into high gear. Marilyn had neither Vivien's intellect nor her sophistication, but she knew how to read men better than any analyst, knew them in all their strength and weakness, knew their almost atavistic need to take charge, to rescue a woman just like her. Larry may have had a knighthood, may have been acclaimed as the greatest actor on the British stage, but he wasn't exempt. Was it love or lust he felt, or a combination of both? Or was it the possibility Marilyn offered of restoring him to the pinnacle of show business power, reminding the world that his stardom still resonated, even if his box office did not?

The next morning, he agreed to direct and costar in *The Sleeping Prince* (later retitled *The Prince and the Showgirl*). He would receive $100,000, twice as much as Marilyn; but she would own the rights to the $1.5 million movie—which meant, in effect, that she would be his boss. The two celebrated at the 21 Club, one of Manhattan's redoubtable hangouts, a place to see and be seen, signaling to the entertainment community that two superpowers had brokered a treaty and now their nation-building would begin. "*What* was going to happen?" Larry wondered. "She was so adorable, so witty, such incredible fun and more physically attractive than anyone I could have imagined, apart from herself on the screen."

If he had done his due diligence, he might have reconsidered. Wyler had compared her to Hitler, and another director, Josh Logan (*Bus Stop*), warned Larry that she was incorrigible. "She was strange," Logan reflected. "She was very much of a frightened, wounded, woodland animal who had been so humiliated and ridiculed by press men and photographers as well as thoughtless, selfish directors, that she did not really respond the way a normal girl would."

None of this dampened Larry's excitement, and five months later Marilyn arrived in London to start work on the film. The timing was notable—only forty-eight hours after Vivien had announced her pregnancy—but the weather was not. Rain bucketed down on the hundreds of journalists, paparazzi and security guards who had staked out their spots at the airport, along with Vivien and Larry, ready for Marilyn as she descended from her plane in a light-colored sheath and long white gloves, accompanied by her husband of two weeks, Arthur Miller, along with twenty-seven items of luggage, only three of which were his. If power could be measured by the bag, his suitcases said it all.

The forty-year-old playwright had almost remained in New York. Unflinchingly political, he had become a prime suspect of the House Un-American Activities Committee as it pursued its relentless mission to root out Communists, wherever they might be. He had fully expected his passport to be revoked, only for his prominence as Marilyn's husband to let him off the hook. Not that he seemed happy to be at her side, as an impromptu press conference got underway. He was "as cold as a refrigerated fish," said one observer, "like a morgue keeper left with a royal cadaver."

Larry, however, was almost giddy with joy and even smiled at Marilyn's well-practiced rejoinder when she was asked by a reporter what she wore to bed: "Chanel No. 5." The actor's blissful state persisted when the press conference turned into a frenzy.

As journalists stampeded, trampling one of their own, Vivien asked Marilyn if all her press conferences were like that. "Actually," Marilyn replied, "this is a little quieter than some of them."

An official press conference took place the next day, attended by "two hundred reporters, four thousand fans, two inspectors, a sergeant, six constables, and four teams of police," writes one of Monroe's biographers, Gary Vitacco-Robles. Marilyn was late, partly because three hundred villagers had mobbed her car as it left Parkside House, the Surrey mansion she had rented from the publisher of the *Financial Times*. It was clear at the press conference that, idolize Larry as she might, she knew nothing of his stage work, let alone Vivien's; she told the reporters her dream role was Lady Macbeth, unaware that Vivien had so recently played the part.

Things quickly soured. As the Millers and the Oliviers spent more time together, "Marilyn felt Larry was paying more attention to Miller than to her," says Michael Korda, "and she felt Miller was going out of his way to be more charming to Larry than to her, even though they were married. She was very shrewd. Mostly what she thought was true."

The couples competed for the worst faux pas. When Larry took his guests to see Vivien in *South Sea Bubble*, one of her last performances in the show, Miller asked who had directed this piffle. Olivier himself, he replied. (In fact, it was William Chappell.) He then demonstrated his own lack of tact by telling Marilyn she should brush her teeth with baking soda to make them less yellow.

On July 24, Olivier and Rattigan threw a welcoming party for her at the writer's country home. Guests included some of England's notable names—Gielgud; John Mills and Sybil Thorndike; the ballerina Margot Fonteyn; the socialite and intellectual Diana Cooper; and the Duke of Buccleuch. Even the American ambassador, Winthrop Aldrich, was there, only to be kept waiting, like everyone else, for Monroe, who finally showed up at 11 p.m.

Days later, she arrived at Pinewood with her entourage—a makeup man, hairdresser, cook, secretary, publicist and producer Greene, as well as the usual battalion of bodyguards. The studio was on red alert. "Every vehicle is checked at the gate just like in the RAF," noted Colin Clark, Larry's assistant. "Once inside there are three huge studios joined by a very long concrete corridor. The other side of this corridor are the star dressing rooms....It really is all very like an RAF base with its hangars, offices and officers' mess."

After some preliminary camera tests, Olivier walked the cast through the story, taking all the parts himself. Production began on August 7 with a scene in the grand duke's drawing room, where Larry would seduce Elsie, the showgirl of the title, played by Marilyn.

From the start, she had trouble remembering her lines, and that only got worse as shooting continued. In one scene, meant to take place at Westminster Abbey, she did not even have to talk; she simply had to look up and move in a certain direction— and even that required multiple takes. It took two full days and thirty-four takes just to capture her nibbling caviar (not to mention twenty jars of caviar). Olivier's confidence in her was "minimal" at best, said Clark. "She didn't seem to understand when he spoke and it wasn't clear she even listened."

Their relationship grew tense. When the actor-director told her to "act sexy," she shot back, "Larry, I don't have to act sexy. I *am* sexy."

"Laurence had to learn patience," said Douglas Wilmer, who had a small role in the film. "It was no good getting annoyed with her, because it was just water off a duck's back. When she did arrive he said to her, 'Why can't you get here on time for fuck sake!' and Marilyn said: 'Oh, do you have that word in English, too?' And that was her only reaction. She would say she wanted to go to her caravan to change her dress, and she would sit in there for hours while Laurence paced up and down outside. And when he knocked on the door she would call 'Go away.'...I admired his patience, and his humor [but] I think it spoiled his own performance, because, as he said: 'It's like teaching a dog for the whole day to bark, and at the end of the day it goes "Yap" and steals the picture.'"

When Thorndike (playing the grand duchess) was kept waiting, Olivier exploded, while the veteran kept her cool. She was "a really wonderful old gal," wrote Bushell. "Laurence +/or I will never forget her immaculate behaviour to that black-hearted trollop Monroe....Repeatedly kept waiting for two or three hours for scenes which Monroe knew perfectly well were for the two of them only, she—made up and word perfect on the set on the dot of 9 o'clock—would greet the blowsy hellion with the sort of reserved courtesy she would have extended to a Hottentot princess. It never failed."

Unlike Olivier, Thorndike recognized Monroe's transcendence on-screen and realized "that little girl is the only one here who knows how to act before a camera." But Vivien knew it too, and when she saw the rushes, she began to cry. "I didn't think she would be that beautiful," she told Amy Greene, the wife of Marilyn's business partner. "She has it and I don't."

This didn't dispose Olivier any better toward his costar. "Larry says of [Marilyn] that she has the 'brains of a poussin [a chicken]' & teaching her acting is like teaching urdu to a marmoset," quipped Oswald Frewen.

On September 12, 1956, the gossip columnist Walter Winchell reported that "the Dear One is muffing lines like crayzee— necessitating as many as twenty 'takes.'...Also that she is driving Sir Laurence Olivier netz [nuts]....The Titled One asked Marilyn to do something the other day. She allegedly turned her renowned derriere on him."

While Olivier always spoke to his British colleagues with a "clubby professionalism," he addressed Marilyn like a child, telling the crew to be patient because she wasn't used to their ways, even though he was unable to be patient himself. Nor was that surprising. Bushell recalled that "the hell-hound" Monroe fluffed one line twenty-two times. "I kid you not," he wrote, "I thought if I had to listen to poor Laurence giving her the cue 'a certain euphoria' once more I should walk out and beat her to death."

None of this escaped Marilyn, who had an almost seismographic sensitivity to others' opinions. "He talks to me as if he's slumming," she complained of Larry. On her copy of the script, she scribbled: "What am I doing here with this strange man?"

Clark, despite being Olivier's employee, worried that "Sir," as he called Larry, was "much too remote...he is quite clearly not in any way concerned with her personally. He is the supreme professional, expecting and assuming that everyone else will be professional too [but not] cosy with MM. He's strong and romantic with most women but he only gets 'cosy' with men."

The actress, in turn, only got cozy with her ever-present coach, Paula Strasberg, a zaftig, brown-eyed woman married to Lee Strasberg, the most famous acting teacher in the world; she would repeatedly step in to offer advice, wanted or not. When Logan, the *Bus Stop* director, visited the set, Olivier "came at me with a venomous rush," he recalled, "and said, 'How dare you tell me to have Paula Strasberg on the set? She's a bloody nuisance!' I said, 'I told you that she never appeared on my set,' and suddenly he looked at me, aghast, and said, 'You did? How did I get the idea she was there all the time?'"

"Olivier," said Miller, "was soon prepared to murder Paula outright, and from time to time I would not have minded joining him, for Marilyn, a natural comedienne, seemed distracted by half-digested spitballed imagery and pseudo-Stanislavskian parallelisms that left her unable to free her own native joyousness...."

As for Olivier, with all his limitations in directing Marilyn—an arch tongue too quick with the cutting joke, an irritating mechanistic exactitude in positioning her and imposing his preconceived notions upon her—he could still have helped her far more than Paula with her puddings of acting philosophy."

Those puddings had a healthy dollop of sycophancy mixed in. "You are the most wonderful actress I have ever known in my life, Marilyn," gushed Strasberg. "I have...prayed on my knees for God to give me a great actress. And now He has given me you."

Neither Strasberg nor Olivier knew that Marilyn was going through a personal crisis as her brand-new marriage began to flame out. Days into the shoot, she stumbled upon Miller's journal and discovered that he was having second thoughts, that he felt he had made a mistake almost as soon as the wedding was over. The revelation was harrowing. Marilyn learned "how disappointed he was in me...how he thought I was some kind of angel but now he guessed he was wrong."

Then came a massive surprise: she learned she was pregnant, a fact she kept hidden from her husband. That pregnancy, which has been the subject of much speculation, appears to be confirmed by the recent discovery of her attorney's phone log, detailing calls he made to a London doctor. It was horribly ironic that Marilyn was pregnant at almost the same time as Vivien, with the same devastating result.

Years later, Clark wrote about that and the time he spent alone with Monroe in the middle of shooting. He claimed he was in her bedroom when she miscarried on September 8, while Miller was back in America, taking a break to visit his children. Lying on Marilyn's bed, where he had dozed off, the young man woke to her screams. "I sat bolt upright in the darkness and fumbled desperately for the light," he recalled. "I had fallen asleep on top of the bed and, thank goodness, fully dressed. I had not even taken off my shoes.... Marilyn lay on her back, clutching her stomach. She was as pale as a ghost.... 'The baby! I'm going to lose the baby.' "

That miscarriage had as profound an effect on Monroe as Vivien's had had on her a month earlier, though Vivien knew nothing about it. Marilyn began to retreat further, became impervious to Olivier's direction and even the need to show up for filming except when the mood took her. Her nebulous condition became a druggy haze, her passive resistance turned into active opposition; she was more like a somnambulist than a major star. Realizing his movie was on the brink of collapse, Larry thought of shutting it down but was told the insurers would never cover the costs. When Marilyn returned to work after days away, Olivier could not even bring himself to kiss her, as required in the script, but became "completely rigid," noted Clark, "as if it is agony for him to get so close to her." The actress was "shattered, washed out, in a dream." He added, "If any of us talk to her she looks at them as if they belonged to a different species."

The two were no longer on speaking terms and intermediaries had to convey the most basic information from one to the other. "It was the most dreadful experience of [Olivier's] life," recalled cinematographer Jack Cardiff, one of the few crew members who could tolerate Monroe. "He had greatness. And all that greatness went up against a stone wall when he was working with Marilyn."

The picture wrapped on November 19 and Marilyn did not even bid Olivier farewell. "When MM left the studio," wrote Clark in his diary, "she did so quickly and furtively. She is supposed to come back tomorrow but we all know she won't. She didn't say goodbye to anyone, not even her personal dresser, who has been so loyal and patient, or to Gordon, her hairdresser. We knew we would never see her again and, sad to tell, it was an immense relief."

some people think it's fairly good satire.' He seemed to have been offended by the play, his patriotism apparently wounded."

When Miller insisted, Olivier backed down and on the evening of July 20 or July 21, 1956, they sat in the fading nineteenth-century playhouse, regal in name only, and politically, socially and philosophically poles apart from the sort of palaces Larry loved. But this time boredom gave way to interest, and interest to fascination, as he watched the play's protagonist, Jimmy Porter (Kenneth Haigh), spew insults at his wife and lodger (Mary Ure and Alan Bates), lacerating everything Larry held dear. "At the interval Olivier asked what I thought," wrote Miller, "and I said it was wonderful. At the end of the play he asked again, and I said there were a lot of hanging threads, but who cared? It had real life, a rare achievement."

Look Back in Anger was a watershed in British theater, a semiautobiographical drama loosely based on Osborne's marriage to actress Pamela Lane. It placed working-class characters front and center stage after years in which they had been relegated to the wings; their loathing and bitterness were a reflection of the country's own. This was not a land of hope and glory, but one of rancor and rage as far as its poorer members were concerned, and Osborne tackled their feelings head-on. By no means a masterpiece, his play nonetheless reimagined classic tropes: where Hamlet spoke in soliloquies, Jimmy Porter spoke in tirades; where Shakespeare's hero ruminated on the meaning of life, Osborne's ranted on about its meaninglessness; where optimism had suffused Britain in the wake of the war, pessimism had now seeped into its very marrow.

As the curtain came down, producer George Devine, who headed the Royal Court–based English Stage Company, invited his guests to meet the twenty-nine-year-old playwright, and the four acquaintances huddled around a table by the bar, where Olivier came face-to-face with "the rebellious Osborne," in

CHAPTER 15

⬦

Larry was almost fifty, petrified of that looming watershed and unable to pretend his marriage was any less troubled than his relationship with Monroe. Nor were things easier for Vivien. Her husband was slipping away, as was her career—and, more terrifying still, her grip on reality. "The saddest thing is that we didn't realise that she had an illness," reflected Maxine Audley. "We all thought she was just behaving badly."

On a three-week vacation in Spain, the couple bickered all the time, their irritation exacerbated when Larry's gout flared up, leaving him unable to get out of bed, while Vivien took to her own bed in a different room. It was at this low point that Larry received a letter about a new play that would change his life.

The Entertainer had its origins at the Royal Court Theatre, where Olivier had taken Miller immediately after he had arrived in London. The writer was keen to catch a new work that had taken the city by storm, John Osborne's *Look Back in Anger*, but at first Larry resisted, as he had already seen it. "His reaction was quick and surprisingly negative, even angry," recalled Miller. "'No, no, you don't want to bother with that, find something else.' 'Why? What's wrong with it?' 'Oh, it's just a travesty on England, a lot of bitter rattling on about conditions, although

Miller's words, "who I assumed was his artistic and ideological adversary." He was right: one was a pillar of the establishment, while the other pilloried it; one was largely generous and gracious, while the other was resentful and vindictive. (Later, after his ex-wife's suicide, Osborne would refer to her as Adolf Hitler and say his only regret was not spitting on her grave.) Given this, Miller was incredulous when he overheard Olivier "asking the pallid Osborne—then a young guy with a shock of uncombed hair and a look on his face of having awakened twenty minutes earlier—'Do you suppose you could write something for me?' in his most smiling tones, which could have convinced you to buy a car with no wheels for twenty thousand dollars."

He didn't know that Olivier was bored—fed up with the West End, sick of his sham marriage and sated with his life as a pseudo-baron. A riptide was pulling him away from safety and security, propelling him toward "acts of folly," he acknowledged, as if "an impulse of rebellion, due to what? Amour propre? A postmenopausal flare-up that had to make some statement and hear the last echo of itself?" He couldn't say. But he saw what Osborne could do for him, just as Osborne sensed what Olivier could do for *him*.

The writer was two-thirds of the way through a new play about a washed-up vaudevillian named Archie Rice. He had never even thought of Olivier as the lead, but now he realized what a brilliant coup de théâtre this would be: to cast the stage's greatest success as its most archetypal failure. Over the past year, Osborne had immersed himself in Archie's world, the dying and decaying music halls, Britain's working-class venues where singers, comics and dancers plied their trades. One such performer had mesmerized him: Max Miller, an elderly comedian whose act climaxed in an imitation of Charles Laughton as *The Hunchback of Notre Dame*'s Quasimodo, in which a "smoky green light swirled over the stage and an awesome banality prevailed for some theatrical seconds." It was Miller who gave him the impetus to create Archie.

Olivier, like Osborne, was steeped in theater history; when his library was auctioned after his death, it included David Garrick's memoirs, a life of the late eighteenth-century actress Mrs. Siddons, and the American stage star Edwin Booth's prompt book. But he had only the faintest awareness of such blue-collar titans as Marie Lloyd and Dan Leno, whose absurdist take on *Hamlet* prefigured *Monty Python*: "Ah, what is Man? Wherefore does he why? Whence did he whence? Whither is he whithering?" And yet the music hall was as British as the stiff upper lip, as inherently theatrical as Olivier himself. It had risen with the Industrial Revolution, providing cheap entertainment for the poor men and women who had migrated to the cities—not unlike the audience for the first-ever films—and peaked in the mid-nineteenth century, only to recede as mass media brought an end to its reign. No more than a handful of major music halls remained in the late 1950s; by the mid-1960s, for all intents and purposes, there would be none.

Having done his research, Osborne got down to writing, merging his real-life sources with his fertile imagination to create a portrait not merely of an art form in decline but of an empire. *The Entertainer* may nominally have been about vaudeville, but it was really about England. It told the story of a mediocre comic on his last legs, a Willy Loman of the variety halls, a man of little talent and less principle, whose wife and children despise him almost as much as he does himself. One of the great characters to emerge from postwar theater, Rice was a pathetic figure who would have been tragic if he hadn't lacked grandeur, a man who may once have aspired to greatness—like his nation— but who had long since settled for survival.

This was an extraordinary role for any actor. And yet, to Osborne's amazement, Olivier didn't want it; instead, he saw himself as Archie's father, Billy, a retired star who clings to his vision of a vanishing Britain, rather as Olivier clung to his own. It was this man who drew him, this man he dreamed of making flesh and blood, at least when he read the first part of the play, the part Osborne gave him before he had finished writing. "Olivier's response was immediate and astonishing," he recalled. "Letting him read just two acts had confused everyone."

When Larry reconsidered, "things moved quickly. Sir Laurence was suddenly 'available' and eager in the way of prized actors who come into season with occasional surprising suddenness and have to be accommodated while the bloodstock is raring."

Osborne and his director, Tony Richardson, a young man whose aristocratic manner belied his modest roots, were summoned to the Connaught Hotel, where Vivien and Larry had taken up temporary residence while waiting to move into new and grander accommodations at 54 Eaton Square.

"It is hard to convey what a royal impression these two had made on the press and the public at the same time," wrote Osborne. "In their different ways they had both promoted it. Seeing Vivien Leigh for the first time, I could only remember watching *Gone with the Wind* as a twelve-year-old recovering from rheumatic fever, sitting in my wheelchair and fainting as she fled from the blood and cries of burning Atlanta." In person, "she was strangely robust in a pent-up way, like some threatened animal....Her voice seemed deeper and more rasping than the recollection of Scarlett's 'Great balls of fire' or, even more memorably, Blanche DuBois's 'I have always relied on the kindness of strangers.' I didn't feel she was overtrusting of these two odd-looking young men with their funny old play. Sir Laurence, long regarded by all (including himself) as a bequest to the nation, seemed to be speaking for both of them."

When Larry did so, it was with "dazzling Olivier craftiness," remembered Osborne. After tentatively suggesting they cast a "little actress you may have heard of—Dorothy Tutin" in the role of Archie's daughter, Larry moved on to his wife. "Well now," he wondered, "what about Vivien?" His visitors were perplexed. Surely, having mentioned Tutin, he didn't want Vivien to play his daughter? No, not at all, he said: Vivien should costar as Archie's wife, a dowdy woman who made the plain heroine of *Deep Blue Sea* look like a bombshell. His guests stared at him, appalled. Was he serious? Or was this a test, some clever move to weigh their worth? It was an *Alice in Wonderland* rabbit hole down which neither man wanted to fall.

Before they could decide, Larry swatted away the suggestion, telling them Vivien was far too beautiful ever to play a woman as frumpy as Phoebe Rice, thereby both flattering her and eliminating her from contention. Only, a moment later, he reconsidered. Was it really out of the question, after all? Hadn't Edith Evans aged a hundred years for the 1949 movie *The Queen of Spades*? Couldn't Vivien do the same?

The question hung in the air. It was preposterous, as everyone knew. Evans had spent five hours in a makeup chair each day, tugging on a rubber mask and applying layers of color and hair—and for a film, not a play, a one-off production shot in a narrow time frame, not a theatrical marathon that would have to be repeated day in, day out, for months.

Vivien said nothing, sphinxlike.

Finally, Olivier shrugged it off. He would just have to do the play without her, he sniffed. The visitors exhaled, got up, shook hands, and moments later popped out into the cool, crisp light of day, where they burst into laughter. Just imagine, they said, Vivien in latex! "'What about that!' [Richardson] whinnied. His gnashing laughter cracked out into Mount Street. 'Rubber masks! Oh, my dear God. Rubber masks!'"

Days later, the board of the English Stage Company was

incredulous, but for different reasons. Many were aghast at the thought of Sir Laurence entering their inner sanctum. He was everything they were not: a defender of the status quo, a royalist, a symbol of the class system their company wanted to end. Invite him to the Court? That was akin to ushering the Romans into the second temple. The matter went to a vote and the board cleaved down the middle, leaving the final decision to one member, Lord Harewood. The aristocrat and cousin of the queen, an improbable custodian of the Court's image, came down in Olivier's favor.

On March 12, 1957, Larry arrived at the theater for a month's rehearsals prior to a limited five-week run. What he found was a shabby little building that had been badly bombed during the war and converted into a cinema before it returned to its theatrical roots; it was miles from the elegant theaters he knew and loved—and yet, to everyone's surprise, this interloper embraced it. Eyes twinkling, casually dressed in an open shirt, he was back doing what he did best—and for love, not money, at the same negligible rate of £50 per week that he had been paid for *Private Lives*.

Osborne watched in awe as Olivier built his character line by line, layer by layer, showing "an astonishing skill at throw-away business, like a spastic Jimmy Cagney." While Larry resisted the play's more controversial elements (he convinced Osborne to drop some antimonarchist swipes, only for the writer to restore them later on), he immersed himself in Archie's life, researching the part as thoroughly as he would any work by Shakespeare, visiting the eighteen-hundred-seat Collins Music Hall and even calling on Max Miller's widow, though Osborne was keen to point out the differences between that comedian and his Archie: "[Miller's] humanity was in his sublime sauce," he noted, "Archie's in his hollow desperation."

Larry's own hollow desperation struck him forcefully. "I

suspect that Olivier has a feeling sometimes that he is a deeply hollow man," he observed. "That doesn't mean that he *is* a hollow man, but he knows what it's like to feel hollow....[He] understands that kind of character and his feelings of inadequacy—of being fifth-rate."

Never did any of Olivier's characters resonate with him as profoundly as Archie Rice; never did any of his princes and potentates touch him as personally as this wreck of a man, this shuffling has-been, the kind of figure he suspected he might have been had he possessed less talent—and perhaps the man he feared he still was. "This is really me, isn't it?" he asked.

Vivien observed her husband with fascination and fear. She had been idle for the better part of a year and, at forty-three, knew her options were narrowing. Larry was entering a brave new theatrical world while she was trapped; he was embracing change while she was stuck with the same. And so, during rehearsals, she would join him at the Court, keeping him under surveillance, as if in some way she could wrench him back and stave off the inevitable: his exit from her life.

"Vivien's watchful presence was the most dangerous threat to the production's progress," wrote Osborne, "and everyone from George to the ASMs [assistant stage managers] was aware of it. She would drop in without warning and sit in the dress circle with Bernard [Gilman], her chocolate-uniformed chauffeur, a row behind her. It was usually an unobtrusive entrance, but stardom has no use for tact. Her presence was as distracting as an underwear advertisement at a Lesbians for Peace meeting....If Larry was out of his depth now and then, so were we all, but none more so than Vivien, which made her isolation increasingly obvious."

One Saturday afternoon, when she was sitting in the stalls, Olivier captured his character in whole cloth for the first time. As Archie sang his version of the blues—

Oh, Lord! I don't care where they bury my body,
'Cos my soul's going to live with God!

—he slowly crumpled to the side of the stage. The moment was riveting. "A dozen of us watched, astounded," recalled Osborne. "Vivien turned her head towards me. She was weeping."

Her anguish spilled over on the others. Minutes before the dress rehearsal, she "made a final effort," wrote Osborne. "To do what? I don't know. The production had perhaps become a vehicle containing all her sense of loss to come or already endured." Summoning him to Olivier's dressing room, along with Richardson and Devine, she exploded. "Like a lioness protective of her energy, she was word-perfect in her complaints and criticism. Her feverish fury erupted in the cramped room."

Having let loose, she stormed out, only to turn back and spit one last barb at the mellow, pipe-smoking Devine. "I was always very fond of you, George," she declared. "But I could never stand that fucking awful pipe."

And yet she continued to act in public as if her life with Larry would never end. She was still "super-grand," recalls Victoria Tennant. "My mother told me once that she went to a dinner party at Notley where pheasant was served and it was off. Everyone could smell it, but they waited for Vivien to say something. She took one mouthful and continued eating—and everyone had to eat the pheasant. There was no 'Oh my God! I can't believe this! Oh, we'd better make some scrambled eggs.' No, it was like, 'We're carrying on with the script.'"

Late one night, Vivien's friends and family were gathered at Notley when they realized she'd disappeared. The party broke up, fanning across the house and grounds, searching for her in the moonlight. "We were having our brandy and listening to the gramophone," says Tarquin, "and Gertrude said, 'I'm very worried about Vivien. Where can she have gone? I'm worried she might have gone to the river.'" The river, of course, meant death, either by accident or suicide, a vivid thought for those present, who were all too aware how Virginia Woolf had ended her life. "Dickie, Larry's older brother, said: 'No, no she never goes there. She just wanders around the paddock or the back of the house.' And Gertrude said, 'What do you mean, *usually*?' She was horrified." Minutes later, they found Vivien safe and sound; but from then on Gertrude was unable to deny how ill she truly was.

In May 1957, the Oliviers set off on a six-week tour of Europe with the Shakespeare Memorial Company, the first British troupe to venture that far east since the advent of Communism. They were famous throughout the world and, even if rumors about their marriage kept popping up in the press, believed in keeping up appearances. Quasi-ambassadors, they went forth not just to Western centers of culture such as Vienna but also to Warsaw and Belgrade—if not quite the bull's-eye of the Soviet Union then at least a stripe on the target. Stalin's death four years earlier had briefly melted the Cold War permafrost and it was a golden time for artists, writers, musicians and poets. Change was everywhere: borders were becoming more porous; young people were planning to descend on Moscow for a worldwide festival of youth; and Yugoslavia and Poland, those Soviet satellites, were preparing to welcome foreigners with open arms.

The company stopped off in Paris, where Vivien was presented with the Légion d'honneur medal, though the response accorded her work was lukewarm. Larry was too concerned with his own problems to focus on hers: he had started taking injections of royal jelly, a secretion from bees believed to have medical benefits, but he was depressed, and maybe clinically so. Despite the success of *The Entertainer*, he was weighed down by "a feeling of vacuity and growing despair."

John Standing, then a twenty-two-year-old actor who was thrilled to be part of the tour, was surprised when the Oliviers invited him to dinner, but Larry didn't say a word. He had just celebrated his birthday. "Oh my God!" recalled Standing. "He couldn't even speak. He went through the whole dinner [like that]. He'd gone into a steep decline about being fifty. I spoke to him the following day. He said, 'I can't bear it.' "

That spring was broiling hot, and as the heat began to rise so did the tension. In Venice, the troupe's performance of *Titus* was as muggy as the fetid air. And when they arrived in Belgrade, the heat was even worse. Without air-conditioning, sweat dripped from hands, arms, faces and legs, staining clothes, books, table-cloths and props. It was almost as bad as the nightmare Vivien and Larry had experienced in New York with *Romeo and Juliet*, with this salient difference: Belgrade was also grim. Gray blocks of run-down apartments jutted against the skyline, their balconies strewn with pots and pans and boxes and bicycles, while chain-smoking citizens hung idle on street corners, hoping against hope for something unexpected to shake up their lives. Brutalism, social as well as architectural, was the order of the day.

Vivien was convinced someone was following her, and she was right. Along with government spies came huge crowds trying to get a glimpse of the real-life Scarlett O'Hara, from a movie that many had only recently seen on this side of the Iron Curtain. But the reverence they showed her did nothing to modify her moods. During the day, writes Hugo Vickers, "she was the ideal companion, visiting the art school studios and talking with genuine interest to the students. She climbed into obscure attics, drank a glass of slivovitz [a form of plum brandy] and seldom left without buying a picture." At night, however, her spirits would change. "She used to go out at night, drinking with her chauffeur, whom she'd brought from England," says John Standing, who had joined the cast for the tour. She would party into the wee hours, leaving Olivier as desiccated as the plums that had been squeezed for her brandy. "If you don't like your life, change it," he muttered to an acquaintance, leaving little doubt about his own intentions.

Asked to address the local pooh-bahs at an interminable official dinner in Zagreb, their next stop, Vivien "rose with an angelic smile," continues Vickers, "and, in the knowledge and hope that they did not understand, recited her speech in a lyrical voice. However, far from delivering the polite reply they were expecting, out came a string of four letter words to the effect that she was having the most boring evening of her life, all said with a smile and greeted by cries of 'Ya, Ya.'"

One evening, Vivien smashed a hotel window and vanished into the night. What happened to her then, nobody knows; she was gone for many hours and much of the following day. There are several accounts of how she came back: in one, her driver found her, sitting on a park bench, crying; in another, she was discovered dancing naked in a public garden. Either way, she arrived at the theater so late that she almost missed her performance and Michael Blakemore, a young actor (and later director), thought she seemed drugged or ill.

But, even in this debilitated condition, "she couldn't resist needling [Larry]," said Colin Clark, the Olivier assistant who was traveling with the group. She was "like a bullfighter with a bull."

Once, onstage after Larry had delivered his celebrated speech—

I am the sea; hark, how her sighs do blow!
She is the weeping welkin, I the earth:

Then must my sea be moved with her sighs;
Then must my earth with her continual tears
Become a deluge, overflow'd and drown'd....

—Vivien muttered, "Silly cunt." None of the audience heard her,
but the other actors did. It was all they could do not to laugh.
"Olivier, invincible in Paris, had become ridiculous in Zagreb,"
wrote Blakemore. "He would never forgive her."

The next day, Vivien refused to join him on their train. "Larry
said, 'I can't stand it,'" recalled Clark. "Then the train began to
move and Vivien stood her ground on the platform. And the
police chief, still very much in attendance, simply picked her up
and put her on the train." Vivien rewarded him with a punch in
the eye. When the train stopped in the middle of nowhere, with a
vertiginous cliffside drop to the side, she got out to look around
and the train took off without her. Only later did everyone realize what had happened and asked the engineer to back up.

As tough as she was with Larry, Vivien seemed hypersensi-
tive to anything involving herself. When Maxine Audley laid an
affectionate hand on her arm, "she leapt away as if I was burning
her skin," remembered the actress. Vivien later chased her down
the aisle, throwing bits of bread at her until she had to barricade
herself in a restroom.

Director Peter Brook begged Vivien to see a doctor, but she
refused until he threatened to replace her with an understudy. In
Vienna, he summoned the cast and crew and quietly told them
she wasn't fit to perform, adding that under no circumstances
should they accept any of her invitations—not to drinks, not to
dinner, not to anything. Much to his mortification, in the middle of his speech, Vivien stepped into the room and heard every
word.

Traveling from Vienna to Warsaw, the temperature reached
new highs: a suffocating and soaking ninety degrees. "The train

was full," writes one of Vivien's biographers, Anne Edwards, "no food was served, and the company had to carry their own lunches and bottled water. Vivien paced the corridor nervously, her voice taking on a hard edge. Everyone was alerted, but no one knew what to do. Then suddenly she turned against Olivier and began to run up and down the corridor shouting. He tried to restrain her, but she broke away, picked up someone's makeup case, and hurled it, smashing a train window. Somehow members of the cast subdued her, and Olivier went into another car."

In Warsaw, Vivien waded into a lake and sliced open her foot on a piece of broken glass, leaving Blakemore to bandage it. By now, like Larry, he had had enough. She was no longer an icon but an irritant, acting like "some *principetta* [sic], absolute in her whims"—as if those whims were hers to control.

And yet, at times, the old Vivien would shine through and she would somehow slip free of her mental fog. In those moments, her remorse was absolute. "Oh Colin," she told Clark, "it's so nice when it's over."

The bedraggled company returned to England six weeks after leaving, almost as happy to get back as the group that had traveled to Australia, and Vivien trained her energy on a new mission: the fight to preserve the St. James Theatre.

For decades the 122-year-old building, with its ornate Louis XIV interior and slender columns, had been a home away from home for the Oliviers, the base of many of their productions. They had leased and operated the theater for five years, like the old actor-managers on whose shoulders Larry stood. It was here that they had staged the *Cleopatra*s, but now the building was about to be demolished. Vivien began to organize a demonstration in protest, only to be upset when few of her friends joined in. Taking out her anger before a performance of *Titus*, she clamped her foot on Audley's dress, which ripped as the young woman tried to get away.

Days later, Vivien embarrassed herself in the House of Lords. While attending a debate on the theater's future, she stood up and proclaimed: "My Lords, I wish to protest against the St. James Theatre being demolished." It was a shocking breach of protocol that infuriated even Churchill, her staunch admirer, and the news raced around the world. "The noble peers shot icy glances in Miss Leigh's direction," reported the *Los Angeles Times*. "Very quickly, Sir Brian Horrocks, sergeant at arms, moved in on the 44-year-old actress and escorted her from the premises. Sir Laurence Olivier, who had been sitting beside his wife, blushed."

The next month, while Larry was dozing in his chair, Vivien grabbed a wet cloth and suddenly began to slap his face. He fled into an empty room, locking the door behind him, but Vivien kept hammering and hammering at it, and in that instant, "Something snapped in my brain," he wrote. He "grabbed her wrist, pushed her along the passage, threw open the door and with all my strength—it must be true that in all-possessing rage it is doubled—hurled her halfway across the room to the bed. Before hitting the bed she struck the outside corner of her left eyebrow on the corner of her marble bedside tabletop, opening up a wound half an inch from her temple and half an inch from her eye. I realized with horror that each of us was quite capable of murdering or causing death to the other."

Titus ended its run on August 3, 1957, and so, in effect, did the Oliviers' marriage. Vivien left to join Holman and Suzanne on vacation in San Vigilio, Italy, drawing outraged objections from the press. Even a member of Parliament, Jean Mann, jumped on the bandwagon. "When a woman finds her ex-husband so easy to get on with that she can spend a holiday with him she should have thought a little longer before she cut the knot," sniped the MP.

"CRITICISM ILL-CONSIDERED AND UNMANNERLY," Vivien responded. "PRESENCE OUR DAUGHTER GIVES EXPLANATION HOLIDAY TO ANY REASONABLE PERSON."

Gertrude tried to explain that Olivier liked his quiet time; but privately, he admitted his marriage was all but over and told Holman the same thing. "I do hope when [she] gets back that they will agree to part for the present," confided Holman, "and I think it would be much better if Vivien suggested it. She could have the flat [in Eaton Square] and he Notley."

At this stage, nobody was mentioning divorce. Both Larry and Vivien, after all, had been divorced before, and divorce was still relatively rare: less than one in twelve British marriages would be severed, and while there were 346,903 weddings in England in 1957, only 23,785 couples received a decree nisi the same year. Naively, Holman advised the couple to have their aide and all-around factotum Peter Hiley issue a statement that they were living apart, while insisting that "no question of a divorce was being considered by either of them." This way, Holman believed, "there would be an end to publicity and idle speculation." Olivier wisely disagreed.

He met Vivien at the airport on August 30 but was such a shadow of his former self that the journalists there failed to recognize him. Rather than go home, Vivien went to stay with Kenneth Clark and then traveled to Ireland with her father—a rare holiday with the man who had all but vanished as a significant presence in her adult life—while Olivier moved out of their London apartment and into a friend's cottage.

He was alone and at his most vulnerable when a new woman entered his life.

*   *   *

Joan Plowright was twenty-seven years old and just beginning to reveal her talent when the director Tony Richardson hired her to replace Tutin in the revived *Entertainer*, which was about to transfer to the West End. Her roots were in the provinces, in the lower-middle classes that Larry had fled; she had grown up in the northern town of Scunthorpe, where her father was a local newspaper editor and her mother a gifted amateur performer, part of a dynamic family with a passion for drama (her brother, David, would become chairman of Granada Television). After graduating from the Bristol Old Vic Theatre School, one of the country's best, she had begun working professionally.

An exceptional actress, she was also Vivien's opposite: whereas Vivien seemed aristocratic, Plowright was more earthy—stolid rather than sparkling, sober rather than scintillating. And yet stolidity and sobriety were enormously appealing at this point in Larry's life. She had impressed him in William Wycherley's Restoration comedy *The Country Wife*, and he must have sensed an attraction because, returning to *The Entertainer*, he resolved to keep a distance. He was at the end of a "philandering fit," he claimed, and wanted a different life—though Tarquin never believed it: "He behaved like a libertine; he became a libertine."

A Royal Court stalwart, Plowright felt the excitement when Olivier arrived at the theater. It was "a welcome surprise," she wrote in her 2001 memoir *And That's Not All*. "There may have been a few mutterings about the Establishment 'joining because they couldn't beat 'em' but they certainly didn't come from the actors." Still, Olivier inhabited a different ether, seemed to float "outside the profession, existing on a different plane and in the constant glare of publicity." He was a remote and regal presence, hardly one with whom Joan could imagine a friendship, let alone a romance, until they began to work together;

then he joked, joshed, pretended he couldn't remember her name (Miss Wheelshare, was it?) and set up a "jaunty intimacy" quite unlike his initial forays with Vivien.

"He was bristling with energy and his smile was full of mischief; it was as though he had been let off a leash," recalled Plowright. "Rehearsing in an open-necked shirt with braces holding up his trousers, he had banished all traces of that titled gentleman of the Establishment. He was simply an actor among actors, but one of such extraordinary accomplishment, and with such electricity crackling around him, that I was both exhilarated and exhausted by the end of the day."

She "never dreamt that what was happening to me now could happen, that I could be so spellbound by the flirtatious charm being directed like a laser beam towards me, even though I knew that my predecessor [Tutin] had been the target before me. But what was infinitely more dangerous was the way my heart was touched by the bleakness in his face when he wasn't acting or flirting; by the way Archie's cynicism and gallows humour came so easily to him; and by his admission that his only anchor in life now was the theatre."

Plowright knew Olivier's marriage was dead and so was her own to actor Roger Gage. But she was also cognizant that, at least publicly, Larry and Vivien were still together and that they would attend public events as a couple, unable to break free. And so, unsure about Larry's sincerity, she held back, wary of adding her name to his long list of conquests. She was not, in her words, "a promiscuous girl," and deliberately kept away during their breaks, almost consciously pushing him aside. And yet, as she acknowledged, "none of my evasive tactics was of the slightest use. And finally I knew that I didn't need them; there was a bond between us, a strange feeling of kinship which had nothing to do with casual flirtation. We had fallen very much in love."

In November 1957, the cast of *The Entertainer* left London

for Glasgow, forced to exit the capital temporarily to make way for another production that had been booked into the Palace Theatre. For a while, Larry and Joan were able to dodge the watchful eyes of their spouses. But then Vivien traveled to Scotland to see the show and sensed something was amiss. Wanting to believe Larry's denials, she made no mention of her lurking fears when she wrote to Coward. "I spent the day with Puss in Glasgow," she told him. "He says the Glaswegians hiss slightly at the lewder jokes in the 'Entertainer' which makes them somewhat disconcerting to play to!"

Three weeks later, Olivier and Plowright slept together for the first time; and a few days after that, Larry confessed to Vivien. "Olivier was removing his make-up [backstage at the Palace]," writes Walker. "As he pulled off the bushy eyebrows he wore as Archie Rice, he looked at her reflection in his mirror, and, without turning round, remarked in what was almost a throwaway line: 'I suppose you should know I am in love with Joan Plowright.'"

On December 6, Vivien presided over Suzanne's wedding to Robin Farrington, a Lloyd's insurance broker, and revealed nothing of her anguish.

Suzanne was now twenty-four, a struggling actress who had become far closer to Gertrude than her mother; but Vivien wrote to her tenderly just before the wedding. "I am thinking of you so much & cannot go to sleep without telling you how much I love you & how I hope with all my heart that today will be the beginning of a most wonderful & happy life," she said. "If you ever need me I shall feel it a joy & blessing to be of any help or comfort I can."

The wedding was strained for the Oliviers. Privately, Vivien said she could not understand why her daughter would want to go through such a tortuous routine—expressing the same disillusionment that Gertrude had felt after Vivien's own wedding to Holman. But publicly she was all smiles, even if she stayed at a remove from Larry, who sat in a different part of the church, speaking little, almost trying to make himself invisible. As the bride and groom took their vows and the bells pealed, Vivien departed for the reception on Holman's arm, while Larry stood to one side of the chapel, alone.

Two months later, he traveled to New York, where Joan was appearing in a double bill of Eugène Ionesco's *The Lesson* and *The Chairs*, and where they would soon star in *The Entertainer*. There their relationship "grew deeper and more binding," wrote Plowright. This was "a precious time of happiness together. We told each other everything about our past history and the present state of our marriages. He confided that he had suggested divorce to Vivien two years ago but that she had vehemently opposed it and even threatened to take her own life if he went ahead. She wanted the legend and the marriage to continue, though she conceded that each of them could be free to enjoy liaisons elsewhere. He was adamant that their life together was over and there was no going back. It was hoped that after a time of separation she would recognize the futility of keeping up the pretence and possibly find a new love of her own."

"I'm going to marry Joan," Larry told Gielgud, who was touring America with a one-man show, *The Ages of Man*. "Vivien's given me some of the happiest times in my life, but it has absolutely worn me out knowing that these moods and attacks are coming on and I can do nothing to stop them."

Alone at Notley, Vivien had only Dickie and his wife for company. Dickie was sick with leukemia and getting sicker by the day, while Hester was busy being a mother.

Vivien was in "agony," she told Coward. Her skin, once as perfect as porcelain, sometimes looked puffy from her drinking;

she now hated looking in mirrors and had taken to wearing sunglasses, indoors as well as out, to hide her incipient crow's-feet. Her state of mind alarmed Olivier; even three thousand miles away, he "could not bear the thought that any precipitate action of his might be the cause of some irrational act on her part," noted Plowright. "And he feared even more, and so did I, the effect such a happening would have on our own relationship; we would carry the burden of it for the rest of our lives."

Vivien's mood swings were now so frequent that they had begun to alienate even her closest friends. "My parents found her volatility very difficult to deal with," admits Hayley Mills. Once, "they got a call from Vivien, saying, 'Where are you, darlings? I never see you. Don't you love me anymore? I need you to come down. You must come now.' 'My God,' they thought, 'she sounds like she's not very well.' They had a farm in Sussex, but they jumped in the car and drove a long way to get to Notley and walked into the living room. Vivien was sitting by the window and she turned her shoulder and screamed at them and picked up a bit of china and flung it at them and told them to fuck off."

In April 1958, she got a much-needed boost when she returned to the West End with Jean Giraudoux's *Duel of Angels*, a drama about the clash between a seductress (Vivien) and a spotless innocent (Claire Bloom). It was an immediate hit, but Bloom, Larry's former lover, found Vivien "breakable," with a "terror and anxiety and delicacy and fear." During rehearsals, director Jean-Louis Barrault was astonished to learn she hated her character, and was unaware that she was simply transferring her self-loathing. "She was constantly on the lookout for reasons [not to love Paola]," he recalled. "She attacked her by provoking antipathy. It was only when she had exhausted all the reasons for hating her that she assumed her."

One night before the opening, Vivien snapped. At home in Eaton Square with the actor Peter Wyngarde, her dapper leading man and briefly her lover, she suddenly said, "I've got to go and talk to the chauffeur." Too late, Wyngarde realized that the chauffeur had already gone. "So I went out and found her running around the garden with nothing on," he remembered. Luckily, a policeman stopped Vivien before she could do anything worse, and Wyngarde managed to coax her toward him, then wrapped a blanket around her and took her inside. On another occasion, "after a perfectly wonderful night," he found her "sobbing uncontrollably on the bathroom floor at four in the morning."

Never good at being alone, she reached out to anyone for emotional support, including John Osborne, with whom she formed the unlikeliest of bonds. "She would sometimes ring me up as I settled down in my cupboard-study in Woodfall Street," he recalled. "It was always a shock to hear her voice. 'What are you doing this evening?' There was only one answer. 'Why don't we go to the pictures? Come round now and we'll see what's on.'" She would pick him up in her Rolls, with its VLO1 license plate, and, the playwright admitted, "All sorts of phantom possibilities crossed my mind. Did she expect me to seduce her? Surely not. The presumption was absurd. I was neither Rhett Butler, Laurence Olivier, good red meat nor even Peter Finch. Was it a kittenish plot to involve me as a pawn in a game about which I was ignorant?...The presumption of youth and the sudden appearance of bourgeois caution within me made it all the more baffling and exciting."

When Larry returned from New York, Vivien begged to meet Joan, perhaps hoping to scare her off, as she had scared off Tutin; but he refused and instead convinced her to see a psychiatrist. Unwilling to go back to Netherne, she agreed to meet with a Harley Street practitioner, who reported that she was on the edge of mania, but "managing not too badly at the moment." He added, "We still hope that a major manic episode can be avoided. I am pretty sure that she will be more approachable when she gets more depressed."

In fact, her mania got worse. In September, she lashed out at her mother, claiming, among other things, that she had tried to block her from playing Blanche, in which there was not a shred of truth. Gertrude begged her to take a break and Vivien agreed to accompany her on another brief vacation to San Vigilio. But in the oxygen-starved Dolomites, she went wild, not only tossing a glass of water in Gertrude's face but also picking up a local fisherman, whom she brought back to her hotel. When the manager refused to let him in, she threw a fit. The local carabinieri were summoned and, in the ensuing struggle, Vivien bit two of the policemen's fingers. She was lucky not to be arrested.

Throughout, she was writing to Larry obsessively. "This is the third letter I have written you to-day," she complained. "You must forgive the fact that I make quick decisions. I believe they are the only true + instinctively correct way for people such as I am—to express their feelings—because I have had a day almost entirely on my own—in bed—+ able to think without interruption of our whole situation. I have come to the conclusion—(a fearfully painful one), that a clear and *absolute* break is the only path to follow—so I intend to divorce you on the grounds of desertion—mental + physical—as soon as both our personal chores in the theatre + television are over—we are in any case separated. I did not want to do this until you had finished your work here but our telephone conversation tonight led me to think I was talking to a complete stranger—which is what you have *chosen* to become....I think our lives will lie in quite different directions. I feel confident I shall make my own life—you have *always* made yours."

She quickly changed her mind and, in her nonmanic condition, remained adamantly opposed to divorce.

Back in England, she shared a quiet dinner with Larry, who was still living on his own while Vivien stayed in their London home. It was now, over dinner, that he made clear his desire for a definitive break.

"Larry has asked for a Legal separation," she wrote Coward. "I need not tell you—Noely, what this means to me. It is a very great and terrible shock, and I am, and have been acutely miserable. I always thought that whatever happened between us— eventually we would be completely together as we used to be. It has always seemd [sic] that with a sense of humour and *inate* [sic] loyalty and respect and *love*, one would pull through anything. I shall never ever love anyone as I love him."

In late 1958, Larry returned to New York for a television production of W. Somerset Maugham's *The Moon and Sixpence*, and he was there when he learned his brother had died. As a child, he had revered Dickie and even toyed with the idea of following him to India; later, when Dickie became his dependent and the estate manager at Notley, their relationship had cooled. But now, with Dickie dead at age fifty-four, Larry was overcome and made his way back home, where he arranged for his brother's ashes to be cast out at sea. Only Sybille was left among his immediate family.

After the funeral, Larry spent a final night at Notley, the house he had loved like a mistress, though he slept in the guesthouse rather than his usual room. That evening, Hester heard raised voices and saw Vivien storm across the garden, then hammer at Larry's door, demanding they make love. He refused. "I suffered grievously for her being made to feel so horribly undignified," he wrote later, "and felt no end of a prig saying 'No no no.'"

After Dickie's funeral, Larry flew to Los Angeles to star as the Roman general Crassus, Kirk Douglas's nemesis, in a new sword-and-sandals epic, *Spartacus*. He was in fine fettle physically despite the upheaval, exercising for the role and trying to remain sober after years of attempting "to drown his sorrows," as Plowright observed.

She was beginning to understand the morass into which she had waded and "feared it might be too much for me to cope with. The stolen happiness, the secrecy and the uncertainty as to when, or indeed whether, we would be able to start a proper life together was becoming unbearable. I suggested to Larry that we should have a year's break; we must not meet or phone or write until the year was over and the future clearer." Olivier was so miserable, however, that "I didn't have the heart to insist."

On Christmas Eve, he wrote saying he was desperate to hear her voice and wanted to call but realized that "a phone call which I have been itching like a crazy lunatic to make is I know too dangerous and would anger and worry you.... Oh baby, I do hope I hear some little word from you soon. But I know what it is if you are feeling sort of paralysed."

He was emotionally raw and unafraid to show it, which endeared him to acquaintances like the actor Louis Jourdan, who had found him remote in the past. Alcohol, Jourdan deduced, had made him "quite another person."

But his film was bedeviled at every step. It was already two and a half times over budget before shooting began, and the screenplay (written under a pseudonym by the blacklisted Dalton Trumbo) was changing daily. When production kicked off in February 1959, leading lady Sabine Bethmann was fired; her replacement, Jean Simmons, fell ill for a month, forcing a reorganization of the shooting schedule; and director Anthony Mann left through one door as his replacement, the thirty-year-old Stanley Kubrick, entered through another. Nor did Olivier care for his costar, Douglas, joking to Bushell that he "was remarkable in having achieved stardom when equipped with only two expressions."

The picture was "as full of intrigue as a Balkan government in the good old days," joked another cast member, Peter
Ustinov—and Larry made the most of it. "Since [he] had arrived
a week prior to the majority of us, he had already inspired a
yet newer version of the script in which his role had somewhat
grown in importance. He [had] played sufficient Shakespearean
villains superbly well to have a great confidence in his own powers of persuasion, and it was always amusing to watch him at
work in the wings, in the process of getting his own way. When
discovered, he would give you a mischievous wink, and what had
begun as an artifice ended as a performance, simply because he
was being watched."

Ustinov (who would win an Oscar for his role as the slave
trader Batiatus) was hardly averse to scene-stealing and gave as
good as he got. In one sequence, he recalled, he had to rush up
to Larry as he wandered on horseback through acres of captured
rebel slaves. "If I identify Spartacus for you, Divinity, will you
give me the women and the children?" asked Ustinov's Batiatus.
"There followed the most enormous pause while Larry let his
eyes disappear upwards under his half-open lids, licked his lips,
pushing at his cheeks from within with his tongue, let his head
drop with a kind of comic irony at the quirks of destiny, hardened once again into the mould of mortal divinity, looked away
into the unknown as his profile softened from brutal nobility into
subtlety. 'Spartacus!' he suddenly cried, as though slashing the
sky with a razor, and then hissed, 'You have found him?'"

Startled by the long pause, Ustinov responded with an interminable pause of his own, allowing his expression to run "the
gamut of impertinence, of servility, and of insincerity [just as
Larry's had run the gamut] of vanity, power, and menace. At
long last, when he least expected it, I let a practically inaudible
'Yes' slip from my mouth."

Olivier leaned down. "Dear boy," he said, with barely

disguised annoyance, "d'you think you could come in a little quicker with your Yes?"

"No," replied Ustinov, politely.

The story is delicious, but should be taken with a pinch of salt. Bushell, for one, had a different version of events. "The dialogue led to Laurence asking Ustinov a question to which the answer was No," he wrote. "And in take 1 Ustinov made his pause, + made one of his comical faces just before saying No. Laurence wasn't having this + said 'Dear boy, do you think you could come in with that No just a little quicker?' To which the wicked chap after a v. long think, said No."

Larry longed for Joan, who by now had left her husband. Afraid their letters might be intercepted, she had avoided writing too often and was in such a state that, for the first time in years, she had gone back to the church in search of spiritual guidance.

"Your love has given me a new strength and courage—I want my love to give that to you whether we are together or not," she wrote Larry, breaking her vow to maintain a distance. "Be strong and have faith, my darling wondrous and good man—you are a very special human being with great gifts. My spirit is with you now and for ever more—I love you, I love you, I love you."

Both were determined to stand firm against Vivien, who was threatening to stop seeing Dr. Arthur Conachy, her psychiatrist. That was "blackhearted blackmail," Larry told Joan.

Two and a half months before *Spartacus* wrapped, he wrote Vivien unequivocally. "I am quite sure in my mind and heart that both are firmly made up not to return to our life together when I come back in June," he said. "In fact, I think it best that we do not see each other. And so I shall be going straight to Stratford when I do get back. We have ten weeks before this happens in which to decide what is best to do in the way of announcement or statement if any; and that is why I think it best to reaffirm at this point my decision of last September-October which I have reiterated each time we have communicated since then. I think it's time now that we dropped the legend which is being kept up for press and public, and before I return have some statement ready on the true state of affairs."

Vivien refused, and so the uneasy state of affairs continued when Larry returned from the US in June and started living with Joan in Stratford while working on his second *Coriolanus*, this time for director Peter Hall.

It was an uneasy collaboration, marked by distrust. "Larry had a deep suspicion of intellectuals," recalled Hall. "He liked to bring things down to basics—to the hard sweat of rehearsal or the simple appeal to the audience.... He started off our meetings by amazing me; he announced that all the lines that express Coriolanus's modesty should be cut.... I said that if we took away Coriolanus's pride—which is mainly expressed by his conceited modesty—we should have little more than a simplified Henry V. We were still arguing at three in the morning. Finally, the thick Olivier eyebrows came down in a frown. 'I'll do what you say because you feel so strongly,' he said. 'But you are wrong.'"

Despite this, Olivier gave an unparalleled performance that ended with one of his most dazzling tricks: a death plunge in which he threw himself headfirst from a parapet, only for four spear-carriers to grab him by the ankles in midair just before he hit the ground. This wasn't simply art; it was almost suicidal, making every previous vault, leap and tumble in his acrobatic stack pale by comparison. But Larry found the challenge a relief in the midst of his domestic preoccupations. "My life has been an equal meting out of horror of what I'm going through and guilt for what I plan to go through," he explained. "And then [I] say, 'Oh, thank Christ, for the next three hours I'll be Coriolanus, nothing like me.'"

He and Vivien got together one last time as husband and wife at the party following *Coriolanus's* premiere. It was their last show of togetherness, their final performance as the royal couple of the stage. Both were distracted, perhaps even distraught, and haunted by the reality that their marriage was almost over. Blakemore, the actor who had been with them on tour, was struck by the Olivier he encountered: "There he sat at his table, our host, this pleasant, greying man in a dinner jacket, surveying his guests through heavy, black-framed spectacles. He might have been a surgeon or a successful solicitor [lawyer] celebrating a wedding anniversary."

In December, Vivien lost her father. Ernest was seventy-six years old and had recently been hospitalized for a leg amputation; his zest was gone, his character a shadow of what it had been. "Somehow," writes Vickers, "the jocular, powerful figure that [he] had been in India had been transformed in recent years into a more mute, shuffling figure, sometimes (though by no means always) to be found in a flat in which Gertrude was the ruler."

His death hit Vivien hard, despite their years apart. It added to her sense that everything was crumbling, that her center did not hold. When she visited Coward in Jamaica that Christmas, he found a "deep sadness in her heart and, for one fleeting moment, tears in her eyes," though she "never for one instant allowed her unhappiness to spill over."

In February, she and Larry finally sold Notley, and Vivien knew her life would never be the same. Wandering through her house one last time, moving from room to room alone, she was despondent. "I can hardly write the words," she told Tarquin, who had become closer to her than he would ever be to his father. "I walk from place to precious place and gaze at the beloved views with tears pouring down my face. What memories for all one's life—such unbelievable rare happiness, sweetness and quietude there has been here. I don't forget the other times too, but they seem to me outweighed by blissfulness together. Dear God it is a heartache."

In her loneliness, she made one more futile attempt to reach Finch, but he had left his wife and was in love with another woman, Yolande Turnbull, and didn't respond. Unable to let go, Vivien begged his mother to intercede and arranged a meeting at her Chelsea house, where the actor arrived with a pregnant Turnbull. "She was terribly grand," recalled Yolande. "For the rest of the interview, she never glanced at me. I subsided into an armchair, and Ma watched and listened with undisguised glee. She was glued. I died. Vivien leaned forward. 'Darling. Finchy. I want you back.... Darling'—the emerald eyes were imploring—'I'd live in an attic with you. I'd live in a garret with you.'" When Finch rose to get a drink, Vivien's eyes never left him. "There was a danger in her face and a sort of gentle mad control showed about her pointed mouth. Her eyes were slightly bloodshot, as if she had been crying. Her body was very still, but her glove-encased hands moved about each other like loving snakes. She opened her alligator handbag and took out a cigarette. Finchy stepped forward to light it and she held his wrist. 'Darling?' she whispered."

"It's too late, Viv," said Finch. "Sorry, luv."

Yolande was shaken by his coldness. Was this the real Finch, she wondered, a monster of ego and hardness? Or was he, in fact, just like every other star, ruthless in his self-absorption? "He reminded me," she wrote, "of the camel castrator in Tangiers who, in giving a demonstration to a crowd of tourists, separates the legs of the beast, then takes a brick in each hand and goes thwack, squeezing the animal's testicles to a pulp."

In March 1960, Vivien set out for America and a revival of *Duel of Angels*. She was working again, to her relief, but her face was pale, her eyes hidden behind her omnipresent sunglasses, and she was unable to put Larry out of her mind. "Her longing for him," wrote Coward, "[had] become an obsession."

Arriving in Manhattan, Vivien moved into a suite at Hampshire House, the historic hotel and apartment building on Central Park South. "It was a very difficult time for her, because she was heartbroken—there's no question of that, absolutely heartbroken," says Juliet Mills. "She never thought that Larry would leave her, but of course things got out of hand. She'd talk about him whenever she could, and she knew my parents were in England and seeing him, so she was always wanting news: 'What's he doing? How is he?' It was heartbreaking and made me very sad."

Vivien began rehearsals with her friend, Robert Helpmann, directing and a new costar, Osborne's wife, Mary Ure. Among the cast was an old acquaintance, Jack Merivale—the half brother of John Buckmaster, who had created such a ruckus in Los Angeles during *Elephant Walk*. A handsome forty-two-year-old who was as gracious as he was good-looking, Merivale had toured in the Oliviers' *Romeo and Juliet* but had rarely interacted with them since. He had written to Larry, apologizing profusely for his brother's behavior, and Larry had begged him to "exert all the influence possible to persuading him to stay on the western side of the Atlantic."

When *Duel* began its out-of-town run in New Haven, Connecticut, Merivale and Vivien were drawn to each other, though Merivale initially resisted his attraction, uncertain of her marital status. He had just gone through a painful split-up and was reluctant to feed another couple's woes. "It was obvious things had gone terribly wrong, yet Vivien still seemed obsessively attached to Larry," he explained. "She had photos of [him] all around her. And once, at rehearsal, when I was wearing a plaid suit, she reached out and fondled it and said wistfully, 'Larry's got a suit just like that. Oh God, I wish he were here.'"

As the weeks progressed, however, their relationship became intimate. This was not love of the transfiguring kind Vivien had known with Larry, not the all-consuming physical and emotional desire the Oliviers had felt for one another; but it was no less genuine and no less profound. Vivien needed someone to be there when there was nobody else, and Merivale answered the call. She "seemed to adore him," recalled the actor Patrick Stewart, who would spend time with them the following year. "She would always be touching him and holding his hand and putting her hand in his and putting her arm around him. He was a delightful, charming man."

Their incipient romance was abruptly interrupted when Larry cabled Vivien, hours before her Broadway opening, to ask for a divorce. No matter how often he had demanded it—and regardless of the fact that she had once asked for a divorce too—she was so traumatized that she could barely get onstage.

"I really don't think that she ever fully got over the shock of that message," said Wyngarde, who was also in the cast, though he was no longer involved with her. He backed up Merivale in giving her support. "Right through the performance," he said, "I had to watch intently, steering her as best as I was able."

It was in this state that Vivien made a fateful decision: to go public with the breakup. On May 21, 1960, she issued a statement: "Lady Olivier wishes to say that Sir Laurence has asked for a divorce in order to marry Miss Joan Plowright. She will naturally do whatever he wishes."

Joan was alone at home when the news broke on Larry's fifty-third birthday. "I was woken in my flat in Ovington Square at 8:10 a.m. that Sunday morning by [a call from] a friendly newspaper man," she remembered. " 'Have you heard the eight o'clock news?' I was still half asleep. 'Vivien Leigh has told the press that

Olivier has asked for a divorce in order to marry you,' he said. 'Get out of your flat now.'"

Reporters were congregating outside. Tony Richardson made his way over and managed to whisk Joan out through a back door and across the city to George Devine's, where the maestro of the Royal Court offered his counsel: "Marry him if you must, but don't act with him too often, or he will destroy you."

Joan had been appearing with Larry in Ionesco's *Rhinoceros*, but all the fuss made it impossible to continue and an understudy took her place. Overnight, while hiding at her brother's, she became an object of scorn, disparaged not just by the press but by legions of the Oliviers' fans. She even began to receive death threats, says her son, Richard. This was the termagant who had destroyed the world's greatest romance, this the harpie who had inserted herself into the crack between reality and their admirers' dreams. Few cared to dig beneath the surface, as Joan's friend Maggie Smith discovered when she spoke to a prospective landlady. "You're not a friend of that Joan Plowright, I hope," the woman sniffed.

In Eaton Square, squadrons of journalists had camped out. "Cameras were there to relay live pictures of his firmly closed front door to the television news bulletins," writes Holden. "While trying to work out the consequences of Vivien's statement—which she later told Merivale she did not remember making—he sent his secretary down to read out a heartfelt message, apologizing that the waiting pressmen had been so 'inconvenienced' and saying he had 'no comment at all. I need time to think.'"

"If anyone is going to come out of this looking a shit, let it be me," he told his publicist, Virginia Fairweather. "Do your best not to let them persecute Joanie or Viv."

Reporters fanned across the country, rooting up whatever

truffles of gossip they could find, even tracking down Joan's parents and offering them cash for tips. "The [tabloid] editors gave instructions that she should be found at all costs—and 'costs' was the operative word," recalled Fairweather. "Larry's chauffeur was offered a vast sum, the stage-door keeper and, even, the local barman the same; anyone who had contact with either of them in a menial capacity was offered money. It says a lot that nobody fell for this and let him down. Throughout that week Larry looked grey and drawn and he'd lost pounds in weight."

Osborne, who came to see him in his hideout, a "temporary foxhole in Glebe Place," found him in "wild, terrible pain." Snarkily, he added: "It was as if Nelson had been caught with his hand in the Admiralty till."

Taking a break from her play, Vivien insisted on returning to London. She was in hysterics and "busily employed in making a cracking ass of herself," observed Coward. "She is right round the bend again, as I suspected, and looks ghastly. . . . I went to see her 'alone' and found the flat full of people. She arrived from Notley, where she had been insulting the new owners. She was almost inarticulate with drink and spitting vitriol about everyone and everything."

Only when Conachy, her psychiatrist, administered five ECT treatments did she calm down; a week after arriving in London, she returned to New York and from then on always carried a note the doctor had written: "This lady is normally a person of high intelligence and education, nimble wit and extremely good judgement and reasoning power. She has a quality of determination and ruthlessness which have helped her to reach and maintain eminence in her profession. [But] I feel there can be no doubt that she has a cyclic manic-depressive psychosis."

At last, Vivien was acknowledging she was ill, with no hope of a cure. And with it she acknowledged her marriage was over.

"Pussy-Cat my darling," she wrote Larry, "whatever may

happen let us be friends my dearest one. Conachy has done a really marvellous thing for me—I am feeling as I have not felt for many many years. Perhaps all the interim mistakes have made just too much difference for our life together—I do not know—+ you must leave it to me to do what I think best for the future + in my own time. It will take me a little while to decide...one does not let 25 years go by lightly. I feel very deeply in love with Jack + very dearly grateful to him but it does not alter the fact that I shall love you all my life + with a tenderness + a respect that is all embracing.... Take care of your precious dearest self. My love dear dear Heart—Vivling."

Months later, when the couple had gone through the requisite proceedings and the divorce became official, Larry wrote back. "Darling," he said, "I want to say thank you for undergoing it all for my sake. You did nobly and bravely and beautifully and I am very oh so very sorry that it must have been such hell for you, and I am very dearly grateful to you for enduring it and setting me free to enjoy what is infinitely happy for me. Oh God Vivling how I do pray that you will find happiness and contentment now. I pray constantly that I may take off from you some of your unhappiness onto myself and I must say it seems to work from this end as your unhappiness is a torment to me; and the thought of it a constant nightmare. Perhaps perhaps now it may be allowed to gently lift off and blow softly away."

CHAPTER 16

━━━◆◆◆━━━

In March 1961, Vivien flew to Atlanta for a special screening of *Gone with the Wind*, marking the centennial of the Civil War. It was a remarkable occasion for which the city had amply prepared. Crowds ringed the streets, confetti dropped down on the dignitaries flooding this epicenter of the new South, the place General Sherman had burned to the ground that was now rising as a mecca of the civil rights movement. But for Vivien, returning alone, rebuffed by the love of her life, it was as painful as it was poignant.

Twenty years had passed since her last visit, and Larry's absence was inescapable. Along the way, she had stopped off in New York, pleading to see him and Joan, but he had refused. She and Joan would never meet.

Now Vivien was in Atlanta, and not just without Larry but many of the men and women who were inextricably connected to *Gone with the Wind*. Gable had died of a heart attack four months earlier, right after completing Monroe's last finished film, *The Misfits*, which helped terminate her unlikely marriage to Miller; Hattie McDaniel had succumbed to cancer in 1952, shunned by many African Americans for contributing to a stereotypical portrayal of slaves; and both Victor Fleming and Margaret

Mitchell had passed in 1949—the director from a massive heart attack, the novelist after being hit by a speeding car. Others were also gone, including the two Howards: Leslie's plane had been shot down during the war; and screenwriter Sidney Howard had died weeks before *GWTW*'s premiere, when he cranked his tractor into life, only for it to lurch forward and crush him against a wall. At least Selznick was here, but with none of his former élan. White-haired and corpulent, he had become as addicted to amphetamines as he had once been to writing memos and as obsessed with his wife Jennifer Jones's career as he had once been with his pictures. Only de Havilland, flying in from her new home in Paris, where she had recently married the editor of *Paris Match*, seemed undiminished; she would outlive them all and die in 2020 at the age of 104.

But this was Vivien's moment. Fans congregated along Peachtree Street, screaming for Scarlett, and when she got out of her car she did not let them down. "She had a ballgown designed to look like the one Scarlett might have worn," noted her friend Radie Harris, the *Hollywood Reporter* columnist who had accompanied her to Atlanta. "It was of beautiful white satin, appliquéd with blue flowers over a wide full skirt over a wide petticoat."

Vivien had at last begun to look favorably on her most memorable work, the film that would outlast her and define her for generations to come. But, while she was gracious enough to send Selznick a congratulatory bouquet of flowers, she spent only the requisite time with him and her former colleagues. The night of the screening, as she watched the battle of Atlanta, she turned to de Havilland, "pale as a ghost," as a reporter observed. "Olivia took her hand, and found Vivien was shaking terribly. 'Are you all right, Vivien?' 'I'm tired. And it's so strange, Olivia. I don't remember this. I just don't remember.' "

Once that was over, she flew back to London for a new film,

The Roman Spring of Mrs. Stone. It was then that she learned Larry and Joan had wed.

"We were married at last on 17 March 1961, St. Patrick's Day, and no small date in the American calendar," recalled Plowright. The two had done everything to keep their wedding a secret. "Elaborate preparations were made with the help of Arnold Weissberger, our lawyer and great friend, for a clandestine marriage outside New York; and we spent our pre-wedding night with friends, Nedda and Josh Logan, at their house in Connecticut. After our respective shows that night [Olivier was appearing on Broadway with *Becket*, Joan with *A Taste of Honey*], we went our separate ways and succeeded in losing the attentions of ever-vigilant reporters. I went back to Angela Lansbury's house, ostensibly for supper, and Larry practised the same deception with his co-star in *Becket*, Anthony Quinn. Leaving our friends' houses by the back doors, where our cars were waiting, we drove separately to the Logans' house, and were married inconspicuously in Wilton, Connecticut, the next morning."

Larry remembered signing the marriage license and hoping he wouldn't be recognized by the clerk.

"Name?" asked the little old lady.

"Laurence Olivier," he replied with a gulp.

"Profession?"

"Actor."

"Are you?" she said. "How very nice."

Vivien was terribly upset and the marriage punctured any dreams she might have had of reconciliation. When she arrived on the set of *Roman Spring*, "she had obviously been crying her eyes out," said assistant director Charles Castle. "She looked awful— woebegone and bloated. She was in the middle of doing her big love scene with Warren Beatty, too, where she had to act tenderly and affectionately. [Director] José Quintero had to handle her very carefully. Until her dying day, I don't think Vivien believed Olivier was beyond recall."

The movie, adapted from Tennessee Williams's story about a broken widow looking for love with a gigolo, was the last on which Vivien had any clout, and she used it to pick her on-screen lover, Beatty, who had made a mark in Kazan's *Splendor in the Grass* and impressed her with his hunger for the role. During his audition, the twenty-three-year-old had lit her cigarette, and when Vivien noticed his trembling hand, she understood how much he wanted the job. He was a man of ungodly good looks, a skilled Hollywood player with a practiced charm lathered over a burning ambition. Bushell believed he and Vivien had an affair, even though she was now seeing Merivale, and Beatty has never confirmed or denied it.

Sarah Miles, who made her screen debut in the picture, could feel the sparks between them. "The moment I appeared on the set Warren did a double-take, which Vivien caught," she recalled. "From then on, I felt distinctly uncomfortable, with Vivien's vixen eyes glued to either Warren or me all day. It was obvious to me that they were having an affair. If only I could have pacified Vivien by telling her that Warren's advances meant nothing to me—he wasn't my type at all—the day might have turned out quite, quite differently. But I found Vivien to be a distinctly brittle, dark and jealous woman."

"Brittle" was an apposite word for Vivien at this stage of her life, when she had neither fully released Larry nor found a way to brake the increasing velocity of her mood swings. She was in that most tortured position for an actress of her age: a woman on the brink of losing her extraordinary looks, a leading lady who would soon be relegated to "character" parts. It was all well and good to have two Oscars, but not even a shelfful could have helped her find the right roles.

Like so many times before, her private and professional lives intersected in an almost uncanny way, noted screenwriter Gavin Lambert. "As in Vivien's life, the odds against her are greater each time, and the effect increasingly poignant." She was "under great strain," he believed, though she no longer denied her illness and would occasionally leave their meetings for further ECT, telling him about it with "no crack in her composure, personal or professional. Like her character, Mrs. Stone, she disciplined her terror."

Weeks later, in June 1961, she returned to Australia for a new tour with three plays: *Twelfth Night*, *The Lady of the Camellias* and *Duel of Angels*. It was a stab at recapturing the past, though a strange one, given that her last trip Down Under had ended in gloom.

Attempting to drum up interest, Merivale misguidedly arranged for *Gone with the Wind* to be shown in Melbourne, only for the film's potency to overpower the plays. How could this tiny woman onstage compete with herself on-screen, her blue-green eyes lustrous in Technicolor, each close-up thirty feet high? In a letter to Gertrude, Merivale blamed the audience for being "too busy looking at itself and being sensible of its own importance to pay full attention to the play."

If Vivien was disappointed, she hid it well and her manners were impeccable. "She was always very, very nice to me," recalls Patrick Stewart, then a junior member of the cast. "But she wasn't always nice to others, particularly the actresses in the company. She was polite but didn't really make friends with the other actresses—she loved to have men around her. People whispered that she wasn't too well. There were rumors about breakdowns and health and stuff, but she was doing eight shows a week for fifteen months, playing leading roles, and she never missed an entrance or a performance."

When Stewart heard that she had trouble sleeping, he and his friends took turns keeping her company late at night. "A list was drawn up—I think this was only the men," he continues. "Four or five or six of us would be invited to her hotel or wherever she was living with Jack Merivale and we would have a party every night unless there were formal events she had to go to. And what she loved to do was play charades. We would divide into two or three teams and we would play into the early hours of the morning. Eventually Vivien would tire and she would say, 'All right, it's breakfast time,' and she would go to the kitchen and cook breakfast for everyone. This would be about four in the morning. While we were eating breakfast, she went to bed. I am told she would sleep into the afternoon. And then she would get up, get ready and come to the theater."

After performing in Melbourne, Brisbane, Sydney and Adelaide, and then New Zealand, the troupe moved to the Americas, starting in Mexico City and working its way south toward Brazil. There the audiences seemed more interested in Vivien's clothes than her performance, more shocked by her out-of-date outfit than her now-exhausted efforts onstage. Her energy was fading, her enthusiasm for the daily grind of traveling and then acting was fast wilting. The strain spilled over in Buenos Aires, where she arrived in April 1962. After arguing with Jack in their hotel room, writes Walker, "Vivien picked up a brass eight-day travelling clock and threw it through the (fortunately) open window of their forty-fourth-floor suite." Merivale rushed into the street, but it was gone.

He was in an impossible position, both wanted and unwanted, embraced and rebuffed. He was the most supportive of companions, "an *angel*, funny and kind," as Vivien told Coward, "and has been a life saver for me over all these months." But he was not Larry. And if he ever thought otherwise, Larry's image would set him right, staring at him from the bedside table where Vivien always kept his photo. "He was very kind to her, very good to her, and he looked after her," says Juliet Mills. "But her passion was still for Larry. That never changed. Never, never, never changed."

Merivale could handle that, but not Vivien's drinking. While she claimed she had almost given up alcohol, the opposite was true: she consumed champagne and cocktails all through the day and hard liquor well into the night. "She drank a terrifying amount after L. left her," noted Bushell, though he believed, contrary to some others, that "it never affected her beauty."

A year after returning to England, Vivien was back in New York with *Tovarich*, a lightweight musical comedy about two aristocrats fleeing the Russian Revolution who find work as servants in Paris. Away from home and struggling to master the songs, she felt her familiar depression sapping her strength. "I have been so really worryingly low + with your dear little letter with me my spirits took a leap," she wrote Larry. "Thank you darling so very much. There is an awesome amount of work to be done on 'Tovarich' some of it not written yet—the thought of new numbers naturally alarms me dreadfully."

Depression, as always, was a prelude to mania, and when the play opened on March 18, 1963, Vivien's delirium swept back in a flood. Trying to rein her in, Merivale took her away for a week, traveling to Katherine Cornell's Hudson Valley home, before bringing her back to Broadway. But that didn't impede her illness. At a September 28 matinee, Vivien erupted onstage and flew at her costar, Jean-Pierre Aumont. "She began to claw me, slap me in the face, and kick me in the balls," recalled the actor. "Since it was a quarrel scene I tried to make the audience believe that this boxing exhibition had been planned."

As soon as the matinee was over, Merivale took Vivien home and tried to keep her there, to no effect. Back at the theater, she had to be restrained. Kay Brown, the former Selznick aide who had discovered *Gone with the Wind*, was summoned to help, and Merivale also called Laurence Evans, the Oliviers' agent, who bought a plane ticket and urged Merivale to bring Vivien to England.

She consented, only for another scene to occur onboard the plane, followed by an enforced sedation. In London, she was carried off on a stretcher, her face covered so that photographers could not see her. Her run in *Tovarich* was at an end.

Following treatment, Vivien recuperated at her new home, Tickerage Mill, a seventeenth-century cottage set on 115 acres of land. It was an idyllic house and "took the breath away," wrote Bushell. Concealed in a hollow, it was set amid "bull rushes, flags + yellow irises, water lilies + swans." Vivien had purchased the mill for £20,000, either consciously or unconsciously seeking to be closer to Larry, whose Brighton townhouse was only eighteen miles away.

After years of increasingly irregular contact, Larry—advised by a doctor to keep a distance—nonetheless agreed to see Vivien at last and drove out to Tickerage one afternoon.

"His car pulled up in front of the house," recalled the nurse who was attending Vivien, "and we were up on the first floor bedroom and I said to her: 'Oh! He's here. Quick. You'd better go down.' And she said, 'Oh no! I can't.' And she was like a little schoolgirl and here I was, old enough to be her daughter and I was saying, 'Miss Leigh you must go down.' And then his voice came up the stairs: 'Vivien, are you coming down or am I coming up?' I nearly ran straight down into his arms—the voice alone. She just took off like a little schoolgirl meeting her boyfriend."

The two reminisced for hours, as if no conflict had ever got in the way of their love, no bitterness tarnished their legendary union, until they were interrupted by a call from Plowright and Larry had to leave. "Oh, it was beautiful," said the nurse, "and they walked by the lake together."

*　　*　　*

As the years passed, Larry's letters to Vivien grew more sporadic, their wording more perfunctory. Three years before her death, he could not even find the time to write but instead dictated one of his final notes, which was typed by a secretary and sent unsigned. When she came to see him onstage in John Ford's *The Broken Heart*, he avoided her altogether.

"I was sharing a dressing room with lovely Joan Greenwood," says the actress Rosemary Harris, "and we sat side by side looking at this mirror that covered the wall, and at the end of the show Miss Leigh came to our room and stood there looking into the mirror. And Joanie Greenwood jumped up and said, 'Miss Leigh, we're so sorry. Sir Laurence was really feeling rotten last night and [has no voice]. It's so awful that he's not playing.' And she just said, 'Isn't it strange? He's never lost his voice before.'" Harris averted her eyes and stared into the dressing room mirror, where she could see Vivien's reflection. "And I looked in the mirror and her eyes were filled with tears."

In Los Angeles for her final film, 1964's *Ship of Fools*—and away from Merivale, who was shooting a picture of his own—Vivien couldn't disguise her distress. "Simone Signoret came over and said there's been a terrible row at the studio and Vivien's not well," remembered Gielgud, "and I rushed off to Katharine Hepburn who was with George Cukor...and they got a doctor and she had some treatment all that week and in spite of that she'd go out, put on a little wig which suited her marvelously and go out to parties every night. [Then] she'd put on her gramophone in the morning with her record of *Tovarich* that she was very proud of and it would play full out for three or four hours through the house and it drove her nearly mad and she would suddenly after being so considerate, so courteous, so beautifully mannered, she'd suddenly become hostile and mischievous and sort of wanting to put people in the wrong."

"This was [a] time of loneliness, I think, for Vivien," said her director, Stanley Kramer. "She gave parties to have people around her. She would give parties for the entire José Greco [flamenco] troupe. It would be Spanish night at Vivien Leigh's. And then a party for all the prop men at Columbia Studio for some strange reason. Not wanting to be alone, I think, and alone meant not having fifty people there."

Somehow, Vivien retained her sense of humor, simultaneously conscious of and oblivious to her behavior, as she kept working on the film. "Stanley," she teased, when she could feel his irritation rising, "if you think this kind of modified bitchery is difficult, wait until you hit Katie Hepburn."

Once, when she was slow to emerge from makeup, Kramer went to find her. "I can't do it today," she said quietly. He understood that she was ill. "[She] couldn't do it," he recalled. "I'll never forget that look....She was ill, and the courage to go ahead—the courage to make the film—was almost unbelievable."

When the movie was over, for the first time since she had left India, Vivien returned to the land of her birth, traveling to New Delhi and Kathmandu. Merivale, still shooting, was unable to join her and so she went with her friends Hamish Hamilton and his wife, Jean. Here, for the first time in half a century, Vivien beheld the Himalayas, the soaring mountains that had towered over the Darjeeling house where she was born in 1913. She was awed by what she saw, by the "peaks of blue white you think *must* be clouds," as she told Merivale. And yet, this close to her childhood haunts, she chose not to go on to Darjeeling or Calcutta, the towns where she had been brought up and where she had spent her idyllic first years And so she never visited the homes Ernest and Gertrude had built; never viewed their summer villa in the shadow of Mount Kanchenjunga; never strolled through the Bengali estate that had been her parents' pride and joy.

*   *   *

Back in England, she invited friends to a screening of *Gone with the Wind*, along with several of her castmates from the tour. "Vivien suddenly called out, 'Patrick! Come here. I want you to sit beside me,'" remembers Stewart. "I couldn't believe it. I was breathless with excitement and overwhelmed by this great honor, which came as something of a surprise to me, I must say. Of course, she was seated first and, of course, the audience went rapturous. They were on their feet cheering and applauding because they couldn't believe they were about to watch that movie with Vivien in the audience."

But once the screening had started, her spirits changed. "We got about fifteen, twenty minutes into the film," continues Stewart, "and she turned to me and she whispered: 'Patrick this is so sad. Everyone in this movie but me is dead. I can't stay and watch this. Forgive me.' And she stood up and left."

In May 1967, Vivien started to cough once again. She thought it was her smoking or the flu, but her tuberculosis had returned— a horrible irony, given that she had just played a woman who dies from the disease in Chekhov's *Ivanov*. A chest x-ray revealed the full extent of her illness, but Vivien rejected the necessary care. She should have been hospitalized; instead, she insisted on staying at home where, rather than rest, she wandered around her apartment, watering the flowers and resisting the medication Merivale tried desperately to give her.

"Her room was like a mini Chelsea flower show and it took her two hours every morning to arrange and trim them," reported one newspaper. "There were piles of books as well—and an open script of the latest play she wanted to do in the autumn or as soon as the doctors allowed her up."

There were antibiotics now; but a full dose was twenty-four

tablets a day, with nausea and stomachache and other miserable side effects. Her treatment would have involved para-aminosalicylic acid (PAS) and that was "a tough drug to take," says Thomas M. Daniel, author of *Captain of Death: The Story of Tuberculosis*. Vivien complained that the medicine was making her worse, not better. "The drugs they fill me with make me feel very peculiar," she wrote to one of her friends, telling another: "They have given me new types of pills this time....I can only get up for an hour a day and I find it difficult to read."

Brian Aherne—the actor Larry had disparaged before his then wife, Joan Fontaine—came to see her at the beginning of July and found her "looking as radiantly beautiful as she had ever looked at any time I have ever seen her. It was rather like a scene from *Camille*.... 'Oh,' she said, 'you know, I had a physical last October and they said I was perfect...nothing wrong with me at all. And then for this play I had to go to a doctor about insurance. He examines me and says I've got a hole as big as this in my lung. But it's ridiculous. They want to send me to a hospital at once, and I refuse to go. I'm not going to go; I'm going to be here and have a party every afternoon and all my friends are going to come and see me. Have a drink, have a drink.' "

She was in denial and, even in this precarious state, forced to remain at home, insisted on rehearsing a new play, Edward Albee's *A Delicate Balance*. Each time the cast joined her for read-throughs, they were interrupted by a stream of visitors. "She drank and smoked," said the play's producer, Toby Rowland. "She had a lot of people smoking in her bedroom."

"I had tea with her and she wasn't feeling well," says Juliet Mills. "She was in bed and resting and said she felt tired all the time. She wasn't doing so much work; she was getting older; her looks were fading. I felt she had lost the will, more than any-thing, the will to fight this disease."

Laurence Evans, her agent, dropped by on July 7 and noted how shakily she put on her makeup. She was doing everything to stay beautiful and yet nothing to stay alive.

The following evening, Merivale called home from the Phoe-nix Theatre, where he was appearing in Frederick Lonsdale's *The Last of Mrs. Cheyney*. He found Vivien's voice weak, but her mood stable; she seemed happy and gave no cause for alarm. "I said I'll be home in whatever time it took—at that time of night about 45 minutes," he remembered.

Arriving at the flat after his show, he "looked in the bed-room and there she was, asleep, with [her cat] Poo Jones curled up beside her. And I went into the kitchen to make myself some soup out of a tin. I had that, and I went back into the bedroom, and she was lying on the floor. So I tried to wake her, with no result, and then she wasn't breathing so I tried mouth to mouth resuscitation, what I knew of it, and no result whatsoever. Then I was pretty sure she was dead."

Larry was in the hospital, receiving treatment for prostate can-cer, the first of many long and debilitating illnesses, when Meri-vale called early the next morning. He left at once.

"Guessing there would be one or two pressmen hovering about in front of the flat in Eaton Square, I went in through a secret side-entrance on the basement floor," he wrote. "Jack was waiting just inside the front door to the flat. Guessing my feelings, he then opened the bedroom door and quietly closed me in to be alone with the one with whom I had shared a life that resembled nothing so much as an express lift skying me upwards and throwing me downwards in insanely non-stop fashion."

He looked back on his failures, on his inability to make Vivien understand "at those times when she was sadly disappointed in the results of my intimate passionate endeavors, that all *that* had gone into my acting, and that you can't be more than one kind of athlete at a time."

Alone with his love—the woman for whom he had given up his wife, his son and even his reputation; his bride of twenty years; the source of his greatest joy and greatest pain, now dead at the age of fifty-three—he could not help noticing the pool that had spread beneath her on the floor. Later, he would be criticized for noting this detail in his memoirs, but for now he reflected on the "ulcer" in their relationship, the malignancy that had grown and spread until it consumed everything that had been so good.

"It has always been impossible for me," he observed, "not to believe that I was somehow the cause of Vivien's disturbances, that they were due to some fault in me." Left in the room they had shared, "I stood and prayed for forgiveness, for all the evils that had sprung up between us."

The years had been good to Larry. Living with Joan, he had done some of his best work as artistic director of the new Chichester Festival Theatre, built in 1962 and only thirty miles from Brighton, where the couple lived. There he mounted productions that were still spoken of with awe half a century later, from Chekhov's *Uncle Vanya* to Shaw's *Saint Joan*, while juggling a new life as the father of three children: Richard (born in 1961); Tamsin (born in 1963); and Julie-Kate (born in 1966).

But more and more, there seemed to be two Oliviers: the exceptional artist who pushed himself to breathtaking heights in such plays as *The Dance of Death*, *Three Sisters* and *Long Day's Journey into Night*; and the rather dull fellow who shunted back and forth on the train to London in a suit and tie, his thick glasses hiding his gunpowder-gray eyes, looking like a salaryman off to earn his keep, "an ordinary man with an extraordinary talent," as his friend and associate Peter Hiley observed.

Olivier's greatest efforts were reserved for his dream of building a national theater similar to ones in Germany and France. More than his films, more than his plays, more than any of his previous achievements, he believed this would be his legacy. In 1963, fifteen years after he and Ralph Richardson had been dismissed as artistic directors of the Old Vic Company, Larry returned there to become the first director of England's new National Theatre, which he would lead until 1976, when it moved to its own building on the South Bank of the river Thames. His name now graces the National's biggest stage, with a life-size statue of him as Hamlet outside the building.

But the stress of fighting over the National took its toll, as Michael Caine discovered when the two men costarred in 1972's *Sleuth*. He was surprised to see Olivier popping valium at a time when the National was being wrested from his grip. (Peter Hall would become its new leader, to Larry's dismay.) Caine adored his costar, found him "a very sensitive man and very gentle, with extraordinary emotional depth," and yet he wasn't oblivious to the turmoil inside, to a darker and more driven fellow who was still propelled by a ferocious desire to win. Caine was startled in one scene when Olivier had to pull out a gun. "It was quite stunning how vicious it became," he recalls. "It showed me something else about him." It was a quality Frank Langella noticed, too, when they filmed 1979's *Dracula*. Larry called himself a "monster," said he needed to be as a star. "I was always keenly aware of the fact that I was dealing with a deadly cobra capable of striking without notice," wrote Langella.

Early in Larry's marriage to Joan, he began an affair with Sarah Miles, then only eighteen and fresh off her few days of work on *Roman Spring*. They were starring in a small British film, *Term of Trial*, about a sympathetic teacher who's falsely accused of having an affair with one of his pupils; soon, they became involved in real life. Looking back, Miles believes the very forbiddenness of the relationship was part of its appeal. "He loved living on the edge, seeing me whenever he could," she says. "That's life at its utmost. He loved that feeling of naughtiness and he did like danger."

Olivier opened up to the young woman as he rarely did to others, though it's impossible to know how much of what he said was true and how much designed to impress. "At one point," Miles remembers, "he toasted and said, 'I'm going to be the first lord of the theater!'" Indeed, in 1970 he became the second Baron Olivier, almost half a century after his uncle Sydney had been elevated to the peerage. "He did have that ambition," Miles continues. "He'd wanted it since he was a little boy."

Larry claimed he was bisexual, she adds, and said he "wanted to marry me. But I didn't want to marry him at that point. I was very happy with how I was." Did he mean what he said? Or was he simply playing yet another role? Not even Plowright could be sure. Later, Olivier told his son, Richard, "I've played over 200 parts in my life and I know them all better than I know myself."

Fifteen years after meeting Miles, he caught up with her again in Los Angeles. He was there to shoot the 1976 thriller *Marathon Man*, while Miles had moved to California after splitting with her husband, writer Robert Bolt. Still married, Olivier was sixty-eight years old and in terrible health: he had had cancer, kidney trouble and a thrombosis of the leg, not to mention physical complications from being attacked by a burglar at home. Worse still, two years earlier he had been diagnosed with dermatopolymyositis, an excruciatingly painful skin disease that made the slightest touch agony and left him hospitalized for months with no certainty he would survive. "He was in a coma for a long time," says Hayley Mills. "And he told me later that [at one time] he was able to hear people talking about him and heard a doctor

[say], 'He's not going to make it.' And it made him so angry. He said, 'I was absolutely fucking furious.' And that was the turning point. That's when he started to fight back."

After inviting Miles to a star-studded Hollywood party, "he took her home, sent his driver away, and asked himself in," writes Terry Coleman. By now he was addicted to valium and Mogadon, a sedative and antianxiety medication. "He feared the nights. He told [Miles] he was not able to give her what he once had, but she led him to bed and they lay quietly together. He was frail and shrunk. He showed her his sore fingers and explained that was why he could not hold her hand. He left after dawn."

"His bravery struck me hugely," says Miles. "He never spoke about it, didn't complain. He had this terrible pus coming out of his hands [and was] very aware of time. But he kept questioning and questioning, [asking] things about me and my new life. He really wanted to know. He was forever curious." Alone with his lover, Larry kept returning to a line of Osborne's, "that there isn't a third act in life any more[.] Life used to be full of third acts bringing everything nicely to a comfortable close, with a satisfying solution. It isn't like that any longer."

On March 21, 1974, he gave his last live performance, playing a Glaswegian communist in *The Party*, written by Trevor Griffiths. "I was onstage with him at the Old Vic," says actor Gawn Grainger. "He had this huge speech, a twenty-minute speech. And I sat next to him on the sofa when he made the speech, and you could feel the fireworks going on: 'Can I get through it? Can I get through it?' And he did. And there was this extraordinary moment when he knew and the audience knew that it was his last time and he walked slowly down to the front as the audience rose, and kissed the stage."

Later, on occasion, Grainger would visit him at his modest country home, the Malt House, twenty-seven miles from his Brighton residence. "One night I said, 'What does it feel like,

knowing that you're going to be buried in Westminster Abbey?'
And he said, 'Westminster Abbey is just as cold as a village
churchyard. I don't want to die.'"

His muscles were shriveled, his arms thin and wasted, and he
wore gloves to protect his fragile fingers. He would have relished
more company, but visitors were fewer than before. Plowright
"openly hated all his old friends + put up a barrier against them
that I never got past," noted Bushell—though Richard Olivier
disputes that, explaining that it was simply harder for the old
friends to talk about their past when Joan was around, and so "I
assume there was a natural diminution of some relationships."

Inevitably, Plowright felt the strain of looking after a much
older man. But they remained together, says Richard, even if his
mother now spent most of her week in London, leaving Olivier
alone. For a while, at least, he had Richard to keep him company. After returning from UCLA, the young man lived with his
father and drew close to him in his final years. "He had had a
series of debilitating illnesses and he was on steroids for a long
time, which didn't help his peace of mind," says Richard. "But if
anything, it was his sense of identity that was the greatest deficit
at the end."

Michael Blakemore, the actor who'd toured with the Oliviers (before becoming a well-known director), saw Larry one last
time in 1989. He was now eighty-two and attended by nurses.
Propped up with cushions, he sat in a small sunroom, where
he reminisced about their work and the roles he had made his
own—*Coriolanus* and *Titus Andronicus* and *Richard III*. Then a
nurse came to take him for a rest, "and it was only when they got
him to his feet that I realized how frail he had become," writes
Blakemore. "The cortisone which he had been taking in such
large quantities, and for so long, appeared to have softened the
vertebrae in his spine and his head had now sunk deep between
his shoulders. Just to move, he needed a helper on either side, and

as they turned and eased him, all pain and infirmity, towards the open door, his outline evoked for a moment a pale ghost of his most famous part [Richard III]: 'Deform'd, unfinish'd, sent before my time / Into this breathing world, scarce half made up.' "

As Larry aged, guilt merged with nostalgia, pleasure with regret. A few years before his death in 1989, he visited New York to work on his memoirs with Michael Korda (the nephew of producer Alex Korda, by now a distinguished book editor) and insisted on finding a steakhouse where he and Vivien had eaten together, "intent on recreating that meal," says Korda. Once there, Larry sat at the same table and ordered exactly the same thing Vivien had done, "none of which he ate."

Once, says the actress Rosemary Harris, Larry began to recite one of Shakespeare's sonnets: "Let me not to the marriage of true minds / Admit impediments. Love is not love / Which alters when it alteration finds." The sonnet ends with a warning: "Love alters not with his brief hours and weeks, / But bears it out even to the edge of doom. / If this be error and upon me prov'd, / I never writ, nor no man ever lov'd." Remembering it, "I felt he was talking about Vivien," says Harris. "I felt there was heartbreak in the back of his voice."

Passion sears, it scalds, it convulses, it disrupts. It creates and destroys in equal measure. At times it can seem like a mental illness, not all that different from the "mixed state" of bipolar disorder that fuses two apparent opposites, mania and depression, into a third, hallucinatory condition, unlike anything most of us have ever known. That's why Larry compared it to a sickness and why his first wife, Jill Esmond, said she had encountered true passion only once, and prayed she would never do so again.

And yet without it, would either Vivien or Larry have soared to such heights? Vivien's career took off only after she met Larry; but he may have benefited even more. "It was Vivien's illness that made Olivier the great actor he became," says the actor and biographer Simon Callow. "He was forced to engage with overpowering emotions and to acknowledge that willpower was not the solution to everything."

In the end, neither willpower nor anything else could save his marriage. "You can reach a point," he reflected, "where it's like a life raft that can only hold so many. You cast away the hand grasping it. You let go. You do not take it onboard because otherwise it's both of you. Two instead of one. Then you go on living and there you are, with it, knowing what has happened, remembering its details. Yet what else is there to do?"

In his final years, when he was frail and sick; when his third marriage was strained; and when he was no longer the colossus of the stage but simply an old man, left with his memories and regrets, thoughts of Vivien would pierce his thick carapace of self-protection. A friend, visiting him at home shortly before he died, found him alone, watching one of her movies. His eyes were full of tears.

"This, this was love," he said. "This was the real thing."

ACKNOWLEDGMENTS

When I began work on this book five years ago, half a century had passed since Vivien's death and psychiatrists had made giant leaps in understanding mental illness. I wanted to apply that to the past and ask: How different does a relationship look with new knowledge? How much should we reevaluate our judgment of people and perhaps life itself?

That would have been impossible without the doctors, academics and psychiatrists who gave me their time. I'm particularly grateful to Paul Edelstein of the University of Pennsylvania's Perelman School of Medicine; Kay Redfield Jamison of the Mood Disorders Center of Johns Hopkins University; Terence Ketter and Po Wang of the Stanford Bipolar Disorders Clinic; John Geddes, Guy Goodwin and Lalita Ramakrishnan of Oxford University; and authors Thomas M. Daniel and Edward Shorter.

Similarly, this book could not have existed without the prior research of other biographers, including Terry Coleman, Anne Edwards, Anthony Holden, Alan Strachan, Hugo Vickers and Alexander Walker. I'd especially like to thank Strachan and Vickers for sharing some of their findings and conclusions with me.

Equally important to anyone with an interest in the Oliviers is Kendra Bean, editor of the website VivandLarry.com. Kendra has been consistently supportive and even supplied photos from her private collection. I owe her enormous thanks, as I do this book's wonderful photo editor, Jennifer Laski.

Members of the Olivier and Leigh families were unfailingly kind and forbearing, especially Richard Olivier, Tarquin Olivier and Neville Farrington (Vivien's grandson). I was also lucky enough to speak to several of the Oliviers' colleagues and contemporaries, notably Don Bachardy, Warren Beatty, Michael Caine, Gawn Grainger, Rosemary Harris, Anthony Hopkins, Waris Hussein, Michael Korda, Miller Lide, Sarah Miles, Hayley Mills, Juliet Mills, Helen Mirren, John Standing, Patrick Stewart and Victoria Tennant.

From the beginning, this book was given a huge boost of enthusiasm by my editor, Suzanne O'Neill, and her team at Grand Central Publishing: Jacqui Young, Jeff Holt, Deborah Wiseman, Roxanne Jones, Alana Spendley, Colin Dickerman and Ben Sevier. I'd also like to thank Little, Brown's Fiona Hill and my astute and thoughtful agents, ICM Partners' Jennifer Joel and Curtis Brown's Gordon Wise.

I spent many wonderful weeks in archives in London, Los Angeles and Austin, Texas, and was given endless help by their staff, especially the extraordinary Keith Lodwick of the Victoria and Albert Museum; Brett Service and Ned Comstock of the USC Warner Archive; Eric Colleary and Steve Wilson of the Harry Ransom Center at the University of Texas at Austin; Louise Hilton of the Academy of Motion Picture Arts and Sciences' Margaret Herrick Library; Alan Brodie, who represents the Noël Coward estate; and Dan O'Rourke of Paramount Pictures. Thanks, too, to Universal's Jeff Pirtle and Aaron Rogers; the staff of the British Library and Wesleyan University's Reid Cinema Archives; and my researchers Mary Mallory, Karie Bible and the exceptional Sophia Hall.

Much to my disappointment, during two weeks of research in India, I was unable to find more than the thinnest traces of Vivien's early life there. Her family home in Kolkata has been knocked down and turned into an apartment building, and there is no sure way of knowing which of several contenders was the genuine Hartley house in Darjeeling. Still, I was greatly helped by Shreya Bansal, Squadron Leader (Ret.) Rana TS Chhina, Pranay Gupta, the Reverend Joy Halder, Reeti Roy and Narendra Pratap Singh. Thanks too to Chelsea McGill of Immersive Trails for all her work unearthing the Kolkata locales.

Mike Medavoy, Avra Douglas and Austin Wilkin were kind enough to grant me access to the Marlon Brando archive. I'd also like to thank David Leonard of Dance Books, along with Anita, Charles and Samantha Finch, for permission to quote from Tamara Tchinarova Finch's *Dancing Into the Unknown: My Life in the Ballets Russes and Beyond*; and Edward Perks of Currey & Co. LLP for permission to quote from the letters of Anthony Bushell.

For additional help and support, I'm grateful to my colleagues at Chapman University and my former colleagues at the *Hollywood Reporter*. Special thanks go to Matthew Belloni, Carolyn Pfeiffer Bradshaw, Dan Bronson, Alison Brower, John Burland, Simon Callow, Liz Chater, Clare Conville, Alan Cowie, Clarissa Dalrymple, Jonathan Dana, Scott Feinberg, Alejandro Franks, Stephen Fry, Nicholas Goldsborough, Richard Green, Sarah Jackson, Michelle Kass, Nick Kazan, Tom Kemper, Pat Kingsley, Rocky Lang, Sherry Lansing, Nicholas Meyer, Janice Min, Sharon Moore, William Niven, David Omissi, Tom Parry, Deborah Dozier Potter, David Stenn, Rochelle Stevens, Kenia Suarez, Ben Svetkey, Katherine Tulich, Tracy Tynan and Stephen Ujlaki. Love goes to my family—Mark Galloway, Norman Galloway and Janine Webber.

NOTES

ABBREVIATIONS

DOS: The David O. Selznick Collection at the Harry Ransom Center, University of Texas at Austin. The archive includes the papers of Selznick's brother, agent Myron Selznick.

LOA: The Laurence Olivier Archive at the British Library, London.

MHL: Margaret Herrick Library, Academy of Motion Picture Arts and Sciences, Beverly Hills.

STENN COLLECTION: Anthony Bushell's letters to Michael Dempsey, the David Stenn Collection, at the Margaret Herrick Library, Beverly Hills.

VLA: The Vivien Leigh Archive at the Victoria and Albert Museum, London.

PROLOGUE

2   **It sometimes felt almost like an illness:** Laurence Olivier, *Confessions of an Actor* (New York: Simon & Schuster, 1982), 100–101.

2   **Real passion:** Tarquin Olivier, *My Father Laurence Olivier* (London: Headline, 1992), 67.

3   **something about Viv:** Thomas Kiernan, *The Life of Laurence Olivier* (London: Sidgwick & Jackson, 1981), 173.

CHAPTER 1

5   **My father used to describe:** Laurence Olivier, *Confessions of an Actor* (New York: Simon & Schuster, 1982), 18. The story may sound suspicious, with its generically named English doctor, but a Dr. John Dunnell Rawlings did in fact live in Dorking, according to the 1901 census. Gerard later presided over his funeral.

6   **a storming, raging tornado**: Thomas Kiernan, *The Life of Laurence Olivier* (London: Sidgwick & Jackson, 1981), 10.

6   **I see little glory**: Winston Churchill to J. Moore Bayley, December 23, 1901, https://www.churchillarchiveforschools.com/themes/the-themes/key-developments-in-british-and-empire-history/why-did-british-politicians-see-the-need-for-welfare-reforms-in-the-early-1900s/the-sources/source-2.

6   **hopelessly degraded**: Russ Willey, "Notting Dale, Kensington and Chelsea," *Hidden London* (blog), n.d., https://hidden-london.com/gazetteer/notting-dale/.

6   **hell on earth**: Jerry White, "Life in 19th-Century Slums: Victorian London's Homes from Hell," *History Extra* (blog), October 26, 2016, https://www.historyextra.com/period/victorian/life-in-19th-century-slums-victorian-londons-homes-from-hell/. For more information on the prevalent conditions, see "The Potteries and the Bramley Road Area and the Rise of the Housing Problem in North Kensington," in *Survey of London*, ed. F. H. W. Sheppard, vol. 37, *Northern Kensington* (London: London County Council, 1973), 340–355, *British History Online*, https://www.british-history.ac.uk/survey-london/vol37/pp340-355.

7   **Many sons react against**: Laurence Olivier, "A Soliloquy in an English Hamlet," *Los Angeles Times*, November 24, 1963.

7   **a thundering love affair**: Sybille Olivier Day to Laurence Olivier, May 7, 1939. LOA Add MS 79891.

7   **from one seaside town to another**: Sybille Olivier Day, "He That Plays the King" (unpublished manuscript), 20. Sybille mistakenly recalled the year as 1912. LOA Add MS 80591.

7   **deaths by heat**: Julie Nicholson, "Long, Hot Summer: The Great British Heatwave of 1911," *The Independent*, September 17, 2011, https://www.independent.co.uk/climate-change/news/long-hot-summer-the-great-british-heatwave-of-1911-5329910.html.

8   **never took kindly to family life again**: Day, "He That Plays the King," 22.

8   **the most enchanting person**: Richard Meryman, "First Lord of the Stage," *Life*, December 2, 1972.

8   **Mrs. Olivier was a darling**: Sybille Thorndike, interview by Ronald Proyer, January 8, 1973, transcript, Vivien Leigh Archive, Victoria and Albert Museum. VLA GB 71 THM/420/35.

8   **Her disease was at first wrongly diagnosed**: Day, "He That Plays the King," 43.

9   **abomination of the body:** Erving Goffman, *Stigma: Notes on the Management of Spoiled Identity* (New York: Simon & Schuster, 1963), chapter 1.

9   **Larry came to the old Rectory:** Day, "He That Plays the King," 43.

9   **Praise Him! Praise Him!** Sybille Olivier Day to Laurence Olivier, May 7, 1939. LOA Add MS 79891.

9   **My heaven, my hope:** Olivier, *Confessions*, 18.

9   **There was undoubtedly:** Olivier, "Soliloquy."

10   **How she loved you:** Sybille Olivier Day to Laurence Olivier, October 9, 1976. LOA Add MS 79891.

10   **pipeline to childhood pain:** Joan Plowright, *And That's Not All* (London: Weidenfeld & Nicolson, 2001), 48.

10   **There was this little gap:** Sarah Miles, interview with author, June 8, 2019.

10   **Calcutta:** I use this spelling for historical references and Kolkata when referring to the city today.

11   **the lower rungs of Anglo society:** Liz Chater, "Armenian: Something Vivien Leigh and her Cousin Xan Fielding a British Spy Had in Common," *Chater Genealogy* (blog), August 12, 2015, http://chater -genealogy.blogspot.com/2015/08/armenian-something-vivien-leigh -and-her_12.html. I'm grateful to Chater for the additional research into the Olivier family that she conducted for this book.

13   **an agonising dilemma:** Anne de Courcy, *The Fishing Fleet: Husband- Hunting in the Raj* (New York: HarperCollins, 2014), 292–293.

14   **Precious blood of our lord Jesus Christ:** See Antonia White's novelized account of life in the school, *Frost in May* (New York: Dial, 1978).

14   **There was rigid discipline:** Hugo Vickers, *Vivien Leigh* (Boston: Little, Brown, 1988), 14.

14   **If Vivian, in her misery:** Victoria Tennant, interview with author, June 21, 2018.

15   **Maureen O'Sullivan:** "I just couldn't take it at all," the actress told author Anne Edwards. "It just wasn't my thing, you know, but Vivien was very happy there. She loved it, she loved the nuns, she loved the care they gave her." Maureen O'Sullivan, interview by Anne Edwards, unpublished transcript, Anne Edwards Papers, Charles E. Young Research Library, University of California, Los Angeles, Box 21.

CHAPTER 2

16   **I first set eyes:** Laurence Olivier, *Confessions of an Actor* (New York: Simon & Schuster, 1982), 100.

17   **who remained in love:** Ashcroft "stayed in passionate and success-
     ful love for at least the run of *Romeo and Juliet*," noted Olivier's
     friend Anthony Bushell to Michael Dempsey, September 21, 1991.
     Stenn Collection.

17   **alarmingly loose:** Oswald Frewen, unpublished diary, June 28,
     1937, quoted in Hugo Vickers, *Vivien Leigh* (Boston: Little,
     Brown, 1988), 77.

17   **cretinous romanticism:** Tarquin Olivier, *My Father Laurence Oliv-
     ier* (London: Headline, 1992), 7.

17   **She wasn't "dazzling":** Ibid., 6.

17   **There was nothing of the passionate:** Alex Knox, interview by
     Anne Edwards, undated, unpublished transcript, Anne Edwards
     Papers, Charles E. Young Research Library, University of Califor-
     nia, Los Angeles, Box 21.

18   **[His] modesty was unnatural:** T. Olivier, *My Father*, 13.

18   **I suppose our happiest moment:** Ibid., 18.

18   **Was it their "imp":** Jill Esmond to Olivier, May 7, 1930, quoted in
     Terry Coleman, *Olivier* (New York: Henry Holt, 2005), 39.

18   **All this gadding about:** Olivier gave this decidedly downbeat version of
     events to a fan magazine when he was already beginning to be disillu-
     sioned. Edward Churchill, "He Got the Habit: Laurence Olivier Had
     a Love Scene in a Play…The Play Is Ended, but Larry Keeps On with
     the Scene Any How," *Silver Screen*, March 1932.

19   **Kim Darling…just a little word:** Isobel Buchanan Ronaldson
     Olivier to Laurence Olivier, July 24, 1930, quoted in Coleman,
     Olivier, 42.

19   **Olivier during the unhappy period:** Anthony Bushell to Michael
     Dempsey, May 13, 1988. Stenn Collection.

20   **bounded to the window:** T. Olivier, *My Father*, 61–62.

20   **In the garden he used to sit:** Ibid., 55.

20   **As soon as he saw:** Ibid., 62.

20   **Jill visited him, so did Larry:** Ibid., 73.

21   **she slapped her face:** Vickers, *Vivien Leigh*, 25.

21   **a dull man, dry, cerebral:** Olivier, *Confessions*, 101.

21   **Drove round and saw Holman estate:** Vivien Leigh, diary, Decem-
     ber 28, 1931. VLA GB 71 THM/433/7/3.

22   **Dinner + show with Leigh:** Ibid., January 25, 1932. VLA GB 71
     THM/433/7/3.4.

22   **All I remember was how thin:** Gwen Robyns, *Light of a Star: The
     Career of Vivien Leigh* (New York: A. S. Barnes, 1970), 23.

22   *Wonderful* day: Vivien Leigh, diary, December 20, 1932. VLA GB 71 THM/433/7/1–31.

22   terribly sad: Vickers, *Vivien Leigh*, 35.

22   That's the man I'm going to marry: Ibid., 44.

22–23   You can't stop her: Ibid., 46.

23   Vivien Leigh: She altered the spelling of her first name when a producer said this way was more feminine.

23   I was influenced: Vickers, *Vivien Leigh*, 48.

23   literally shook from head to foot: Ibid., 48.

24   The miracle had happened: Ibid., 49.

24   [He] pointed across to Larry: David Lewin, "Vivien Tells: When She Met Olivier," *Daily Express*, August 16, 1960.

24   we went and we played football: Ibid.

24   "Vivien Leigh," using her full name: Laurence Olivier, diary, January 27, 1936. LOA Add MS 79802.

25   I was making up for a matinée: Olivier, *Confessions*, 100.

26   trumpeted the putative £50,000 pact: Alexander Walker, *Vivien: The Life of Vivien Leigh* (New York: Grove, 1987), 60.

27   "You know," Larry teased her: Chester Erskine at Vivien Leigh's March 17, 1968, memorial service at the University of Southern California. *An Appreciation of Vivien Leigh* (Los Angeles: University of Southern California, Friends of the Libraries, 1969), 13.

28   Korda then sent a spy: Vickers, *Vivien Leigh*, 68.

28   every day, two, three times: Ibid., 69.

28   I don't think I have ever lived: Godfrey Winn, *The Positive Hour* (London: Michael Joseph, 1970), 397.

28   didn't pay it any attention: Walker, *Vivien*, 78.

28   We're in love: Ibid., 77.

28   had the whisper of an idea: Ibid., 78.

28   defenceless and looking her worst: T. Olivier, *My Father*, 65.

29   punctured the membrane: Ibid., 66.

29–30   Vivien was "so natural": Walker, *Vivien*, 80.

30   I am restless to have you back: Leigh Holman to Vivien Leigh, n.d. VLA GB 71 THM/433/2/8.

30   it would be fun to see Jill & Larry: Vickers, *Vivien Leigh*, 71.

30   Terrified, Vivien muttered the name: Walker, *Vivien*, 80.

30   Larry, the other side of the hall: Ibid., 80.

31   Vivien suffered a "crise de nerfs": Vickers, *Vivien Leigh*, 73.

31   I was so depressed Friday: Ibid., 67–68.

31   I am so unhappy when you are in London: Ibid., 68.

31   He "had been away filming": Walker, *Vivien*, 78.

32   Despite herself: T. Olivier, *My Father*, 67–68.

32   I am loveless because you have it all: Leigh Holman to Vivien Leigh, n.d. VLA GB 71 THM/433/2/8.

32   "Olivier," noted the actor Anthony Quayle: Walker, *Vivien*, 79.

32   Her language, he said: Anthony Quayle, *A Time to Speak* (Reading, England: Sphere, 1990), 263.

33   two years of furtive life: Olivier, *Confessions*, 101.

33   All [Vivien] wanted to do: Vickers, *Vivien Leigh*, 73.

33   the high water-mark: Jonathan Croall, *Gielgud: A Theatrical Life* (New York: Continuum, 2002), 123.

33   With all its physical virility: Thomas Kiernan, *The Life of Laurence Olivier* (London: Sidgwick & Jackson, 1981), 166.

34   On the opening night: Quayle, *A Time to Speak*, 263.

34   I remember how beautiful: Alan Dent, *Vivien Leigh: A Bouquet* (London: Hamish Hamilton, 1969), 84.

34   Ernest, nearly splitting a gut: Olivier, *Confessions*, 191.

35   This welding closeness: Ibid., 101.

CHAPTER 3

37   She torments herself: Helen Spencer to Olivier, November 24, 1938. LOA Add MS 80619.

37   David Niven, Milord Olivier: Anthony Bushell to Michael Dempsey, August 17, 1987. Stenn Collection.

38   alleges that Olivier had an affair: Donald Spoto, *Laurence Olivier: A Biography* (New York: HarperCollins, 1992), 228.

38   My mother was spitting angry: Victoria Tennant, interview with author, June 21, 2018.

38   I think I would have known: Gawn Grainger, interview with author, June 21, 2018.

38   the homosexual act: Laurence Olivier, *Confessions of an Actor* (New York: Simon & Schuster, 1982), 86.

39   I had got over: Ibid., 85–86.

39   Their probable fling: Terry Coleman, *Olivier* (New York: Henry Holt, 2005), 79.

39   "Christ!" Ainley writes: Ibid., 78.

39   extravagantly camp: Tarquin Olivier, *So Who's Your Mother?* (Wilby, England: Michael Russell, 2012), 292.

39   "Christ no," he said: T. Olivier, *My Father*, 256.

40   baby that refused to be suckled: T. Olivier, *My Father*, 67.

40   a myriad purple veinlets: Ibid., 53.

41   To do it once is forgivable: Hugo Vickers, *Vivien Leigh* (Boston: Little, Brown, 1988), 86.

41   Bless me, Reader, for I have sinned: Olivier, *Confessions*, 9.

42   I couldn't believe it: Vickers, *Vivien Leigh*, 82.

42   we got on v. well together: Bushell to Dempsey, October 8, 1988. Stenn Collection.

43   had no feeling for the child: Vickers, *Vivien Leigh*, 40.

43   He still hopes to get her back: Ibid., 86.

43   a wave of promiscuity: Ibid., 85.

43   She said flatly: Ibid., 85–86.

43   I'm terribly afraid: Ibid., 83.

44   Quayle, the actor: Anthony Quayle, *A Time to Speak* (Reading, England: Sphere, 1990), 112.

44   appear to be as much in love: Vickers, *Vivien Leigh*, 83.

44   of nightmares for us: Ibid., 83.

44   And now, please, may I be serious: Henry Ainley to Olivier, January 10, 1938. LOA Add MS 79766.

45   Fewer than five thousand: "Divorce Rates Data, 1858 to Now: How Has It Changed?," Data Blog, *The Guardian*, accessed on, https://www.theguardian.com/news/datablog/2010/jan/28/divorce-rates-marriage-ons.

45   Leigh says, in essence: Olivier to Leigh, April 22, 1939. VLA GB 71 THM/433/1.

45   When she left me for Larry: Vickers, *Vivien Leigh*, 82.

45   "Leigh," Vivien told her husband: Ibid., 83.

46   I can never be sure of myself: Ibid., 91.

46   My poor darling Viv: Leigh Holman to Vivien Leigh, March 3 (no year given). VLA GB 71 THM/433/2/8.

46   her hair turned white: Tarquin Olivier, interview with author, August 2, 2019.

47   She couldn't bear any kind of tenderness: T. Olivier, *My Father*, 73.

48   One friend, running into Olivier: Thomas Kiernan, *The Life of Laurence Olivier* (London: Sidgwick & Jackson, 1981), 158.

48   The first night he was asked: Bushell to Dempsey, March 22, 1989. Stenn Collection.

48   He had "a sting": Alexander Walker, *Vivien: The Life of Vivien Leigh* (New York: Grove, 1987), 101.

49   **Vivien curtsied; Helpmann bowed:** Ibid., 102.

49   **It was a very dressed-up evening:** Hayley Mills, interview with author, May 13, 2021.

49   **dreadfully upset at the turn:** Sybille Olivier Day, "He That Plays the King" (unpublished manuscript), 127. LOA Add MS 80591.

49   **melted at last:** Ibid., 127.

50   **building her own art collection:** Artists were as fond of Vivien as she was of them—sometimes too fond, as she discovered during a sitting for Augustus John. "Vivien ran into the charming side of the old devil's nature when friends clubbed together + persuaded her to go there for a portrait," remembered Anthony Bushell. "John spent her first visit dashing off pencil drawings like his wonderful T. E. Lawrence one, + then flogging them, as Vivien found out later, for a quick £100 each for his pocket money. And at the second sitting he actually had the bloody, or drunken, nerve to try the manhandling lark. He got the back of Vivien's hand, + the biggest flea he'd ever had in his ear + no further visit from her ladyship." Bushell to Dempsey, January 31, 1989. Stenn Collection.

50   **I have chosen no particular period:** Kendra Bean and Lena Backström, "Inside the Oliviers' Love Nest," *vivandlarry.com* (blog), March 5, 2016, http://vivandlarry.com/guest-post/inside-oliviers -love-nest/.

50   **two rooms upstairs:** Ibid.

51   **even his suits seemed shabby:** Walker, *Vivien*, 93.

51   **She was the adored of all us bad boys:** Bushell to Dempsey, February 11, 1988. Stenn Collection.

52   **Her shoes hurt her so much:** Walker, *Vivien*, 94.

52   **She wasn't shouting now:** Ibid., 95–96.

52   **an axillary swelling:** Vickers, *Vivien Leigh*, 92.

53   **Laurence worked on his voice:** Bushell to Dempsey, May 31, 1987. Stenn Collection.

53   **the nearest thing we have:** Anthony Holden, *Olivier* (London: Little Books, 2007), 135.

54   **when Vivien spoke, you could hear Larry:** Walker, *Vivien*, 106.

54   **straying across the Rhône:** Olivier, *Confessions*, 103.

54   **ARE YOU INTERESTED:** Holden, *Olivier*, 136.

55   **box office poison:** Advertisement in the *Hollywood Reporter*, May 4, 1938, reproduced in "Poison at the Box Office," *Vienna's*

Classic Hollywood (blog), June 1, 2020, https://viennasclassicholly wood.com/2020/06/01/poison-at-the-box-office/.

55–56   **Goldwyn had immense presence:** David Niven, *Bring On the Empty Horses* (New York: G. P. Putnam's Sons, 1975), 125.

56   **THOUGHT HIM ONE:** Ben Hecht to Samuel Goldwyn, May 5, 1938. A. Scott Berg. *Goldwyn: A Biography* (New York: Knopf, 1989), 322.

57   **He was "hollow":** Curtis Bill Pepper, "Talking With."

57   **found her sitting on an old chest:** Olivier, *Confessions*, 93.

57   **I went into the role:** Virginia Maxwell, "The Amazing Story Behind Garbo's Choice of Gilbert," *Photoplay*, January 1934.

57   **In Heaven's name:** Karen Swenson, *Greta Garbo: A Life Apart* (New York: Scribner, 1997), 310.

57   **You say she was in love:** Laurence Olivier, "A Soliloquy in an English Hamlet," *Los Angeles Times*, November 24, 1963.

58   **smelled of Goldwyn corn:** Laurence Olivier, *On Acting* (New York: Simon & Schuster, 1987), 258.

58   **I had seen him in a play:** William Wyler to Ronald Proyer, May 8, 1973. VLA GB 71 THM/420/38.

58   **I will play Cathy or nothing:** Ibid.

58   **HAVE FOUND HEATHCLIFF:** William Wyler to Samuel Goldwyn, July 7, 1938. Berg, *Goldwyn: A Biography*, 322.

58   **NEWTON OUT OF QUESTION:** Samuel Goldwyn to William Wyler, July 12, 1938. Ibid.

59   **"Yes," answered his friend:** Olivier, *Confessions*, 106.

59   **Blind with misery:** Coleman, *Olivier*, 98.

59   **Larry drowned his sorrows:** Ibid., 102.

59   **Darling have just received:** Olivier to Leigh, November 15, 1938. VLA GB 71 THM/433/1.

60   **I am learning a great deal:** Ibid.

60   **I awoke at 20 to 8:** Ibid.

60   **She spent the whole time:** Helen Spencer to Olivier, November 24, 1948. LOA Add MS 80619.

60   **My dear dear darling:** Olivier to Leigh, November 17, 1938. VLA GB 71 THM/433/1.

61   **The sort of hope, the self-deceiving:** Ibid.

61   **Jimmy Townsend [a colleague] told me:** Olivier to Leigh, November 15, 1938. Ibid.

62   **I went in to see Sam:** Olivier to Leigh, November 17, 1938. Ibid.

62 They're going to fix tapes: Ibid.

62 What's a little spit: Berg, *Goldwyn: A Biography,* 325.

62 pockmarked face: Holden, *Olivier,* 138.

62 in which we were both trembling: Coleman, *Olivier,* 101.

63 One reporter observed: Gene Schrott, "A New Kind of Lover," *Silver Screen,* August 1939.

63 at least a pat on the shoulder: Merle Oberon, interview by Ronald Proyer, n.d., transcript, Vivien Leigh Archive, Victoria and Albert Museum. VLA GB 71 THM/420/27.

63 Goldwyn would regularly let fly: Anthony Bushell to Michael Dempsey, August 6, 1994. Stenn Collection.

63 Sam Goldwyn never seriously considered: William Wyler to Ronald Proyer. VLA GB 71 THM/420/38.

63 Whereas Garbo was cold: Holden, *Olivier,* 138.

63 Look, I've done it: Olivier, *On Acting,* 258.

63 For Christ sake: Coleman, *Olivier,* 100.

64 *think* of Vivien and *act* with Merle: Ibid., 101.

64 "Well, really," he told Vivien: Olivier to Leigh, November 17, 1938. VLA GB 71 THM/433/1.

CHAPTER 4

65 crouched in the back of a car: Laurence Olivier, *Confessions of an Actor* (New York: Simon & Schuster, 1982), 107.

65 a long interview: Olivier to Leigh, November 15, 1938. VLA GB 71 THM/433/1.

66 no soul: Terry Coleman, *Olivier* (New York: Henry Holt, 2005), 223.

66 regarded the view: Anthony Bushell to Michael Dempsey, August 26, 1988. Stenn Collection.

66–67 When one colleague had mentioned: Hugo Vickers, *Vivien Leigh* (Boston: Little, Brown, 1988), 84.

69 Los Angeles city desks: Roland Flamini, *Scarlett, Rhett, and a Cast of Thousands: The Filming of "Gone with the Wind"* (New York: Macmillan, 1975), 149–151.

69 The last burning structure: Ibid., 154.

70 "Here, genius," he said: Ibid., 154.

70 rocked by her looks: Irene Mayer Selznick, *A Private View* (New York: Knopf, 1983), 215.

70 took one look [at Vivien] and knew: David Thomson, *Showman: The Life of David O. Selznick* (New York: Knopf, 1992), 281.

71   I remember my office was nearby: Gwen Robyns, *Light of a Star: The Career of Vivien Leigh* (New York: A. S. Barnes, 1970), 64.

71   I don't think she had ever heard: George Cukor at Vivien Leigh's March 17, 1968, memorial service at the University of Southern California. *An Appreciation of Vivien Leigh* (Los Angeles: University of Southern California, Friends of the Libraries, 1969), 10.

71   She had the same well-bred, arrogant beauty: Robyns, *Light of a Star*, 64–65.

71   Vivien slept very little: Ibid., 65.

72   don't Scarlettize until I get there: Thomson, *Showman*, 283.

72   You will never guess what has happened: Vickers, *Vivien Leigh*, 104.

73   George is busily engaged: Rudy Behlmer, *Memo from David O. Selznick* (New York: Modern Library, 2000), 200.

73   In the next five days: Flamini, *Scarlett, Rhett*, 163.

74   Vivien was exactly the opposite: Charlotte Chandler, *It's Only a Movie* (New York: Simon & Schuster, 2005), 127.

74   Oh, by the way, we have made our choice: Robyns, *Light of a Star*, 67.

75   [My] attention was caught: Olivier, *Confessions*, 90.

75   Hepburn's deal wasn't signed for months: Donald Spoto, *Laurence Olivier: A Biography* (New York: HarperCollins, 1992), 69.

75   Larry tried in every way: Thomson, *Showman*, 284.

76   he would become a "laughingstock": Ibid.

76   Vivien would earn a total of $25,032.33: In an undated letter to accountant E. G. Hathcock, the Myron Selznick agency notes that Vivien earned $31,916.66 from January 23 to June 28, 1939. Of that, $28,541.66 was salary paid at the rate of $1,250 per week; $3,375 was for expenses at $150 per week. After agency fees and tax deductions, her net salary was $25,032.33. Later, Vivien learned she would have to pay British taxes on the income as well as American taxes. Thy Myron Selznick Archive, Ni–On, File 1, DOS.

76   She is certainly pretty: Thomson, *Showman*, 285–286.

76   THE MOST INTERESTING GIRL: Carole Lombard to David O. Selznick, January 14, 1939. DOS Box 179, Folder 1.

76   CONGRATULATIONS ON SUCCESSFUL CASTING: William Bankhead to David O. Selznick, January 16, 1939. DOS Box 179, Folder 1.

76   WE RESOLVE TO WITHHOLD OUR PATRONAGE: Mrs. Raymond B. Bullock to David O. Selznick, January 18, 1939. DOS Box 179, Folder 1.

77 the almost unbelievable news: Jennifer Frost, *Hedda Hopper's Hollywood: Celebrity Gossip and American Conservatism* (New York: New York University Press, 2011), 70.

77 The papers are full of you: Gertrude Hartley to Vivien Leigh, n.d. VLA GB 71 THM/433/2/8.

77 Tape them up: Alexander Walker, *Vivien: The Life of Vivien Leigh* (New York: Grove, 1987), 121.

78 ability to snap on and off: Flamini, *Scarlett, Rhett*, 221. The words are Flamini's, not de Havilland's.

78 I can't do it, she's hurting me: Ibid., 216.

78 I hated that role: Art Harris, "The Reluctant Butterfly," *Washington Post*, March 13, 1989, https://www.washingtonpost.com /archive/lifestyle/1989/03/13/the-reluctant-butterfly/94322dca -cc06-4269-919b-23f7bbd51c23/.

78 a large mobile dressing room: Flamini, *Scarlett, Rhett*, 224.

79 Don't let it get cold: Ibid., 225.

79 If you want to know the truth: Otto Friedrich, *City of Nets: A Portrait of Hollywood in the 1940s* (Berkeley: University of California Press, 1986), 106.

79 seemed too demure to me: Clark Gable, as told to Ruth Waterbury, "Vivien Leigh, Rhett Butler, and I," *Photoplay*, February 1940.

79 I'll walk out of this picture: Walker, *Vivien*, 122.

80 gun whose shaft was shaped like a penis: Flamini, *Scarlett, Rhett*, 249.

80 great intolerances: Patrick McGilligan, *George Cukor: A Double Life* (Minneapolis: University of Minnesota Press, 2013), 149.

80 a closely guarded battle: Flamini, *Scarlett, Rhett*, 206.

80 We couldn't see eye to eye: Lloyd Shearer, "Gone with the Wind," *New York Times*, October 26, 1947, https://archive.nytimes.com /www.nytimes.com/packages/html/movies/bestpictures/wind-ar6 .html.

80 Ashley, at that moment: Michael Sragow, *Victor Fleming: An American Movie Master* (New York: Pantheon, 2008), 318.

80 I couldn't accept the fact: I. M. Selznick, *Private View*, 216.

81 George was coming to the house: Ibid. 216.

81 The efficient Ginsberg: Flamini, *Scarlett, Rhett*, 232–233.

81 We got this news: Rochelle Reed, ed., *Dialogue on Film*, Volume 4, Number 3 (The American Film Institute, December 1974), 5.

82 Miss Leigh called me: Sig Marcus, memo, February 18, 1939. The Myron Selznick Archive, Le–Li, File 1.

82   If you quit this film: Walker, *Vivien*, 124.

82   I'm sure that no one can teach you: Olivier to Leigh, March 8, 1939. VLA GB 71 THM/433/1.

83   You know I would give anything: Olivier to Leigh, March 30, 1939. Ibid.

83   If we loved each other: Quoted in Hannah Ellis-Petersen, "Laurence Olivier's Steamy Letters to Vivien Leigh See Light of Day," *The Guardian*, February 2, 2015, https://www.theguardian.com /stage/2015/feb/02/laurence-olivier-vivien-leigh-love-letters.

83   I am sitting naked: Ibid.

83   I love and worship you: Olivier to Leigh, April 18, 1939. VLA GB 71 THM/433/1.

83   "Darling," wrote Larry: Olivier to Leigh, June 10, 1939. Ibid.

84   extremely masculine breed: Sragow, *Victor Fleming*, 324.

84   nervous as a thoroughbred horse: Ibid., 317.

84   I've been working too hard: Ibid., 317.

85   replacing the word "witch": "Ding, Dong the Witch Is Dead," *Newsweek*, June 27, 1999, https://www.newsweek.com/ding-dong -witch-dead-167334.

85   On the fourth day: Sragow, *Victor Fleming*, 323.

85   Everyone is *hysterical* about this film: Vickers, *Vivien Leigh*, 108.

85   I had to keep this a secret: Reed, *Dialogue on Film*, 7.

86   a mere workaday hack: Sragow, *Victor Fleming*, 321.

86   Ham it, baby, just ham it: Ibid., 333.

86   For Christ's sake, let's get a good look: Flamini, *Scarlett, Rhett*, 250.

86   Miss Leigh, you can take this script: Walker, *Vivien*, 126.

86   couldn't sleep: Roger Carroll, "The Woman behind Scarlett," *Motion Picture*, February 1940.

86   Several times: Sunny Alexander to Olivier, June 8, 1939. LOA Add MS 79775.

86   As rehearsals: Olivier, *Confessions*, 109.

87   a scholarly and devoted priest: "A Former Addington Rector," *Buckingham Advertiser & Free Press*, April 8, 1939.

87   withdrawal of tender intimacies: Olivier, *Confessions*, 73.

87   a heavy gold Albert watchchain: Anthony Bushell to Michael Dempsey, January 17, 1989. Stenn Collection.

87   no protective influence: Olivier, *Confessions*, 29.

88   Once [Larry] became famous: Richard Olivier, interview with author, June 8, 2021.

88   **I don't think you can ever know:** Isobel Buchanan Ronaldson Olivier to Laurence Olivier, July 24, 1930. LOA Add MS 79890A.

88   **a marble effigy:** Sybille Day Olivier to Laurence Olivier, May 7, 1939. LOA Add Ms 79891.

88   **God be with you till we meet again:** Ibid.

89   **Sometimes we were only given:** Robyns, *Light of a Star*, 75.

89   **a dreadful milk-sop:** Ronald Howard, *In Search of My Father* (New York: St. Martin's, 1982), 18.

89   **He scarcely bothered to look:** Leslie Ruth Howard, *A Quite Remarkable Father* (New York: Harcourt, Brace, 1959), 258.

89   **Before a scene:** Behlmer, *Memo*, 152.

89   **The hours were the most punishing:** I. M. Selznick, *Private View*, 217.

90   **the miasma of fatigue:** Thomson, *Showman*, 298.

90   **He gravely told me:** Sragow, *Victor Fleming*, 338.

90   **What do you take me for:** Ibid., 340.

90   **the realtor:** Flamini, *Scarlett, Rhett*, 276.

91   **exhausted and impatient:** Vickers, *Vivien Leigh*, 113.

91   **a false pregnancy scare:** Thomson, *Showman*, 298.

91   **Urrrrrggh! Urrrrrrgh!** Coleman, *Olivier*, 119.

91   **Ways to Kill a Baby:** Thomson, *Showman*, 299.

91   **veered erratically:** Flamini, *Scarlett, Rhett*, 292.

92   **My God, you look so old:** Robyns, *Light of a Star*, 77–78.

92   **Oh David:** Flamini, *Scarlett, Rhett*, 294.

92   **$100,000 over budget:** A. Scott Berg, *Goldwyn: A Biography* (New York: Knopf, 1989), 327.

92   **the worst responses:** Ibid., 328.

93   **It is Goldwyn at his best:** Frank S. Nugent, "The Screen," *New York Times*, April 14, 1939, https://www.nytimes.com/1939/04/14/archives/the-screen-goldwyn-presets-film-of-wuthering-heights-at-rivolithe.html.

93   **a synonym for the fiery, impetuous lover:** Gene Schrott, "A New Kind of Lover," *Silver Screen*, August 1939.

93   **mercurial as the month of March:** Ibid.

93   **Life is very dull:** Anthony Holden, *Olivier* (London: Little Books, 2007), 146.

94   **absolutely transfixed:** Olivier to Leigh, June 12, 1939. VLA GB 71 THM/433/1.

94   **You have got to justify yourself:** Olivier to Leigh, n.d. Ibid.

94   **was not a thing:** Vickers, *Vivien Leigh*, 112.

95   SOUND THE SIREN: David O. Selznick to John Hay Whitney, June 27, 1939. DOS Box 3341, File 1.

CHAPTER 5

97   that was partly an industry: Otto Friedrich, *City of Nets: A Portrait of Hollywood in the 1940s* (Berkeley: University of California Press, 1986), 110. The words are Friedrich's.

98   landed the book: Leonard J. Leff, *Hitchcock and Selznick: The Rich and Strange Collaboration of Alfred Hitchcock and David O. Selznick in Hollywood* (Berkeley: University of California Press, 1987), 38.

98   a radio adaptation: David Thomson, *Showman: The Life of David O. Selznick* (New York: Knopf, 1992), 239. For more, see "Campbell Playhouse: *Rebecca*," Orson Welles on the Air, 1938–1946, https://orsonwelles.indiana.edu/items/show/1975.

98   Worried that playing a murderer: In a cable to Hitchbock, Selznick warned, "REGRET TO INFORM YOU COLMAN SO FEARFUL ABOUT MURDER ANGLE AND ALSO ABOUT POSSIBILITY OF PICTURE EMERGING AS WOMAN STARRING VEHICLE THAT HE WILL NOT DO IT UNLESS HE SEES TREATMENT AND WE MIGHT FIND OURSELVES IN JAM BY WAITING." David O. Selznick to Alfred Hitchcock, January 9, 1939. DOS Box 170, File 7.

98   Called Olivier in Baltimore: Nat Deverich to David O. Selznick, April 12, 1939. DOS Box 937, File 5.

99   He was not au fond a witty man: Anthony Bushell to Michael Dempsey, June 7, 1991. Stenn Collection.

99   if he were able to spend: Nat Deverich to David O. Selznick, April 12, 1939. DOS Box 364, File 2.

100   He talked all the big stars: Thomson, *Showman*, 331.

100   Anne Baxter, Bette Davis: In a memo to Selznick, Hitchcock gave notes on each contender, observing of Fontaine: "Tested. Possibility. But has to show fair amount of nervousness in order to get any effect. Further test to see how much we can underplay her without losing anything." Alfred Hitchcock to David O. Selznick, July 19, 1939. DOS Box 170, File 7.

100   The last test of Joan Fontaine: John Hay Whitney to David O. Selznick, August 21, 1939. DOS Box 3340, File 2.

101   Miss Leigh told me this morning: David O. Selznick to Alfred Hitchcock and Daniel O'Shea, April 25, 1939. DOS Box 627, File 4.

101   I didn't like having to plead: Charlotte Chandler, *It's Only a Movie* (New York: Simon & Schuster, 2005), 127.

101 **inform Mr. Olivier:** David O. Selznick to Daniel O'Shea, June 12, 1939. DOS Box 627, File 4.

101 **signed a contract:** A copy of the contract exists in Selznick's legal files. Dated July 1, 1939, it says Olivier will receive $4,166.66 per week, plus the balance if the picture is finished within twelve weeks. A March 29, 1940, memo notes that Olivier's total pay ended up at $54,861. DOS Box 937, Files 4 and 5.

101 **Scarlett in a cardigan:** Kendra Bean, "Vivien Leigh and the Search for 'Rebecca,'" *vivandlarry.com* (blog), February 2, 2010, http://vivand larry.com/classic-film/vivien-leigh-and-the-search-for-rebecca/.

102 **Sherwood and Cukor:** David O. Selznick to John Hay Whitney, August 18, 1939. Rudy Behlmer, *Memo from David O. Selznick* (New York: Modern Library, 2000), 300–1.

102 **My first choice has been:** John Hay Whitney to David O. Selznick, August 21, 1939. DOS Box 170, File 7.

102 **DEAR LARRY PLEASE SEE MY WIRE:** David O. Selznick to Olivier, August 18, 1939. DOS Box 170, File 7.

103 **DEAR VIVIEN WE HAVE TRIED:** David O. Selznick to Leigh, August 18, 1939. DOS Box 3341, File 1.

103 **Now that, that is something:** Stephen Galloway, "'King Kong' or 'Gone with the Wind'? Investigating Hitler's Bizarre Hollywood Obsessions," *Hollywood Reporter*, October 18, 2019, https://www.hollywoodreporter.com/movies/movie-news/king-kong-investigating-hitlers-bizarre-hollywood-obsessions-1244456/.

103 **At 1115 BST:** "1939: Britain and France Declare War on Germany," *On This Day*, BBC News, n.d., http://news.bbc.co.uk/onthisday/hi/dates/stories/september/3/newsid_3493000/3493279.stm.

104 **Larry felt "blighted":** Laurence Olivier, *Confessions of an Actor* (New York: Simon & Schuster, 1982), 110.

104 **This is the end:** Logan Gourlay, ed., *Olivier* (New York: Stein and Day, 1975), 83.

104 **one of the few times:** Alan Dent, *Vivien Leigh: A Bouquet* (London: Hamish Hamilton, 1969), 83.

105 **People felt strongly:** Michael Korda, interview with author, February 8, 2019.

106 **she was not a good enough actress:** Leff, *Hitchcock and Selznick*, 74.

106 **Well, maybe if you slapped me:** Ibid.

106 **His technique:** Joan Fontaine, *No Bed of Roses* (New York: William Morrow, 1978), 116.

106　**I have an inferiority complex:** Fontaine, interview by Scott Feinberg, May 4, 2013, unpublished, courtesy of Feinberg.

106　**Couldn't you do better than that:** Fontaine, *No Bed of Roses*, 116.

107　**Hollywood was full of phony Englishmen:** Korda, interview.

107　**Acting for films:** Anthony Holden, *Olivier* (London: Little Books, 2007), 140.

107　**be a little more Yiddish Art Theater:** David O. Selznick to Alfred Hitchcock, October 11, 1939. DOS Box 170, File 7.

107　**habit of throwing away lines:** David O. Selznick to Alfred Hitchcock, October 23, 1939. DOS Box 170, File 7.

107　**nearly as attractive:** David O. Selznick to Ray Klune, October 11, 1939. DOS Box 170, File 7.

108　**moods and descriptions:** Ibid.

108　**Larry's silent action:** David O. Selznick to Alfred Hitchcock, October 13, 1939. DOS Box 170, File 7.

108　**He seemed uncertain:** Irene Mayer Selznick, *A Private View* (New York: Knopf, 1983), 223–224.

109　**replace her with Joan Crawford:** Greer Garson at Vivien Leigh's March 17, 1968, memorial service at the University of Southern California. *An Appreciation of Vivien Leigh* (Los Angeles: University of Southern California, Friends of the Libraries, 1969), 18.

109　**The story we do is so dreary:** Hugo Vickers, *Vivien Leigh* (Boston: Little, Brown, 1988), 120.

109　**Hate Hollywood though she did:** Alexander Walker, *Vivien: The Life of Vivien Leigh* (New York: Grove, 1987), 139.

110　**I am awfully distressed:** Thomson, *Showman*, 321.

110　**She wanted to take the first plane:** David O. Selznick to Kay Brown, December 7, 1939. DOS Box 627, Folder 4.

110　**Then I won't be going either:** Walker, *Vivien*, 137.

110　**Oh, they're playing the song:** Roland Flamini, *Scarlett, Rhett, and a Cast of Thousands: The Filming of Gone with the Wind* (New York: Macmillan, 1975), 327.

110　**De Havilland believed:** Arvind Acharya, "Clark Gable Almost Went with the Wind: Olivia," *Deccan Chronicle*, July 1, 2016, https://www.deccanchronicle.com/opinion/op-ed/010716/clark -gable-almost-went-with-the-wind-olivia.html.

111　**[William] Hartsfield:** "Cinema: G with the W," *Time*, December 25, 1939, http://content.time.com/time/magazine/article/0,9171, 762137,00.html.

111   Life's pattern pricked: "Inscribed 'Gone with the Wind' in Vivien Leigh's Collection at Sotheby's," *Fine Books and Collections*, July 17, 2017, https://www.finebooksmagazine.com/news /inscribed-gone-wind-vivien-leighs-collection-sothebys.

111   "Lord," one young woman gasped: "Cinema: G with the W." *Time*.

112   the greatest motion mural: Frank S. Nugent, "The Screen in Review," *New York Times*, December 20, 1939.

112   This is more than the greatest: " 'Gone with the Wind' Magnificent, Supreme Triumph of Film History," *Hollywood Reporter*, December 13, 1939.

112   there was a hush: Thomson, *Showman*, 324.

112   He couldn't claim ignorance: Jennifer Schuessler, "The Long Battle Over 'Gone with the Wind,' " *New York Times*, June 14, 2020.

113   While responses to the finished film: Ibid.

113   McDaniel persuaded him to go: Acharya, "Clark Gable."

114   If you're happy: Hedda Hopper, "Happiness Is a State of Mind," *Photoplay*, July 1954.

114   I knew it was a marvellous part: Gwen Robyns, *Light of a Star: The Career of Vivien Leigh* (New York: A. S. Barnes, 1970), 78. Years later, Vivien changed her mind and began to feel a nostalgia for the film, telling her goddaughter Juliet Mills how much she loved it. Juliet Mills, interview with author, May 22, 2021.

114   Victor Fleming came on: Thomson, *Showman*, 296.

114   a note of near panic: Walker, *Vivien*, 116.

115   I HAVE CAUTIONED VIVIEN: William Hebert to David O. Selznick, July 11, 1939. DOS Box 187, Files 10–11.

115   There is no longer any secret: Gene Schrott, "A New Kind of Lover," *Silver Screen*, August 1939.

115   It's an accepted conclusion: James Reid, "Here's Scarlett at Long Last," *Motion Picture*, April 1939.

115   It took the naïve question: Cedric Chalmers, "A Love Story Hollywood Had to Hide" (syndicated), December 1939, http://viv andlarry.com/wp-content/uploads/2011/05/article_lovestoryhide.png.

116   "A Love Worth Fighting For": Ruth Waterbury, "A Love Worth Fighting For," *Photoplay*, December 1939.

CHAPTER 6

118   I'd been forgotten: Irene Mayer Selznick, *A Private View* (New York: Knopf, 1983), 221.

118   the *Los Angeles Times* had spilled: Anthony Breznican, "Olivia de Havilland Got Early Word Hattie McDaniel Defeated Her at the Oscars," *Vanity Fair*, July 27, 2020, https://www.vanityfair.com/hollywood/2020/07/olivia-de-havilland-hattie-mcdaniel-gone-with-the-wind-oscars.

119   If I were to mention: A film clip of her speech is available on the website Oddball Films at https://www.oddballfilms.com/clip/13162_9845_academy_awards4.

119   De Havilland, who had reportedly fled: Breznican, "Early Word."

120   a then-record $500,000: "Leigh 'Gone with the Wind' Oscar Sells for $510,000," *Los Angeles Times*, December 16, 1993.

120   It was all I could do: Tarquin Olivier, *My Father Laurence Olivier* (London: Headline, 1992), 86.

121   roaring boy: Alexander Walker, *Vivien: The Life of Vivien Leigh* (New York: Grove, 1987), 143.

121   The stage was like an oven: Laurence Olivier, *Confessions of an Actor* (New York: Simon & Schuster, 1982), 115.

121   not merely weak or spotty: The review can be read on the *vivandlarry.com* blog at http://vivandlarry.com/the-oliviers/articles/romeo-and-juliet-review/.

122   all their savings: $96,000: Olivier, *Confessions*, 115.

122   For sheer, savage, merciless cruelty: Ibid., 114.

122   drowning themselves: Anthony Holden, *Olivier* (London: Little Books, 2007), 159.

123   It was absolutely hilarious: Hugo Vickers, *Vivien Leigh* (Boston: Little, Brown, 1988), 128.

123   At that time: Walker, *Vivien*, 150–151.

124   Larry was asked: Garson Kanin, *Tracy and Hepburn: An Intimate Memoir* (New York: Bantam, 1972), 77.

124   The last one you'll get: Holden, *Olivier*, 164.

124   "Finally," continues Kanin: Kanin, *Tracy and Hepburn*, 77.

124   no recollection of anyone: Walker, *Vivien*, 151.

124   Too bad it got out: Garson Kanin at Vivien Leigh's March 17, 1968, memorial service at the University of Southern California. *An Appreciation of Vivien Leigh* (Los Angeles: University of Southern California, Friends of the Libraries, 1969), 22.

125   roll of dishonor: Holden, *Olivier*, 160.

125   "deserters" and "isolationists": Ibid.

125   Larry, you know Lady Hamilton?: Olivier, *Confessions*, 116.

126　**Captain Whitby was unable to speak:** Christopher Hibbert, *Nelson: A Personal History* (New York: Hachette, 1996), 379.

126　**the neurotic I discovered:** Laurence Olivier, *On Acting* (New York: Simon & Schuster, 1987), 266.

126　**My dear Vivien:** Alan Dent, *Vivien Leigh: A Bouquet* (London: Hamish Hamilton, 1969), 60.

126　**I am extremely dubious about it:** Vickers, *Vivien Leigh*, 127.

127　**he started popping:** Tom DeVane, "Lady Hamilton," *Hollywood*, March 1941.

127　**We made Lady Hamilton in six weeks:** Paul Tabori, *Alexander Korda: A Biography* (London: Oldbourne, 1959), 224–225.

127　**Nelson had the most:** Olivier, *On Acting*, 266.

127　**Saturday I did my big scene:** Michael Powell, *A Life in Movies* (New York: Knopf, 1987), 363.

127　**I went off the deep end:** This was not Olivier's only battle with his friend Korda. "I was his right hand and dealer and communicant with the lower levels of his employees for two years and never a cross word," recalled Anthony Bushell. "I was his buffer in all his relations with Laurence O. and oh my word how they did shout at each other." Bushell to Michael Dempsey, May 31, 1996. Stenn Collection.

127　**You cannot possibly:** Holden, *Olivier*, 165.

128　**the admirable fidelity:** Bosley Crowther, "That Hamilton Woman," *New York Times*, April 4, 1941.

128　**In real life:** Alex von Tunzelmann, "That Hamilton Woman: A Tale of Two Halves (for Better or for Worse)," *The Guardian*, January 6, 2011.

129　**It sounds like a suicide pact:** Tom Kemper, *Hidden Talent: The Emergence of Hollywood Agents* (Berkeley: University of California Press, 2010), 170.

129–130　**Hitler's secret weapon:** Olivier, *Confessions*, 117.

130　**Overdramatic as it may well seem:** Ibid., 118.

130　**from an aeroplane in the dark:** Olivier to Leigh, March 12, 1939. In that letter, he told Vivien, "The *rock* I am hugged to on the beach I have landed on, is *you*." VLA GB 71/THM.433/1.

130　**about halfway home:** Olivier, *Confessions*, 119.

CHAPTER 7

131　**just a hole in the ground:** Hugo Vickers, *Vivien Leigh* (Boston: Little, Brown, 1988), 120.

131   It is most strange: Leigh to David O. Selznick, February 14, 1941. DOS Box 3340, File 1.

132   The only topic of conversation: Leigh to Daniel O'Shea, May 28, 1942. DOS Box 922, File 6.

132   Vivien's former brother-in-law: Vickers, *Vivien Leigh*, 129.

132   rushed to her dressing-room: Tom DeVane, "Lady Hamilton," *Hollywood*, March 1941.

132   I don't suppose living: Vickers, *Vivien Leigh*, 129.

133   Families from the East End: Rose Staveley-Wadham, "The Blitz and the London Underground—Safety beneath the Streets in the Second World War," *British Newspaper Archive* (blog), November 6, 2019, https://blog.britishnewspaperarchive.co.uk/2019/11/06/the-blitz-and-the-london-underground/.

133   Thousands of men, women and children: John Simkin, "Underground Stations as Shelters," *Spartacus Educational* (blog), January 2020, https://spartacus-educational.com/2WWunderground.htm.

133   We had our first really bad air raid: Leigh to David O. Selznick, March 10, 1941. DOS Box 811, File 4.

134   when the nuns learned: Vickers, *Vivien Leigh*, 133.

134   bequeathing Mrs. Hartley his stocks and shares: Last will and testament of John Lambert Thomson, October 5, 1938. Courtesy H. M. Courts & Tribunals Service.

135   I heard from the Admiralty: Laurence Olivier, *Confessions of an Actor* (New York: Simon & Schuster, 1982), 120.

135   did not quite pass the medical exam: Leigh to David O. Selznick, February 14, 1941. DOS Box 811, File 4.

135   consisted of a large hill: Olivier, *Confessions*, 120.

135   of notorious incompetence: Michael Korda, interview with author, February 8, 2019.

135   Having gained [his pilot's wings]: Anthony Bushell to Michael Dempsey, April 19, 1988. Stenn Collection.

135   shoot up a friend: Olivier, *Confessions*, 121.

136   It was an amazingly different: Hattie Grimstead, "Vivien Leigh Today," *Screenland*, July 1944.

136   "One gets 'shore leave'": Laurence Olivier, "Olivier Reporting," *Photoplay*, January 1941, http://vivandlarry.com/wp-content/uploads/2010/08/Untitled-1.jpg.

137   more than $1 million: David Thomson, *Showman: The Life of David O. Selznick* (New York: Knopf, 1992), 458.

137   just over $700,000: Ibid., 379.

138 CLIPPER IMPOSSIBLE: Leigh to David O. Selznick, January 25, 1941. DOS Box 3341, Files 1–10.

138 This is a very difficult letter: Leigh to David O. Selznick, February 14, 1941. DOS Box 3340, File 1.

139 I think it would be a lovely picture: Leigh to David O. Selznick, March 10, 1941. DOS Box 811, File 4.

139 she wasn't a good enough actress: Anthony Holden, *Olivier* (London: Little Books, 2007), 170.

140 one of the coldest winters: Alexander Walker, *Vivien: The Life of Vivien Leigh* (New York: Grove, 1987), 161.

140 The war meant: Richard Huggett, *Binkie Beaumont: Eminence Grise of the West End Theatre 1933–1973* (London: Hodder & Stoughton, 1989), 274.

141 One of them asked me: Ibid., 275.

141 It was believed: Ibid.

141 She was charming: Ibid., 279.

142 The production proposal: "And They're Over There Too," *Photoplay*, January 1942, http://vivandlarry.com/wp-content/uploads/2010/08/vivienlarry.jpg.

142 fragile because she had had: Alan Dent, *Vivien Leigh: A Bouquet* (London: Hamish Hamilton, 1969), 19.

143 older & more tired: Vickers, *Vivien Leigh*, 137.

143 Time is very precious: Walker, *Vivien*, 162.

143 could hardly believe he was sleeping: Robert Stephens with Michael Coveney, *Knight Errant: Memoirs of a Vagabond Actor* (London: Hodder & Stoughton, 1996), 71–72.

144 His manner was naval: Holden, *Olivier*, 171.

144 When the friends heard: Ibid.

144 I found him quite changed: Olivier to Gertrude Hartley, September 25, 1942. VLA THM/433/2/8.

145 the sort of life one had forgotten: Ibid.

145 I had, at first, a Russian lady: Olivier, *Confessions*, 123.

145 scoutmaster: Ibid., 103.

146 We pulled up a couple of chairs: Michael Powell, *A Life in Movies* (New York: Knopf, 1987), 602.

146 They got him drunk as a skunk: Donald Spoto, *Laurence Olivier: A Biography* (New York: HarperCollins, 1992), 166.

147 I could think of the play sideways: Laurence Olivier, *On Acting* (New York: Simon & Schuster, 1987), 269.

147 the old masters: Ibid., 276.

147   I was amazed how easily: Ibid., 269.

148   To hell with the purists: Ibid., 271.

148   I felt there was a quarrel: Ibid., 279–280.

148   The elusive animal: Olivier, *Confessions*, 124.

149   [Olivier] very foolishly *guaranteed*: Jenia Reissar to Robert H. Dann, September 19, 1944. DOS Box 811, File 2.

149   I remember the tremendous vigour: Jesse Lasky Jr. with Pat Silver, *Love Scene: The Story of Laurence Olivier and Vivien Leigh* (Brighton, Australia: Angus & Robertson, 1978), 147.

149   [I] had never been in command: Olivier, *Confessions*, 127.

149   I may sometimes be asking: Ibid., 128.

150   Larry nearly went mad: Jenia Reissar to Selznick, n.d. DOS Box 922 File 2.

150   Larry had a railroad track: Charles Bennett, "Laurence Olivier: The Power and the Glory," *Close-Ups: Intimate Portraits of Movie Stars by Their Co-stars, Directors, Screenwriters, and Friends*, ed. Danny Peary (New York: Workman, 1978), 109.

150   The finder hit my upper lip: Olivier, *Confessions*, 129.

151   Things, I suppose: Olivier to Leigh, June 7, 1943. VLA GB 71 THM/433/1.

152   I shall think of you so hard: Terry Coleman, *Olivier* (New York: Henry Holt, 2005), 149.

152   warned against: Sgt. Len Scott RAPC, "Race Relations in Algiers," *WW2 People's War* (blog), May 28, 2004, https://www.bbc.co.uk /history/ww2peopleswar/stories/70/a2676170.shtml.

152   The sight of this small, beautiful woman: Vickers, *Vivien Leigh*, 146.

153   I am so miserable: Leigh to Olivier, n.d. LOA Add MS 80618.

153   One's emotions: Leigh to Olivier, June 10, 1943. Ibid.

153   I get more + more anxious: Olivier to Leigh, June 3, 1943.

154   My sweet sweet Larry boy: Leigh to Olivier, June 22, 1943. LOA Add MS 80618.

CHAPTER 8

155   Later, the Oliviers would learn: Anthony Bushell to Michael Dempsey, February 6, 1985. Stenn Collection.

156   a somewhat humiliating inspection: Hugo Vickers, *Vivien Leigh* (Boston: Little, Brown, 1988), 149.

156   little bag of bones: Michael Powell, *A Life in Movies* (New York: Knopf, 1987), 607.

156   like to have a nervous breakdown: Vickers, *Vivien Leigh*, 150.

156   [taking] up her chair: Hattie Grimstead, "Vivien Leigh Today," *Screenland*, July 1944.

156   from choosing costumes: Hattie Grimstead, "Sir Laurence and His Lady," *Screenland*, August 1948.

156   meticulously to the best: Ibid.

157   She sat in front of my dressing table: Ibid.

157   it was after midnight: Vickers, *Vivien Leigh*, 151.

158   Before the work: Laurence Olivier, *Confessions of an Actor* (New York: Simon & Schuster, 1982), 133.

158   I am a man who: Anthony Holden, *Olivier* (London: Little Books, 2007), 184.

159   It was Vivien's: Jenia Reissar to Daniel O'Shea, January 13, 1944. DOS Box 921, File 8.

160   Despite anything: Jenia Reissar to David O. Selznick, September 6, 1944. Ibid.

160   Do you think so?: Alexander Walker, *Vivien: The Life of Vivien Leigh* (New York: Grove, 1987), 164.

160   Production began: Marjorie Deans, *Meeting at the Sphinx: Gabriel Pascal's Production of Bernard Shaw's Caesar and Cleopatra* (London: MacDonald & Co., undated), 89.

160   Never had there been: Michael Holroyd, *Bernard Shaw: The Lure of Fantasy*, vol. 3, *1918–1950* (New York: Random House, 1991), 475.

161   gabbling tonelessly: Walker, *Vivien*, 168.

161   the budget soared: Arthur Austin, "The Most Expensive Film They Ever Made," n.d. DOS Box 796.

161   No film—not even: Ibid.

162   except when he actually directed: Jenia Reissar to David O. Selznick, September 19, 1944. DOS Box 811, File 2.

162   he remained moodily: Holden, *Olivier*, 187.

162   Don't you love Sergius: Laurence Olivier, *On Acting* (New York: Simon & Schuster, 1987), 121.

163   *What* do you suppose: Vickers, *Vivien Leigh*, 156.

164   plenty more: Walker, *Vivien*, 169.

164   She never forgave Pascal: Granger, *Sparks Fly Upward* (London: Granada, 1981), 83.

164   were both terribly disappointed: Jenia Reissar to David O. Selznick, September 19, 1944. DOS Box 811, File 2.

164   very much a feature: Guy Goodwin, interview with author, April 27, 2021.

164   She stopped dead: Walker, *Vivien*, 170.

165   attributed her collapse: Ibid.

165   one-sixth what it would be: "All in the Mind: Mental Health
       Evolves," BBC News, July 1, 1998, http://news.bbc.co.uk/2/hi/events
       /nhs_at_50/special_report/124368.stm.

166   She appeared to make: Walker, *Vivien*, 170.

CHAPTER 9

167   surrounded by several ranges: Amit Ranjan Basu, "A New Knowl-
       edge of Madness—Nineteenth-Century Asylum Psychiatry in Ben-
       gal," *Indian Journal of History of Science* 39, no. 3 (July 6, 2004):
       261.

167   mania chronic, cause unknown: Liz Chater, "Armenian: Some-
       thing Vivien Leigh and her Cousin Xan Fielding a British Spy Had
       in Common," *Chater Genealogy* (blog), August 12, 2015, http://
       chater-genealogy.blogspot.com/2015/08/armenian-something
       -vivien-leigh-and-her_12.html.

168   Cruel as the natives: T. Hastings, "Lunatic Asylums in Bengal,"
       Calcutta Review 26, no. 52 (1856): 592. A map of the asylum can
       be found in Waltraud Ernst, *Mad Tales from the Raj: Colonial
       Psychiatry in South Asia, 1800–58* (London: Anthem, 2010). The
       1856 report in the *Calcutta Review* notes that "insanity is not
       more prevalent in India than at home" (604).

168   the gardens were beautiful: Basu, "New Knowledge of Mad-
       ness," 262.

168   a genetic element: "As with many mental disorders, there is almost
       certainly a genetic component, but we've never been able to iden-
       tify any single gene," says John Geddes, professor of psychiatry at
       the University of Oxford. "There've now been a number of genes
       that confer increased risk. How they work, what the mechanism is,
       what protein they code that makes the difference—we simply don't
       know. There's almost certainly a major contribution from the very
       early environment, childhood and later life events, which inter-
       act with the genes for the unique predicament of each individual
       human and decide whether or not you're going to become ill." John
       Geddes, interview with author, June 18, 2021.

168   there is no history: Dr. Arthur Conachy, report on Vivien Leigh's
       psychiatric condition, June 20, 1961, Jack Merivale Collection at
       the British Film Institute, London, JME-4-6.

168   she had had such trouble sleeping: Hugo Vickers, *Vivien Leigh*
       (Boston: Little, Brown, 1988), 9.

169 **If you look at those kids:** Po Wang, interview with author, April 25, 2021.

169 **Maureen O'Sullivan, later:** Maureen O'Sullivan, interview by Anne Edwards, unpublished transcript, Anne Edwards Papers, Charles E. Young Research Library, University of California, Los Angeles, n.d. Box 21.

169 **terribly miserable:** Vivien Leigh diary, July 27, 1930. VLA GB 71 THM/433/7/2.

169 **feeling blue + down:** Vivien Leigh diary, January 9, 1931. Ibid.

169 **often happens within a year:** Wang, interview.

169 **Beaumont said he could:** John Gielgud, interview by Anne Edwards, n.d., unpublished transcript, Anne Edwards Papers, Charles E. Young Research Library, University of California, Los Angeles, Box 20.

170 **It may be that over time:** Geddes, interview.

170 **Bipolar disorder is the chameleon:** Francis Mark Mondimore, *Bipolar Disorder: A Guide for Patients and Families*, 2nd ed. (Baltimore: Johns Hopkins University Press, 2006), 1–2.

170 **[That] perpetuates the notion:** Kay Redfield Jamison, *An Unquiet Mind: A Memoir of Moods and Madness* (New York: Vintage, 2011), 182.

171 **What has driven her:** *The Noël Coward Diaries*, ed. Graham Payn and Sheridan Morley (Boston: Little, Brown, 1982), 441.

171 **"Personally," he added:** Ibid., 280.

171 **Olivier's sister, Sybille:** She was not the only member of Olivier's extended family to have mental health issues. In two letters to his son, Gerard Olivier describes visiting an "Uncle Willie" in an asylum, though he seems to be referring to his second wife Ibo's relative, not his own. "Willie has been in there for over a year now," he writes in one of the letters (undated). "He's much worse than ever before, and occasionally goes on 'hunger strike' and has to be 'fed forcibly.'" LOA Add MS 79890 A.

171 **a pair of fools:** "'A Pair of Fools' in the Divorce Court," *Illustrated Police News*, March 1, 1928.

172 **how my young wife:** G. W. L. Day, *Rivers of Damascus* (London: Rider, 1940), xii.

172 **a terrible change:** Ibid., 23.

172 **assortative mating:** Terence Ketter, interview with author, May 1, 2021.

172 **once the unconsciousness:** C. G. Jung, *Psychological Types* (Princeton, NJ: Princeton University Press, 1990), 522.

173 the monster stared back: Laurence Olivier, *On Acting* (New York: Simon & Schuster, 1987), 125.

173 "An actor," he reflected: Olivier, *On Acting*, 118.

173 one of the most sexually attractive: Garry O'Connor, *Darlings of the Gods: One Year in the Lives of Laurence Olivier and Vivien Leigh* (London: Hodder & Stoughton, 1984), 65.

173 for the first time in his career: Anthony Holden, *Olivier* (London: Little Books, 2007), 189.

173 Stories had been circulating: Michael Powell, *A Life in Movies* (New York: Knopf, 1987), 606.

174 Larry called my parents: Hayley Mills, interview with author, May 13, 2021.

174 rushed to the throne: Anthony Bushell to Michael Dempsey, May 31, 1987. Stenn Collection.

174 Nothing prepared us: Powell, *Life in Movies*, 606–607.

175 There it was: Laurence Olivier, *Confessions of an Actor* (New York: Simon & Schuster, 1982), 138.

175 Nothing could [have been] more gentle: Charles Bennett, "Laurence Olivier: The Power and the Glory," *Close-Ups: Intimate Portraits of Movie Stars by Their Co-Stars, Directors, Screenwriters and Friends*, ed. Danny Peary (New York: Workman, 1978), 111–112.

175 an indication of what: Holden, *Olivier*, 179.

175 the most difficult, annoying: Ibid., 179.

176 a sea monster: Curtis Bill Pepper, "Talking With," *New York Times*, March 25, 1979.

176 Do you know, Larry: Holden, *Olivier*, 10.

176 a stout and filthy prebendary: John Strype, *Memorials of the Most Reverend Father in God Thomas Cranmer* (Oxford: Oxford University Press, 1840), 158.

177 Olivier has just bought a house: Jenia Reissar to Sir Lancelot Joynson-Hicks, February 10, 1945. DOS Box 811, File 5.

177 At Notley I had an affair: Olivier, *On Acting*, 200.

177 Many people in Britain: "What You Need to Know about VE Day," Imperial War Museum, accessed on January 15, 2021, https://www.iwm.org.uk/history/what-you-need-to-know-about-ve-day.

178 All the shops: "Fact File: VE Day," *WW2 People's War* (blog), October 15, 2014, http://www.bbc.co.uk/history/ww2peopleswar/timeline/factfiles/nonflash/a1057448.shtml.

178 We came back: Winston Churchill, "End of the War in Europe," speech, House of Commons, London, May 8, 1945, International

Churchill Society, https://winstonchurchill.org/resources/speeches /1941-1945-war-leader/.

178 It is high time: David O. Selznick to Daniel O'Shea and Jenia Reissar, February 12, 1942. DOS Box 922, File 4.

179 You may think I am nuts: David O. Selznick to Daniel O'Shea, July 31, 1940. DOS Box 627, Folder 4.

179 We talk of actors: Jenia Reissar to David O. Selznick, June 22, 1942. DOS Box 922, File 4.

179 a far deeper person: Jenia Reissar to Robert H. Dann, September 19, 1944. DOS Box 921, File 2.

179 her exclusive services: Quoted in "Vivien Leigh," an unsigned memo about the history of Selznick's dealings with his star, n.d. DOS Box 811, File 6.

180 Char lady Vivien: "Vivien Leigh Might Be a Char—Counsel," *Daily Mail*, February 24, 1945.

180 she collapsed: Hattie Grimstead, "It Happened to Laurence Olivier," *Screenland*, March 1946.

181 In the decades before: Sue Bowden and Alex Sadler, "Getting It Right? Lessons from the Interwar Years on Pulmonary Tuberculosis Control in England and Wales," *Medical History* 59, no. 1 (January 2015): 101–135, https://www.ncbi.nlm.nih.gov/pmc/arti cles/PMC4304552/.

181 An ambulance took Vivien: Grimstead, "It Happened to Laurence Olivier."

181 to feel that you are sad: Olivier to Leigh, June 30, 1945. VLA 71 THM433/1.

182 was a spectre: Chester Erskine at Vivien Leigh's March 17, 1968, memorial service at the University of Southern California. *An Appreciation of Vivien Leigh* (Los Angeles: University of Southern California, Friends of the Libraries, 1969), 7.

182 although he was only admitted: Grimstead, "It Happened to Laurence Olivier."

182 a worm in the blood: Vickers, *Vivien Leigh*, 165–166.

CHAPTER 10

183 the miraculously soft warmth: Laurence Olivier, *Confessions of an Actor* (New York: Simon & Schuster, 1982), 138–139.

183 tremendous erudition: Hugo Vickers, *Vivien Leigh* (Boston: Little, Brown, 1988), 167.

184   Isaiah Berlin's: Isaiah Berlin, *The Hedgehog and the Fox* (London: Weidenfeld & Nicholson, 1953).

184   Tchee: Hattie Grimstead, "Sir Laurence and His Lady," *Screenland*, August 1948.

184   howl of an ermine: Olivier, *Confessions*, 145.

185   one such dream: Olivier to Leigh, March 12, 1939. VLA 71 THM433/1.

185   At 5:35 p.m.: Terry Coleman, *Olivier* (New York: Henry Holt, 2005), 175.

186   the most magnificent: Ibid.

186   she risked being "boring": Olivier to Leigh, n.d. VLA 71 THM433/1.

187   In depression: William Styron, "Why Primo Levi Need Not Have Died," *New York Times*, December 19, 1988.

187   Throughout his heaviest season: Anthony Holden, *Olivier* (London: Little Books, 2007), 207.

187   that horrible mother: Gertrude Hartley to Leigh, August 15, 1966. VLA GB 71 THM433/2/8.

188   gave way to a fit of fury: Olivier, *Confessions*, 191.

188   made her behave: Hayley Mills, interview with author, May 13, 2021.

188   Just as he was wondering: Vickers, *Vivien Leigh*, 168.

188   An attitude circulated: Gwen Robyns, *Light of a Star: The Career of Vivien Leigh* (New York: A. S. Barnes, 1970), 114.

189   I remember when we were staying: Juliet Mills, interview with author, May 22, 2021.

190   Leigh dominates: "Anna Karenina," *Daily Variety*, December 31, 1947.

190   For some reason: Vickers, *Vivien Leigh*, 176.

190   I would have liked to have found: Holden, *Olivier*, 214.

191   Dear Larry, anybody: Michael Powell, *A Life in Movies* (New York: Knopf, 1987), 578.

191   when Vivien wasn't in front: Grimstead, "Sir Laurence and His Lady."

192   We had a perfect double: Anthony Bushell to Michael Dempsey, August 9, 1987. Stenn Collection.

192   Laurence's first + v. strong intention: Bushell to Dempsey, June 7, 1988. Stenn Collection.

192   constipated: Bushell to Dempsey, March 29, 1988. Stenn Collection.

193   Larry forbade everybody: Grimstead, "Sir Laurence and His Lady."

193   Handsome mobile-faced Larry: Ibid.

194   I could kill myself: Olivier, *Confessions*, 152–153.

194   Olivier was nervous: Donald Spoto, *Laurence Olivier: A Biography* (New York: HarperCollins, 1992), 210.

194   Vivien, sitting nearby: Grimstead, "Sir Laurence and His Lady."

CHAPTER 11

195   a great struggle theatrically: Hugo Vickers, *Vivien Leigh* (Boston: Little, Brown, 1988), 181.

195   entirely destructive: Ibid., 179.

195   who never lets a chance slip: Ibid., 180.

196   between a quarter and a half: Garry O'Connor, *Darlings of the Gods: One Year in the Lives of Laurence Olivier and Vivien Leigh* (London: Hodder & Stoughton, 1984), 22.

196   white hot needles: Ibid., 37.

196   God and the Angel: Anthony Holden, *Olivier* (London: Little Books, 2007), 228.

196   Peter Cushing: O'Connor, *Darlings of the Gods*, 36.

196   The cast were devoted: Vickers, *Vivien Leigh*, 181.

196   Clara the alley cat: O'Connor, *Darlings of the Gods*, 40.

197   Sir Lady: Leigh to Meriel Richardson, July 28, 1948. Ralph Richardson Archive Collection, the British Library, London, Add MS 82044.

197   One is always on one's feet: Leigh to Meriel Richardson, May 15, 1948. Ibid.

198   Vivien Leigh came into the wardrobe: Michael Redington, quoted in O'Connor, *Darlings of the Gods*, 49.

198   2,280 Australians: Ibid., 49.

198   We were the first company: Laurence Olivier, "A Soliloquy in an English Hamlet," *Los Angeles Times*, November 24, 1963.

199   They [had] expected: O'Connor, *Darlings of the Gods*, 54.

199   Vivien shrieked with joy: Ibid., 59.

199   felt almost a physical weariness: Ibid., 65.

199   better than ever: Ibid., 74.

199   Miss Vitamin B: Ibid.

199   a strange woman: Ibid., 40.

200   damned awful fuss: Holden, *Olivier*, 230.

200   piss-elegant and nervously smug: O'Connor, *Darlings of the Gods*, 78.

200   We have better *Richard III*s: Ibid., 79.

200   *Charley's Aunt*: Ibid., 77.

200   she was going to float away: Ibid., 137.

200   Ever so slightly: Ibid., 119.

200   I once thought I'd like: Ibid., 102.

201   splendid fury: Kenneth Tynan, "Laurence Olivier," in *Profiles* (New York: Random House, 1998), 243.

201   Sir Laurence remembered: Vickers, *Vivien Leigh*, 183.

201   "Next day," writes O'Connor: O'Connor, *Darlings of the Gods*, 104.

202   by men, however able: Terry Coleman, *Olivier* (New York: Henry Holt, 2005), 195.

202   "O ME," he cabled Burrell: Ibid., 196.

202   he claimed all he could do: Laurence Olivier, *Confessions of an Actor* (New York: Simon & Schuster, 1982), 158.

202   the rogue elephant: Holden, *Olivier*, 239.

202   and attributed it: O'Connor, *Darlings of the Gods*, 133.

202   Somehow, somewhere: Olivier, *Confessions*, 158.

203   a blazing row: O'Connor, *Darlings of the Gods*, 143.

203   walking corpses: Ibid., 146.

CHAPTER 12

204   It came like a small bolt: Laurence Olivier, *Confessions of an Actor* (New York: Simon & Schuster, 1982), 161–162.

204   felt as if I had been told: Ibid., 162.

204   There's no nice way: Kay Redfield Jamison, interview with author, March 14, 2019.

204   occasional acts of incest: Olivier, *Confessions*, 162.

205   When she had the breakdowns: John Gielgud, interview by Anne Edwards, n.d., unpublished transcript, Anne Edwards Papers, Charles E. Young Research Library, University of California, Los Angeles, Box 20.

205   the best quality twill: Terry Coleman, *Olivier* (New York: Henry Holt, 2005), 206.

205   the most extraordinary powers: John Lahr, *Tennessee Williams: Mad Pilgrimage of the Flesh* (New York: W. W. Norton, 2014), 196.

206   Female Moneybags: Tennessee Williams to James "Jay" Laughlin, April 9, 1947, *The Selected Letters of Tennessee Williams*, ed. Albert J. Devlin and Nancy M. Tischler, vol. 2, *1946–1957* (New York: New Directions, 2004), 92.

206   supposed to have: Ibid., 91.

206   overwhelmed by its power: Irene Mayer Selznick, *A Private View* (New York: Knopf, 1983), 296.

206   I was speechless: Ibid., 295.

207   the actor Richard Harris: Nadine Holdsworth, *Joan Littlewood's Theatre* (Cambridge, England: Cambridge University Press, 2011), 26.

208   TREMENDOUSLY ENTHUSIASTIC: I. M. Selznick, *Private View*, 319.

208   Apparently in London: Ibid.

208   By the time we reached Claridge's: Ibid., 320–321.

209   The prestige of his name: Tennessee Williams to Audrey Wood, February 15, 1949, *Selected Letters of Tennessee Williams*, 234.

209   You have evidently: T. Williams to I. M. Selznick, mid-February, 1949, Ibid., 232.

209   fastened her hopes: Olivier, *Confessions*, 163.

209   I thought, if her critics: Ibid., 166.

209   Vivien in essence: I. M. Selznick, *Private View*, 322.

210   We heard his footsteps: Ibid., 323.

210   There were no auditions: Ibid., 324.

210   Oh, the old boy: Ibid.

210   cannot be altered: T. Williams to I. M. Selznick, March 23, 1949, *Selected Letters of Tennessee Williams*, 236.

210   a Negress: Philip C. Kolin, *Williams: A Streetcar Named Desire* (Cambridge, England: Cambridge University Press, 2000), 66.

211   You are absolutely in the right: Sam Staggs, *When Blanche Met Brando: The Scandalous Story of "A Streetcar Named Desire"* (New York: St. Martin's, 2006), 105.

211   willing to listen: I. M. Selznick, *Private View*, 326–327.

211   You must *know*: Olivier to Tennessee Williams, T. Williams Collection. Correspondence, Harry Ransom Center at the University of Texas at Austin.

212   Dame Irene's: Ibid.

212   capriciousness: Ibid.

212   Advance booking started: Richard Huggett, *Binkie Beaumount: Eminence Grise of the West End Theatre 1933–1973* (London: Hodder & Stoughton, 1989), 418.

213   women fainted: Ibid., 419.

213   It is only Olivier: Kolin, *Williams*, 67.

213   If the play lasts in London: Ibid., 68.

213   like apes: Coleman, *Olivier*, 218.

213   illustration of the way: Kenneth Tynan, *He That Plays the King* (Harlow, England: Longman, 1950), 142–143.

214   bulldozed: Hugo Vickers, *Vivien Leigh* (Boston: Little, Brown, 1988), 196.

214   go through it: Ibid.

214   No sooner had I stripped: *The Diaries of Kenneth Tynan*, ed. John Lahr (New York: Bloomsbury, 2001), 133.

214   There's a secret drawer: Ibid., 134.

215   She would dismiss: Alexander Walker, *Vivien: The Life of Vivien Leigh* (New York: Grove, 1987), 198.

215   tipped me into madness: Ibid.

215   He buttonholed Elia Kazan: Scott Eyman, *Lion of Hollywood: The Life and Legend of Louis B. Mayer* (New York: Simon & Schuster, 2005), 404.

216   a piece of filth: Elia Kazan, *Kazan on Directing*, ed. Robert Cornfield (New York: Vintage, 2009), 160.

216   non-existent: *Selected Letters of Tennessee Williams*, 230.

216   to get it up twice: Jeff Young, *Elia Kazan: The Master Director Discusses His Films* (New York: Newmarket, 1999), 79.

216   This kind of casualness: Jessica Tandy to Marlon Brando, January 30, 1948, in the Brando Estates Archive (Private Collection).

217    $100,000 for the film: Warner Bros. production budget, July 25, 1950. USC Warner Bros. Archives, University of Southern California, *Streetcar* file.

217   *Don't* listen to Leigh: T. Williams to Elia Kazan, June 16, 1950, *Selected Letters of Tennessee Williams*, 323.

217   I have read the script: Leigh to Kazan, June 16, 1950. VLA GB 71 THM/433/4/3/11.

217   I may be totally wrong: Ibid.

218   I think we might trim: Kazan to Leigh, n.d. VLA GB 71 THM/433/2/11.

218   Why do you always wear scent?: Walker, *Vivien*, 202.

218   150 feet wide: "Much of our story takes place in the two rooms of Stanley's home," said art director Richard Day. "I never exaggerate size on screen. These rooms are normal sized rooms.... Our acting space in the main room is 12 by 20 feet, 240 square feet in all. In the bedroom, it is 12 by 14. Not much space for Director Kazan to move his camera around in, but he wanted the real thing

and he's got it." Internal Warner Bros memo, August 24, 1950. USC-WB, *Streetcar*.

218   out of limits at all times: Internal Warner Bros. press memo, August 16, 1950. Ibid.

219   Brando, quietly: Warner Bros. press memo, n.d. Ibid.

219   friends like Humphrey Bogart: Internal Warner Bros. memo, September 31, 1950. "You've come at the psychological moment," Kazan told Hubbard. "I'm just going into a scene between Miss Leigh and Brando. Come and watch it." Ibid.

219   Because of the strenuous: Warner Bros. press memo, n.d. Ibid.

219   opened her big, blue eyes: Louella Parsons, *In Hollywood with Louella Parsons*, n.d. DOS 3341, Files, 1–10.

220   I don't know what that Method is: Lewis Funke and John E. Booth, *Actors Talk about Acting: Fourteen Interviews with Stars of the Theatre* (New York: Random House, 1961), 239.

220   For the first three weeks: Young, *Elia Kazan*, 80.

220   Have you ever been with: Ibid., 85.

220   I wanted to show: William Baer, ed., *Elia Kazan: Interviews* (Jackson: University Press of Mississippi, 2000), 135.

220   Pasha: David Richards, "Elia Kazan: The Director and His Gifts," *Washington Post*, December 4, 1983, https://www.washington post.com/archive/lifestyle/style/1983/12/04/elia-kazan-the-director -and-his-gifts/133b4027-968a-4acf-852b-4ebc063f851b/.

221   we got to like: Young, *Elia Kazan*, 80.

221   She had a small talent: Elia Kazan, *A Life* (Boston: Da Capo, 1997), 387.

221   pick her up: Karl Malden, *When Do I Start? A Memoir*, with Carla Malden (New York: Limelight Editions, 1997), 192.

221   Kazan also allowed: Internal Warner Bros. memo, November 6, 1950, USC-WB, *Streetcar*.

221   Gadg is doing a brilliant job: T. Williams to I. M. Selznick, September 26, 1950, *Selected Letters of Tennessee Williams*, 349.

221   While the average length: Warner Bros. press release, September 21, 1950, USC-WB, *Streetcar*.

222   pleasant, unpleasant: Marlon Brando, unpublished and undated transcript of taped interviews for his autobiography in the Marlon Brando Estates Archive.

222   $1.9 million: A Warner Bros. weekly production cost summary dated March 22, 1952, states that the exact cost was $1,897,471.68, USC-WB, *Streetcar*.

222 **At the wrap party:** Internal Warner Bros. memo, November 6, 1950. The crew gave Kazan a fishing rod and tackle. There's no record of what Vivien gave Kazan. Ibid.

222 **Elizabeth Taylor:** Jan Herman, *A Talent for Trouble: The Life of Hollywood's Most Acclaimed Director, William Wyler* (New York: G. P. Putnam's Sons, 1995), 321.

223 **DOUBLE DEALING:** Ibid., 322–333.

223 **I remember pausing:** Kazan, *A Life*, 143–144.

223 **"I'm doing the 'Caerey downt…'":** Coleman, *Olivier*, 223.

224 **Larry could be warm:** Herman, *Talent for Trouble*, 329.

224 **It was my first real experience:** Walker, *Vivien*, 201. Suzanne was planning to attend RADA, like her mother, who told the press: "I don't recommend a career in the theater. I believe it's too trying, too difficult a life. I would like to see her turn to a less exacting profession. I think she would be happier….I want Suzanne to be sure that she desperately wishes to become an actress. I want her to burn with the ambition. Because, otherwise, she won't be able to take the disappointments." Internal Warner Bros. memo, August 24, 1950, USC-WB, *Streetcar*.

224 **Her mind began to wobble:** Marlon Brando, *Brando: Songs My Mother Taught Me*, with Robert Lindsey (Random House, 1994), 152.

225 **We had to be careful:** Scotty Bowers, *Full Service: My Adventures in Hollywood and the Secret Sex Lives of the Stars*, with Lionel Friedberg (New York: Grove, 2012), 160.

225 **accused her of picking up strangers:** Michael Korda, interview with author, February 8, 2019.

225 **had a more tenuous relationship:** Malden, *When Do I Start?*, 192.

225 **Mona sat there:** Ibid., 192.

226 **counting on the freighter:** Internal Warner Bros. memo, October 23, 1950, USC-WB, *Streetcar*.

226 **forty thousand boxes:** Warner Bros. press release, n.d. Ibid.

226 **It is interesting:** Olivier, *Confessions*, 164. In a letter to Katharine Hepburn after Vivien's death, Olivier made a similar point, comparing himself to her partner, Spencer Tracy: "I have often thought we both sensed an affinity in our fates, as people well might who feel that their lives are a bewildering mixture of incredibly good and incredibly bad fortune." Olivier to Katharine Hepburn, July 10, 1967. LOA Add MS 80619.

226 **For the first time:** Ibid., 169.

CHAPTER 13

227   **of two such demanding roles:** Michael Korda, *Charmed Lives: A Family Romance* (London: Allen Lane, 1980), 304.

227   **They all drank far too much:** Juliet Mills, interview with author, May 22, 2021.

228   **People tended to be around Vivien:** Michael Korda, interview with author, February 8, 2019.

228   **the movies he and Vivien:** Korda, *Charmed Lives*, 305.

229   **went swimming and fishing:** Ibid., 304.

229   **Charm was Vivien's "secret weapon":** Ibid.

229   **the only person in the world:** Ibid., 305.

229   **high-pitched nervous laughter:** Ibid., 231.

229   **began to giggle:** Ibid., 305.

229–230   **one three-month period:** Terry Coleman, *Olivier* (New York: Henry Holt, 2005), 206.

230   **Donald Wolfit:** Hugo Vickers, *Vivien Leigh* (Boston: Little, Brown, 1988), 244.

230   **He was consumed with jealousy:** Rosemary Harris, interview with author, January 17, 2019.

231   **Between good and great acting:** Quoted in Dominic Shellard, *Kenneth Tynan: A Life* (New Haven, CT: Yale University Press, 2003), 84.

231   **If you try to muddle:** Philip Ziegler, *Olivier* (London: MacLehose, 2013), 176–177.

232   **she began to sweat:** Vickers, *Vivien Leigh*, 202.

232   **She picks at the part:** Kenneth Tynan, *Curtains* (New York: Atheneum, 1961), 10.

232   **twenty-five tons:** Anthony Holden, *Olivier* (London: Little Books, 2007), 268.

233   **[Olivier] interprets Antony:** Alice Venezky, "Shakespeare Conquers Broadway: The Olivier *Antony and Cleopatra*," *Shakespeare Quarterly* 3, no. 2 (April 1952): 121–124.

233   **I think you're the only actor:** See *One Hundred Books from the Library of Lord Olivier, Including Two Inscribed to Vivien Leigh*, Bernard Quaritch Ltd., List 2017/13, https://www.quaritch.com/wp-content/uploads/2017/10/100-Books-from-the-Library-of-Lord-Olivier.pdf.

234   **She is smoldering and sensual:** Brooks Atkinson, "First Night at the Theater: 'Antony and Cleopatra' Put On by the Oliviers as the Second of Their Twin Bill," *New York Times*, December 21, 1951,

https://www.nytimes.com/1951/12/21/archives/first-night-at-the
-theatre-antony-and-cleopatra-put-on-by-the.html.

234   funny little child-like: Laurence Olivier, *Confessions of an Actor* (New York: Simon & Schuster, 1982), 172.

234   shivering with weakness: Vickers, *Vivien Leigh*, 207.

234   exquisite unreality: Ibid.

234   Nonsense: Olivier, *Confessions*, 174.

234   in a pitiful state: Vickers, *Vivien Leigh*, 208.

235   Kubie has gone down in history: Theodore Lidz, "Caring for the Bird," *New York Review of Books*, August 15, 1985, https://www.nybooks.com/articles/1985/08/15/caring-for-the-bird/.

235   a slick bit of goods: Gore Vidal, "Immortal Bird," *New York Review of Books*, June 13, 1985.

235   I am sure: Olivier, *Confessions*, 181.

236   *Le malade imaginaire*: Tamara Tchinarova Finch, *Dancing into the Unknown: My Life in the Ballets Russes and Beyond* (Alton, England: Dance Books, 2007), 128.

236   You bring that clever husband: Ibid., 129.

237   I suppose I had encouraged it: Olivier, *Confessions*, 158.

237   a mixture of elation and sadness: Finch, *Dancing*, 129.

237   eating whale meat: Ibid., 130.

237   When finally an invitation came: Ibid., 131.

237   The stalls were pitch black: Trader Faulkner, *Peter Finch: A Biography* (London: Pan Books, 1980), 158.

238   W. A. Darlington: Ibid., 161.

238   Forgive me, dear Larry: Olivier, *Confessions*, 186.

239    $150,000: Alexander Walker, *Vivien: The Life of Vivien Leigh* (New York: Grove, 1987), 210.

239   On a frosty January night in 1953: Finch, *Dancing*, 134.

239   the remains of a roast: Ibid., 135.

239   sad little kiss: Coleman, *Olivier*, 238.

239   Great God in heaven: Ibid. The words were written by Olivier and then discarded from an early draft of his autobiography. Coleman, *Olivier*, 238.

240   MY DEAREST PLEASE: Leigh to Olivier, cable, January 28, 1953. LOA Add MS 80618.

240   MY LOVE HAVE MET: Leigh to Olivier, cable, January 30, 1953. LOA Add MS 80618.

240   Tormented by sleeplessness: Beverly Linet, "This Is Vivien Leigh Today: A Shaken Woman Coldly Discarded by Sir Laurence Olivier

after 20 Years of Marriage. This Is Her Story," *Modern Screen*, September 1960.

240 **If she did sleep:** Bevis Bawa, *Bevis Bawa's Brief: The Sometimes Irreverent Memoirs of a Gentleman in 20th Century Sri Lanka* (Beruwala, Sri Lanka: Brief Publications, 2011), 156.

241 **swallowed a chicken bone:** Ibid., 158.

241 **shaking like a leaf:** Elaine Dundy, *Finch, Bloody Finch: A Life of Peter Finch* (New York: Holt, Rinehart and Winston, 1980), 181.

241 **Dana Andrews:** Finch, *Dancing*, 155.

241 **swinging from being tense:** Dundy, *Finch, Bloody Finch*, 182.

241 **It was a drive:** Bawa, *Bevis Bawa's Brief*, 158.

242 **suddenly started talking:** Ibid., 159.

242 **I could find no blame:** Olivier, *Confessions*, 187.

242 **understandably exhibited:** Dundy, *Finch, Bloody Finch*, 189.

242 **of the wretched waste of time:** Olivier, *Confessions*, 187.

242 **My Darling Vivien:** Leigh Holman to Vivien Leigh, February 25, 1953. VLA GB 71 THM/433/2/8.

242 **It was apparent:** Dundy, *Finch, Bloody Finch*, 184.

243 **[She] suddenly unfastened:** Ibid., 184–185.

243 **a very high physical energy:** Kay Redfield Jamison, interview with author, March 14, 2019.

244 **the doors flew open:** Finch, *Dancing*, 139.

244 **Vivien began to rush down:** Ibid., 141–142.

245 **our bedroom door:** Ibid., 143.

245 **thunderbolt:** Ibid.

246 **There's very little:** Jamison, interview.

246 **she cried, imploring:** Finch, *Dancing*, 144.

246 **Bellevue Hospital:** Vickers, *Vivien Leigh*, 213.

247 **"Mista David," she screamed:** David Niven, *Bring On the Empty Horses* (New York: G. P. Putnam's Sons, 1975), 284.

248 **choking and gasping:** Finch, *Dancing*, 149.

248 **submerged in an overflowing bath:** Ibid., 154.

249 **She looked like:** Ibid.

249 **Vivien Leigh is suffering:** Paramount Pictures press release, March 15, 1953. (Private source.)

249 **She's stopped breathing:** Coleman, *Olivier*, 245.

250 **screaming appalling abuse:** Olivier, *Confessions*, 191.

250 **Actress Vivien Leigh:** "Vivien Leigh, in Tears, Pulled Aboard Plane," *Los Angeles Times*, March 20, 1953.

250   **Wan but smiling radiantly:** Maurice Fagence, "Tired Olivier Brings Home a Smiling Vivien," *Daily Herald*, March 21, 1953.

250   **Poor Olivier:** Finch, *Dancing*, 156.

CHAPTER 14

251   **excellently looked after:** Sybille Olivier Day to Laurence Olivier, August 19, 1949. LOA Add MS 79891.

252   **There are about 1600 patients:** Eleanor Roosevelt, "My Day," May 3, 1948 (syndicated), Eleanor Roosevelt Papers, Digital Edition, https://www2.gwu.edu/~erpapers/myday/displaydocedits.cfm ?_y=1948&_f=md000956.

252   **All sorts of treatments:** William Sargent and Eliot Slater, *An Introduction to Physical Methods of Treatment in Psychiatry* (London: Churchill Livingstone, 1972), 89.

252   **would have had a muscle relaxer:** Edward Shorter, interview with author, November 13, 2018.

253   **quite humane:** Ibid.

253   **There was the risk:** Po Wang, interview with author, April 25, 2021.

253   **When convalescent myself:** Sybille Olivier Day to Laurence Olivier, March 30, 1953. LOA Add MS 79891.

253   **The treatment is progressing:** R. K. Freudenberg to Olivier, March 29, 1953. LOA Add MS 80619.

254   **I'll never forget Netherne:** Alexander Walker, *Vivien: The Life of Vivien Leigh* (New York: Grove, 1987), 214.

254   **she started in floods:** *The Noël Coward Diaries*, ed. Graham Payn and Sheridan Morley (Boston: Little, Brown, 1982), 211.

254   **the Waltons wrapped him:** Terry Coleman, *Olivier* (New York: Henry Holt, 2005), 247.

254   **I had never known her:** Tarquin Olivier, *So Who's Your Mother?* (Wilby, England: Michael Russell, 2012), 14–15.

255   **I do most desperately feel:** Coleman, *Olivier*, 246.

255   **not being more alive:** Laurence Olivier, *Confessions of an Actor* (New York: Simon & Schuster, 1982), 194.

255   **five additional ECT treatments:** Walker, *Vivien*, 214.

255   **totally numbed:** Ibid.

255   **I can only describe:** Olivier, *Confessions*, 195.

256   **I did some hard thinking:** Anthony Holden, *Olivier* (London: Little Books, 2007), 280.

257 a trifle about Kings and Queens: Geoffrey Wansell, *Terence Rattigan: A Biography* (London: Oberon, 2009), 246.

257 a quilted cushion: Dominic Shellard, *Kenneth Tynan: A Life* (New Haven, CT: Yale University Press, 2003), 83.

257 subordinating his career: Wansell, *Terence Rattigan*, 257.

257 my flimsy little fairy tale: Ibid.

258 Sometimes he would break: Holden, *Olivier*, 281.

258 ham fat: Ibid., 282.

259 seventeen weeks: Ibid., 285.

259 Esmond Knight: Douglas Wilmer, interview by Ronald Proyer, March 28, 1973, transcript, Vivien Leigh Archive, Victoria and Albert Museum. VLA GB 71 THM/420/37.

259 I well remember: Anthony Bushell to Michael Dempsey, August 24, 1989. Stenn Collection.

260 far different in character: Claire Bloom, *Leaving a Doll's House* (Boston: Little, Brown, 1996), 90.

260 fatal combination: Ibid.

260 a dryness: Ibid., 91.

260 Notley Abbey was absolutely hers: Ibid., 92.

261 Baby, what are you doing here: Trader Faulkner, *Inside Trader* (London: Quartet, 2012), 126.

262 My new love: Olivier, *Confessions*, 223.

262 He was really upset: Tarquin Olivier, interview with author, August 2, 2019.

264 He had this theory: Hugo Vickers, *Vivien Leigh* (Boston: Little, Brown, 1988), 220–221.

264 Larry came down to see her: Kenneth More, *More or Less* (London: Hodder and Stoughton, 1978), 166.

264 petulant, spoilt: Alan Dent, *Vivien Leigh: A Bouquet* (London: Hamish Hamilton, 1969), 82.

264 Peggy A. was unforgettable: Bushell to Dempsey, May 28–29, 1988. Stenn Collection.

265 she started to go strange: Vickers, *Vivien Leigh*, 229.

265 She'd lose her looks: John Gielgud, interview by Anne Edwards, n.d., unpublished transcript, Anne Edwards Papers, Charles E. Young Research Library, University of California, Los Angeles, Box 20.

265 The truth is: *Sir John Gielgud: A Life in Letters*, ed. Richard Mangan (New York: Arcade, 2004), 180.

266   Jewish hairdresser: John Gielgud, *An Actor and His Time* (New York: Applause, 1997), 118.

266   armed with a battering ram: Peter Brook, *Threads of Time* (Washington, DC: Counterpoint, 1998), 90.

266   a strangely hidden man: Ibid., 89.

266   Onstage and on the screen: Ibid.

267   polite and attentive: Ibid., 91.

267   Olivier put his hand down: Vickers, *Vivien Leigh*, 242.

267   at the very summit: Bushell to Dempsey, May 31, 1987. Stenn Collection.

267   Poor Vivien: Anthony Quayle, *A Time to Speak* (Reading, England: Sphere, 1990), 470.

268   Most Macbeths: Vickers, *Vivien Leigh*, 225.

268   in his old age: Laurence Olivier, "A Soliloquy in an English Hamlet," *Los Angeles Times*, November 24, 1963.

268   the greatest theatrical emotion: See *From the Library of Lord Olivier*, Bernard Quaritch Ltd., 2011, https://www.quaritch.com/wp-content/uploads/2014/12/1408-From-the-Library-of-Lord-Olivier.pdf.

268   shook hands with greatness: Holden, *Olivier*, 294.

269   Vivien Leigh's Lady Macbeth: Ibid.

269   With only two hours of sleep: Olivier, *Confessions*, 202.

269   She was not too difficult: Ibid.

270   talked at supper wildly: *Noël Coward Diaries*, 278.

270   They have made a pact: Vickers, *Vivien Leigh*, 275.

270   Vivien, more and more: Tamara Tchinarova Finch, *Dancing into the Unknown: My Life in the Ballets Russes and Beyond* (Alton, England: Dance Books, 2007), 160.

271   Vivien was on edge: Trader Faulkner, *Peter Finch: A Biography* (London: Pan Books, 1980), 186–187.

271   Ginette Spanier: Vickers, *Vivien Leigh*, 231.

271   He was invited to Notley: Faulkner, *Peter Finch*, 188.

272   Larry said to Vivien: Victoria Tennant, interview with author, June 21, 2018.

272   It was impossible: Finch, *Dancing*, 163.

272   How could one resist: Ibid., 162.

272   Vivien found Betty's cottage: Ibid., 161.

273   The publicity this attracted: Coleman, *Olivier*, 266–267.

273   It *saddens* and *saddens*: Leigh to Noël Coward, July 3, 1956. Noël Coward Archive, London.

273 The hysterical, disorganized silliness: *Noël Coward Diaries*, 330–331.

274 I am so terribly distressed: Leigh to Noël Coward, n.d. Noël Coward Archive, London.

274 They couldn't save the baby: Beverly Linet, "This Is Vivien Leigh Today: A Shaken Woman Coldly Discarded by Sir Laurence Olivier after 20 Years of Marriage. This Is Her Story," *Modern Screen*, September 1960.

275 I'm sorry: Holden, *Olivier*, 305.

275 He would receive $100,000: Warner Bros. production-distribution agreement, August 29, 1956. USC-Warner Bros. Archives, *The Prince and the Showgirl*.

275 *What* was going to happen: Olivier, *Confessions*, 206.

276 She was strange: Joshua Logan to Ronald Proyer, February 12, 1973. VLA 71 THM/420/22.

276 twenty-seven items: Gary Vitacco-Robles, *Icon: The Life, Times, and Films of Marilyn Monroe* vol. 2, *1956 to 1962 and Beyond* (Albany, GA: Bear Manor Media, 2014), 29.

276 as cold as a refrigerated fish: Ibid., 30.

277 "Actually," Marilyn replied: Ibid., 30.

277 two hundred reporters: Ibid., 32.

277 Marilyn felt Larry: Michael Korda, interview with author, February 8, 2019.

277 Olivier himself: Vitacco-Robles, *Icon*, 2:34.

278 Monroe, who finally showed up: Wansell, *Terence Rattigan*, 284.

278 Every vehicle is checked: Colin Clark, *My Week with Marilyn* (New York: Weinstein, 2011), 162.

278 It took two full days: Holden, *Olivier*, 308.

278 "minimal" at best: Clark, *My Week*, 197.

278 Laurence had to learn patience: Douglas Wilmer to Ronald Proyer. VLA GB 71 THM/420/37.

279 a really wonderful old gal: Bushell to Dempsey, n.d. Stenn Collection.

279 that little girl: Holden, *Olivier*, 309.

279 I didn't think: Vitacco-Robles, *Icon*, 42.

279 Larry says of [Marilyn]: Vickers, *Vivien Leigh*, 240.

279 the Dear One: Walter Winchell, "Of New York," *Daily Mirror*, September 12, 1956.

280 clubby professionalism: Vitacco-Robles, *Icon*, 36.

280 the hell-hound: Bushell to Dempsey, April 25–26, 1988. Stenn Collection.

280   He talks to me: Vitacco-Robles, *Icon*, 37.

280   What am I doing here: Ibid.

280   much too remote: Clark, *My Week*, 175.

280   came at me with a venomous rush: Joshua Logan to Ronald Proyer.

280   "Olivier," said Miller: Arthur Miller, *Timebends: A Life* (New York: Grove, 1987), 420–421.

281   You are the most wonderful: Clark, *My Week*, 207.

281   her attorney's phone log: Vitacco-Robles, *Icon*, 47.

281   I sat bolt upright: Clark, *My Week*, 96.

282   completely rigid: Ibid., 269.

282   shattered, washed out: Ibid., 241.

282   If any of us talk to her: Ibid., 288.

282   It was the most dreadful: Holden, *Olivier*, 309.

282   When MM left: Clark, *My Week*, 304.

CHAPTER 15

283   The saddest thing: Hugo Vickers, *Vivien Leigh* (Boston: Little, Brown, 1988), 231.

283   His reaction was quick: Arthur Miller, *Timebends: A Life* (New York: Grove, 1987), 416.

284   At the interval: Ibid., 417.

284   the rebellious Osborne: Ibid., 417.

285   Osborne would refer to her: John Osborne, *Almost a Gentleman: An Autobiography*, vol. 2, *1955–1966* (London: Faber and Faber, 1991), 258.

285   acts of folly: Laurence Olivier, *Confessions of an Actor* (New York: Simon & Schuster, 1982), 204.

285   smoky green light: Osborne, *Almost a Gentleman*, 35.

287   Olivier's response: Ibid., 36.

287   It is hard to convey: Ibid.

287   dazzling Olivier craftiness: Ibid., 37.

288   little actress: Ibid.

288   What about that!: Ibid.

289   negligible rate: Terry Coleman, *Olivier* (New York: Henry Holt, 2005), 276.

289   [Miller's] humanity: Osborne, *Almost a Gentleman*, 39.

289–290 I suspect that Olivier: Logan Gourlay, ed., *Olivier* (New York: Stein and Day, 1975), 150.

290   This is really me: Anthony Holden, *Olivier* (London: Little Books, 2007), 318.

290   Vivien's watchful presence: Osborne, *Almost a Gentleman*, 41–42.

291   A dozen of us: Ibid., 42.

291   made a final effort: Ibid.

291   super-grand: Victoria Tennant, interview with author, June 21, 2018.

291   We were having our brandy: Tarquin Olivier, interview with author, August 2, 2019.

292   he had started taking: Coleman, *Olivier*, 305.

293   a feeling of vacuity: Olivier to Jack Merivale, August 16, 1960. Jack Merivale Collection, British Film Institute, London, JME-1-2.

293   Oh my God!: John Standing, interview with author, May 16, 2021.

293   Vivien was convinced: Vickers, *Vivien Leigh*, 245.

293   to modify her moods: "That really sudden switching is really hard to explain from any genetic, biological deficit, unless you see it as a problem with some kind of regulatory system," says Oxford's John Geddes. "But quite honestly, we don't know what that is." John Geddes, interview with author, June 18, 2021.

293   was the ideal companion: Vickers, *Vivien Leigh*, 245.

294   She used to go out: Standing, interview.

294   If you don't like your life: Vickers, *Vivien Leigh*, 245.

294   rose with an angelic smile: Ibid., 245–246.

294   smashed a hotel window: Ibid., 246.

294   she couldn't resist: Ibid., 248.

295   Silly cunt: Michael Blakemore, *Arguments with England: A Memoir* (London: Faber and Faber, 2004), 167.

295   Larry said: Vickers, *Vivien Leigh*, 246.

295   she leapt away: Ibid., 245.

295   Peter Brook: Ibid., 246.

295–296   The train was full: Anne Edwards, *Vivien Leigh: A Biography* (Lanham, MD: Taylor Trade, 2013), 217.

296   some *principetta*: Blakemore, *Arguments*, 162.

296   Oh Colin: Vickers, *Vivien Leigh*, 247.

297   The noble peers: "Vivien Leigh Ejected from House of Lords," *Los Angeles Times*, July 12, 1957.

297   Something snapped: Olivier, *Confessions*, 222.

297   When a woman finds: Vickers, *Vivien Leigh*, 256.

298   CRITICISM ILL-CONSIDERED: Ibid.

298   I do hope: Ibid., 257.

298   346,903: "Marriage Rates in the UK," Data Blog, *The Guardian*, accessed on June 12, 2018. https://www.theguardian.com/news/datablog/2010/feb/11/marriage-rates-uk-data.

298   no question of a divorce: Vickers, *Vivien Leigh*, 257.

299   philandering fit: Coleman, *Olivier*, 290.

299   He behaved like a libertine: T. Olivier, interview.

299   a welcome surprise: Joan Plowright, *And That's Not All* (London: Weidenfeld & Nicolson, 2001), 42.

299   outside the profession: Ibid.

300   jaunty intimacy: Ibid., 45.

300   He was bristling with energy: Ibid.

300   never dreamt that: Ibid., 47.

300   a promiscuous girl: Ibid., 48.

300   none of my evasive tactics: Ibid.

301   I spent the day: Leigh to Noël Coward, November 8, 1958. Noël Coward Archive, London.

301   Olivier was removing: Alexander Walker, *Vivien: The Life of Vivien Leigh* (New York: Grove, 1987), 236.

301   I am thinking of you: Vickers, *Vivien Leigh*, 259.

302   grew deeper and more binding: Plowright, *And That's Not All*, 49.

302   I'm going to marry Joan: John Gielgud, interview by Anne Edwards, n.d., unpublished transcript, Anne Edwards Papers, Charles E. Young Research Library, University of California, Los Angeles, Box 20.

302   Vivien was in "agony": Leigh to Noël Coward, November 12, 1958. Noël Coward Archive, London.

303   could not bear: Plowright, *And That's Not All*, 49.

303   My parents found: Hayley Mills, interview with author, May 13, 2021.

303   breakable: Claire Bloom, *Limelight and After: The Education of an Actress* (London: Penguin, 1982), 150.

303   She was constantly: Vickers, *Vivien Leigh*, 261–262.

304   I've got to go: Ibid., 263.

304   after a perfectly wonderful night: Ibid.

304   She would sometimes: Osborne, *Almost a Gentleman*, 66–67.

304   managing not too badly: H. M. Segal to Olivier, October 24, 1958. LOA Add MS 80619.

305   picking up a local fisherman: Vickers, *Vivien Leigh*, 266.

305   This is the third letter: Leigh to Olivier, November 2, 1958. LOA Add MS 80618.

306   I need not tell you: Leigh to Noël Coward, November 12, 1958. Noël Coward Archive.

306   Hester heard raised voices: Coleman, *Olivier*, 300.

306   I suffered grievously: Ibid.

307   to drown his sorrows: Plowright, *And That's Not All*, 59.

307   feared it might be too much: Ibid., 55.

307   a phone call: Ibid., 56.

307   quite another person: Ibid., 59.

307   was remarkable: Anthony Bushell to Michael Dempsey, October 13, 1988. Stenn Collection.

308   as full of intrigue: Peter Ustinov, *Dear Me* (London: Arrow, 1998), 294–295.

308   If I identify: Ibid., 297.

309   The dialogue led: Bushell to Dempsey, June 8, 1988. Stenn Collection.

309   Your love has given me: Plowright, *And That's Not All*, 57.

309   blackhearted blackmail: Ibid., 58.

309   I am quite sure: Ibid.

310   Larry had a deep suspicion: Peter Hall, *Making an Exhibition of Myself* (London: Oberon, 2000), 140–141.

310   My life has been an equal: Curtis Bill Pepper, "Talking With," *New York Times*, March 25, 1979.

311   There he sat: Blakemore, *Arguments*, 224.

311   "Somehow," writes Vickers: Vickers, *Vivien Leigh*, 273.

311   deep sadness: *The Noël Coward Diaries*, ed. Graham Payn and Sheridan Morley (Boston: Little, Brown, 1982), 427.

311   I can hardly write the words: Leigh to Tarquin Olivier, February 19, 1960. LOA Add MS 80619.

312   She was terribly grand: Yolande Finch, *Finchy* (New York: Wyndham, 1981), 61–62.

312   He reminded me: Ibid., 62.

313   Her longing for him: *Noël Coward Diaries*, 424.

313   It was a very difficult time: Juliet Mills, interview with author, May 22, 2021.

313   exert all the influence: Olivier to Jack Merivale, April 17, 1953. LOA Add MS 80619.

313   It was obvious: Walker, *Vivien*, 245.

314   seemed to adore him: Patrick Stewart, interview with author, December 18, 2017.

314   I really don't think: Tina Wyngarde-Hopkins, *Peter Wyngarde: A Life amongst Strangers* (London: Austin Macauley, 2020), 110.

314   Lady Olivier wishes: Walker, *Vivien*, 250.

314   I was woken in my flat: Plowright, *And That's Not All*, 73–74.

315   Marry him if you must: Ibid., 150.

315 **She even began:** Richard Olivier, interview with author, June 8, 2021.

315 **You're not a friend:** Plowright, *And That's Not All*, 74.

315 **Cameras were there:** Holden, *Olivier*, 345.

315 **If anyone is going to come:** Virginia Fairweather, *Cry God for Larry: An Intimate Memoir of Sir Laurence Olivier* (London: Calder & Boyars, 1969), 26–27.

316 **The [tabloid] editors:** Ibid., 33–35.

316 **a temporary foxhole:** Osborne, *Almost a Gentleman*, 161.

316 **busily employed:** *Noël Coward Diaries*, 441.

316 **This lady is normally:** Dr. Arthur Conachy, report on Vivien Leigh's psychiatric condition, June 20, 1961. Jack Merivale Collection, BFI, JME-4-6.

316 **Pussy-Cat my darling:** Leigh to Olivier, June 20, 1960. LOA Add MS 80618.

317 **"Darling," he said:** Olivier to Leigh, December 4, 1960. VLA GB 71 THM/433/1.

CHAPTER 16

319 **She had a ballgown:** Alexander Walker, *Vivien: The Life of Vivien Leigh* (New York: Grove, 1987), 265.

319 **pale as a ghost:** Olivia de Havilland, as told to Jane Ardmore, "Gone with the Wind—Fate Broke Its Promises," *Photoplay*, August 1961.

320 **We were married:** Joan Plowright, *And That's Not All* (London: Weidenfeld & Nicolson, 2001), 90.

320 **Name?:** Laurence Olivier, *Confessions of an Actor* (New York: Simon & Schuster, 1982), 236.

320 **she had obviously been crying:** Walker, *Vivien*, 265–266.

321 **Bushell believed:** "Vivien's leading man in this disaster was a then unknown Mr. Warren Beatty + I don't have to tell you what that led to," Bushell wrote to Michael Dempsey, October 28–29, 1989. Stenn Collection.

321 **The moment I appeared:** Sarah Miles, "'Larry Thought He'd Killed Her': Laurence Olivier's Secret Lover of 20 Years Reveals How the Actor Confessed to a Violent Row with His Adulterous Wife Vivien Leigh," *Daily Mail*, August 17, 2013, https://www.dailymail.co.uk/news/article-2396200/Laurence-Oliviers-secret-lover-reveals-actor-confessed-violent-row-adulterous-wife-Vivien-Leigh.html.

322   **As in Vivien's life:** Gavin Lambert, "Vivien Leigh's Internal Struggle," *Close-Ups: Intimate Portraits of Movie Stars by Their Co-Stars, Directors, Screenwriters and Friends*, ed. Danny Peary (New York: Workman, 1978), 314–316.

322   **too busy looking at itself:** Hugo Vickers, *Vivien Leigh* (Boston: Little, Brown, 1988), 293.

322   **She was always:** Patrick Stewart, interview with author, December 18, 2017.

323   **A list was drawn up:** Ibid.

323   **Vivien picked up:** Walker, *Vivien*, 272.

323   **an *angel*:** Leigh to Noël Coward, n.d. Noël Coward Archive.

324   **He was very kind:** Juliet Mills, interview with author, May 22, 2021.

324   **She drank a terrifying amount:** Bushell to Dempsey, February 17, 1995. Stenn Collection.

324   **I have been so really worryingly low:** Leigh to Olivier, February 11, 1963. LOA Add MS 80618.

324   **She began to claw me:** Jean-Pierre Aumont, *Sun and Shadow* (New York: W. W. Norton, 1977), 233.

325   **took the breath away:** Bushell to Dempsey, October 8, 1988. Stenn Collection.

325   **His car pulled up:** Vickers, *Vivien Leigh*, 310.

326   **I was sharing a dressing room:** Rosemary Harris, interview with author, January 17, 2019.

326   **Simone Signoret came:** John Gielgud, interview by Anne Edwards, n.d., unpublished transcript, Anne Edwards Papers, Charles E. Young Research Library, University of California, Los Angeles, Box 20.

327   **This was [a] time of loneliness:** Stanley Kramer at Vivien Leigh's March 17, 1968, memorial service at the University of Southern California. *An Appreciation of Vivien Leigh* (Los Angeles: University of Southern California, Friends of the Libraries, 1969), 36.

327   **"Stanley," she teased:** Ibid.

327   **I can't do it today:** Ibid.

327   **peaks of blue white:** Vickers, *Vivien Leigh*, 317.

328   **Vivien suddenly called out:** Stewart, interview.

328   **Her room was like:** Alex Harvey, "I'm Worried about Larry-Boy," *The People*, July 9, 1967.

329   **a tough drug to take:** Thomas M. Daniel, interview with author, April 27, 2021.

329   **The drugs they fill me with:** Leigh to Miller Lide, n.d. Courtesy of Miller Lide.

329 They have given me new types: Harvey, "I'm Worried."

329 looking as radiantly beautiful: Brian Aherne in *Appreciation*, 11.

329 She drank and smoked: Vickers, *Vivien Leigh*, 324.

329 I had tea: Juliet Mills, interview.

330 I said I'll be home: Vickers, *Vivien Leigh*, 325.

330 I am weary: Private Collection courtesy of Judith Koop.

330 Guessing there would be: Olivier, *Confessions*, 273.

331 at those times: Ibid., 274.

331 ulcer: Ibid., 275.

331 I stood and prayed: Ibid., 274.

332 an ordinary man: Richard Olivier, interview with author, June 8, 2021.

332 a very sensitive man: Michael Caine, interview with author, July 24, 2017.

332 a "monster": Frank Langella, *Dropped Names: Famous Men and Women as I Knew Them* (New York: Harper Perennial, 2013), 73–75.

333 He loved living on the edge: Sarah Miles, interview with author, June 8, 2018.

333 At one point: Ibid.

333 Larry claimed he was bisexual: Ibid.

333 I've played over 200 parts: R. Olivier, interview.

334 He was in a coma: Hayley Mills, interview with author, May 13, 2021.

334 he took her home: Terry Coleman, *Olivier* (New York: Henry Holt, 2005), 405.

334 His bravery struck me hugely: Miles, interview.

334 there isn't a third act: Laurence Olivier, "A Soliloquy in an English Hamlet," *Los Angeles Times*, November 24, 1963.

334 I was onstage with him: Gawn Grainger, interview with author, June 21, 2018.

334 One night, I said: Ibid.

335 openly hated: Bushell to Dempsey, July 12, 1989. Stenn Collection.

335 Richard Olivier disputes: R. Olivier, interview.

335 He had had a series: Ibid.

335 and it was only when they got him: Michael Blakemore, *Stage Blood: Five Tempestuous Years in the Early Life of the National Theatre* (London: Faber and Faber, 2013), 338–339.

336 intent on recreating: Michael Korda, interview with author, February 8, 2019.

336 **Once, says Rosemary Harris:** Rosemary Harris, interview with author, January 17, 2019.

336 **It was Vivien's illness:** Simon Callow, email to author, August 23, 2021.

337 **You can reach a point:** Curtis Bill Pepper, "Talking With," *New York Times*, March 25, 1979.

337 **This, this was love:** Anthony Holden, *Olivier* (London: Little Books, 2007), 112.

INDEX

ABOUT THE AUTHOR

Stephen Galloway is the dean of Chapman University's Dodge College of Film and Media Arts. Before joining Chapman in 2020, he was for many years the executive editor of *The Hollywood Reporter*.